P9-DNB-817

HF   Steinbock, Dan
5415.1265   The Birth of
.S735   Internet
2000   Marketing
             Communications

OUACHITA TECHNICAL COLLEGE
LIBRARY/LRC

3 9005 00009 0344

The Birth of
Internet Marketing
Communications

The Birth of Internet Marketing Communications

DAN STEINBOCK

QUORUM BOOKS
Westport, Connecticut • London

OUACHITA TECHNICAL COLLEGE

Library of Congress Cataloging-in-Publication Data

Steinbock, Dan.
    The birth of Internet marketing communications / Dan Steinbock.
        p.   cm.
    Includes bibliographical references and index.
    ISBN 1–56720–303–5 (alk. paper)
        1. Internet marketing.   2. Communication in marketing.   3. World
    Wide Web (Information retrieval system)   4. Internet (Computer
    network)   I. Title.
    HF5415.1265.S735   2000
    658.8'00285'4678—dc21   99–13713

British Library Cataloguing in Publication Data is available.

Copyright © 2000 by Dan Steinbock

All rights reserved. No portion of this book may be
reproduced, by any process or technique, without
the express written consent of the publisher.

Library of Congress Catalog Card Number: 99–13713
ISBN: 1–56720–303–5

First published in 2000

Quorum Books, 88 Post Road West, Westport, CT 06881
An imprint of Greenwood Publishing Group, Inc.
www.quorumbooks.com

Printed in the United States of America

The paper used in this book complies with the
Permanent Paper Standard issued by the National
Information Standards Organization (Z39.48–1984).

10 9 8 7 6 5 4 3 2 1

HF
5415.1265
.S735
2000

The Internet is like a 20-foot tidal wave coming, and we are in kayaks. It's been coming across the Pacific for thousands of miles and gaining momentum, and it's going to lift you and drop you. We're just a step away from the point when every computer is connected to every other computer, at least in the U.S., Japan, and Europe. It affects everybody— the computer industry, telecommunications, the media, chipmakers, and the software world. Some are more aware of this than others.

Andy Grove, CEO of Intel
"A Conversation with the Lords
of Wintel," *Fortune*, July 8, 1996

Contents

Preface

The Birth of Internet Marketing Communications results from my research program, "Competition, Strategy, and Marketing: From Marketplace to Marketspace" (1997–2000). The program originates from a joint project with Intel Corporation. In the next few years, it will generate several book-length studies on competitive strategy, online and offline brands, new media planning, and telecommunications. This work is one of the first comprehensive studies of Internet marketing. It focuses on marketing strategies and the critical early years of the Internet.

Since 1997, I have served as "virtual" Professor of Management and Organization at Helsinki School of Economics (i.e., conducting all courses and lectures with Intel's videoconferencing systems).[1] My interest in the Internet stems from issues of competitive strategy and industrial organization in the digital convergence. This subject led to my first book in the United States, *Triumph and Erosion in the American Media and Entertainment Industries* (1995).[2] *The Birth of Internet Marketing Communications* has also been preceded by several pilot studies I have conducted on Internet marketing, convergence, and electronic commerce initiatives.[3] The work on the projects began after I had served as the rapporteur for the OECD on global electronic commerce (1997–1998).[4]

In my works, I have focused on firm-level characteristics, paying special attention to issues of competitive strategy, marketing management, valuation, and industrial organization. With different perspectives, all throw light on emergent industries that are often characterized by dynamic strategy and dynamic positioning, as well as discontinuous technologies. This approach is not unrelated to the empirical work I have done on industrial clusters, with the advice and intellectual inspiration of Professor Michael E. Porter, Harvard Business School.[5] The cluster studies have greatly enhanced my analyses of new media, interactive agencies, and the nascent Internet retail, or electronic commerce, in the United States. In effect, the inherent multidimensionality of the cluster theory is well equipped to properly capture the inherent richness and complexity of the emerging new media clusters in California (Silicon Valley), New York City (Silicon Alley), and elsewhere.

All of these research projects share a similar framework and approach that makes them somewhat unique, collectively. Unlike most studies in the field, mine tend to focus on firm-level determinants. Aggregate studies tend to downplay the risks and the uncertainty that are an integral part of these particular business activities. Moreover, macroeconomic studies tend to ignore the very presence of industries and business segments that are in the process of formation. Finally, the manifestos of the Internet pundits, as fascinating as they can be in their futuristic faith in the Web that "will change everything," almost entirely neglect the significance of the most critical determinant of the cluster theory—*location*.

True, it is not just a Web. It is a *World Wide* Web. But while we may spend quite a lot of time *on* the Web, we live in our physical world. It is our location that connects us into the Web, that enables us to access and navigate the Web, and that interconnects us with this wonderful "other world" of ours in the very process of formation. Physical distance hardly exists in the virtual world, but it is and will remain a reality in the physical world. These two worlds—the physical and the virtual—and their parallel business equivalents—the marketplace and the marketspace—exist in parallel. But they are *not* identical. Therefore, location is not gone. It is and will remain present in our physical world and its marketplace. In an ironic way, perhaps, it is now more significant than ever before. Despite the rhetoric on the "disappearance of distance," some 70%–80% of current Internet traffic, and as much of web-driven transactions, occurs in the United States, one nation alone. Even a superficial glance at the infrastructure, hardware, software, content/aggregation, and media industries that, directly or indirectly, make up the Internet or Internet-driven and Internet-related industries, reveals a stunning fact: *in almost all these industries, the top 20 companies worldwide are exclusively American.* And even more: the headquarters or core activities of almost all of these top 20 American firms are located either in California's Silicon Valley or in New York City's Silicon Alley, or both.

Once a journalist asked Arthur Miller to define American theater. Amused, the playwright said something to the effect: It's within 42nd Street and 50th Street and Broadway and 9th Avenue. So it is with the new media. Of course, things may change; or they may not. Silicon Valley is situated close to the Hollywood studios. New York City houses not just Silicon Alley, but the headquarters of traditional media, the marketing and advertising giants of Madison Avenue, the massive conglomerates of the *Fortune* 500—and, perhaps most importantly, Wall Street and financial services. Venture capital lives next to new media, stock exchanges thrive in the proximity of more traditional forms of media and entertainment, computing, and telecommunications.

For all of these reasons, *The Birth of Internet Marketing Communications* is not only about those American companies and activities that are currently creating entirely new forms of industries, companies, and business activities. It is also specifically about those particular entities and entrepreneurs of whom most reside in these two clusters of frantic rivalry and hectic activity. It is this simple social fact that accounted for my decision to interview many of the most critical implementors of these new industries. Also, I sought persons who were representative, or whose work was *representative*, in some critical sense of the word; in this study, they do not represent their own accomplishments only but those of their colleagues, friends, and rivals. Finally, in order to "get the story straight," I have interviewed key figures in both the core areas of Internet activity and those whose role has been more poignant in the related and supporting industries. The line between the two is relevant for analytical purposes only; in practice, it is a line drawn in waters.

In addition to keeping things real and empirical, I also consider it extremely important—perhaps even urgent these days—to pay heed to the classic body of work in these disciplines. Most contemporary theories, fashionable books, and trend-setting theories on these subjects downplay the value and significance of history and tradition in management and marketing. Yet, it would be naïve to try to understand the present or even the future, without a firm sense of the past. The resulting intellectual amnesia is a dangerous hobby. "Those who do not remember the history," says the philosopher, "are condemned to live it again." In contemporary America, these business segments *also* serve as the locomotive of the technology sector which, in turn, functions as the financial generator of the U.S. economy and thereby global finance. As a result, intellectual amnesia is not just an intellectual self-deception; it can ruin fortunes of people, companies, even entire industries.

But even if one tries to explore the present and the potential future with the assistance of the past, how enduring is a work like *The Birth of Internet Marketing Communications* that, by definition, studies a very rapidly growing cluster of industries? If the Internet truly is in a state of constant flux, a legitimate concern involves the durability of the material. Yet, there are three good reasons why, with a proper approach, such a work is possible and probably necessary.

First of all, we do not know and, by definition, *cannot* know the future evolution of the Internet; it is not predictable. In brief, we cannot tell the *narrative* (i.e., the sequence of the critical elements). However, on the basis of the early phase of the Internet (fragmentation, emergence, growth), we already know many of the crucial elements of the story (i.e., the elements as distinct components but without proper understanding of their specific contribution in the future evolution of the entire system). This particular element of the story—the early years of the Internet— will *not* change. For instance, it is indisputable that between 1993 and 1995 sponsored banner advertising emerged as the primary source of revenues for the leading Internet companies. That's an element of the story of Internet marketing. Yet, we have no assurance that this element will not change, or acquire a different function in the future. Take, for instance, the inflated hopes that once, not so long ago, were attached to the push technology as a proper substitute for the browsers.

Second: why, then, is it meaningful to tell this story? Of course, any story may always have descriptive interest, but there's more to this one. It is not only interesting as a piece of history but as a configuration of the *primary determinants* of the coming infrastructure. Focusing on the early years of a nascent industrial cluster where one layer of activities is built upon another, each major strategic decision is bound to include some potential future paths and exclude others. Think of telecommunications and Internet telephony and microprocessors. Think of software applications based on that infrastructure and hardware. Think of content and aggregation products and services based on that software and the underlying infrastructure and hardware. Think of media based on that content and aggregation, and so on. In each case, certain critical strategic decisions rule some solutions in and some out.

Third, it is this *path-dependent nature of the nascent industry evolution* that is so crucial to the understanding of its future manifestations. In that sense, good strategy formulation is always based on a multifaceted knowledge of business history—not just this-or-that case but also those frameworks that we use to approach these cases and that, in a true sense of the word, make them "cases." This process is tragic and heroic at once. It is about the existential choices and commitments of entrepreneurs, companies, and industries in situations of high risk and uncertainty.

These three factors—the critical role of the early years, the emergence of the primary determinants, and the path-dependent nature of industry evolution—account for the durability of the book and its cases and materials.

I have tried to look underneath the process of industry evolution to see what really drives it. I have tried to capture this cluster of industries in its initial structure, with those entry barriers, buyer and supplier power, and so on that exist when the industry comes into existence. Of course, this structure may be a far cry from the industry's final configuration.[6] Still, that final configuration will have to evolve from this initial structure.

The Birth of Internet Marketing Communications, as well as the coming books and studies, I hope, will provide the students, practitioners, researchers, and professionals empirical and real life insight. In general, I prefer to focus on *real-life issues of strategy and marketing*. Moreover, it is important to distinguish between the analytical and the descriptive. The former may produce great insights, as well as some truly bad writing; the latter can provide great journalism, but lousy theories. As I have sought to illustrate the analytical with the descriptive, I have incorporated longer segments of some interviews that—to my mind—capture something essential of the issues, agendas and approaches. In that capacity, these particular segments hopefully serve as testimony of their times, as well as interesting and often provoking introductions to the subject matter. I have chosen to study a field that is highly dynamic and controversial. It would be strange if some of those who set the standards and practices in these fields were not highly dynamic and controversial. Many of them are persistent entrepreneurs who started with a dream, a sense of mission—and very little of anything else, except for an ironclad discipline. If these characteristics did not show in the interviews, something would probably be missing.

The Birth of Internet Marketing Communications can be read as a comprehensive source and reference on the most recent developments in American marketing communications. First and foremost, it serves the researchers and practitioners of marketing and advertising management, media planning, film, television and communication studies, as well as information systems. Due to the digital convergence, it is as important to those in the fields of computers and telecommunications as it is to those in venture capital and corporate finance. It should also prove a handy reference on new media, Internet, and electronic commerce for executives, financial analysts, investors, journalists, as well as general readers.

As a narrative, *The Birth of Internet Marketing Communications* opens with the now famous "crisis speech" by Edwin Artzt, former chairman and CEO of Procter & Gamble. The second chapter explores the context that gave rise to that speech and its concern for the fate of mass marketing in a competitive environment that is about to fragment the marketplace. The third chapter focuses on the rise of Internet marketing in and through relationship marketing and business-to-business marketing. The fourth chapter tells the story of consumer marketing on the Web. The fifth chapter explores the rise and evolution of industry practices, from online branding to both online and offline advertising, hybrids, online communities, and ad networks. The sixth chapter studies some implications of the Web in global marketing and for global marketers.

I dedicate *The Birth of Internet Marketing Communications* to those young Americans, diverse and yet similar in their boldness of thought, optimism of spirit, idealism and pragmatism, who initiated a revolution in the nation's infrastructure—a revolution that began at the close of the 20th century but whose implications will carry well into the new millennium.

NOTES

1. Finland, as the reader may know, has the highest relative Internet and cellular penetration in the world.

2. Dan Steinbock, *Triumph and Erosion in the American Media and Entertainment Industries* (Westport, CT: Quorum Books 1995).

3. See Dan Steinbock, *Verkkobisnes* [*Internet Business Economics*] (Helsinki: Edita 1997); Dan Steinbock, *Pentagonista elektroniseen kauppaan: Amerikkalainen tietoyhteiskuntakeskustelua* [*From Pentagon to Electronic Commerce: American Discourses on the Information Highways*] (Helsinki: SITRA 1998); Dan Steinbock, *Internet and the Transformation of Marketing Communications* [*Internet ja markkinointiviestinnän muodonmuutos*] (Helsinki: Edita 1998); *Internet markkinointi Suomessa* [*Internet Marketing in Finland*] (Helsinki: Edita 1998).

4. For my OECD report, see Dan Steinbock, *Dismantling the Barriers to Global Electronic Commerce*, Turku, Finland, November 19–21, 1997, An International Conference and Business-Government Forum, February 1998. It is available on the OECD website, http://www.oecd.org.

5. Dan Steinbock, *The Competitive Advantage of Finland: From Cartels to Competition?* (Helsinki: ETLA, Taloustieto 1998), with Foreword by Professor Michael E. Porter, "The Competitive Advantage of Nations—The Finnish Case."

6. In his *Competitive Strategy*, Michael E. Porter makes this point very distinctly: "The evolutionary processes work to push the industry toward its *potential structure*, which is rarely known completely as an industry evolves. Imbedded in the underlying technology, product characteristics, and nature of present and potential buyers, however, there is a range of structures the industry might possibly achieve, depending on the direction and success of research and development, marketing innovations, and the like." See Michael E. Porter, *Competitive Strategy* (New York: The Free Press 1980), p. 163.

Acknowledgments

In the course of my research program, "Competition, Strategy, and Marketing: From Marketplace to Marketspace" (1997–2000), I have interviewed many industry leaders and academic researchers. *The Birth of Internet Marketing Communications* would not have been possible without my interviewees. For the *framework* of this study, I remain in gratitude for Professor Michael E. Porter, and Professor Emeritus Theodor Levitt of Harvard Business School, and Regis McKenna, Chairman of The McKenna Group (whose arguments on interactivity and relationship marketing were so convincing that I needed to review the entire book).

I would also like to thank several other interviewees for significant contributions to this particular project and the program itself: David A. Aaker (E. T. Grether Professor of Marketing and Public Policy, Haas School of Business, University of California, Berkeley), Robert Allen (President, Modem Media), Craig R. Barrett (President and CEO, Intel Corp.), Jan Brandt (Senior VP of Marketing, America Online), George F. Colony (President and CEO, Forrester Research, Inc.), C. Samuel Craig (Professor, Department of Marketing, NYU), Gene DeRose (Chairman and CEO, Jupiter Communications), Marco Iansiti (Associate Professor, Technology & Operations Management, Harvard Business School), Rosabeth Moss Kanter (Professor, Harvard Business School), Philip Kotler (Professor, International Marketing, J. L. Kellogg Graduate School of Management, Northwestern University), Mark Kuamme (Chairman of USWeb/CKS Group), Ira Magaziner (Senior Policy Advisor, Clinton Administration), F. Warren McFarlan (Albert H. Gordon Professor of Business Administration, Harvard Business School), Geoffrey E. Moore (Chairman, The Chasm Group), Nathan Myhrvold (Chief Technology

Director, Microsoft Corp.), Martin Nisenholtz (President, New York Times Electronic Media Co.), Kevin J. O'Connor (Chairman, CEO, DoubleClick, Inc.), Fergus O'Daly (former President of CKS Partners/ East Coast), Don Peppers (Partner, Peppers and Rogers Group), Martha Rogers (professor and Partner, Peppers and Rogers Group), Louis Rossetto (former CEO and Editorial Director, Wired Ventures), Don E. Schultz (Professor, Integrated Marketing Communications, Medill School of Journalism, Northwestern University), John Julius Sviokla (Adjunct Professor, Harvard Business School), Steve Telleen (Managing Director, Electronic Commerce IT Practices, Giga Information Group), Lester Wunderman (Chairman, Wunderman Cato Johnson), and Albert Yu (Senior VP, General Manager, Microprocessor Products Group, Intel Corporation).

I also would like to single out a few people who have had a specific role in this project. I am especially grateful to Eric Valentine, publisher of Quorum Books, for his interest, confidence, and seemingly endless patience in the project, and to John Donohue of Rainsford Type for editorial assistance. I am indebted to my project partners, Thomas Jöhnsson, IT manager of IntelSweden responsible for the Northern European Territory, and Hannele Pöysä-Mikkola, project chief in charge of Edita's new media operations. Finally, I am indebted to my colleagues and students at the Helsinki School of Economics, as well as to my research assistants, Yael Ines Hernandez and Shirley M. Brito.

Thanks to Latin rhythms and my dance partners for the *salsa y sabor* that so many times lifted my spirits and cleared my thoughts in the course of this project. And, finally, thanks to my family, my parents and my brother, all of whom I see too seldom and miss daily.

The Birth of
Internet Marketing
Communications

1

Prologue: The Crisis Speech

From where we stand today, we can't be sure that ad-supported TV
programming will have a future in the world being created—a world
of video-on-demand, pay-per-view and subscription television.[1]

In May 1994, Edwin L. Artzt, then-chairman and chief executive of Procter & Gamble (P&G), addressed the American Association of Advertising
Agencies (AAAA) on the future of television advertising. He was not
about to paint a rosy picture of the impending prospects. He wanted to
shock the community. He urged the advertising community to take
charge of what many observers called the interactive media.

As the CEO of P&G, Artzt represented the leading U.S. and global
mass marketers. His words counted. He wanted to make the ad community aware of what might be coming. He sought to prepare the industry for change. He knew exactly the kind of impact he was about to
achieve in the advertising community. He wanted to provoke.

At the time, most industry observers spoke of "interactive advertising," not quite yet of the Internet revolution which would pick up the
momentum later in 1994. Many feared interactive advertising would
eclipse traditional media, both broadcasting (the "Big Three" networks)
and narrowcasting (the multiple station operators on cable). Mass advertising was vital to a mass marketer like P&G, which spent almost 90%
of its $3 billion advertising budget on broadcasting. Big advertisers and
ad agencies were still licking their wounds after the M&A wave of shake-
out and consolidation in the 1980s. Business was no longer "as usual."
Things had changed, irreversibly. In less than a year, the launch of the

World Wide Web, Mosaic, and an aggressive Internet upstart, Netscape, would alter the industry structure that had practically ensured mass marketers' profitability for the past 40 years.

"Within the next few years—surely before the end of the decade—consumers will be choosing among hundreds of shows and pay-per-view movies," noted Artzt. "They'll have dozens of home shopping channels. They'll play hours of interactive video games. And for many of these—maybe most—no advertising at all."[2]

If advertisers and media would *not* intercede, Artzt thought that interactive television (ITV) could emerge as a mostly ad-free medium. Consequently, advertisers could no longer count on broadcast television, the broadest medium of all, to reach a mass audience.

P&G's chief executive delivered his speech at the pinnacle of the hype over interactive TV, offering video clips from such ITV champions as Time Warner Chairman-CEO Gerald Levin, Tele-Communications Inc. President-CEO John Malone, and Barry Diller, then chairman of QVC. If QVC could sell 20,000 pairs of earrings in five minutes on the home shopping channel, that was terrific for a company that sold impulse items, Artzt argued. But all of this meant little to P&G and other *mass marketers*. P&G alone had to sell 400 million boxes of Tide annually. In order to build and nurture brand loyalty, it needed mass markets. It needed broad reach to launch, retain, and expand its brands. If cable had segmented mass markets, the Web promised to fragment them.

Insofar as Artzt was concerned, if advertisers were to remain bystanders, they were digging their own graves. "If that happens," he concluded, "if advertising is no longer needed to pay most of the cost of home entertainment, then advertisers like us will have a hard time achieving the reach and frequency we need to support our brands."[3]

Artzt's "crisis speech" energized advertisers and agencies, and not a moment too soon. In May 1994, for instance, IBM, in the largest shift of advertising history, dismissed more than 40 agencies it had worked with around the world and moved its entire account to a single shop. The decision reverberated for months in the ad industry, while its underlying motive—consolidation by rapid industry change—anticipated sweeping changes on Madison Avenue.

Yet, in retrospect, Artzt's "crisis speech" would be as famous for its catalytic role as it would for its mistaken premises. Yes, mass marketing had eclipsed; but, no, interactive television did not replace traditional media advertising—the *Internet* would.

In December 1994, Time Warner Inc. activated its highly touted interactive television network in Orlando, Florida. The so-called Full Service Network (FSN) was initially portrayed as the centerpiece of the company's ambitious plans to dominate the "information superhighway." The FSN allowed its 4,000 customers to order movies, pizza, and stamps, as well as play interactive games with other subscribers. Each customer was equipped with a cable box that was 10 times more powerful than a contemporary PC with a 486 microprocessor. Since each set-top box cost thousands of dollars and Time Warner spent tens of millions of dollars, the high-tech cable system proved far too costly to introduce nationwide.

By the mid-1990s, development efforts in the interactive world were almost exclusively focused on the Internet, not dedicated cable systems. In September 1997, TW said it planned to unplug the FSN, all but abandoning plans to use its cable systems for a national interactive entertainment-and-shopping service. Following the industry leader's announcement, other cable and phone companies also largely dropped such plans. Time Warner Chairman Gerald Levin acknowledged that the company's focus on the FSN had been "off the mark," but he also noted that the explosion of interest in the Internet validated the company's focus on developing a major interactive presence. "He who makes a living from a crystal ball must learn to eat ground glass," Levin joked.[4]

After the mid-1990s, ITV sank under its own hype, unable to generate the bandwidth needed to deliver the product. Few had regrets. The future belonged to the Internet. Oddly enough, when Edwin Artzt delivered his crisis speech, he had *missed* the emergence of the new medium. Why?

In the late 1990s, Bob Herbold served as the executive vice president chief operating officer of Microsoft. In May 1994, he was still P&G's senior vice president of information services and advertising. Insofar as he was concerned, the specifics of the contemporary predictions were less relevant than the broader call to action to prepare Madison Avenue for the new media. By 1997, he defended the do-or-die message in the address. "It was an appropriate thing to do given everything that was known at that juncture."[5]

Of course, Artzt was not alone in failing to forecast the explosion of the Internet. Only a month before the crisis speech, Netscape began to develop the first commercial web browser. Still, most ad industry observers discovered the Internet phenomenon far, far behind the Silicon Alley. Even the titans of the PC revolution in the 1980s were latecomers: Microsoft did not join the bandwagon until 1995. Three years later, Microsoft had become the largest advertiser on the Web, just like P&G had placed its bet on the Internet.

In September 1997, Herbold drew the lessons from the crisis speech: Don't blindly believe long-term predictions about technology. Accept the more important point that the new media realm is changing the marketing game. And be prepared to modify the game plan continually.

Of course, Procter & Gamble was neither the first nor the last to face what would become known as the digital tornado. In the next few years, many other legendary American companies, *both* consumer marketers *and* business-to-business marketers, would have to face a very different competitive environment. Occasionally, the ad practitioners would revive the debate on Artzt's crisis speech, while young MBA candidates would earn course credits digging new details on the ITV debacle.

Historically, Artzt's speech was critical. It was far more than just a side effect of a new emerging industry. It reflected a crucial shift in the very ground of American marketing. Something similar had taken place at the turn of the 20th century, when the United States completed the transition from an agricultural to an industrial society. In her *Satisfaction Guaranteed*, a historical study of the making of the American mass market, Susan Strasser has described the birth of the new economy, new society, and new culture with breathtaking freshness:

New ways of relating to the objects of everyday life—the material culture of American society—developed along with this physical and economic landscape. During the decades around the turn of the century, branded, standardized products came to represent and embody the new networks and systems of production and distribution, the social relationships that brought people the things they used. Household routines involved making fewer things and purchasing more; consumption became a major part of the work of the household. Formerly *customers*, purchasing the objects of daily life from familiar craftspeople and storekeepers, Americans became *consumers*. They bought and used mass-produced goods as participants in a national market composed of masses of people associating with big, centrally organized, national-level companies. As they came to depend on complex goods from distant sources, they came to understand less about how things were made, how they worked, how they could be fixed.

This combination of private and public change amounted to nothing less than a major cultural shift that entailed new kinds of needs.[6]

After two to three decades of massive transitions in the American economy, technology, society, and culture, something very similar occurred in the 1990s. Just as the turn of the 19th century had witnessed new ways of relating to the objects of everyday life, the material culture of the late 20th century American society saw its own transformations. Ultimately, *these changes* would problematize even "materiality" and "physicality," through the virtualization of entire economies, organizations, and industries, as well as products and services.

During the decades around the turn of the 21st century, branded and standardized products lost much of their appeal. Product development accelerated. Private brands proliferated. Mass-customized production came to represent and embody the new networks and systems of production and distribution. None of these changes took place at once; each was layered on the previous one. Through the evolutionary cycle of substitution economics, minicomputers invaded niches in the mainframe markets, personal computers replaced minicomputers, just as Internet-enabled systems would substitute for stand-alone PCs.

During the 1880s, inventors had developed new machinery that made flow production possible in the manufacture of soap, cigarettes, matches, breakfast cereals, canned goods, and many other products. But that alone was not enough. As Strasser puts it, "New techniques for national marketing emerged in tandem with the mass-produced products they promoted. People who had never heard of toothpaste had to be told that they needed it. . . . A population accustomed to homemade products and unbranded merchandise had to be converted into a national market for standardized, advertised, brand-named goods in general."[7] By the 1980s and 1990s, new technologies made possible entirely new modes of production, through virtualization, digitalization, miniaturization, and distributed computing. But now, just as before, that alone would not be enough. These new techniques were no longer just national. With the *World Wide* Web, the globalization of highly cost-efficient marketing strategies emerged in tandem with the mass-customized products they promoted. People who had never heard of browsers had to be told they needed them, if only to access the wonders of the "Net." A population accustomed to factory-made products and branded merchandise had to be converted from an early adopter niche mixture of PC nerds, sophisticated professionals, and faddish consumers to a worldwide market for new, or newly digitized goods.

In June 1996, *Business Week* managed to capture the ethos of the new era in its special report on the information appliance as software's Holy Grail. Just as a century ago, Procter & Gamble had to introduce the idea of soap to sell Ivory, the leading business weekly touted the "user-friendly" values of the "information appliances" of the Internet era:

Whether it's the PC or one of the new "Web cruisers" that are under development, the information appliance that brings the masses into cyberspace will have to have software that's more intuitive, more forgiving, and a lot better at simplifying the digital experience. . . . The solution, however, may be at hand—or at least the path to a solution. It is the Web-browsing software used to navigate the World Wide Web. The browser filled a simple need: It provided a standard way to view, from any type of computer, information stored on the Web. Anyone with a browser and a modem could reach the thousands of computers on the Web, jumping from one to another by simply clicking a mouse on highlighted words on a Web page. . . .

So the scramble is on to create a new wave of network-based software and services that will take advantage of the Web and deliver on the vision of the information appliance. . . . Eventually, the Net will be brimming with multimedia information that's accessible from virtually any place where there's an information appliance.

Once the digital deluge begins, the next software challenge will be to help consumers keep their heads above water.[8]

A century ago, Americans had become consumers. By the 21st century, they were becoming sophisticated consumers who no longer bought and used simple mass-produced goods, but increasingly used a multitude of different and specialized marketing channels to find what they were searching for. They had become quite aware of the impact of the seasonal changes on advertising and promotions and had also become active participants in international markets.

In his *New and Improved: The Story of Mass Marketing in America*, Richard S. Tedlow has identified three phases of consumer product marketing in the United States: fragmentation (prior to the 1880s), unification (1880s–1950s), and segmentation (1950s–1990s). Certain strategic characteristics and infrastructure mark the progression through these three phases. Historically, the railroad and the telegraph made possible the pre–World War II national market and mass marketing; it formed a marketplace based on high volume and low margin (unification). The post–World War II era exploited the rise of commercial television (and later cable), as well as market/audience research in the segmentation of the national market(s); it formed a marketplace based on high volume and value pricing (segmentation).[9] Each stage gave rise to businesses existing within the infrastructure—with legal, technological, political, and a whole host of other attributes—that both provided opportunities for profitable expansion and limited the options available.[10]

The most recent stage is no exception. Just as the 1880s and 1950s represented a profound paradigm shift in consumer product marketing, so do the 1990s, which is witnessing the explosive emergence of the Internet-enabled marketing systems that would previously have been impossible (Exhibit 1-1).

In the famous third chapter of *The Wealth of Nations*, Adam Smith had argued that "the division of labor is limited by the extent of the market." This power of exchange and division of labor is no longer limited by those geographic boundaries that formed the first (nationally limited) mass markets.[11] At the turn of the 21st century, the Internet-enabled marketing systems are rapidly transforming and defining the infrastructure of the U.S. economy—through the Internet revolution and the digitalization of information and communications industries, as well as the rapid commercial exploitation of the Web, from intranets and extranets to the nascent electronic commerce.

In the process of this massive transformation, the principles of high volume and value pricing continue to influence marketing, even if their *context* has drastically shifted. If the strategy of profit through volume, for instance, was a breakthrough concept in the development of the mass

Exhibit 1-1
The Four Phases of Consumer Product Marketing in the United States*

Phase	Strategic Characteristics	Defining Infrastructure
I. Fragmentation (To the 1880s)	• High margin • Low volume • Geographically limited markets	• Incomplete railroad network • Incomplete exploitation of telegraph • Political and economic instability
II. Unification (1880s–1950s)	• High volume • Low margin • Incorporation of the whole nation in a mass market	• Railroad and telegraph network complete • Political stability • Economic cycles
III. Segmentation (1950s–1990s)	• High volume • Value pricing • Demographic and psychographic segmentation	• Rise of commercial television (and later new media)
IV. Internet-Enabled Marketing Systems (1990s–Present)	• High volume, differential pricing • Behavioral rather than attitudinal database drivers • Interactivity through (globalized?) relationship marketing and/or integrated marketing communications	• Internet revolution and digitalization of information and communication industries • Rapid leveraging of the Web (from intranets/extranets to electronic commerce) • Penetration strategies within the horizontal layers of the new infrastructure

*Slightly modified; the first three phases adapted from Richard Tedlow (1990), *New and Improved* (New York: Basic Books 1996), p. xxii.

market, it remains so with the emergence of the virtual "marketspace."[12] In the past, first-mover advantages were quite real, leading to high profits not despite but because of low prices. In turn, these advantages served as barriers to the entry of new competition. Toward the late 1990s, such first-mover advantages have become even more critical. As agility and time-based competition in the deregulated, new and emergent markets replace the regulated, old and mature markets, speed economies have become crucial to competitive strategy.

In the process, differential pricing may displace or augment value pricing as the price paradigm.[13]

Complementing the traditional demographic and psychographic segmentation, behavioral rather than attitudinal database determinants are taking the spotlight in the marketing systems with the assistance of the new technologies. Simultaneously, feedback loops are being incorporated with the formerly one-directional marketing approaches to ensure interactivity through relationship marketing or integrated marketing communications. And, due to new cost-efficient solutions, the Internet-enabled marketing systems are being globalized. On the firm level, the strategy of profit through volume, the commitment of individual managers, mass-customization, first-mover advantages, imitation and innovation strategies, adaptability to change—these characteristics typify many of the leading marketers of the new era.

Reflecting on the significance of the Internet revolution, Andrew Grove, president and CEO of Intel in the mid-1990s, concluded that even the most powerful industry giants would have to be prepared to modify the game plan continually. The Internet was changing *both* the consumer *and* the business-to-business marketing game, irreversibly. As Intel embarked on a whole new way of doing business, Grove would later argue that the company had stumbled onto a "strategic inflection point."

Strategic inflection points can be caused by technological change but they are more than technological change. They can be caused by competitors but they are more than just competition. They are full-scale changes in the way business is conducted, so that simply adopting new technology or fighting the competition as you used to may be insufficient. They build up force so insidiously that you may have a hard time even putting a finger on what has changed, yet you know that something *has*.[14]

In the spring of 1994, Edwin Artzt had had a hunch of a massive ongoing transition which was about to subvert all conventional industry wisdom. He felt it. He saw it. But, at the time, he just could not put a finger on the change. Others would—not least because of the energizing impact that Artzt's speech had, from New York's Madison Avenue and then-miniscule Silicon Alley to California's Hollywood and Silicon Valley.

American marketing would never be the same again.

NOTES

1. See "P&G's Artzt: TV Advertising in Danger," *Advertising Age*, May 23, 1994.

2. Ibid.

3. Ibid.

4. Eben Shapiro, "Time Warner Will Pull the Plug On Its Interactive-TV Network," *Wall Street Journal*, May 1, 1997.

5. Bradley Johnson, "Bob Herbold Reflects on '94 Speech He Wrote," *Advertising Age*, September 2, 1997.

6. Susan Strasser, *Satisfaction Guaranteed: The Making of the American Mass Market* (New York: Pantheon Books 1990), see chapter 1, especially pp. 15–16. For a practitioner's account on mass production and segmentation, see Alfred P. Sloan, Jr. (1962), *My Years with General Motors* (New York: Doubleday 1996). On the history of strategy and structure in mass production and mass marketing, see Alfred D. Chandler, Jr., *Strategy and Structure: Chapters in the History of the American Industrial Enterprise* (Cambridge, MA: The MIT Press 1962); *The Visible Hand* (Cambridge, MA: Belknap Press of Harvard University Press 1977); and *Scale and Scope* (Cambridge, MA: Belknap Press of Harvard University Press 1994). On the transition from mass production to mass customization, see B. Joseph Pine III, *Mass Customization* (Cambridge, MA: Harvard Business School Press 1993).

7. Strasser, *Satisfaction Guaranteed*, p. 7.

8. Amy Cortese, "The Information Appliance Software's Holy Grail: No-Fuss Clicking Is What Consumers Need Most," *Business Week*, June 24, 1996.

9. Richard S. Tedlow (1990), *New and Improved: The Story of Mass Marketing in America* (New York: Basic Books 1996).

10. For a contemporary treatment of segmentation in strategic marketing, see Vithala R. Rao and Joel H. Steckel, *Analysis for Strategic Marketing* (Reading, MA: Addison Wesley Longman 1998).

11. Compare Adam Smith (1776), *The Wealth of Nations: Books I–III* (London: Penguin Books 1986), pp. 121–126.

12. In future research projects, I intend to explore some specific implications of this transition—from the physical marketplace to the virtual marketspace—especially its effects on competitive strategies from the Internet to electronic commerce, the virtualization and leveraging of "offline" brands, and so on. For the pioneering investigations on the transition impact in value chains, see, e.g., Jeffrey Rayport and John Sviokla, "Managing in the Marketspace," *Harvard Business Review*, November–December 1994; Jeffrey Rayport and John Sviokla, "Exploiting the Virtual Value Chain," *Harvard Business Review*, November–December 1995; Arthur G. Armstrong and John Hagel III, "Real Value of On-Line Communities," *Harvard Business Review*, May–June 1996; Stephen P. Bradley and Richard L. Nolan (eds.), *Sense & Respond: Capturing Value in the Network Era* (Boston: Harvard Business School Press 1998).

13. On information rules and differential pricing, see Carl L. Shapiro and Hal R. Varian, *Information Rules: A Strategic Guide to the Network Economy* (Boston: Harvard Business School Press 1998).

14. Andrew S. Grove, *Only the Paranoid Survive: How to Exploit the Crisis Points That Challenge Every Company and Career* (New York: Doubleday 1996), pp. 3–5. To Grove, himself, it was the Pentium debacle that would serve as *the* metaphor of an underlying structural industry change (i.e., strategic inflection point).

2

The First Years: From Home Pages to Websites and Portals

In December 1992, John Malone, CEO of TCI, announced that TCI planned to introduce digital compression technology that would let the company provide 500 or more channels to cable subscribers. It was his statement that popularized the notion of a "500-channel universe."[1]

But the dream never materialized. In 1993, Malone again tried to jump start the revolution by merging the nation's powerful cable giant with Bell Atlantic. The deal did not work out. Malone disappeared from the digital arena. He had set out to be the "Vanderbilt of the information highway."[2] But the convergence would be highly complex, both technologically and financially. Ultimately, it would require the fusion of video, interactive data, and telephone service over broadband pipes into every American household throughout the nation and internationally. In the United States, such dreams were predicated on strategic alliances between carriers, local telcos, media and entertainment conglomerates, chip and computer manufacturers, software giants, and others. Such plans would not be easy, and they would take more than a handful of companies to realize.

By the summer of 1996, only four years had passed since the nation's first digital debate, but it felt like an eternity. Even as Malone had been touting the 500-channel universe, a handful of relatively unknown researchers had launched the World Wide Web at CERN, Netscape had charmed Wall Street and Main Street alike, the first Internet IPO (initial public offering) boom had arrived and crashed, and the browser wars were climaxing.

In the end of July in 1996, Intel hosted a symposium for 1,500 techies in Silicon Valley. By then Andy Grove, CEO of Intel, had come to the realization that it would take years before computer networks had enough capacity or bandwidth to carry the multimedia Internet to the masses. To bridge the gap, and stimulate demand for PC microprocessors, Intel came up with a new strategy. The world's biggest chipmaker would focus on *hybrid applications*. Of course, Intel had not (and did not claim to have) invented the concept, and many hybrids already existed (e.g., the features of Microsoft's Encarta encyclopedia).[3] The notion was merely a pragmatic realization that one had to do with what one had *now*. Hybrids would stretch and extend technology that already existed to offer souped-up multimedia experiences, even if they were not yet quite as advanced as those promised once the telecommunications capacity increased. "The myth of the Internet is that there is plenty of bandwidth," Grove said in the symposium. "The hybrid application is what we will use for a long time to overcome the limits of the available bandwidth."[4] Excited about the prospects of emerging digital technologies and the Internet, Grove pranced onstage before a cheering throng of techies. He saw an era of not just "500 channels, but . . . *500,000 channels!*"[5]

In the early 1990s, the idea of 500 TV channels had been embraced by the nation's leading media, computing, and telecommunications conglomerates. Now—after the mid-1990s—the nation's leading microprocessor manufacturer was ridiculing the old capacity and pioneering the way toward half a million marketing channels. Hollywood and Silicon Alley may have loved Grove's statements, but in Madison Avenue, they triggered fear and loathing. What meant paradise to the former indicated a nightmare to the latter.

Media planners, in particular, felt distraught. Deregulation, cable revolution, and alternative media options had already shattered the old and cozy status quo. As the "big three" networks lost control of the prime time audience, promotions were invading ad volumes and brand loyalty was rapidly becoming a remnant of history. Interactive television threatened to re-fragment the already fragmented markets. And now Silicon Valley was dreaming of 500,000 channels? That did not mean a simple channel multiplication any longer; instead, it meant far more—a revolution in the entire channel infrastructure and the ensuing demise of all conventional industry wisdom. How on earth could anybody gain adequate reach and frequency, not to speak of branding, in such a chaotic universe of marketing channels?

How did the dream of Silicon Valley become the nightmare of Madison Avenue?

FROM MASS MARKETING TO INTERNET DYNAMICS:
THE PROLIFERATION OF MARKETING CHANNELS

Since the mid-1980s, American markets have been swept by the emergence of digital marketing communications. In the past, mass marketers conceived of, organized and implemented the marketing paradigm, which originated from the *consumer markets*. Toward the end of the 20th century, marketers were conceptualizing and launching a new marketing paradigm. It evolved in *business-to-business markets*. If Procter & Gamble heralded the era of mass marketing, Federal Express seemed to anticipate the new one of digital marketing communications. In the long term, these systems would also proliferate in the consumer markets. The new environment puzzled even the hard-nosed veterans. Industry wisdom had become a competitive disadvantage. Old rules no longer worked. The world had changed. In 1991, well before the rise of the Web, *Business Week* aired a lot of these sensations in a cover story, "What Happened to Advertising":

Madison Avenue was always a street that had just one side: sunny. The ad game, after all, is about optimism and the power of positive thinking. Advertising legend David Ogilvy regularly exhorted his top lieutenants to "encourage exuberance" and "get rid of sad dogs who spread gloom." Well, welcome to Madison Avenue, 1991: It's the gloomiest kennel you ever saw. This once-buoyant business is suffering through the deepest and most prolonged ad drought in 20 years. Advertising has muddled through its share of recessions. But this downturn has sent an unusual shiver through the industry. The gloom has even reached Chateau de Touffou, the 12th century French castle where Ogilvy now lives in retirement. The advertising world, says the 80-year-old adman, is haunted by "a pervasive atmosphere of fear."[6]

Ad agencies, as well as the publishers and broadcasters who depended on ad sales for much of their revenues, had come to believe that the current hard times could be only a foretaste of much slower growth to come. *That* was new in a business that had prided itself on optimism and limitless boom, and not entirely without a reason. From 1976 through 1988, total U.S. ad spending grew faster than the economy as a whole.

Of course, technological advances were not the only trend affecting marketers and advertisers in the 1980s and early 1990s. Instead, leading interactive ad agencies, for example, saw themselves amidst a longer-term structural transition. Within the U.S. and international business communities, several trends had been causing deep changes in the marketing communications needs of businesses throughout the world. These trends included the following:

- Corporate downsizing, which had led many corporations to reduce the size of their in-house marketing departments, which in turn had led to an increased need to outsource the creation and coordination of such corporations' marketing strategies.

- Shortening product life cycles and preparation times for marketing campaigns, which increased the need for rapid development and execution of marketing strategies.

- The emergence of new media, such as the World Wide Web, proprietary online services, CD-ROMs, laptop PC presentations and interactive kiosks, as well as the increasing availability of sophisticated digital delivery, storage, and multimedia enhancement tools and technologies.

- The advent of narrowly focused media delivery vehicles, such as proprietary online services, the World Wide Web, satellite television and special interest magazines, which allowed greater market segmentation but demanded coordination of multiple variations of marketing messages aimed at particular market sub-segments.[7]

In the course of the 1990s, each and all of these determinants would be instigated by Internet-related technological advances. Marketers, advertisers, ad agencies, market research providers, website developers, traffic measurement and analysis companies—they and many other in related industry segments soon found themselves in the very heart of the "digital tornado."

THE ECLIPSE OF MASS MARKETING

Due to economies of scale and scope, the American media marketplace is not only larger but far more specialized than any other environment worldwide. Also, historically, marketing and advertising, in particular television and electronic media, have had a far more significant role in the United States than elsewhere. Since 1960, advertising volume, measured against gross domestic product, has varied around 2 to 2.4%. Cyclical fluctuations account for most peaks and troughs. Downcycles of the economy have often triggered deep decreases in total advertising volume and television advertising volume. These abrupt turns can best be seen through annual changes.

Advertising and Promotional Spending. Even prior to the dawn of the web, the traditional advertising market remained huge in America, but its composition was changing. Total U.S. advertising and promotional spending consists of three basic segments:

- Measured media (broadcast and cable TV, radio, daily newspapers, and magazines);

- Non-measured media (direct mail, yellow pages, outdoor, weekly newspapers, sports or event sponsorships, and so on);
- Promotions (consumer promotions such as point-of-purchase, coupons, and premiums and trade promotion such as meetings, conventions, trade shows, and incentives).

In 1995—that is, with the onset of the first Internet IPO boom—measured media advertising amounted to some $100 billion and non-measured media advertising to $96 billion, whereas promotional spending had soared to $170 billion.[8] Since the 1980s, the tide had moved toward promotions.

Changes in Measured TV Advertising. Moreover, there had been significant shifts in the composition of measured media ad spending. The evolution of TV ad volume, as a portion of total ad volume, illustrates both the long-term growth trend *and* its changing characteristics since the mid-1980s. Except for the severe years of the energy crisis around 1973–1974, TV ad volume, as a portion of total ad volume, has been steadily climbing since 1960 (around 14%) to the present (almost 25% after the mid-1990s). Even if TV ad volume has steadily increased, its composition has gone through a transformation. In 1987, broadcast TV accounted for $23 billion and cable less than $1.2 billion, whereas, a decade later, the former had grown to $43 billion and the latter to $10 billion. In measured TV advertising, the portion of mass television had declined from 95% to 81%, while that of cable had boomed from 5% to 19%.

The Decline of the Big Three Networks. The penetration of American mass television evolved between the late 1940s and late 1950s. During this decade, the "Big Three" networks (NBC, CBS, and ABC) captured the business and held onto it until well into the 1980s. Until the late 1970s, the incumbent networks (NBC, ABC, CBS) dominated in excess of 90% of America's prime time audience. In the course of the 1980s, the combined share of the "Big Three" declined drastically. The struggle for eyeballs shifted network programming strategies from the ratings race to a profit rivalry. By 1990, for example, CBS won the Nielsen ratings, but ABC captured the "demographic cream" of the audience. If American advertising was born with mass marketing, the 1980s witnessed the splintering of the mass market. Deregulation of cable provided a powerful boost to market segmentation. By the late 1980s, the audience segments had to be sufficiently large for scale economies. Now pricing went hand in hand with the value that the segment placed on the product, not production costs. The bargaining power shifted toward the buyer.[9]

Historically, the erosion of the audience base has been discernible for more than four decades. In relative terms, the ratings were highest with the launch of the new broadcast media at the turn of the 1950s, when the top four TV shows could still each garner almost 50% of the audience. After the first generation of TV sets had been sold, the top shows could still attract almost 30% of the viewers in the mid-1960s. It was this mature competitive environment, stabilized by regulation and controlled by the "Big Three" that, essentially, prevailed until the 1980s. With the onset of cable deregulation around 1982 to 1984, the "cable revolution," as well as the rapid proliferation of independent TV stations and syndicated television, fragmented the marketplace. At the turn of the 1990s, the most successful TV show could attract hardly 20% of the audience. By October 1998, only the most solid performers, such as *E.R.*, *Friends*, or *Frazier* could achieve ratings of 15 to 20%.[10]

Moreover, even these numbers downplayed the full audience losses. At the time, there were an estimated 98 million TV households in the United States. A single ratings point represented 1%, or 980,000 households. That was not all. Ratings are based on audience *shares*. Share is defined as the percentage of TV sets tuned to a specific program. Between 1950 and the early 1980s, the Big Three controlled more than 90% of American prime time viewers; at the close of the 1990s, that figure is around 45 to 55%, depending on the source. In other words, while audience *ratings* had declined to less than a third of the peak years, half of the *share* of the audience was gone, too. Not only had the Big Three lost almost half of their clients; the remaining ones had become very expensive (Exhibit 2-1).

The Rising Costs of Network Television and Audiences. From the mid-1960s to the early 1980s, the number of households viewing prime time network TV had climbed steadily from 10 million to a peak of 15.2 million in 1983. With the rise of cable, the audiences began to decline rapidly, shrinking to 9.5 million in 1997—to a *pre*-1965 level. Despite the erosion of ratings and shares, costs per 30 seconds of average prime time programming soared from less than $20,000 in the mid-1960s to nearly $108,000 in the mid-1980s and, again, to $122,200 in 1990. It was not until the 1990–1991 recession that the costs of prime time programming were contained. Costs per 1,000 homes (CPMs) followed the pattern of costs for programming, booming from $1.98 in the mid-1960s to $9.00 in 1991. Since then, however, they have *not* been contained. They began a steep rise after the 1990–1991 recession climbing to $11.18 in 1997. Despite the losses in audiences, costs of television and audiences continue to rise.

The Shrinking Commercials. Until the mid-1960s, almost 100% of American prime time TV consisted of 60 second commercials (Exhibit 2–1). Between 1970 and 1980, their portion declined from 75% to less than 2%, whereas the portion of 30-second commercials soared from 25% to almost 95%. Between 1980 and 1997, the portion of 30-second commercials declined to 64%, while the portion of 15-second commercials soared from nothing to more than 33%. In the course of three decades, the length of an average prime time TV commercial was only half or a fourth of what it had been in the mid-1960s. The more the commercials shrank, the

Exhibit 2-1

TV Costs and Commercials: From the Mid-1960s to Late 1990s (Network TV Costs and CPM Trends: Nighttime Average Programs)

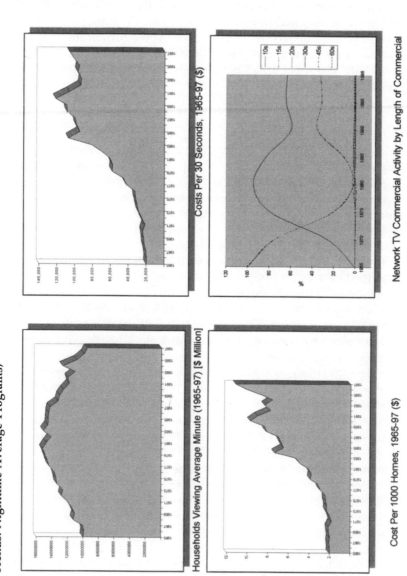

Source: A.C. Nielsen Co. (February each year) [viewing]; CMR + MediaWatch [commercials]. Television Bureau of Advertising, Inc. (1998). All rights reserved.

faster they had to make their pitch. By the early 1990s, the senseless pace of homogeneous commercials served as a constant reminder of the eclipse of mass marketing. The recession had laid bare forces that were giving advertising a permanently diminished role in the selling of goods and services. Argued *Business Week*:

Cynical consumers are wearying of the constant barrage of marketing messages. They're becoming less receptive to the blandishments of Madison Avenue. And their loyalty to brands has eroded as they see more products as commodities distinguished only by price. At the same time that consumers have changed, technology and the proliferation of media are transforming the science of marketing to them. Now, companies increasingly can aim their messages to carefully pinpointed consumers through direct mail. General Motors Corp. is rolling out its new Cadillac Seville with a mailing offering a videocassette to 170,000 young and affluent consumers. Or they can advertise on one of the new and sharply targeted media. To reach young children, Levi Strauss & Co. used to advertise mostly during Saturday morning cartoons on the networks. Now the company also advertises on MTV and a new music channel on cable called Video Jukebox Network.[11]

In the light of the Internet and its direct potential, these targeting options remained narrow and one-sided. Based on a broadcast model, they made real time interactivity impossible.

In summary, since the 1960s and well *before* the rise of the Internet, American prime time TV, the right arm of mass marketing, had been characterized by several structural, long-standing developments:

- Despite the steady increases in total TV ad volume, TV advertising had gone through an internal "new deal," especially since the cable revolution in at the turn of the 1980s.
- Since and due to the cable revolution, independent TV stations, syndicated television, and other media options, the Big Three networks had lost half of their audience, even before the Internet revolution.
- Despite significant losses in ratings and shares, the costs of prime time television were barely contained until the turn of the 1990s, while the costs of network audience would continue to soar.
- In the process, the average length of American prime time commercial was halved at best and declined by two-thirds at worst.

It is important to note that all of these trends *preceded* the rise of the Internet. Even before the launch of the Web, American marketers were paying increasingly more for increasingly less.

From Remote and Zapping to Internet and Clicking. It is quite possible that even these distressing figures overstate the size of the viewing audiences. To a great extent, the numbers disregard or entirely neglect the extraordinary rise of remote control and home video since the early 1980s. With the rise of these new *buyer reception* technologies, the creative producers became quite aware of the shift in the bargaining power. In the past, program schedules had directed viewing, but by the 1980s, *audiences* made up their "own" schedules. As Brandon Tartikoff, NBC's legendary programmer, put it in the mid-1980s:

When you've got a Zap Box in your house, and the average number of channels in the typical household is somewhere in the 25–30 range, you've got much more control and many more choices. . . . Lucille Ball said that television changed with the invention of the remote control device. As soon as a guy doesn't have to get up from his chair to switch the channel, television becomes a new ball game. Viewer inertia, which supported many an uninspired show, has given way to viewer impatience.[12]

But even that was only the beginning. As the mouse replaced the remote and zapping gave way to clicking, the old conventional wisdom was no longer a solution, but part of the problem.

One might suspect that by the early 1990s advertisers and brands would have turned their back to mass television, but that was not the case. As America grew more diverse and audiences became highly specialized, advertisers and brands did not leave *en masse*. On the contrary, they stayed and grew steadily. In 1970, there had been 427 advertisers and 2,348 brands using network TV; by the mid-1990s, there were some 750 advertisers and 3,496 brands.[13] Even though the competitive environment had gone through a wholesale transformation and marketing channels had proliferated, advertisers and brands continued to rely on mass television—against all evidence, against all reality. Of course, mass marketers knew well what was happening, but they saw cable and segmentation as a threat rather than an *opportunity*—just as they would see the Internet only a decade later.

The rise of integrated marketing communications toward the end of the 1980s had precipitated the coming changes in Madison Avenue, in particular the shift of bargaining power toward buyers—consumers and advertisers rather than ad agencies.

The First Stages of Internet Advertising. In the early 1990s, the biggest American advertisers were primarily consumer products companies, such as General Motors, Procter & Gamble, Philip Morris, Chrysler, Ford, Sears, Roebuck, and Walt Disney. In the very first years of the Web, advertising expenditures on the Internet were generated by portals and IT-based companies, such as Microsoft, IBM, Excite, Yahoo!, Netscape, Infoseek and Lycos. By 1997, however, major national advertisers were joining the game in droves, including auto manufacturers (GM, Toyota, etc.), telecommunications (AT&T, Bell Atlantic, etc.), and many others.

Indeed, many of these were investing significant amounts of capital in the business-to-business markets (intranets, extranets) where expenditures were hard to track. Still, Web advertising remained top-heavy: with more than 900 sites selling advertising on the Web after the mid-1996, the top ten highest grossing revenue sites accounted for 57% of total Web ad revenue. Also, many of these leading Web advertisers—mainly portals and browsers and content/aggregators—were also among the biggest recipients of Web advertising revenue.[14]

Estimates of Internet advertising varied, but directional significance was relatively clear (Exhibit 2-2). Between 1996 and 2000, subscriptions revenues were expected to rise from $120 million to $966 million; advertising revenues from $312 million to $5 billion; and transactions from $518 million to $6.6 billion. The contemporary media executives shrugged off such figures as insignificant, but such gestures reflected only strategic signaling and maneuvering. Certainly, it was true that, in comparison to mainstream ad vehicles and media pipelines, Web advertising was miniscule. In 1996, direct mail accounted for $34.9 billion, TV networks more than $13 billion, and radio almost $2.7 billion—as against the Internet's $312 million. In the long term (and even in the not-so-long term), what really mattered was that every media had to start its rise from zero—and that, historically, the Internet was growing faster than any other media. Around 1996 and 1997, many observers expected the Internet revenues to top the radio ad revenues by the year 2000.

By the end of the 1990s, the Internet threatened to speed up the demise of mass marketing. In the early 1990s, many advertisers and some agencies put their faith in integrated marketing communications, hoping that it would resolve the issue of channel multiplication.

Information Revolution and Integrated Marketing Communications

"The days of traditional mass marketing are over. Technology ended them. They will not return." This opening of the 1993 book, *The New Marketing Paradigm: Integrated Marketing Communications*, was provocative. It was intended to be so. The authors, Don E. Schultz, Stanley I. Tannenbaum, and Robert F. Lauterborn, were convinced that American marketing had entered an era of information revolution that made possible *integrated marketing communications* (IMC). For a few years, these ideas had been "in the air," but the authors gave them structure and clout.[15]

The proponents of IMC argued that the marketplace had changed dramatically in the 1980s, both domestically and globally. Mass marketing had evolved in a marketplace that had been subject to the laws of mass production, economies of scale, homogeneous consumer markets, as well as national brand domination of a limited number of channels. By the

Exhibit 2-2
Internet Advertising: Internet Revenues, 1996–2000 (estimated); Online
Revenues, Advertising and Subscriptions, 1995–2000 (estimated); and Total
Ad Volumes and Internet Revenues

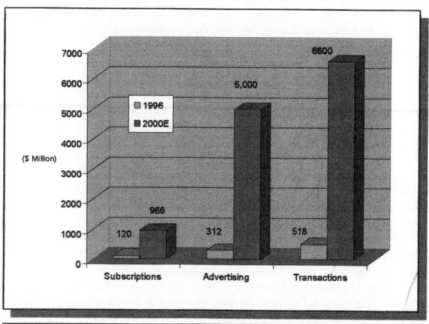

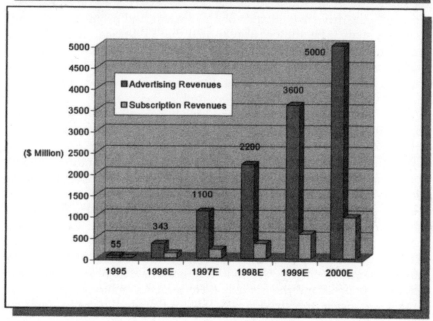

Exhibit 2-2 (continued)

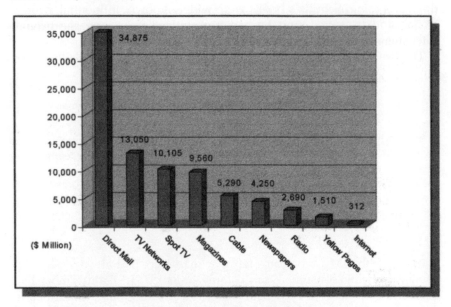

Sources: Jupiter Communications; Forrester Research; McCann-Erickson.

late 1980s, that marketplace had become unrecognizable. The marketing methods business had relied on were no longer working. They had been replaced by the relentless focus on new products, generic competitive strategies, the drive to generate volume growth, and promotional pricing to obtain share. The authors also argued that traditional marketing and marketing organizations had become equally obsolete. Since traditional marketing was irrevocably altered, traditional communication programs had become increasingly irrelevant. "Mass advertising is dying," the authors wrote. "Mass media is in deep trouble. Big, ponderous advertising agencies are sinking in the ooze. The 1990s call not just for a re-engineered approach to communications but for a re-invention of the entire marketing communications process."[16]

Of course, the message was not exactly new. Many industry practitioners had become acutely aware of the problems in the course of the 1980s. What made *The New Marketing Paradigm* unique was not just its message but the messengers. They were no longer industry "gurus" or "visionaries" with little or marginal significance in the business or the academia. Don Schultz, for instance, served as professor of Integrated Marketing Communications (IMC) at the Medill School of Journalism, Northwestern University.[17] He had authored dozens of significant articles in trade press and the academia. He served as editor or co-editor of several significant industry journals. He participated in critical industry functions ranging from direct marketing to marketing research and media advertising. Schultz's books were widely known, influential, professional, and respected, and he had proselytized new converts through intensive international lecture tours.[18]

The IMC proponents were industry insiders. If *they* were disillusioned with the "old marketing paradigm," that reflected the views of the industry and researchers quite extensively. According to Schultz, the pressure toward IMC arose

in the early 1980s, as the money began to shift from media advertising into promotion. As a result, advertising agencies began to buy direct marketing agencies. They were trying to find some way to put all of these venues together. At the time, we had done quite a bit of work with ad agencies. Most of our students graduated and went to work for very large agencies, primarily as account managers, account directors, and so on. We learned about these developments quite early.[19]

In effect, the IMC advocates felt that marketers had always given lip service to being consumer- or customer-oriented. In reality, most had been and continued to be product- or service-focused; they continued to favor top-down strategies. Instead of more old receipts, the IMC advocates spoke for an entirely new approach. Interestingly enough, that approach would prove not that dissimilar with the views, methods, and techniques of the new generation of marketers who considered the Internet and interactivity crucial in the 21st century.

Successful marketing in the 1990s and beyond required *real* customer orientation, argued Schultz and his colleagues. It meant communicating with individuals, not shotgunning markets. Based on long-term relationships between buyer and seller, user and supplier, it was a two-way relationship where the marketer and the customer acted, reacted, and interacted to the benefit of both. Based on customer satisfaction, it was quality driven. The authors of the new paradigm called for integrated, coordinated, cohesive marketing communications programs that would inform, involve, and persuade customers and prospects. They would not work inside-out, but *outside-in*—they intended to start with the customer or consumer, and adapt to suit the customer's needs. They wanted to speak specifically to individuals, not generically to markets. They would focus on what customers and prospects wanted or needed to know about products and services, not just what marketers wanted to tell them. They sought dialogue. But, most significantly, they believed in being accountable. Modern marketers, they argued, measure success not just in soft terms like awareness and favorability but in the hard currency of return on marketing communications investment.[20]

IMC was the implementation process for the new marketing paradigm.

By the mid-1990s, it was no longer known just in the physical market-place. Trendsetting interactive ad agencies, such as CKS Group, embraced and adopted the tenets of IMC in marketspace. By 1997, the IMC had moved from the "what is it?" to the "how can we do it?" stage of development in the United States.[21] While academic textbooks presented IMC as a fait accompli, Schultz himself saw integration as far more difficult. According to research, agency leaders believed IMC to be an important concept and approach, just as they believed that their clients felt the same. There were, however, concerns as to how IMC programs should or could be evaluated. Also, integration would have to come from the client. Unless the client led the way, even the most capable agencies would not be able to integrate a client's marketing communications programs. The issues were organizational, but stemmed from the information revolution, in particular the rise of the Internet and *open standards*. According to Don Schultz,

To a certain extent, the Web has been driven by the promotion end. Much of its explosive growth is the result of the availability of data. In the past, the databases of most organizations were legacy systems. Now we have seen the rapid development of servers, the ability to manage quite a bit of data. It is now becoming affordable to manage, capture, store, and manipulate on customers' prospects. To a certain extent, most organizations, at least on the corporate side, are beginning to realize that they have a tremendous amount of data internally that they don't use. Organizations have always wanted to integrate their data, but it has been extremely difficult to achieve and, historically, they haven't had a way to really organize it. In the past, they couldn't use the data to look at *customers* as a unit. The growth of the technology changed the situation.[22]

The IMC advocates viewed Artzt's crisis speech in 1994 as reflective of a channel conflict rather than the general rise of the new interactive media. Procter & Gamble was able to trigger some changes, but these did not pertain to the new competitive environment, only certain relevant industry environments. "What Artzt really said was, 'We're going to go back and find different ways of dealing with customers and consumers.' He was trying to stop the promotion spiral," argues Schultz.

To a certain extent, that *has* occurred. Couponing is still out there but, as an issue, it's not nearly as critical. Still, the firms have not reduced trade promotions, which have actually gone up. Artzt focused the marketing organization in terms of recognizing the *channel*. And today you do see a tremendous amount of emphasis on co-marketing between the manufacturer and the channel trying to approach the customer in a joint effort. Still, the problem for the manufacturer is that the retailer wants to become a brand, whereas the manufacturer is a brand. Manufacturers resist retailers' efforts to gain power in the channel. They believe *they* are the brand, and they don't believe retailers have a brand. Yet, if you look at organizations like Wal-Mart, Home Depot, and others, they are very brand conscious. The firms that have the best data and are best able to put it together are the ones that are going to win.[23]

According to Schultz, most of the successful contemporary organizations were ones that had direct customer contact.

It doesn't necessarily mean they sell direct, but that they have direct access to information about customers, consumers, and users. Many operate in business-to-business arenas, including the financial services and service organizations. In effect, we've seen almost a 180-degree shift in terms of the sophisticated marketer models. If one could go back to the mid-1980s and ask, "Who are the most sophisticated marketing organizations of the world?" most people would have listed consumer package organizations. In the late 1990s, however, there's a wide recognition that these companies are probably further behind than most other firms in terms of understanding and dealing with customers. In the past, it was the business-to-business marketing organizations that were considered very old, slow—though safe. Today, probably the most sophisticated marketing organization in the world is Federal Express. They know who their customers are. They know what their customers are worth. They know the share requirement on their customers' business. They manage income flows. They allocate resources based on the value of customers. They have a tremendous internal marketing organization that really deals with and ties organizations to them. You can even use their software to track your Federal Express package from your own PC. That's the model that's driving the business.[24]

Insofar as Schultz was concerned, the agencies had lost the leadership they had in the post–World World II era. More importantly, the very intermediary function of agencies, their raison d'être, was being questioned.

Today, there's much more knowledge inside the client organization than in the agency. To some extent, agencies fell into the trap of thinking that they were only a creative group putting all the emphasis on the creating department but conducting little research. The clients lead in terms of thinking about how markets and communications work. As a result, agencies have been pushed more and more into the position of being vendors. They do ads. In the early 1980s, the agency used to be in charge. Now the clients have taken the intellectual leadership away from the agencies.[25]

Toward the late 1990s, Schultz and the IMC proponents argued that marketing and marketing communication were in a flux, moving from the historical marketing approaches of the 1960s (4Ps), via the current and transitional marketplace, to a new and interactive marketplace in the 21st century. As information technology shifted from one to another, definitive changes took place in the need for communication. These necessitated a new approach to marketing communication.[26]

The Historical Marketplace. This is the arena perfected in the 1950s and 1960s by such marketing and communication pioneers as Procter & Gamble, Nestle, Unilever, Shell, Philip Morris, and other mass market, mass media-driven organizations committed to product differentiation. Using IT, such as consumer research, mass distribution systems, mass media, and the like, these organizations developed dominant brands for their differentiated products and captured much of the marketplace for their product categories. Aggressive and skilled marketing organizations dominated the distribution channels, the media, and the consumer, using differentiated products or services that were not easily replicated.

The Current Marketplace. In the 1970s, the market began to change as products proliferated, while the media became increasingly fragmented and specialized. During this same period consolidation occurred within the channel segment. Strong wholesalers, agents and retailers acquired weaker competitors and expanded their franchises into new regions and markets. Retailing, which traditionally had been a localized business, became regional, then national and even international in scope. That gave channel buyers significant clout in negotiating with manufacturers. At the same time, IT shifted from the manufacturers/marketers to the distribution channels. The universal product code (UPC), computers, scanners, and magnetic-strip bank and credit cards made it easy, fast, and cheap to capture data on consumers. The channels had closer contact and relationships as well as more information than their marketer/suppliers. By the mid-1990s, in most consumer categories, retailers dominated the consumer relationship. Now organizations, such as Wal-Mart, Tesco, Carrefour, and others defined the terms under which *they* would stock and sell manufacturers' brands.

The 21st-Century Marketplace. This arena will be dominated by the consumers who control the IT. Through already developed systems (i.e., toll-free numbers, internationally accepted credit cards, overnight delivery services, and the like), information and technology will shift to the hands of the consumer. This is the arena of the Internet, the World Wide Web, and electronic commerce. It is continuously evolving, interactive, easy, fast, and puts the consumer in control.[27] Both the historical and current marketplaces are driven by the marketer (i.e., *outbound* only) who offers what he/she makes. The new marketplace, however, will be driven by what customers want, when they want it, and under what conditions and through what means of distribution they desire it. Since current marketing and marketing communication concepts and approaches were designed for the historical and current marketplaces, both will have to change.

The full implications of what the Internet is all about are still not clear, Schultz cautions.

The Internet is nothing more than another distribution system. That's really all it is. Yet, it is a different form of distribution and information delivery. The critical ingredient that organizations don't understand is that the Internet really makes them global and forces them into global competition, whether they compete globally or not. This is due to the fact that the Internet arms the consumer or the customer with information. Any organization that has the most information is always the one to have the most power in the marketplace. Marketing organizations historically have had more knowledge, more information about products and services and customers. Now *customers* have more knowledge It's simply a shift of marketplace power. Yet, most organizations do not understand that they no longer have power in the marketplace, and that's what creates difficulty for them. They continue to market as if the old rules of the game prevailed. The bargaining power has shifted to the consumer, and that's the difference. It's terribly hard for the organizations to acknowledge this shift. In effect, part of the problem with the Internet is that it continues to be viewed as a medium. Organizations see it as an assurance of more power in the marketplace. In fact, the Internet means less power for them in the marketplace, and that's what they don't understand.[28]

It was this peculiar *dynamics* of the Internet that many firms found so difficult to comprehend.

The Internet Dynamics

The current Internet can be traced to ARPANET, a network developed in the late 1960s with funding from the Advanced Research Projects Administration (ARPA) of the U.S. Department of Defense. From the late 1950s to the late 1980s, the U.S. government and an elite group of the nation's research universities controlled the Internet backbone.

Advanced Research Projects Administration (ARPANET). ARPANET linked together computers at major universities and defense contractors, allowing researchers at those institutions to exchange data. The TCP/IP protocol was adopted as a standard to allow the interconnection of these networks which consisted of many different types of computers. The potential of commercialization became more tangible in 1986, when the National Science Foundation initiated the NSFNet, a series of high-speed (56 kbps) networks connecting the NSF's supercomputers. With the NSFNet in place and the military using a separate Defense Data Network (DDN), the dismantling of the ARPANet was almost complete.[29]

National Science Foundation Net (NSFNet). As the new NSFNet backbone connected the various regional networks, the term "Internet" was formally adopted. At the time, there were few if any *commercial* business models. By 1989 and 1990, the use of the Internet was becoming more commercial. Since that was inconsistent with the NSF policies, it soon began to withdraw funding of commercial traffic. These years witnessed the accelerating speed and expansion of the networks, coupled with the eclipse of the Cold War. The same years also witnessed the expanding role of the U.S. carriers (MCIMail, ATTMail, Sprintmail) and the online service providers (CompuServe). Now these commercial carriers and OSPs, together with NSFNet, formed the new backbone.

From 1986 to April 1995, the primary backbone of the Internet, NSFNet (National Science Foundation Net), was federally funded and intended for noncommercial use. Still, the Internet was rapidly heading toward privatization. In 1990, the Commercial Internet Exchange (CIX), a universal connection point to the Internet, was formed to allow *commercial* networks to connect to the Internet. By the spring of 1995, NSFNet began the two-year phased withdrawal from its funding role, even though it continued to support a backbone intended mainly for academia.

Concurrently, the U.S. government adopted the role of a critical catalyst and accelerated the expansion of the Internet backbone and the proliferation of new commercial applications. In these developments, the coming deregulation of American telecommunications, accompanied by the phased privatization of the Internet, would play a crucial infrastructural function. The change was not evolutionary; it was revolutionary. Dramatic changes were occurring simultaneously in computing and telecommunications—and, in time, marketing would bring them together.[30]

From Information Infrastructure toward Electronic Commerce. During the 1992 campaign, Bill Clinton and Al Gore had vowed to rebuild America. One of their policy priorities was the creation of "a national information network to link every home, business, lab, classroom, and library by the year 2015. . . . To expand access to information, we will put public records, databases, libraries, and educational material on line for public use."[31] Starting in 1992 and 1993, the National Information Infrastructure (NII) initiative became an inherent part of the Clinton administration's political agenda, which directed significant private and public allocations into the building of the "electronic superhighways." Despite the Clinton administration's "high-tech activism," much of the NII was overtaken by events that took place between 1992 and 1994.[32]

Due to the twin deficit, the U.S. government lacked the funds to launch the infrastructure, and corporate America was not willing to wait for one to be built. Indeed, the Internet's growth rate has actually been quite stable for some time, with the number of hosts roughly doubling every year. "Electronic superhighways" were being built even prior to new government policies and legislative changes by America's leading international carriers, local telcos, cable operators, computer and Internet companies, and Hollywood studios.[33] For all practical purposes, the principal objectives of this agenda, policies, and priorities are reflected by three critical government documents: *The National Information Infrastructure: An Agenda for Action* (1993), *The Global Information Infrastructure: An Agenda for Cooperation* (1994), and *A Framework For Global Electronic Commerce* (1996) (Exhibit 2-3, Exhibit 2-4).[34]

Since the termination of federal funding for the NSFNet backbone, the Internet has continued to evolve, grow, and expand very rapidly. Despite increases in capacity, usage has grown even faster, leading to concerns about congestion.[35] As the government proceeded to facilitate electronic commerce, the research and education community, with the support of the White House and several federal agencies, announced the "Internet II" or "Next-Generation Internet" initiative to establish a new high-speed Internet backbone dedicated to noncommercial uses.[36]

By the late 1990s, the Internet had become synonymous with the Web. Still, the old, text-based Internet did not enter the new, graphic and user-friendly Web era until the first *browsers* were launched; they shoved the Web toward mass markets. By the mid-1990s, a powerful initial public offering (IPO) boom, reminiscent of the PC era, swept the nation's stock markets. Between 1980 and 1995, the PC industry had created more than $250 billion in net shareholder value. As the industry began to tap the base of an estimated 150 million PC users worldwide who in time would become more active Internet users, analysts believed that the shareholder value created by the Web revolution could exceed that created in the course of the PC revolution.[37]

The times and the technologies were different, but the transitions had a common denominator. In both cases, it was the *user-friendly evolution* of a new technology (Apple's Macintosh, PC clone manufacturers, Microsoft's Windows; the World Wide Web, Mosaic, Navigator) that triggered the expansion, first in the nation's *business-to-business markets* and thereafter in the *consumer markets*.

The 1980s had been about the PCs; the 1990s would be about the Web. But both were about digitalization. Or as Nicholas Negroponte has put it, "The information superhighway is about the global movement of weightless bits at the speed of light. As one industry after another looks at itself in the mirror and asks about its future in a digital world, that future is driven almost 100 percent by the ability of that company's product or services to be rendered in digital form."[38]

The Genesis of the "New Media." In the late 1970s, a decade before the young media planners in ad agencies and media buying houses even began to use the term for the cable channels, Ted Leonsis, America Online's programmer, reportedly coined the phrase "new media": "The companies that understand marketing and brands and how to weave together areas of interest and communities of interest will win in the

OUACHITA TECHNICAL COLLEGE

Exhibit 2-3
Evolution of the Internet: From the Early 1970s to the Late 1990s*

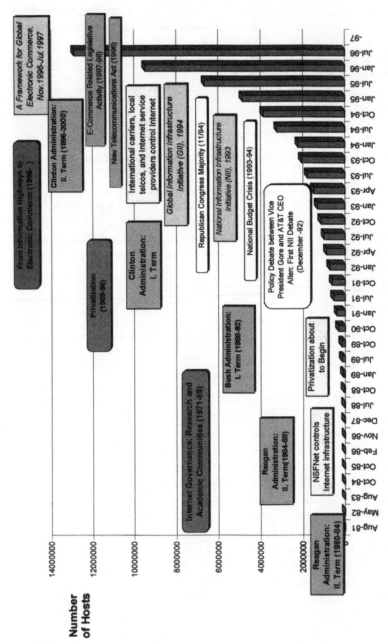

*The Internet is notoriously difficult to measure. A "host" is a computer directly connected to the Internet. The figure gives a quantitative indication of the size of the Internet, but it does not accurately reflect the actual number of Internet users. In the spring of 1997, America Online, for example, had some 8 million subscribers—yet it had only a handful of host computers which the users relied on for their Net connectivity.

Exhibit 2-4

Government Policies (1993–1997): The Fundamental Principles

The National Information Infrastructure (NII) (1993)	*A Framework For Global Electronic Commerce* (1997)

The National Information Infrastructure (NII) (1993)

All Americans have a stake in the construction of an advanced National Information Infrastructure (NII), a seamless web of communications networks, computers, databases, and consumer electronics that will put vast amounts of information at users' fingertips . . .

Our efforts will be guided by the following principles and objectives:

- Promote private sector investment, through appropriate tax and regulatory policies . . .

- Extend the "universal service" concept to ensure that information resources are available to all at affordable prices . . .

- Act as a catalyst to promote technological innovation and new applications . . .

- Promote seamless, interactive, user-driven operation of the NII . . .

- Ensure information security and network reliability . . .

- Improve management of the radio frequency spectrum, an increasingly critical resource . . .

- Protect intellectual property rights . . .

- Coordinate with other levels of government and with other nations . . .

- Provide access to government information and improve government procurement . . .

The benefits of the NII for the nation are immense. An advanced information infrastructure will enable U.S. firms to compete and win in the global economy, generating good jobs for the American people and economic growth for the nation . . .

A Framework For Global Electronic Commerce (1997)

PRINCIPLES

1. The private sector should lead.

2. Governments should avoid undue restrictions on electronic commerce.

3. Where governmental involvement is needed, its aim should be to support and enforce a predictable, minimalist, consistent and simple legal environment for commerce.

4. Governments should recognize the unique qualities of the Internet.

5. Electronic Commerce over the Internet should be facilitated on a global basis.

The Internet is emerging as a global marketplace. The legal framework supporting commercial transactions on the Internet should be governed by consistent principles across state, national, and international borders that lead to predictable results regardless of the jurisdiction in which a particular buyer or seller resides.

Source: U.S. Government Information Infrastructure Task Force: *The National Information Infrastructure: Agenda for Action,* September 15, 1993; *A Framework for Global Electronic Commerce,* July 1, 1997.

long term. We call the online world 'new media' but at some point this won't be new media. It will be *the* media."[39]

The development of American new media began in the late 1980s with the ascent of first movers like CUC International, America Online, and the first interactive ad agencies, such as Modem Media, CKS Group, Poppe Tyson, and many others. During the first half of the 1990s, government policies, deregulation of enabling industries, and intense entrepreneurial activity in California's Silicon Valley and New York City's Silicon Alley prompted the emergence of hundreds of tiny, flexible, and aggressive new media firms and interactive ad agencies.[40] As technology companies, they were familiar with software; as media companies, they knew how to use the traditional techniques of media advertising and sales promotion. Overall, they represented a curious amalgam of the old and the new—the kind of *dynamic* and web-driven technology integration that reflected and would accelerate the convergence of American media and entertainment, marketing and advertising, computing and telecommunications.[41]

Since the early 1990s, many observers, practitioners, and analysts have compared the Internet to a "tidal wave" or a "digital tornado." Such metaphors suggest a popular perception of flux, dynamics, and change. It can actually be quite useful heuristically to examine the evolution of the Internet as a sequence of product life cycles affecting (and being affected by) strategy, marketing, and competition. A structural framework provides context and order into the seemingly chaotic progression.

Life Cycles of IT/Internet

Historically, the starting point for analyzing industry evolution has been the classic product life cycle, or technology adoption life cycle.

Stages of Life Cycle. The idea is that an industry passes through a number of stages—introduction, growth, maturity, and decline. These stages are defined by inflection points in the rate of growth of industry revenues. In an ideal case, industry growth is expected to follow an S-shaped curve because of the process of innovation and diffusion of a new product. The flat introductory stage tends to reflect the difficulty of overcoming buyer inertia and stimulating trials of the new product. Rapid growth ensues when buyers and rivals rush into the market after the product has proved its success. When the marketplace becomes saturated, the rapid growth will stop and eventually level off. Finally, the growth is expected to taper off as new substitutes replace the initial product.[42]

As the industry goes through its life cycle, the nature of competition will shift. From the standpoint of strategy and marketing, the specific nature of these shifts is particularly important in issues affecting, among other things, buyers and buyer behavior, products and product change, traditional marketing functions, overall strategy, and competition (Exhibit 2-5).[43] As we shall see, most Internet-related business theories and models, from the penetration strategies of the browsers to the growth of the virtual communities, go back to the classic life cycle theory—even if and when the original concepts have been renamed and repackaged.[44]

IT/Internet-Enabled Systems: Four Stages. With each step in the evolution of computing from mainframe to minicomputers and to PCs and Internet-enabled systems no company that dominated one generation of computing has managed to dominate the next. Each became wedded to its legacy systems and cash flow. Also, analysts believe development of the Internet industry will follow a pattern similar to the beginning of personal computers in the early 1980s, with three distinct phases (compare Exhibit 2-6). In the early years, *hardware/infrastructure* will dominate, but over time, value will shift first to enabling technology (like an operating system and *software and services* to manage the interactive environment) and ultimately to programming, *content, and aggregation.*[45] Since the mid-1960s, this evolution has been made possible by "Moore's Law," a prediction by the Intel co-founder Gordon Moore that transistor density on microprocessors would double every two years. This prediction, so far, has proven amazingly accurate. As a result, the number of transistors on a chip has increased from 2,300 on the 4004 in 1971 to 7.5 million on the Pentium II processor.[46] Similarly, toward the end of the 1990s, the shift from low-speed modems to cable modems and DSL is expected to accelerate the evolution and convergence of computing and telecommunications.

This IT/Internet evolution has had several basic characteristics:

- Externally, each stage of computing has been layered horizontally on the previous one (external evolution).
- Internally, each stage has progressed from hardware/infrastructure to software/services to replacement or substitute technologies (internal evolution).
- With the onset of each new stage, the number of buyers has drastically increased as more and more people have gained control of their computing capabilities (buyer evolution).
- At each stage, smaller and cheaper computing systems have made the control more economical (price and size evolution).
- Finally, this progression of stages represents a rapid transition from sales-driven business-to-business markets (mainframes, minicomputers) to marketing-driven consumer markets (PCs, Internet-enabled systems) (marketing evolution).

Most of the visionary Internet marketers have had a relatively clear conception of this evolution.[47] Following Intel's example of *proactive* strategic management (microprocessor production, information appliances),

Exhibit 2-5
Stages of Life Cycle: Issues of Marketing and Strategy

	Introduction	Growth	Maturity	Decline
Buyers and Buyer Behavior	High-income purchaser, innovators; low sales; high cost per customer	Widening buyer group; early adopters; rapidly rising sales; average cost per customer	Mass market; middle majority buyers; peak sales and saturation; repeat buying; low cost per customer	Customers are sophisticated buyers of the product; stress on laggards; low cost per customer
Products and Product Change	Basic product; low quality; product development key; product variations; absence of standards	Technical and performance differentiation; reliability key for complex products; competitive product improvements; product extensions; higher quality	Brand diversification; superior quality; less product differentiation; standardization; less rapid product changes; trade-ins become significant	Little product differentiation; phasing out weak items
Marketing	Product awareness and trial; high advertising/ sales (a/s); high-growth price strategy (creaming, skimming); high marketing costs	Maximization of market share; high advertising (but lower percent of sales than introductory); intensive distribution	Maximization of profit while defending market share; market segmentation and focus strategies; efforts to extend life cycle and broaden product lines; stress on service and deals, and packaging important	Reduction of expenditures and milking the brand; low a/s and other marketing
Advertising	Building product awareness among early adopters and dealers	Building awareness and interest in the mass market	Stress on brand differences and benefits; competitive costs; "marketing effectiveness" key	Advertising reduction to level needed to retain hard-core loyals
Competition	Few companies, pioneers	Entry; many competitors; mergers & acquisition activities; casualties	Price competition; shakeout; increase in private brands	Exits; fewer competitors

Source: Adapted with slight modification from Chester R. Wasson, *Dynamic Competitive Strategy and Product Life Cycles* (Austin, TX: Austin Press 1978); Michael E. Porter, *Competitive Strategy* (New York: The Free Press 1980), pp. 156–162; and Philip Kotler, *Marketing Management: Analysis, Planning, Implementation, and Control*, Ninth Edition (Upper Saddle River, NJ: Prentice-Hall 1997), see chapter 12.

Exhibit 2-6
From Mainframes to Internet-Enabled Systems

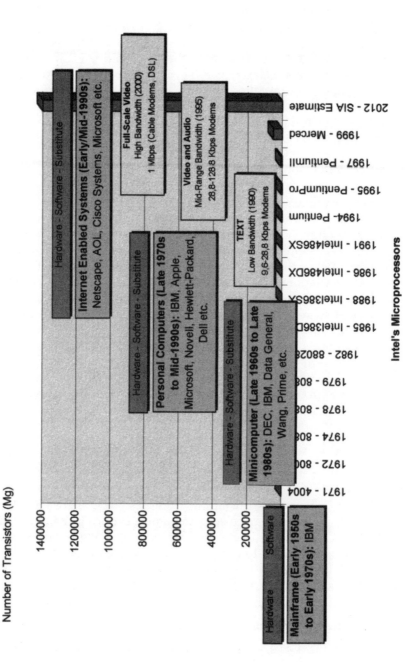

Number of Transistors (Mg)

Source: Based on Dan Steinbock, "The Virtual Revolution in American Business and Management," The XIII Nordic Conference on Mass Communication Research, Jyvaskyla, 9–12 August 1997, *Nordicom Review,* 19(1), June 1998.

these firms those reflected, reflected on, and purposefully instigated the pace of IT/Internet developments, or what America Online has called the "new media programming evolution" (Exhibit 2-7). It was this vision, one based on certain predictable developments in chip performance and rising access speed, that motivated the *direction* of AOL's strategy.

As the first Internet marketers began to explore ways to exploit the rapid expansion of the Web, they had to re-think the idea of industry evolution as a *diffusion* of an innovation. In the recent past, chief executives like Intel's Andrew Grove had explained the new industry forces by recourse to strategic inflection points.[48] That was legitimate in the business-to-business markets where strategic decisions originated from the supply side (i.e., innovation among the suppliers and producers). Since many new media and interactive agencies focused on the demand side and operated in consumer markets, they preferred to explore the industry forces by recourse to diffusion among the buyers. It was the diffusion of innovations that now became the key concern of the marketers.[49]

As mass customization provided both business-to-business and consumer marketers the technological means to view masses and individual buyers as variations of identical entities, the differences between the two would begin to blur toward the late 1990s. The history of the first movers shows that such distinctions were relatively marginal to the pioneers in business-to-business and consumer markets. Both had grown weary with traditional mass marketing. Both had a personal distaste for the manipulation inherent in mass media advertising. Both sought for new means to create direct and interactive long-term relationships with their clients. As the two groups would find later in the 1990s, the affinities far exceeded the dissimilarities.

BROWSERS, HOME PAGES, AND WEBSITES

In fact, the first generation of Internet marketers had been trained in the late 1980s and early 1990s by the launch of the first national commercial online services, including CompuServe, America Online, and Prodigy. Except for CompuServe, the online service providers were preceded by CUC International, the first cybermall that inspired, trained, and provided a model to a generation of online marketers and managers—from interactive ad agencies like Modem Media to online service providers such as America Online.

CUC International and Online Service Providers

Through the 1980s, CompuServe, the pioneering online service provider, expanded globally and initiated several now-standard services (i.e., e-mail, forums). Despite initial first-mover advantages, it did not

Exhibit 2-7
America Online: New Media Programming

1. Iron Age: 1985+
(text-based; low speeds; small audience)

- Member-generated content
- Branded, repackaged ("repurposed") content areas
- Reference database materials
- Icons for information areas and logos for ads
- Rudimentary transactions

2. Bronze Age: 1994+
(text/picture-based; higher speeds; niche audiences)

- Channel creation and new media programming
- Packaging of multiple content streams
- Shopping malls for commerce (with text and photos)
- Interactive marketing areas as information providers
- Celebrity events and vertical communities

3. Silver Age: 1996+
(multiple media; higher speeds; critical mass audiences)

- Original content
- Less "repurposed" content
- Commerce as a programmed area
- New channels to serve new markets
- Network initiated, purchased, or produced shows
- Member-generated content via home pages, personal websites, road trips, intelligent message boards
- New HTML original content areas
- Few partners; better service and increased promotion

4. Gold Age: 1999+
(full-motion video; speed not an issue; mainstream media)

- The next thing: cable and telephony and datacom and Hollywood blended together
- Advertisers/marketers pay the freight
- More consumers using PCs in prime time than TVs
- Promise of interactive services achieved

Source: Copyright 1998 America Online, Inc. All Rights Reserved.

manage to exploit those benefits with the rise of the Internet. In particular, CompuServe did not add an icon-based, color, graphical user interface until 1991. In 1984, IBM, Sears, and CBS founded Prodigy as a joint venture. Still, the company did not really launch its first operations until 1988 and made a national debut only in 1990, adding a multitude of services a year later.

At the turn of the 1990s, CompuServe and Prodigy, as well as a slate of new entrants, struggled for the U.S. online market leadership. Half a decade later, both had lost to a relative newcomer that would consolidate the marketplace with an aggressive growth strategy. In 1989, Quantum launched a nationwide service for IBM-compatible and Apple computers. Three years later it went public. It would become better known as America Online.

In the early 1990s, the online service providers and—following the 1996 Telecommunications Act—the international carriers and local telcos accelerated the expansion of the Internet consumer markets and thereby the evolution of the new marketing channels by providing Web access to millions of Americans eager to "surf the Net." In turn, America Online began offering a Windows version of its online software a year later, even if did not offer Internet access. *Before* the Telecommunications Act, these online and Internet service providers made their revenues from subscriptions. *Following* the Act, advertising revenues emerged as the driving industry force. *In the long run*, all major players sought to establish business models relying on transactions. Ultimately, it was Internet retail, or what would become known as electronic commerce, that would deliver the promise of CUC International—the pioneer of the online retail world.

CUC International and Online Retail

In 1997, HFS, a hospitality franchisor, merged with direct marketer CUC International to form Cendant, the world's largest hotel franchisor, with more than 5,500 middle- and economy-priced properties. After the merger Cendant was swept by a bitter controversy. It all stemmed from the discovery of hundreds of millions of dollars in "fictitious revenues" and other accounting problems at CUC. While these alleged abuses cast a dark cloud on the future online retail pioneer, they do not refute the historical accomplishments of the company.

Prior to the merger, CUC explained the mission of the company as follows:

CUC International Inc. is a leading membership-based, consumer-services company that provides access to travel, shopping, auto, dining, timeshare exchange, financial, and other services to more than 66 million consumers worldwide.

Headquartered in Stamford, Connecticut, CUC works in partnership with leading banks, retailers, oil companies, credit unions, charities, and other organizations to offer consumers convenience and significant savings when purchasing a wide array of high-quality goods and services. Our goal is to be the leading consumer-content provider, delivering value to consumers in every aspect of their lives. To accomplish this ambitious goal, we continuously strive to provide superior customer service in addition to offering new or enhanced consumer services. We are also focused on broadening our membership base through untapped distribution channels, global expansion, and the newest delivery technologies. With more than 15,000 employees worldwide who are dedicated to pursuing these objectives, we are confident that our goals are attainable.[50]

CUC's Killer Product: Shoppers Advantage. Formed in 1973 as Comp-U-Card of America, the company's most popular product was Shoppers Advantage, introduced in 1981. Consumers paid an annual membership for the service, which entitled them to call the company's operators on a toll-free line or to use online computer access seven days a week to inquire about price and/or buy brand-name products. In 1983, Comp-U-Card of America went public and was renamed CUC International in 1987.

By the late 1980s, Shoppers Advantage offered more than 250,000 brand-name and specialty items, including a written description of the product, the manufacturer's suggested retail price, the vendor's price, features and availability. All of these products could be purchased through CUC's independent vendor network (e.g., manufacturers, distributors, and retailers nationwide).

Individual members were entitled to an unlimited number of toll-free calls seven days a week to the company's shopping consultants, who accessed the merchandise database to obtain the lowest available fully delivered cost from participating vendors for the product requested and accepted any orders that the member may place. The program informed the vendor providing the lowest price of the member's order and that vendor then delivered the requested product directly to the member. Acting as a conduit between its members and the vendors, CUC did not maintain an inventory of products.

By 1997, CUC had capitalized on its Shopper Advantage experience by introducing a variety of other membership-based products, ranging from shopping and travel to auto, dining, and financial products. CUC made large marketing investments to build memberships in these new programs. Indeed, after the mid-1990s, variations of these fundamental membership service variations would "re-emerge" as some of the most thriving categories of transactional websites. Many of the latter emulated the CUC models.

Membership Base and Financial Reporting Debate. CUC also exploited a then-controversial financial reporting practice that, years later, many Internet companies would imitate, with variable success. Since current marketing outlays provided significant future benefits, CUC's management decided the company should capitalize membership solicitation costs in financial statements and amortize them over three years at rates of 40%, 30%, and 30%. "Many companies spend money on acquiring plant and equipment, and they capitalize these costs," noted Stuart Bell, Executive VP and CFO of CUC. "Our business does not require major investments in plant and equipment. Instead, it requires investments in membership acquisitions."[51] CUC's assets were no longer things; its assets were people. Interestingly enough, CUC's practice was endorsed by Ernst & Whinney, the company's auditors, and the Securities and Exchange Commission when the company went public. Still, the practice resulted in a controversy that anticipated similar debates in the mid-1990s when several growth-oriented Internet companies tried to replicate CUC's choices—and its success.[52]

It was CUC's large membership base that allowed it to negotiate attractive discounts on the products offered in its catalog. As a result, it guaranteed its subscribers the lowest prices available on goods it sold. The programs thrived on the success of Shoppers Advantage which, in turn, was made possible by the high-volume membership base. Through Compu-U-Card Services, Inc., CUC's discount shopping program provided product price information and home shopping services to its members. CUC's "secret of success" *was* its membership base which, in turn, would have been inconceivable without America's major credit card issuers. In effect, CUC acquired a large proportion of its new members through agreements with leading credit card issuers, who provided the company access to *their* lists of cardholders. The latter were solicited by three direct marketing approaches: billing statement inserts, solo mailings, and telemarketing.

A decade later, these practices would be eagerly emulated in Internet marketing, as well as in the business models of the first generation of Internet retail companies, starting with the IPO of Amazon.com in the summer of 1997. Among other things, these characteristics involved membership-based products leveraged on the success of a few "killer programs," massive membership base, strategic alliances with credit card issuers, direct marketing approaches in new member solicitations, as well as the new and initially controversial practices of capitalizing membership solicitation costs in financial statements.

These very same practices provided the American Internet entrepreneurs with a competitive edge, especially in comparison to their European colleagues. While, for instance, the European "information society" projects were debating the privacy issues and technology components of Internet retail, CUC and its followers were busily implementing the first transactional experiences with the assistance of the leading U.S. credit card issuers.[53]

The trial-and-error experiences of CUC would be studied carefully by the first new media firms and interactive ad agencies in California's Silicon Valley and New York's Silicon Alley. By the mid-1990s, Modem Media was considered one of the leading interactive ad agencies in America. The senior management of the rapidly growing agency readily acknowledged its apprentice lessons in CUC International. Indeed, both of the two founding partners—G. M. O'Connell and Douglas Ahlers—came out of CUC, recalls Robert "Bob" Allen, president of Modem Media.

As a direct marketing company, CUC sold primarily affinity-based or membership programs, like in travel clubs and shopping clubs, etc. In the early 1980s, it was one of the first firms to explore what would become known as electronic commerce. At the time, only a few American companies had such closed online services (e.g., General Electric, CompuServe, Adelphi). At CUC, they certainly had the vision to recognize that sometime in the future—they probably thought sooner than later—people would be shopping more and more from computers. So they got into electronic direct marketing, with direct marketers and traditional cataloguers. They used new forms of electronic communication (e.g., PC-based, online services) to reach out and build better relationships with the customers and sell products online.[54]

Amidst the Internet momentum and the "browser wars" in the mid-1990s, many agency observers presumed that Internet *advertising* would be the dominant, if not the sole, form of marketing on the Web. Such a view was based on a very narrow and unhistorical understanding of the Internet potential. The latter was based on *direct marketing and interactive dialogue*. That was the lesson of CUC. "CUC International was clearly one of the leading early entrants, a first mover among the electronic direct marketers", argues Allen of Modem Media. "Many executives and managers who started in CUC went on to start Internet companies that would later thrive. In retrospect, CUC served as a sort of a greenhouse for the pioneering enterpreneurs."[55]

The Vision of Interactive Television and "500 Channels"

Between 1992 and 1994, the public debate on the new *interactive* access devices, as well as their funding strategies and potential revenue models, focused on several interactive television (ITV) projects. Many were triggered by the "convergence strategy"—the fusion of video, interactive data, and telephone service over broadband pipes—of John Malone, chairman and CEO of Tele-Communications, Inc., the most powerful cable MSO in the early 1990s.

With the deregulation of the cable TV industry in 1984, TCI bought more than 150 cable companies by the end of the decade.[56] Recognizing that the systems needed a variety of programming in order to compete with the networks, Malone also began financing nascent channels in exchange for stock. TCI soon held shares in the Discovery Channel (1986) and Turner Broadcasting (1987). The convergence momentum ensued with the end of the national recession. In a 1991 transaction, TCI spun off its interests in QVC Network, other networks, and various cable systems as Liberty Media. The MSO also sold the UAE theater division in 1992 and kept the cable division. The following year TCI joined with Microsoft and Time Warner to form Cablesoft, a venture exploring interactive cable TV. Meanwhile Liberty Media returned to TCI's fold in 1994.

It was during these years that Malone developed his highly touted vision of a "500-channel universe" of interactive TV channels. He set out to bring convergence into the homes of America with a 1992 promise of "500 channels" of interactive TV channels. The vision never materialized. In 1993 he tried to jump start the revolution by merging TCI with Bell Atlantic. After months of efforts, the $33 billion deal failed to materialize. In the 1997 strategic turnaround, Malone acknowledged that the vision had been too ambitious, overhyped, and impossible to carry out on schedule. In its place, TCI was pursuing a much-diminished strategy and scrambling to make a major retreat to its roots in cable. "We were just chasing too many rabbits at the same time," Malone said. "The company got overly ambitious about the things it could do simultaneously." TCI was no longer set to become the powerful lord of the new information superhighway, using cable to deliver phone service, the Internet, and other futuristic interactive goodies. "If you read our annual report last year, you'd think we're one-third data, one-third telephone and one-third video entertainment, instead of 100% video entertainment and two experiments," he acknowledged. The hype "influenced our staffing and the market's perception of the business."[57]

Backing off Malone's vaunted promise of a 500-channel universe, TCI was upgrading the capacity and speed of its cable systems by using cheaper alternatives such as digital compression and, on top of TVs, digital set-top boxes. "When it ultimately turns out to be everything we hoped it would be and more, then I think we'll be vindicated," he thought.[58]

However, Malone was hardly the only one to bet on the 500-channel interactive vision. After the mid-1990s, instead of developing the once-promised instant access to TV shows, the broadcast networks were lining up to provide news and entertainment in cyberspace. Similarly, the rush of Hollywood studios to deliver movies on command had taken a back seat to promotions and contests on the Web. In the early 1990s, hardware and software computing companies such as Microsoft, Oracle, and Silicon Graphics had been among the biggest boosters of interactive TV; now all had re-engineered those systems for the global computer network. Even Tele-TV, an interactive programming venture of Bell Atlantic, Nynex, and Pacific Telesis, shelved its TV plans.[59]

Manufacturers of set-top boxes were racing to transform their technology to make it Web-ready. In 1992, they had promised the advent of digital set-top boxes that would be the gateway for interactive TV. After the mid-1990s, few of the souped-up devices had been shipped. They turned out to be far more complicated to design and build than imagined. By the late decade, the same companies were hawking the cable modem (among others, TCI was pouring money into an online venture called @Home). Coupled with a cable Internet link, it promised to deliver Web content to homes much faster than ordinary phone lines. By 1996, Time Warner had revamped the shopping feature it designed for its much-vaunted interactive TV network in Orlando, Florida, so it could work on its burgeoning website, Pathfinder. Touted three years before as the first city in a nationwide rollout, the Orlando "Full Service Network" (FSN) remained an extravagantly expensive experiment serving only 4,000 homes, while the company's website could potentially be reached by millions.

What went wrong with the interactive-TV dream? Most importantly, the promoters vastly underestimated the difficulty and cost of the undertaking and overestimated the financial returns that would pay for it. By the mid-1990s, the Web had arrived, while interactive TV remained a distant promise. Combining color photos, text, and even sound and video, the Web, even in its primitive form, brought many of the promised features of interactive TV—*cost-efficiently.*

Advertisers eagerly awaited the results of the ITV projects. In retrospect, however, the development programs had been an exercise in futility. "Modem Media was involved in many interactive TV trials in the United States," recalls Robert Allen, president of Modem Media.

Our clients were very interested in experimenting with the technology in local test markets, including Time Warner in Orlando and AT&T in Castro Valley, California. The technology was neat, but we saw two obstacles. First, one would have to roll out ITV technology across the entire United States in order to achieve critical mass of customers and garner major advertisers. Such a rollout would be very expensive. Second, the process of creating this rich, full-blown interactive media that would run on the ITV trials was very, very expensive. Certainly, advertisers were interested in achieving addressable advertising or the ability to nurture one-to-one relationships with the customers. However, the ITV technology simply was not sophisticated enough. Moreover, the costs would be prohibitive for both advertisers and providers. Instead of ITV, we began to look for something else that could deliver a lot of the ITV promise but at a lower cost for the service providers, the advertisers, and the customers.[60]

The pioneering new media firms and interactive ad agencies were about to discover the advertising potential of the Internet. But how could the telecommunications giants ignore the rapid rise of the Internet? And why were they unable to accomplish the kind of R&D that would have provided them first-mover benefits? In brief, why did they need Modem Media and other pioneering interactive agencies to show *them* the way?

"At AT&T, one might look at the issue from two perspectives," thinks Modem's Robert Allen.

First, one would take a network perspective and ask: Would people make telephone calls over the Internet rather than the existing telecommunications? Perhaps they did not think that the Internet would become a strategic threat to their business. And, for the first seven years, they were probably right. After all, there were many companies that were blindsided by the expansion of the Internet; they presumed that the Internet would evolve very rapidly as a venue of electronic commerce. Second, one might look at things from an advertising perspective, which is the *real* issue. Unfortunately, AT&T did not have anybody looking at the Internet as an advertising media. As traditional advertisers, they were accustomed to using direct marketing, the mail, television, print, and so on. There really was not anybody in the organization who was figuring out how you could use the Internet as an advertising vehicle. Yet that is the perspective they should have had.[61]

It was not the incumbent carriers and telcos but the early online service providers that first understood the significance of advertising revenue in funding the accelerating Internet activities. If Wired Ventures would pioneer *Web* advertising in late 1994, Prodigy was the first to establish *Internet* advertising as a key funding resource.

Prodigy: The First Internet Advertising Deals

Founded as Trintex in 1984 by IBM, Sears, and CBS, Prodigy launched its first service in 1988 in Hartford, Connecticut, and White Plains, New York.[62] It was never meant to follow in the footsteps of industry founders such as H&R Block's CompuServe. At that time, most online pioneers offered consumers electronic versions of familiar messaging tools such as mail, bulletin boards, and real-time "chatting." Instead, IBM and Sears executives envisioned a new advertising medium that would *build audiences* for marketers much as niche TV channels do. In addition, Prodigy's audience would be able to buy products on the spot, with two strokes on the keyboard.[63] In this sense, its aggregator function and content production anticipated later developments among the online service providers, in particular America Online. By the mid-1980s, Prodigy conceived business models and audience uses that would become familiar only in the mid-1990s (for its graphic interface in the late 1990s).

Led by former IBM executive Theodore Papes, the company marketed itself as a household shopping and banking service for busy women. In 1989, it changed its name to Prodigy and made its national debut a year later. Concurrently, it went online. In 1991 followed the added new services. As its then-corporate parents IBM and partner Sears, Roebuck recognized the potential for bringing the information revolution to consumers, Prodigy Services Co. offered push-button access to all sorts of information, an electronic shopping mall, and e-mail ("for just $9.95 a month!"). In two years, a million people signed up.

Prior to the commercialization of the Internet *and* the creation of the Web and the first browser generation, Prodigy adopted advertising as a revenue source. At the time, rival online service providers shunned Internet advertising. It was alone in experimenting the new arena. Although CompuServe had gone online in 1979, it sold its first sponsorship only in 1995 when AOL made Web advertising a part of its strategy. Prodigy had some 200 different advertisers on its network and many sold products online. After its initial success, however, the company stumbled and fell behind America Online. Essentially, Prodigy ignored the fundamentals of the very same business models and audience functions it had developed: while the company tried to boost transactions, its members sought online-community activities.[64]

Wrong Pricing Model: The Magazine Approach. While most online service providers charged users for each minute online, Prodigy adopted a magazine pricing model. The flat monthly subscription rate was never intended to cover operating costs. Instead, Prodigy was to sell one-fifth of each screen to *advertisers* and receive *commissions* from sales made online. As originally conceived, Prodigy's fixed monthly cost was expected to encourage users to browse its hundreds of menus, ostensibly generating more sales leads for advertisers. Graphics capabilities were another innovation, allowing marketers to create billboards and infomercials to stir consumers. As Prodigy went on to build its "field of dreams," the users did not follow. The Internet is not a magazine. The pricing model did not apply in an online environment and Prodigy's ad revenues did not materialize as planned. Between 1989 and 1991, according to Harris 1993 report, Prodigy derived about 41% of its income from customer charges, 30% from advertising, 13% from sale of start-up kits, 3% from online sales commissions, and 13% from other sources.[65]

Soon Prodigy had even more pressing problems.

Wrong Industry Vision: Mistaken Consumer Behavior Predictions. Even though Prodigy did provide a user-friendly environment, the technology was not yet sophisticated and the system was too slow. Betrayed by its own market research, Prodigy overestimated consumer interest in computer-based shopping and underestimated the volume of e-mail and bulletin board activity that the system would carry. Such a nightmarish combination of mistakes generated a double whammy that was bound to shake the very survival of the company. *American Demographics* reported that Prodigy's planners estimated e-mail usage from the number of personal letters sent between households via postal delivery. That model proved to be a proper predictor for 95% of Prodigy's members. The problem arose from the other 5%, who posted 3.7 million messages. In 1992, for example, Prodigy's subscriber base grew an impressive 45% percent, but postings on its bulletin boards grew 500%, to more than 40 million messages a year.[66]

Wrong Marketing Concept: Magazine Model, Online Environment. In the long term, the delay of the response time was not as serious as the confused marketing concept. The advocates of one-to-one marketing have found it surprising that "on the front end the [Prodigy] system operates as if it were a totally non-addressable mass medium. . . . Prodigy wants national advertisers despite the fact that for any service to be genuinely interactive it should be a low-barrier tool for local marketers."[67] Although capable of one-to-one marketing, Prodigy still saw itself as a magazine, trying to push and impose the old broadcast model into a rapidly fragmenting marketplace. Unlike America Online, which would dominate online services through its focus on context and communication, Prodigy not only priced like a magazine, it thought it had a magazine business model. Yet, online users were not interested in online content (which was not yet even original and was easier to browse in the offline world), but in *communicating* with one another (which the company was not prepared for).

Briefly put, Prodigy was in the right time in the right place with the right funding source; but its wrong business model undid all benefits it could reap from its timing, online services, or revenue base. As the OSP began to understand the implications of its strategic decisions, the online industry was changing drastically. Until the mid-1990s, the incumbents had provided their services in a proprietary marketplace; each player had a different interface for the consumer. Now the Web and the first browser generation changed the rules of the game.

The Rise of the Web and the First Browser Generation

"The Internet is interactive television on training wheels," said James Clark, chairman of Netscape Communications in 1996. "Unquestionably, interactive television will come right out of the Internet." As chairman of Silicon Graphics, he helped light the fire under the ITV movement in 1993, signing high-profile deals to help cable and phone companies revamp their systems for video-on-demand. A year later, he quit SGI to found a company to create software for interactive TV. "But after a few months of trying to figure out how you can actually build a business," Clark recalled, "I concluded there wasn't a business to be built because it was too far in the future."[68]

Few executives foresaw the shift from interactive television to the Internet more clearly than Clark, with the assistance of Marc Andreessen. The two teamed up to found Netscape Communications to commercialize the young programmer's college project: a way to get around the Web using a simple graphic user interface. Yet, Navigator would have been inconceivable without the infrastructure of the Web and the first browser program, Mosaic, on which it was founded.

From World Wide Web to Mosaic. Many of the existing Internet technologies were developed and launched by the early 1990s, including the World Wide Web, which Tim Berners-Lee invented while working at CERN, the European Particle Physics Laboratory. These technologies, however, were slow, text-based, and often ridden with incompatibilities. Neither the online service providers, the telecommunications builders of the Internet backbone, nor Washington's information policies "created" the new media. The network and Internet technologies were necessary, but not sufficient. They had to be made user-friendly in order to attract a critical mass of consumers. The true genesis of American new media began in January 1993 when Mosaic, the first Web browser, was introduced and distributed through the Internet at the National Center for Supercomputing Applications (NCSA).

Established in 1985 with a National Science Foundation grant, the NCSA opened to the national research community in January 1986. It is a high-performance computing and communications facility designed to serve U.S. computational science and engineering communities.[69] NCSA created Mosaic, the foundation of Netscape Navigator and Microsoft's Internet Explorer. Mosaic was a network navigational tool that allowed one to access networked information easily with the click of a mouse button.[70]

The NCSA Software Development Group (SDG) gave the Internet a human face or, more precisely, a *graphic user interface* which syncronized features that used to be incompatible. Since Mosaic was conceived of and developed in an academic environment, it was distributed free of charge. It was Mosaic that educated the first Web techie generation into the use of the mouse and mouse buttons, through which the NCSA Mosaic Document View provided a transparent window into the cyberspace.

Netscape Navigator. In April 1994, Marc Andreessen and Jim Clark hired a half dozen of the most experienced Mosaic developers away from the NCSA and founded Mosaic Communications which, for licensing reasons, had to be rechristened Netscape Communications. Two months later, Digital Equipment Corporation announced the shipment of a version of Mosaic, enhanced by Spyglass Inc., with every machine it sold. In October, after a furious R&D period, Netscape offered Netscape Navigator, the first *commercial* Web browser, free on the Internet. Concurrently, *Wired* magazine, the voice of the "digital generation," touted the merits of Mosaic and declared that the "second phase" of the Internet revolution had begun. The interfaces of the closed and proprietary online service providers had become defunct:

Don't look now, but Prodigy, AOL, and CompuServe are all suddenly obsolete—and Mosaic is well on its way to becoming the world's standard interface. When it comes to smashing a paradigm, pleasure is not the most important thing. It is the only thing. If this sounds wrong, consider Mosaic. Mosaic is the celebrated graphical "browser" that allows users to travel through the world of electronic information using a point-and-click interface. Mosaic's charming appearance encourages users to load their own documents onto the Net, including color photos, sound bites, video clips, and hypertext "links" to other documents. By following the links—click, and the linked document appears—you can travel through the online world along paths of whim and intuition. Mosaic is not the most direct way to find online information. Nor is it the most powerful. It is merely the most pleasurable way, and in the 18 months since it was released, Mosaic has incited a rush of excitement and commercial energy unprecedented in the history of the Net. Intense efforts to enhance Mosaic and similar browsers are underway at research institutes around the world. At least six companies are gearing up to sell commercial versions of Mosaic.[71]

For all practical purposes, Netscape's Navigator was a faster, more reliable, and more sophisticated version of Mosaic. The faster Navigator's market share expanded, the more rapid was the decline of Mosaic.[72]

Faced with Netscape's substitute threat, the NCSA Mosaic "What's New Page" on the Net announced that it also was seeking sponsors. But that was too little too late. *Now* marketers began to pay heed to the Web developments: even as Edwin Artzt, the chief executive of Procter & Gamble, delivered his crisis speech to Madison Avenue, Navigator was being downloaded by tens of thousands of users across America and internationally. New media firms were hurriedly studying the principal features of this new and fascinating screen called the "browser." All sought ways to integrate the graphic user interface with *their* products. The new industry, the new practices, the new companies, the new Internet-related technologies—all of these began to grow dramatically with the first browser generation.[73]

Microsoft's Strategic U-Turn: From Avoid and Neglect to Embrace and Ex-

tend. Although many analysts doubted Microsoft's ability to compete in the Internet, it was the software giant's strategy that, in the long term, would greatly influence the evolution of the Internet. In the beginning of 1995, Microsoft seemed to be so far behind Internet upstarts that industry analysts wondered if the company whose software had dominated the PC era might be sidelined in a new age of Internet computing. Between 1990 and 1993, when the Internet was about to enter its rapid expansion, Microsoft was growing explosively, tripling sales to $3.8 billion, and boosting its payroll from 5,600 to 14,400—mainly with the success of Windows. As the early adopters discovered the Web in 1993, it was little more than a curiosity at Microsoft headquarters. "I wouldn't say it was clear it was going to explode over the next couple of years," thought Chairman Bill Gates at the time. "If you'd asked me then if most TV ads will have URLs [Web addresses] in them, I would have laughed."[74]

In the summer of 1995, Microsoft engaged in a strategic U-turn, which had been prepared for months. Under the leadership of Bill Gates, the software giant adopted an "embrace and extend" strategy, whose fundamental objective was to integrate the operating system and the application software, both of which *it* dominated, with the Internet, relying on the Microsoft Internet Explorer 1.0, the company's first browser program. The strategy *also* included Microsoft Network (MSN), an online community whose launch coincided with Windows 95. A year later, as Microsoft was preparing for a massive marketing campaign to launch Windows 95, *Business Week* published a highly-touted cover story, "Inside Microsoft," which was subtitled, "The Untold Story of How the Internet Forced Bill Gates to Reverse Course."[75] While the story had not been told, Microsoft's assistance implied the company saw the publicity as a marketing device for its new Internet strategy.[76] Yet, the strategic U-turn was no sham; it penetrated the entire corporate organization, from Bill Gates, Steve Ballmer, Nathan Myhrvold, and the senior management to software programmers. It was a stunning triumph of change management.

Historically, this dramatic redefinition of strategy was reminiscent of the classic auto wars in the 1920s. Unlike Ford, Gates and Microsoft's senior management knew it would be futile to resist technological change; instead, they would embrace it. And so they did. As an anonymous Microsoft employee paraphrased the strategy in the "Battle Hymn of the Reorg," cited in *MicroNews*, the in-house newsletter, "Oh, our eyes have seen the glory of the coming of the Net, We are ramping up our market share, objectives will be met. Soon our browser will be everywhere, you ain't seen nothin' yet, We embrace and we extend!"[77]

A few years later, the Department of Justice would sue Microsoft for its strategy, for alleged monopolistic abuse. In August 1995, however,

Microsoft's entry into the market accelerated the growth in the Internet adoption worldwide. As the world's greatest software company began aggressive Internet marketing mobilizing its massive installed customer base, it contributed to the popularity of the Web and the Internet IPOs among the investors.

The First Sponsored Browsers. "With the coming of the first browsers, we began building websites for companies that were using the Internet as a *commercial* media," recalls Fergus O'Daly, Jr. "It had always been a scientific and research media, but we were interested in the *commercial* applications."[78] A seasoned advertising agency veteran, O'Daly did not start in the digital Web business, but had spent his entire career in the agency business—over 30 years. He spent the first 20 on the creative side. With Fred Poppe, he founded Poppe Tyson, later acquired by BJK&E in 1988. From the new media pioneer, he switched to CKS, a major rival, in 1997.[79] As the nascent new media was swept by M&A activity starting in the fall of 1996, he was regularly quoted in all the major media covering the emergence of the WWW.[80] Through Poppe, he also saw some of the development with the earliest Navigator versions:

Years ago, Poppe Tyson owned an office in Silicon Valley. One of the accounts we handled was Silicon Graphics. At the time, SGI's CEO was Jim Clark, current chairman of Netscape; he had a business association with my partner, Dave Carlick. After Clark left SGI, he was looking for something new to do. He discovered the Internet and Mark Andreessen, who'd been developing Mosaic. Clark returned to Silicon Valley with Andreessen. They wanted to build a "browser." At the time, nobody really understood what the name or the technology was all about. Clark hired us to develop Modzilla, a prototype of Navigator 1.0 and the first Internet browser ever produced. We also helped to design the home page of Navigator 2.0. In the process, I became very enamored with the Internet. When we finished Modzilla and realized what a browser was all about or what it could do, I just quickly presumed there could be a good business in it.

So we set up a small team to begin building websites for companies that were on the very cutting edge of the Internet as a commercial media. Among the first websites that we did were Hewlett-Packard and Intel. To me, it was history in the making. I've never got tired of it. I was really interested in what the Internet could accomplish. I got visionary about it. You don't get many chances in a lifetime to be part of the development of a whole new medium. Here was a chance to be part of the Internet. I jumped at it.[81]

Fergus O'Daly saw the business and marketing potential of the Internet well before others in the ad business. He had two reasons for curiosity:

First, my background was creative. I was a creative director for fourteen years and I've been involved in many aspects of creative edge. And although I've done a lot of TV, most of the creative work was in the print area. Second, a lot of the work I've done was in the business-to-business, and it seemed that the Internet would be one of the great business-to-business communication mediums of all time. You could put up endless amounts of information on the Internet, including questions and applications that would show schematics. You could bond interactively. I saw the Internet as a world-class tool for business-to-business communications.[82]

Indeed, in the early years of the Internet, the "action" was primarily in the business-to-business markets. The consumer markets would follow with the rapidly expanding household penetration. For many relationship, direct, and business-to-business marketers, the Internet represented the ultimate dialogue media. They expected the Web to revolutionize the prevailing rules and practices. And they were right.

NOTES

1. See Mark Robichaux, "Need More TV? TCI May Offer 500 Channels," *Wall Street Journal*, December 3, 1992. On the struggle for the new distribution pipelines, see Dan Steinbock, *Triumph and Erosion in the American Media and Entertainment Industries* (Westport, CT: Quorum Books 1995), see especially chapters 6–7.

2. Edward W. Desmond, "Malone Again," *Fortune*, February 16, 1998.

3. At the Intel gala, 3DO demonstrated a far richer hybrid: Meridian 59, a computer game in which hundreds of players could congregate in an online medieval computer-animated world. Intel itself had launched the new Intercast technology, which allowed web pages to be displayed on TV monitors.

4. Hybrids would offer ways to download via telephone modems increased amounts of graphics or video off a website and then store it on a PC's hard drive. The data could then be quickly accessed. Intel was refocusing and developing new software tools and other technologies that could, for example, convert a TV screen so that it could run images from favorite websites, or make video flow from a website to a computer far faster. Intel would supply millions of dollars worth of engineering support and research to help other companies develop hybrids. Hybrids, declared Grove, would enhance the PC, making it into a communications tool that could supplant old-style or newer-style appliances like TV sets, telephones, and the cheaper network computers. See Intel press releases.

5. Dean Takahashi, "Intel Bets on Hybrid Tools to Enhance Multimedia," August 6, 1996. See also Amy Cortese, "Special Report: The Information Appliance Software's Holy Grail," *Business Week*, June 24, 1996.

6. Mark Landler, Walecia Konrad, Zachary Schiller, and Lois Therrien, "What Happened to Advertising," *Business Week*, September 23, 1991.

7. On the characteristics of the crisis, see Form 10-K for CKS Group Inc., filed on February 28, 1997.

8. McCann-Ericksson, research releases.

9. On the fragmentation of American media, see Steinbock, *Triumph and Erosion in the American Media and Entertainment Industries*, especially chapters 1–3.

10. Nielsen Media Research.

11. See Landler, Konrad, Schiller, and Therrien, "What Happened to Advertising."

12. Quoted in Richard Levinson and William Link, *Off Camera: Conversations with the Makers of Prime-Time Television* (New York: A Plume Book 1986), pp. 245–265.

13. CMR—MediaWatch.

14. Jupiter Communications, Press Releases, 1996.

15. Don E. Schultz, Stanley I. Tannenbaum, and Robert F. Lauterborn, *The New Marketing Paradigm: Integrated Marketing Communications* (Lincolnwood, IL: NTC Business Books 1993), see "Preface."

16. "What Is the New Marketing Paradigm?" in ibid.

17. Schultz's articles have appeared in *Advertising Age, Journal of Advertising Research, Journal of Advertising, Marketing Communications, Business Marketing, Journal of Direct Marketing, Journal of Business Strategy, Journal of Database Marketing*, and *Marketing News*. He was also a regular columnist of Marketing News. Even more importantly, he was the first editor of the *Journal of Direct Marketing* and the associate editor of the *Journal of Marketing Communications*, and on the editorial review board for a number of trade and scholarly publications

18. He is author/co-author of seven books, *New Marketing Paradigm: Integrated Marketing Communications, Strategic Advertising Campaigns* (now in fourth edition), *Essentials of Advertising Strategy* (now in third edition), *Essentials of Sales Promotion* (now in second edition), and *Sales Promotion Management* and *Strategic Newspaper Marketing*. After a career in ad agencies and public relations, he had become one of the leading advocates of IMC—the call for "the integrated management of all corporate communications to build positive and lasting relationships with customers and vital stakeholders" (Definition used by Integrated Marketing Communications at the Medill School of Journalism, Northwestern University. See www.medill.nwu.edu/imc/.)

19. Dan Steinbock, Interview with Don E. Schultz, Professor of Integrated Marketing Communications, the Medill School of Journalism, Northwestern University.

20. Ibid.

21. Toward the late 1990s, compensation, measurement, and IMC developments in terms of execution and implementation of integrated programs appeared to be the key areas for future research. See Philip J. Kitchen and Don E. Schultz, "Integrated Marketing Communications in U.S. Advertising Agencies: An Exploratory Study," *Journal of Advertising Research*, September–October 1997, pp. 7–18. On the state and evolution of IMC in the United States and internationally, see also C. Caywood, D. Schultz, and P. Wang, "Integrated Marketing Communications: A Survey of National Goods Advertisers," Unpublished report, Medill School of Journalism, Northwestern University, June 1991; T. Duncan, "The Concept and Process of Integrated Marketing Communication," *Integrated Marketing Communications Research*, 1, 1995, pp. 3–10; A. F. Grein and S. J. Gould, "Globally Integrated Marketing Communications," *Journal of Marketing Communications*, 2(3), 1996, pp. 141–158.

22. Steinbock, Interview with Don E. Schultz.

23. Ibid.

24. Ibid.

25. Ibid.

26. This differentiation and account of three marketplace forms derives from Don E. Schultz and Heidi F. Schultz, "Transitioning Marketing Communication into the Twenty-first Century," *Journal of Marketing Communications*, 3, 1998, pp. 9–26.

27. Still, Schultz was skeptical about the future of relationship marketing. "There's a relatively small number of products and services that people really want to have a relationship with. I don't particularly want to have a relationship with a plastic garbage bag manufacturer." The skeptic's verdict was unambiguous: Even if Americans could be sold on the idea of interactive media, it would not be a panacea for every industry, product, or service. Many products might never need this information-age marketing approach or the interactive relationship that goes with it.

28. Steinbock, Interview with Don E. Schultz.

29. These paragraphs on the ARPANET and NSFNet are derived from Mary Meeker and Chris DePuy, *The Internet Report* (New York: HarperBusiness 1996). For a history of the *early* Internet, see Katie Hafner and Matthew Lyon, *Where Wizards Stay Up Late: The Origins of the Internet* (New York: Simon & Schuster 1996). See also Jack Rickard, "Internet Architecture," available on the Web at http://www.boardwatch.com/isp/archit.htm, and Henry Edward Hardy, "A Short History of the Net," in Gary Welz, *The Internet World Guide to Multimedia on the Internet*, available on the World Wide Web at http://found.cs.nyu.edu/found.a/CAT /misc/welz/internetmm/02history/history1.html.

30. "For decades, advances in the various components of information processing and transmission (data collection, analysis, and so forth) have been proceeding continuously, often independently in more-or-less evolutionary fashion. Now, however, the cumultaive effects of the simultaneous changes in the individual components have converged and resulted in a fundamental discontinuity—a qualitative change in the capacity to collect, store, process, and transmit information. Hence, a revolution." See Robert C. Blattberg, Rashi Glazer, and John D. C. Little (eds.), introduction to *The Marketing Information Revolution* (Boston: Harvard Business School Press 1994).

31. Bill Clinton and Al Gore, *Putting People First* (New York: Times Books 1992), pp. 9–11. Many of these principles stemmed from the studies of the "new Democratic" Progressive Policy Institute (PPI), see, e.g., Will Marshall and Martin Schram, The Progressive Policy Institute, *Mandate for Change* (New York: Berkley Books 1993). On the political ties between the Clinton administration and the PPI, see Paul Starobin, "Aspiring to Govern," *National Journal*, May 9, 1992, pp. 1103–1110.

32. On the public and private interests in the building of the U.S. national information infrastructure, see Steinbock, *Triumph and Erosion in the American Media and Entertainment Industries*, especially chapter 6. For a concise policy study of the NII and its international spinoffs, see Brian Kahin and Ernest Wilson III (eds.), *National Information Infrastructure Initiatives: Vision and Policy Design* (Cambridge, MA: The MIT Press 1997).

33. Ibid.

34. See U.S. Government Information Infrastructure Task Force, *The National Information Infrastructure: An Agenda for Action*, September 15, 1993; *Global Information Infrastructure: An Agenda for Cooperation*, March 1994–February 1995; *A Framework For Global Electronic Commerce*, December 1996–July 1997. I shall explore this evolution—firm and industry-level strategies, as well as government policies—in a forthcoming study, tentatively entitled *The Virtual Hand: From the Internet to Electronic Commerce* (Mahwah, NJ: LEA 2000).

35. In the mid-1980s, the NSFNet operated at a speed of 56 kbps; in the late 1980s, it was upgraded to T-1 (1.5 mbps). In the early 1990s, it was upgraded to T-3 (45 mbps).

36. *See* "Clinton Announces Moves for Improving Access to the Internet," *Wall Street Journal*, October 11, 1996, p. B5; "Internet 2 Project General Information," available on the World Wide Web at http://www.internet2.edu/about_i2/.

37. See, e.g., Mary Meeker and Chris DePuy, *The Internet Report* (New York: HarperCollins 1995), p. 1–2.

38. Nicholas Negroponte, *Being Digital* (New York: Random House 1995), p. 12.

39. John Brockman, *Digerati: Encounters with the Cyber Elite* (San Francisco: Hardwired 1996), p. 180.

40. On these early days of the Web and the first new media enterpreneurs, see, e.g., Robert H. Reid, *Architects of the Web: 1,000 Days that Built the Future of Business* (New York: John Wiley & Sons 1997).

41. Here the term *technology integration* is used in a specific sense. In his fascinating account on the development of new and innovative technologies, Marco Iansiti applies his concept primarily in R&D. Yet, his definition is wide enough to fit the purposes of Internet marketing (just as he illustrates the notion with product development at Yahoo! and Netscape): "Technology integration is defined as the set of investigation, evaluation, and refinement activities aimed at creating a match between technological options and application context." See Marco Iansiti, *Technology Integration* (Boston: Harvard Business School Press 1998), p. 21. Similarly, though in a wider sense, we should view the scope of technology integration in Internet marketing as an effort to create an effective match between available technologies and application context. As we shall see, this is precisely what, for example, Modem Media did in its Zima campaign— the history's first major consumer marketing campaign (see chapter 4).

42. On industry evolution and strategic positioning, see Michael E. Porter, *Competitive Strategy* (New York: The Free Press 1980), pp. 156–162. On the uses of life cycle management in marketing, see Theodor Levitt, "Exploit the Product Life Cycle," *Harvard Business Review*, November–December 1965; Philip Kotler, *Marketing Management*, 9th ed. (Upper Saddle River, NJ: Prentice Hall 1997), chapter 12.

43. On the criticism and limitations of the life cycle theories, see Porter, *Competitive Strategy*, pp. 158 and 162.

44. For a lucid introduction to the issues of strategy, information systems, and the evolution of the IT architecture, see Lynda M. Applegate, F. Warren McFarlan, and James L. McKenney, *Corporate Information Systems Management: The Issues Facing Senior Executives*, 4th ed. (Chicago: Irwin 1996).

45. Meeker and DuPuy, *The Internet Report*, chapter 1.

46. See Intel's accounts on Moore's Law and its significance: www.intel.com.

47. This presentation is a very rough *sketch* of the complex links between dominant designs, new technologies, and change. On the relationships between technological change and business success, see in particular, Christopher Clayton, *The Innovator's Dilemma: When New Technologies Cause Great Firms to Fail* (Boston: Harvard Business School Press 1997); Stephen P. Bradley and Richard L. Nolan (eds.), *Sense & Respond: Capturing Value in the Network Era* (Boston: Harvard Business School Press 1998). For a thorough introduction to the problems of technology, strategy, and innovation, see Robert A. Burgelman, Modesto A. Maidique, and Steven C. Wheelwright, *Strategic Management of Technology and Innovation*, 2nd ed. (Chicago: Irwin 1996).

48. Andrew S. Grove, *Only the Paranoid Survive: How to Exploit the Crisis Points That Challenge Every Company and Career* (New York: Doubleday 1996).

49. The roots of diffusion research extends back to the European beginnings of social science (Gabriel Tarde and imitation, the British and German-Austrian diffusionists, etc.). For a history of the research field, see Everett M. Rogers [1962] *Diffusion of Innovations*, 4th ed. (New York: The Free Press 1995). Yet, diffusion research proper began outside of the academic field of communication, with the classic hybrid corn study by two anthropologists. See Bryce Ryan and Neal C. Gross, "The Diffusion of Hybrid Seed Corn in Two Iowa Communities," *Rural Sociology*, 8:15–24.

50. The home page of CUC International, Inc., 1997. For background, see CUC's 10-K's from 1987 to 1996.

51. Arguing that because the membership renewal rates were high and steady, Bell believed that it was "important for accounting to reflect future benefits from spending money on membership acquisition in the current period. While expensing these costs is conservative, it fails to reflect their true nature." See *1988 Annual Report, CUC International, Inc.*

52. When CUC made its IPO, the company had only a limited following among analysts and institutional investors. As the company grew larger, it sought to broaden its investor base. It was then that some analysts got concerned that capitalized marketing costs would subsequently have to be written off as losses because of high uncertainty about future renewal rates. They argued that deferring current marketing costs lowered the firms earnings quality. For a case study on CUC's financial management choices, see Paul Healy and Krishna Palepu, "CUC International, Inc. (A)," Harvard Business School case 9–192–099.

53. As a result, a direct marketing online company like Amazon.com could structure its transactional operations with Visa, American Express, MasterCard, and other alternative payment options. There was no pressing *need* for a recourse to "cybercash" or other more esoteric alternatives that were intensely debated by the American and European "digerati" but proved obsolescent in the marketplace. True, such options might become available, perhaps even necessary, in the long term. Yet, no new Internet retail company could base its business model on future viability only; the practice of quarterly statements made fun of such technological utopias.

54. Dan Steinbock, Interview with Robert Allen, President of Modem Media, June 1998.

55. Ibid.

56. For the rise and glory years of TCI, Inc., see chapter 3 ("Telecommunications, Inc.: The Deal Machine"), in Steinbock, *Triumph and Erosion in the American Media and Entertainment Industries*. For an informative but highly opinionated account on the company's fortunes, see L. J. Davis, *The Billionaire Shell Game: How Cable Baron John Malone and Assorted Corporate Titans Invented a Future Nobody Wanted* (New York: Doubleday 1998).

57. In particular, Malone took personal blame for the industry's two-year delay in delivering the new digital cable boxes that will match some of the most appealing features of digital satellite services, including scores of additional channels, on-screen viewer guides, and higher-quality sound and pictures. "This is my brainchild, I invested in it, I started it, I believe in it, and I'll take all the blame for its tardiness," he said. See Mark Robichaux, "TCI to Return to Its Roots As Phone Plans Fail to Pan Out," *Wall Street Journal*, January 2, 1997.

58. See Robichaux, "TCI to Return to Its Roots."

59. On the demise of interactive TV experiments, see, e.g., Bart Ziegler, "An Autopsy on the 'Next Big Thing': How the Web Toppled Interactive TV," *Wall Street Journal*, March 28, 1996.

60. Steinbock, Interview with Robert Allen.

61. Ibid.

62. The presence of CBS was short-lived. When Lawrence Tisch took control of CBS in 1986, he soon began an extensive divestiture program and the company dropped out of all nonbroadcast ventures. On CBS's strategic decisions, see Steinbock, *Triumph and Erosion*, chapter 2: "Loews, Inc./CBS: End of the Tiffany Network?"

63. On the historical evolution of Prodigy, see Robert D. Shapiro, "This Is Not Your Father's Prodigy," *Wired*, December 1993; Paul M. Eng, with Susan Chandler, "Prodigy: A 5-Year-Old Underachiever," *Business Week*, October 30, 1995.

64. By 1992 Prodigy users were more interested in e-mail and bulletin boards than shopping online. Many users switched to CompuServe and AOL.

65. See Shapiro, "This Is Not Your Father's Prodigy."

66. Ironically, most calls lasted far longer than necessary because, unlike most competitors, Prodigy's communications software did not allow users to compose and read messages offline. Through its phone bill, the online service started bleeding cash. The flaw was near-fatal; communications turned out to be among the most desired services on Prodigy. See Shapiro, "This Is Not Your Father's Prodigy."

67. Don Peppers and Martha Rogers, *The One to One Future: Building Relationships One Customer at a Time* (New York: Currency Doubleday 1993), p. 253.

68. See Ziegler, "An Autopsy on the 'Next Big Thing.' "

69. Located on the campus of the University of Illinois at Urbana-Champaign (UIUC), NCSA is funded by the National Science Foundation, the Advanced Research Projects Agency, other federal agencies, the State of Illinois, the University of Illinois, and industrial partners.

70. Mosaic accessed data via protocols such as HTTP, Gopher, FTP, and NNTP (Usenet News) natively, and other data services such as Archie, WAIS, and Veronica through gateways. NCSA Mosaic provided transparent and seamless access to these information sources and services.

71. Gary Wolf, "The (Second Phase of the) Revolution Has Begun, Part 1," *Wired*, October 1994.

72. On Netscape's early years, see Joshua Quittner and Michelle Slatalla, *Speeding the Net: The Inside Story of Netscape and How It Challenged Microsoft* (New York: Atlantic Monthly Press 1998).

73. If Netscape initiated the birth of the new growth industries, it also sought to solidify mass markets while raising the entry barriers. In October 1994, it became the founding member of the W3 Consortium, which sought to standardize the existing Web technologies. Although Netscape had hardly been introduced, it was already trying to create new products and services and influence the future course of the entire marketplace. In particular, it aspired to position itself as solidly as possible before the entry of the traditional industry leaders (especially Microsoft), which would soon "discover" the Web and adapt to Internet-driven competitive strategies.

74. See Kathy Rebello, with Amy Cortese and Rob Hof, "Inside Microsoft: The Untold Story of How the Internet Forced Bill Gates to Reverse Course" (Part 1 and Part 2), *Business Week*, July 15, 1996.

75. Ibid.

76. On Microsoft and its Internet strategy, see Bill Gates, with Nathan Myhrvold and Peter Rinearson, *The Road Ahead* (New York: Viking 1995). On the company's strategic U-turn, see James Wallace, *Overdrive: Bill Gates and the Race to Control Cyberspace* (New York: John Wiley & Sons 1997).

77. Ibid.

78. Dan Steinbock, Interview with Fergus O'Daly, August 3, 1998.

79. O'Daly served as Poppe's chairman, CEO, and a director from 1991 to 1997. In particular, he spearheaded the development of the agency's digital marketing capabilities. It was through O'Daly's visionary leadership that Poppe decided in 1993 to pursue online marketing as a core competency, giving the company a head start in the development of new media capabilities. In May 1997, after Poppe had been swept by internal turbulence, Fergus O'Daly joined CKS, an international integrated marketing communications holding company with headquarters in Silicon Valley. In August 1998, he left his position as president of CKS Partners (CKS Eastern Region). See press releases (CKS Group, Poppe Tyson).

80. O'Daly was named by *New York Magazine* as one of the "Cyber 60," the 60 most influential people building the Internet. The March 10, 1997 issue of *Ad Age*, featured O'Daly, along with Mark Kvamme, CEO of CKS, as "standing head and shoulders above the crowd" as two of three "New Goliaths" of interactive agencies.

81. Steinbock, Interview with Fergus O'Daly.

82. Ibid.

3

Relationship Marketing and Business-to-Business Marketing

If industrial society was based on machine technology, post-industrial society is shaped by intellectual technologies. And if capital and labor were the major structural features of industrial society, information and knowledge are those of the post-industrial society. In *The Coming of Post-Industrial Society*, Daniel Bell documented the transition of America from an industrial society to a post-industrial one based on services and the accelerating significance of the "economics of information."[1]

The first infrastructure in society is transportation—roads, canals, rail, air—for the movement of people and goods. The second infrastructure has been the energy utilities—oil pipeline, gas, electricity—for the transmission of power. The third infrastructure has been telecommunications, principally the voice telephone, radio, and television. But with the explosive growth of computers and terminals for data and the rapid decrease in the costs of computation and information storage, the question of hitching together the varied ways information is transmitted in the nation had become a major issue of economy and society.[2]

In the era of mass marketing, the core of this social structure emerged in the industrial East Coast. The new information infrastructure, however, began to evolve in California's Silicon Valley, the future hotbed of America's technological innovation and economic growth. Prompted by microprocessors and PCs, digitalization and miniaturization, as well as the convergence of computing and telecommunications, the 1990s "Internet revolution" was merely an extension of this historical transformation.

TECHNOLOGY MARKETING: IDEAS AND CAMPAIGNS

As the marketing channels of entire industries were changing, the value chains of distinct companies would have to follow. If, indeed, the entire infrastructure of the economy were changing, clearly such shifts would not take place without substantial consequences in strategic marketing management.

The more perceptive observers began to question the absence of *time* in marketing practices. That paved way to future ideas on various forms of speed economies (i.e., agility, flexible production, time-based competition, and so on). In the past, marketing managers had focused on transactions, persuasion, and broadcasting, without active or reactive feedback. The new marketing managers began to focus on relationships, dialogue and interactivity, and feedback loops.

As the center of gravity in a dynamic new sector shifted decisively to the west, similar changes occurred in the very characteristics of that center. In particular, the insularity of old-line industrial communities gave way to a far more open, flexible and proactive network economy.[3] As a result, it is hardly surprising that it was in Silicon Valley, too, where the changing concepts and practices of relationship marketing were first realized.

Relationship Management

As the new value chains reflected the accelerating bargaining power of the buyer (e.g., consumers, enterprises, and corporations), intense rivalry in new and emerging industries reflected both the efforts to increase entry barriers *and* the attempts to raise switching costs through *dense seller-buyer relationships*. By the late 1970s and early 1980s, several perceptive observers paid increasing attention to the implications of this shift in bargaining power. Their writings heralded and made way for those ideas and practices that would proliferate in the early years of Internet marketing. In retrospect, the common denominator lies in the centrality given to the idea of *relationship, interactivity*, or *feedback loop*.

The relationship between a seller and a buyer does not end when the sale is made, as Theodore Levitt notes in a classic article, "Relationship Management." In a great and increasing proportion of transactions, the relationship actually intensifies subsequent to the sale. *That*, as Levitt noted, becomes the critical factor in the buyer's choice of the seller the next time around. The sale consummates the courtship; how good the marriage is depends on how well the relationship is managed by the seller. As a result, he urged companies to avoid trouble and enhance their standing by recognizing at the outset the necessity of managing their relationship with customers. Such an understanding implied a significant revision of classic economic theory:

This takes more than what comes normally in good marketing. It takes special attention geared to what uniquely characterizes a relationship. That is *time*. The economic theory of "supply and demand" is totally false in this respect. It presumes that the work of the economic system is time discrete and absent of human interactions—an instantaneous, disembodied sales transaction clears the market at the intersection of supply and demand. This was never so and is increasingly less so as growing product complexity and interdependencies among the institutions of the industrial system intensify. The buyer of automated machinery does not, like the buyer at a flea market, walk home with his purchase and take his chances. He expects installation services, applications aids, parts, postpurchase repair and maintenance, retrofitted enhancements, and vendor R&D in support of the buyer's need to stay competitive in all respects. The buyer of a continuous stream of transactions, like a frozen food manufacturer who buys cartons from a packaging company and cash-management services from a bank, is concerned not with "clearing the market" but rather with maintaining the process.[4]

In these new conditions, a purchase decision is no longer a decision to buy an item, but a decision to enter a *bonded relationship*. This, argued Levitt, requires of the would-be seller a new orientation and a new strategy. In the past (mass marketing), the seller, living at a distance from the buyer, had reached out with his sales department to unload onto the buyer what the *seller* had decided to make. In the past marketing (segmentation), the seller, living closer to the buyer, penetrated the buyer's domain to learn about his needs and desires, and then designed and supplied the product. With increasing interdependence, however, marketing would have to reach for long-term relationships between sellers and buyers.

Exploring the evolution of fundamental categories of competition (from items and value to lead time and distribution), Levitt noted that relationship management was in a rapid state of change. In the past, the item itself had been synonymous with the product; by the early 1980s, the increasing complexity of the products had evolved into hybrids, such as augmented products; and in the future, the customers could be expected to look for more extensive solutions, such as system contracts. Similarly, in the past, service had been modest and strategy based on sales; in the present, service had become important and strategy adapted to marketing; and in the future, service would become vital while strategy would increasingly originate from relationship management.

The future of marketing management would be characterized by more and more intensified relationships, especially in industrial marketing, but also increasingly even in frequently purchased consumer goods. For instance, Procter & Gamble, copying General Mills' Betty Crocker advisory service, soon found out that the installation of a consumer hotline to give advice on its products and their uses raised customer brand loyalty. Only a decade later, companies would begin exploring the potential of Internet marketing in customer service—to enhance the service concept, to benefit strategically (e.g., raising switching costs), and to move from brand loyalty to sales (e.g., Web-driven direct sales).

Assuming that, in time, the Web-driven new entrants and incumbent industry leaders focus on relationship management, how real is the issue of rising switching costs? Commenting on the issue fifteen years after the release of his original essay, Levitt thought "it is possible," but also expressed some caution. Such a situation would not be automatic. Just because it was possible, it would not necessarily be actual. In particular, he argues that the proposition of heightened switching costs rested on two presumptions:

It assumes that the Internet will become an instrument of maintaining a closer and abiding relationship. It also assumes that both parties understand the importance of doing that; that if the seller is particular to the buyer, the buyer gets a lot of advantage from the seller, too. *Then* the relationship will add to the switching cost or at least raise barriers to the new entrants.[5]

Theodor Levitt's classic article on relationship marketing reflected, anticipated, and instigated new developments in American marketing and management. In particular, two developments of relationship marketing would prove particularly important in the 1990s. The first one preceded Levitt's writings and consists of Intel's innovative marketing campaigns. The second entails Regis McKenna's highly influential accounts of the dynamic marketing concepts. The two strands are highly interrelated.

Intel and Customer Education

Intel's history is legendary. The company was founded in 1968 when three engineers from Fairchild Semiconductor launched Intel (a condensation of Integrated Electronics) in Mountain View, California. While Robert Noyce, co-inventor of the integrated circuit, and Gordon Moore handled long-range planning, Andy Grove oversaw manufacturing. Intel's mission would be to develop technology for silicon-based chips. At first, Intel supplied semiconductor memory for large computers. The soaring gains were then reinvested in microprocessor designs that revolutionized the electronics industry. When IBM, in 1981, chose Intel's 8088 chip for its PC, Intel ensured a critical strategic position as the microcomputer standards supplier, just as Microsoft acquired a dominant hold of operating systems and, eventually, applications. Complementing each other's activities, the two functioned as a de facto duopoly of two to three critical computing industries (hence the nickname "Wintel," a contraction of Windows and Intel). By the end of the 1980s, *they* were the industry leaders, whereas IBM was struggling for its survival.

The growth of Silicon Valley and the mass production of microprocessors went hand in hand with the expansion of Intel. Unsurprisingly, then, it would be the first technology company to struggle with customer education. When microprocessors were introduced in the early 1970s, few customers recognized the value of the new chips. To develop new markets, business-to-business companies had to be willing to educate their customers. By the end of the 20th century, such an approach is considered not only necessary but an inherent element of competitive strategy. Initially, however, the concept was often not understood, and sometimes ridiculed. Indeed, the very idea of programmable chips was novel and many engineers took the new product for a "marketing gimmick."[6]

Still, Intel went ahead and the company ran advertisements with suggested applications for the new product. It distributed booklets with descriptions of actual applications, from electronic games to blood analyzers, from milking machines to satellites. Most importantly, perhaps, the company ran seminars for potential corporate customers. "In the first few years, Intel ran hundreds of these seminars, all over the world," recalls Regis McKenna, Silicon Valley's pioneer in business-to-business marketing.[7]

At each seminar, Intel first presented a corporate overview, usually from a top company executive. Next, an Intel marketing manager would give a presentation on the marketing value of microprocessor-based products. Finally, Intel engineers would describe the technical details of the microprocessors. Most of the early customers ordered only a few microprocessor chips. But as the education campaign continued, Intel was able to attract more and more high-volume users.[8] (Exhibit 3-1.)

In the coming years, Intel's concept of customer education has provided a powerful model to other technology companies (e.g., infrastructure, hardware, software, content aggregation, media) followed its example—from Apple's user-friendly Macintosh targeting American households to DoubleClick touting the added value inherent in ad targeting and ad networks.[9] Similarly, Intel's early use of feedback loops in buyer chains would later be enhanced by online communication (e.g., the use of online beta communities by Netscape and Yahoo! in speeding up product development).[10] Toward the end of the 1990s, this concept of interactivity and feedback loop was moving rapidly from the marketspace and the Internet companies to the marketplace and business-to-business and consumer companies.[11] The idea of a dynamic

Exhibit 3-1
Educating Customers

In November 1971, Intel introduced the world's first commercial microprocessor, the 4004, invented by three Intel engineers. Primitive by today's standards, it contained a mere 2300 transistors and performed about 60,000 calculations in a second. Twenty-five years later, the microprocessor is the most complex mass-produced product ever, with more than 5.5 million transistors performing hundreds of millions of calculations each second. (By 1998, Pentium ® II processor, by contrast, contained 7.5 million transistors.)

What was Intel like in the early '70s?

In 1968 Intel was one of the hot new companies, kind of like the Netscape of the '60s and '70s. The prestige of Noyce and Moore made it a special company. They both had this tremendous stature—they had founded Fairchild, the most prolific semiconductor company of its day, which really created Silicon Valley. Noyce was co-inventor of the integrated circuit. There was an aura about them—they were scientists and businessmen, and they were a cut above most of the people in the business.

How did the engineering community receive Intel's first microprocessors?

A lot of my engineering friends scoffed at them as a gimmick. The market really had to be educated. In the early '70s, Intel was conducting dozens of corporate trainings on how to use the microprocessor. Noyce, Moore and Andy Grove went on the road with a traveling educational roadshow. Engineers resisted changing the way they designed products, but Intel appealed to their managers by promoting the idea that they could speed up the time-to-market by using microprocessors—a strategy that worked.

Do you think Intel's founders foresaw what the microprocessor would do?

I think Noyce imagined a world in which computers could be used for educational purposes and that microprocessors would become cheap enough to become as disposable as a lightbulb. I remember hearing him speak in the '70s at an electronics conference and he was talking about distributed computing and the convergence of computing and telecommunications—there were very few people who understood what he talking about or the importance these developments would have.

Source: "Intel Museum Home Page," Intel Corp. 1998 (www.intel.com/intel/museum/25anniv/index.htm).

supplier-buyer relationship, however, originated from Intel's early marketing management.

Intel's pioneering collaboration with customers and complementors began in the 1970s, but it has accelerated with the rising chip performance. Technology companies produce complex products. They operate in a complex environment where the lines between buyers and sellers may get blurry. Since new products tend to be based in complex systems, joint standards are critical for acceptance. That necessitates collaboration with customers and complementors (i.e., manufacturers, hardware developers, software developers, and end users)—all of which depend on one another in a business "ecosystem."[12] Through strategic partnerships, Intel's strategy turned many potential competitors into actual complementors and the competition into co-opetition. Indeed, these new notions of game theory evolved, at least partially, from the observation of Intel's strategic moves,[13] or as the authors of *Co-opetition* readily acknowledged:

The classic example of complements is computer hardware and software. Faster hardware prompts people to upgrade to more powerful software, and more powerful software motivates people to buy faster hardware. For example, Windows 95 is far more valuable on a Pentium-powered machine than on a 486 machine. . . . Though the idea of complements may be most apparent in the context of hardware and software, the principle is universal. A complement to one product or service is any other product or service that makes the first one more attractive. Hot dogs and mustard, cars and auto loans, televisions and videocassette recorders, television shows and *TV Guide*, fax machines and phone lines, phone lines and wide area networking software, catalogs and overnight delivery services, red wine and dry cleaners, Siskel and Ebert. . . . [14]

In microprocessors change has always been constant. If the environment is highly dynamic, what assurances do the executives have that today's complementors will not get hungry and turn into tomorrow's substitutors? None. *In practice*, the idea of complements and the necessity of strategic partnerships with complementors has been as much embraced at Intel as viewed with a suspicious eye. The famous dictum of Andy Grove, "Only the paranoid survive," cautions executives not to view complementors as static partners. Just as the environment is under constant change, so are the complementors. Or as Grove has put it,

Complementors often have the same interests as your business and travel the same road. I think of them as "fellow travelers." While your interests are aligned, your products support each other. However, new techniques, new approaches, new technologies can upset the old order and change the relative influence of the complementors or cause the path of fellow travelers to diverge from yours.[15]

Today's allies may well be tomorrow's enemies. Still, Intel customers were companies. It had no alternative but to build partnerships, even if it would constantly have to watch its back. As its ties grew deeper with the business community, it had to penetrate further into the channel structure.

Collaboration and Channel Structure: From Customers to Customers' Customers

When Intel started out in the semiconductor memory business, the customer relationships were straightforward. Its customers were computer manufacturers, and it dealt with their engineering and purchasing departments through its field sales engineers (FSEs). But when the company entered the microprocessor business, defining the customers became more complex. Now Intel had to address not only the two internal departments, but also the CEOs of its customers. The idea was to assure high-level executives that Intel had a long-term product road map. It was not urging companies to select memory or other products; it was suggesting cooperation to mutual benefit and providing assistance in a critical and strategic long-term decision.

Since designing microprocessor-based systems was fairly complex, Intel also set up in the 1970s a new team of specialists, field application engineers (FAEs) who gave technical support to its customers' engineering staffs. At the time, the concept was new and innovative, assisting customers to design better and faster microprocessor-based systems. In retrospect, Intel was building a feedback loop with its buyer chain. "Because our FAEs are in continuous contact with technical personnel at our customer sites, they are in an excellent position to talk to them about new Intel products," notes Albert Yu, Senior VP and General Manager of the critical Microprocessor Products Group at Intel. "They also gather valuable feedback on what features the customers really want in our products and how we might improve them."[16]

As Intel began to solidify its buyer chain creating feedback systems with its customers, it was only a matter of time until it would have to address the needs of its customers' customers. For two decades, the chip manufacturer had dealt with other companies in business-to-business markets. This channel solution grew more complex by the early stages of promoting the 386 processor in the late 1980s. After Intel had worked hard with its traditional customers—PC manufacturers—to get them to use 386 in their product lines, a number of upstarts—Compaq, Acer, and others—jumped on the 386 opportunity. Meanwhile, IBM, the then-market leader, decided that it did not need 386; the 286 was good enough to serve its needs. That put Intel into a difficult position: the company was eager to push the newer and better 386, but it needed IBM's strong endorsement to move the market to the 386. It was then that Dennis Carter, the then-technical assistant of Andy Grove, Intel's CEO, came up with the idea of addressing PC end users *directly* about the advantages of the 386.[17]

Historically, this decision was crucial. Later it made possible both the success of the "Intel Inside" campaign *and* the turmoil of the Pentium debacle. While it was in Intel's interest to ceaselessly expand the marketplace, this growth came with a price. As the industry grew more complex, its control and ecosystem got more elaborate, too. Says Albert Yu,

This was a novel and risky concept at the time. It was like an engine manufacturer addressing car drivers directly about the virtues of the engine inside their cars. We had never dealt directly with end users before. Besides, our customers, PC manufacturers, might not like us addressing their customers directly. Still, we reasoned that because the microprocessor defined the performance and characteristics of the PC, it was appropriate for us to educate end users as to why they should buy newer and faster 386 PCs rather than older and slower 286 machines.[18]

While Intel had legitimate reasons to be concerned for a channel conflict, it also rode the PC momentum. True, IBM was still the market leader, but the clone manufacturers had caught up with the trendsetter. Compaq had shipped its first computer in 1982, and in 1983 (the year it went public) it recorded unprecedented sales of $111 million. The startup was technologically attuned and capitalized on the extensive base of dealers and suppliers built up around the IBM PC to sell its products. In 1983 Compaq introduced a 28-pound portable computer, some 18 months before IBM. In 1986, it also was first out with a computer based on Intel's 386 chip. Two years later, it became the first company to exceed the $2 billion sales mark within six years of its first product introduction—not least because of its reliance on the Intel processors. By its refusal to participate in the microprocessor evolution, IBM was neglecting the implications of technology change. As a result, the clone manufacturers invaded its market shares and the "Big Blue" would flirt with disaster.

Obsoleting Products

It was Intel's decision to approach its clients directly that prompted the "Red X" campaign in 1989. Unlike previous campaigns, this one was aimed directly at PC users. The company ran ads with a big red X over the 286, and the message, "Now, get 386 system performance at a 286 system price." With this advertising campaign, Intel took the risk of promoting a new product, the 386 at the expense of the earlier (and still popular!) 286 processor. The campaign was a tremendous success, causing a rapid rise in the 386 chip sales.

Besides a success, the campaign proved a watershed event for Intel. "We realized that our customers were not only PC manufacturers but also the end users that bought PCs," recalls Yu.

Once we knew that our customers included end users, several logical steps followed. We mounted the "Intel Inside" advertising campaign, which successfully established the Intel brand name in consumers' minds. In concert with this consumer ad campaign, we worked with our primary customers, PC manufacturers, to encourage them to display the "Intel Inside" symbol in their ads and on their products. We worked hard over many years to execute this campaign, and it was extremely successful all over the world.[19]

If influencing the channel structure would prove crucial in the launch of the product, the purposeful obsoleting of products would provide its fundamental rationale. Understandably, perhaps, initially, the idea of product cannibalization made little sense to many technology companies. It made even less sense to firms in the related or nonrelated sectors. By the late 1980s and early 1990s, fast product development and increasing product proliferation made cannibalization almost inevitable.

The "Red X" campaign was aimed directly at PC users. Intel ran ads with a big red X. Visually, it was dramatic. As a business strategy, it was far more exciting. The company was purposefully obsoleting its own product, the 286 (Exhibit 3-2). Given the pace of technological advances predicted by Moore's Law, Intel learned early that to continue to develop better products, it would have to obsolete its existing products. It was this very concern that motivated Andy Grove's famous dictum "only the paranoid survive." If Intel did not cannibalize its products, someone else would.

Certainly, the ad campaign alone did not account for the popularity of the 386. Functional marketing and advertising were necessary, but not sufficient; most importantly, the new product had to be driven *through the channel structure*. It was the campaign *and* the collaboration with the primary customers that accounted for the success.

The technology sector consists of several constituents that are closely linked through direct buying-and-selling relationships or in some form of collaborative relationship. To prosper, each depends on the other. Competition and collaboration drive the industry. In such a complex amalgam of industries, even Intel could not dictate the pace or terms of the change. However, it could and would try to influence the direction of the change (Exhibit 3-3).

It was the marketing chain, the entire *channel structure*, with its com-

Exhibit 3-2
Obsoleting Products

With this advertising campaign, Intel took the risk of promoting a new product, the Intel 386TM, at the expense of the earlier, still popular, 286 processor. The campaign was a tremendous success, causing a rapid rise in Intel 386 chip sales.

Source: Thirty Years of Creativity & Innovation: 1969 to 1998 (Intel Museum Archives).

Exhibit 3-3
Intel's Influence Map (Late 1990s)

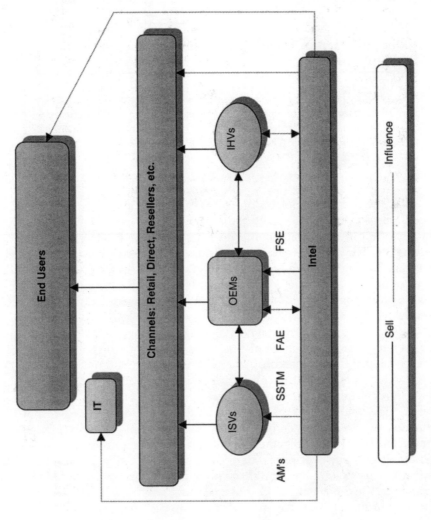

Source: Intel Corp. (1998).

plex sales and influence relationships, that accounted for Intel's success. The company would soon be emulated by other industry players in their pursuit of financial prosperity and technological excellence. Yet, that very penetration of the channel structure would also push Intel into the kind of marketing that, initially, had been entirely foreign to its mission and vision.

Riding the Market Momentum: From "Intel Inside" to Bunny People

H-E-L-L-Oooooooool Who is the paying customer here? Now if Intel were giving away buggy chips, maybe, just maybe I could understand their "profit margin" mentality. Intel . . . after monopolizing the PC industry for so long, you disappoint me as a PREVIOUS customer! You made millions and you still don't understand who got you to where you are/were today . . . THE CUSTOMER!

As if the messages posted on comp.sys.intel were not enough, IBM's press release cracked the jackpot. Big Blue announced it would halt shipments of all IBM personal computers based on the Intel Pentium microprocessor. The action was based on tests conducted by the IBM Research Division. Caught off guard by IBM's decision, Andrew Grove, Intel's president and CEO, offered replacements only to those heavy users who could prove their vulnerability to what the microprocessor company perceived as a minor flaw.

Only months later Grove, who also taught management at the Stanford University Graduate School of Business, came to understand the significance of the Internet revolution, the ensuing transformation of Intel's own value chain, and the company's shifting position in the industry's rapidly changing vertical chain. For some 26 years, *Intel* had decided what the customer needed; it had sold microprocessors to computer makers, not to computer users. It operated in the business-to-business markets; it spoke of consumers but did not deal with *consumers* directly. Now, all of a sudden, Intel was receiving 25,000 daily calls from angry computer users who had bought nothing directly from the company, and demanded a replacement. Yet, in an ironic way, it was the company's marketing muscle that was now threatening its very survival.[20]

In the early 1990s, the company introduced the "Intel Inside" marketing campaign, the biggest the industry had ever seen. Hundreds of manufacturers, domestic and international, displayed a new distinctive logo in their advertising, often with a sticker on the actual computer. Intel spent millions of dollars to promote the brand. The aim was to suggest to the computer user that the microprocessor that was inside his or her computer *was* the computer. By 1994 Intel's research showed that the logo had become one of the most recognized logos in consumer merchandising, like Coca-Cola or Nike. On November 22, 1994, when the newspaper and media stories revealed defects in Intel's top of the line chip, this very success was threatened. "When problems developed with the new flagship chip," wrote Grove, "our merchandising pointed the users directly back to us." Ultimately, Intel had no alternative but to take a write-off of $475 million—the equivalent of half a year's R&D budget or five years worth of the Pentium processor's advertising spending.[21]

Since the early 1970s, Intel had served business-to-business markets. Suddenly, it had become a consumer marketer, without even selling directly to the consumers. The transition had taken a while, but few had noticed the signs. By 1994, when the first browser generation was launched, even a powerful industry giant such as Intel had to be prepared to modify the game plan continually; the consumer marketing *and* the business-to-business markets were only about to get increasingly competitive. The rise of the Internet would merely accelerate the shift of the bargaining power to the buyers. As Intel embarked on a new way of doing business, Grove realized that the company had stumbled onto a "strategic inflection point."[22]

At first, Intel had tried to fight the change. That was futile. Instead, it would embrace the change—and more. In the coming years, it would do its utmost to *anticipate and instigate change*, even if that meant cloning a bunch of disco bunnies dancing to "play that funky music."

In January 1997, Intel's Bunny People made their debut at Super Bowl as a device for the Santa Clara chip maker to transform one of its most esoteric technologies—a set of computer instructions for managing multimedia data—into a household phrase: MMX. Cashing in on the Beanie Babie craze, perhaps, the TV commercials featured the dancing antics of actors clad in colorful versions of the antiseptic "bunny suits" that semiconductor workers must wear when handling the delicate processors. Instead of the traditional techy style, these spots pushed few specifications; the disco dancing Bunnies concentrated on funk and hustle. The campaign was so successful that the following Labor Day weekend saw the company promoting consumer-oriented Pentium II computers by handing out 8-inch Bunny People figures. They had the symbol of Intel's initial marketing gimmick, the Intel Inside logo, emblazoned on their chests (Exhibit 3-4).[23]

Only two months prior to the Super Bowl, Intel's then-CEO Andy Grove had delivered a keynote speech at the Comdex computer show predicting a war "for eyeballs." In fifteen years, microprocessors would be 250 times more powerful than they were in 1997, which would provide enough muscle to put the PC into head-to-head combat with TV

Exhibit 3-4
The Disco Dancing Bunny People

Intel Launches New Ad Campaign For MMX™ Technology That Puts The Fun In Computing
"Seinfeld" Star Jason Alexander and Intel "Bunny People" Featured in New Commercials
Only Technology Company to Debut Ad During Super Bowl
First Time Intel Advertises on Super Bowl

Santa Clara, CA (January 22, 1997)–To showcase how Intel's Pentium® processor with MMX™ technology creates a more fun experience for consumers, Intel said today that it is unveiling a new advertising campaign which includes two series of entertaining commercials. NBC's "Seinfeld" star, Jason Alexander, will debut tonight (Wednesday, January 22), in a tongue-in-cheek commercial featuring Intel's ProShare® videoconferencing technology titled "Blind Date."

A second ad series titled "Bunny People" will debut on Sunday's Super Bowl broadcast. ("Bunny Suits" is the industry term for white outfits worn by manufacturing technicians to maintain a sterile environment in Intel chip fabrication plants. "Bunny People" are those who wear bunny suits.) These ads feature a colorful group of Intel manufacturing workers who illustrate how Intel's MMX technology is more visually lifelike, enables top-quality sound, and—most of all—fun for consumers to use. Intel is the only technology company to advertise during the Super Bowl this year. The company introduced the new Pentium processor with MMX technology on January 8.

At Intel chip fabrication plants, manufacturing technicians work in white outfits known as "Bunny Suits" in order to maintain a sterile environment.

Kicking Off at the Super Bowl
"Over the years, Intel's chip technology has fostered a tremendous growth in the capabilities of the personal computer, which now appeals to a broader range of users than ever before," says Dennis Carter, vice president and director of Corporate Marketing at Intel. "We have chosen to advertise during the Super Bowl because we see it as a great venue to introduce our new Pentium processor with MMX technology to the broad consumer marketplace."

The Super Bowl ads portray a colorful group of dancing "Bunny People" shown adding fun to the new chip. "These commercials are humorous, high-tech fantasies that show how fun computing can be with MMX technology. The spots demonstrate in a playful way the vivid color, quality sound and rich experience consumers can have with a new personal computer based on the Pentium processor with MMX technology," said Ann Lewnes, director of Worldwide Advertising at Intel.

Entertaining Ads Reflect a More Exciting Computer Experience
Directed by Jim Gartner who is known for spots such as Pepsi's "Dad's Blessing," HBO's "Falling TV" and Visa's "Burro," and created by Euro RSCG Dahlin Smith White, two spots called "Blind Date" feature actor Jason Alexander. In each of the two spots, Jason Alexander's character is foiled in his attempts to impress two different blind dates whom he has called using Intel's video phone on a PC featuring the Pentium processor with MMX technology.

In the second series of spots, Intel introduces a group of new characters—"Bunny People"–a take-off on employees in "bunny suits" who work in processor fabrication

Exhibit 3-4 (continued)

plants at Intel. The setting of the first spot is a traditional Intel fabrication plant which is contrasted with a fanciful representation of the "MMX technology department" where Bunny People add the fun ingredient to the processor which will lift consumers' PC experience to exciting, new heights. A second ad focuses exclusively on the "MMX technology department." The ads were directed by Bob Giraldi, famous for Michael Jackson's "Beat It," "Reebok" with Shaquille O'Neal, and Pepsi-Cola spots with Michael Jackson and Lionel Richie. The ad concept was created by Euro RSCG Dahlin Smith White. The first of these ads breaks during the Super Bowl on Sunday, January 26.

     Both the "Blind Date" and "Bunny People" spots will air also during prime time on major networks, as well as news, sports, late night and cable programming. In addition, Intel is complementing the campaign with print ads shortly after the broadcast release. Intel is devoting a record number of advertising dollars to the worldwide Intel MMX technology campaign—part of a wider effort which includes online (http://mmx.com) and retail activities as well.

Source: "Intel Launches New Ad Campaign For MMX™ Technology," Intel Press Release, Santa Clara, CA (January 22, 1997).

and any other type of electronic entertainment device. "In this war," Grove said, "he who captures the most eyeballs wins."[24]

In the 1970s, the Bunny People campaign would have represented the kind of mass advertising that was the polar opposite of Intel's initial marketing efforts. But by the close of the 1990s, even traditional mass marketing and mass advertising was no longer foreign to the company. As Intel was getting used to the idea that, under certain circumstances, potato and microprocessor chips were not that different at all, it embraced the new strategic directives and would try to beat consumer packaged goods in their own game. In the past, the company had never sold directly to consumers. The branding of the chip and the "Intel Inside" campaign had changed the old channel strategy. Now Intel would sell by all means necessary.

Since the 1970s, Regis McKenna, a legendary marketer, had assisted in Intel's campaigns. In the course of the 1980s and the 1990s, he would draw the lessons from these experiences. Earlier than many of his colleagues he understood that these pioneering strategies and campaigns were bound to spread from Silicon Valley to Madison Avenue. In the process, McKenna, Intel, and other pioneering marketers would subvert marketing from within.

FROM RELATIONSHIP MARKETING TO REAL TIME

In 1963, Regis McKenna had left Pennsylvania for Silicon Valley. "Though technology was racing ahead, the ways of doing business in Silicon Valley had not changed very much," he recalls.

Companies were still marketing their products in very traditional ways. It was engineers selling to engineers. Salesmen stressed technical details and prices. In short, the businesses were technology- and sales-oriented. Before long, it became clear to me that these traditional approaches were not well suited to a world of fast-changing markets and complex products. Companies in Silicon Valley needed marketing strategies as new and innovative as their products. So while the engineers of Silicon Valley were experimenting with new technologies, I began experimenting with new ideas in marketing and communications.[25]

After his move to Silicon Valley, McKenna gained marketing experience in General Micro Electronics (the first company to develop and market commercial metal oxide semiconductor products) and National Semiconductor. As marketing services manager, he

was the third person in marketing there. It carried on with the same idea of digitizing circuits and applications to everything from refrigerators to automobiles. The wonderful thing of working in the silicon industry is that you're constantly dealing with end-user applications or companies that are delivering to end-users. The products ranged from automobiles to space satellites and medical devices such as blood analyzers. The position gave one a vast array of exposure to industry and application.[26]

In 1970, McKenna started his own marketing strategy firm; by the late 1990s, The McKenna Group was headquartered in Palo Alto, California, with international offices.[27] He has advised Intel, Apple, Microsoft, and many other companies. He became aware of the Internet and its business potential well before many others.[28]

McKenna had a very broad liberal arts education, majored in philosophy but was trained in languages, history, English, and literature. He was also very interested in physics, science, and technology:

That training enabled me to go into many of these engineering-based companies and to provide a different kind of perspective. At the time, there weren't people who thought about saying, "How is technology changing people?" or "How odd would it be to shape our organization in order to get more people out there to adopt our technology?" "How should our technology be shaped so that we would have a broad market?" Of course, I did not know the answers, but perhaps searching for the answer required us to watch closely the marketplace so that we could evolve the process rather than come up with specific answers. The idea was to age in and with the marketplace. If we can see how things actually evolve, we can supercede our mistakes. Looking at history, we know that early television grew by trying to emulate radio, just as much of the early Internet has been trying to emulate television. New technologies will always forge their own paths and ties. So it is important to keep an open mind, not fixing our views on how things were but the way they have to evolve in order to embrace the future.[29]

McKenna's clients operated on emerging information technology and telecommunications technologies and markets. The strategies sought to create significant leadership and subsequent revenue growth for the clients. The objective was to make the future happen before the competition created first-to-market advantage for the clients.[30] So it was only logical that McKenna would be among the first, if not the first of those marketers who intuitively and persistently began to build, develop, and implement a *dynamic* marketing concept—first in technology industries, but soon in many others, too.

Emergent Industries and Dynamic Positioning

McKenna and other pioneers of early technology marketing arrived in the business in the late 1960s and 1970s. From the start, they got involved with practices and procedures involving emerging industries. These new products, services, and industries were moving rapidly toward mass customization. Yet, many of the early practitioners had been trained in disciplines that were designed to support *mass* production and *mass* marketing. In the course of the years, McKenna would get weary with the classic view of (functional) marketing. The classic view might still "work" in mature industries, which were characterized by static positioning and unsophisticated buyers. But instead of reflecting and anticipating, it distorted the new and emerging markets, which were typified by dynamic positioning and increasingly sophisticated buyers. Through his experiences, McKenna began to

develop a new approach to marketing, an approach that takes into account the dynamic changes in industries and markets. It is an approach that stresses the building of relationships rather than the promotion of products, the communication of concepts rather than the dispersal of information, and the creation of new markets rather than the sharing of old ones. . . . While these marketing ideas were conceived and tested at high-technology companies, they can be applied to many other industries. Indeed, the traditional rules of marketing are breaking down in a growing number of industries. The business world is changing quickly, and marketing ideas are lagging behind.[31]

McKenna saw several forces underlying the need for new approaches to marketing.

- *Pace of Change.* The most important one was the quickening pace of change. Traditional marketing rules were designed for static markets and static industries. The speed-up was most extreme in high-technology industries, but it was accelerating in old-line industries as well.
- *Mass Customization.* The change reflected shifting out of an age of mass-manufactured goods and into an era of custom-made products. Unlike the

mass-produced black automobiles from the Fordian assembly line, the new products came in different shapes, sizes, colors, and varieties. With new technology, diversity no longer cost more than uniformity.[32] In this new environment, marketing managers would have to learn to treat every customer as an individual.

- *Complexity.* Products were becoming more complex than ever before. When a customer bought a new computer, he or she had to understand what types of software and peripherals could be used with it.

All of these determinants—the quickening pace of change, the rise in diversity, the increase in complexity—were creating new challenges in marketing.[33]

Dynamic Positioning. The cornerstone of the "new marketing," McKenna argued, lay in *dynamic* positioning. Positioning is competitive: customers think about products and companies in relation to other products and companies. They set up a hierarchy in their minds, then use that hierarchy when making decisions. At the heart of every good marketing strategy is a good positioning strategy. All of marketing—merchandising, advertising, pricing, packaging, distribution, public relations—grows out of positioning. Modern marketing is, to a large extent, a battle for positioning. Yet, traditional positioning strategies were no longer adequate. They did not take technology and change into account. They assumed a static marketplace where technologies, products, and customer perceptions changed very slowly. In the traditional model, a company first decided how it wanted its product positioned ("low-price," "premium-quality," etc.). Next, the company came up with a slogan that summarized the desired message. Finally, it spent money on advertising and promotions until the slogan achieved broad recognition (e.g., the Avis-Hertz rivalry).[34]

McKenna urged new ideas to differentiate dynamic positioning from traditional approaches to positioning. In particular, he stressed four aspects:

- *Marketing should be dynamic, not static.* It was the market's gravitational forces that drew the product in and helped position it in the minds of the customers. These forces included financial resources, timing, technology, people, market infrastructure, strategic relationships, FUD (fear, uncertainty, and doubt), adaptation sequence, and competition.

- *Marketing should focus on market creation, not market sharing.* In traditional positioning, marketers identified established markets and then tried to find a way to get a piece of that market. In fast-changing industries, however, marketers did not think about sharing markets but about *creating* markets. Traditional market-share strategies do not work well in emerging markets that are small to begin with and require managers to think like enterpreneurs. That requires experimentation and risks, as well as developing new markets. That means taking the time to *educate customers*.

- *Marketing should be a building process, not a promotional process.* Advertising and promotion are a small part of the entire marketing strategy. Advertising can reinforce positions in the market, but it cannot create positions. To build enduring positions in the market, companies first had to build strong relationships with suppliers, distributors, retailers, and the financial community. They simply had to take advantage of the industry's infrastructure.

- *Marketing should be qualitative, not quantitative.* In emerging markets, numbers are rarely reliable. In many cases, quantitative analyses use the past to predict the future. Yet, extrapolating today's trends into the future seldom works. To take a qualitative approach to marketing, managers had to understand the market environment, including all of its gravitational forces (e.g., social trends, relationships, and competition).

According to McKenna, the origins of what would become known as relationship marketing in the latter half of the 1980s evolved from the business-to-business marketing.

Infrastructure Revolutions and Relationship Marketing

"In the 1970s, Intel played a critical role in the emergence of relationship marketing in business-to-business markets," McKenna recalls.

It was trying to establish profitability, new technology, and standards. In a sense, relationship marketing was a natural extension of our contemporary work with our clients, and their clients. These relationships often evolved from a phone call that required sitting down with the client. One would be honest and direct, and go through the relevant issues, such as "Is this product a good idea?" "What do we have to do to improve it?" "How do we have to change in order to keep your business?" and so on. Business-to-business has always been personalized in a number of ways. Take for example engineer-to-engineer businesses. The engineering folks from the high-tech world would sit down with the engineers of the medium-sized companies and say, "How can we work together?" and "How can we design our products and the product system?" That's how I learned to develop marketing.[35]

McKenna traces the origins of relationship marketing to work assignments and lectures that he gave in the early 1980s.[36] Still, "relationship marketing first evolved in certain companies and businesses. The industries came to it later. And certainly the discovery itself came even later."[37]

As the business-to-business expanded and more industries emerged and more companies got into the play, says McKenna, the conduct of business grew far more complex and extensive.

First with Apple and then with others, we began to see that we were moving out into broader and broader markets. That made things difficult. It is hard to build relationships with a thousand, not to speak of a million, people. But the technology is enabling us to manage millions of people. We would have to develop a concept of how to view technology to create, evolve, and develop relationships with a far broader proportion of the public. In the process, you began to ask yourself the question of "How do I maintain a real relationship at this-and-that level?"

That's perhaps where my philosophical upbringing came in. I abhor consumer marketing that often manipulates the customer. If you really start to analyze what is happening, the consumer is now given more and more choice and, in short, that leads to a higher value of the brand. Brand was always something you think about, but when we buy soap, we do that without making a conscious choice or decision. It is also how we make political decisions and there are other types of values and decisions. So you have to look at it in a very broad range in order to engage people in relationships without trying to be manipulative of their choices *and* to use their the feedback to gain as a producer. Through those relationships, I'll learn more from the customers. I can build better products or new products to respond to their needs. In turn, the consumers gain by getting products that are more attuned and adapted to the things that they want and need. Interactivity can only begin if you can understand how to build, direct, and manage technology.[38]

Strategic Relationship Marketing. What worked in the static marketplace was destined to fail in the new and fast-changing industries where products, markets, technologies, and competition were in constant flux. Since the 1980s, for instance, these changes have been reflected by the rapid shifts in ad budget expenditures from media advertising to sales promotions. McKenna urged companies to establish strategies that could survive the turbulent changes in the new market environment. *That* meant (strategic) relationship marketing:

To survive in dynamic marketplaces, companies clearly need a new form of positioning. . . . To do that, companies can't focus on promotions and advertising. They need to gain an understanding of the market structure, then develop strategic relationships with other key companies and people in the market. They must build relationships with suppliers and distributors, investors, and customers. Those relationships are more important than low prices, flashy promotions, or even advanced technology. Changes in the market environment can quickly alter prices and technologies, but close relationships can last a lifetime, if not longer. . . . With this approach, positioning evolves gradually. . . . [A product or company] acquires meaning from its environment, and it changes as the environment changes.[39]

Unlike traditional positioning, dynamic positioning is a multidimensional process. It involves three interlocking stages of product, market, and corporate positioning. Through *product positioning*, a company must determine how it would like its product to fit in the market. *Market positioning* enables the product to gain recognition in the market. In *corporate positioning*, the company had to position not just its products but itself, primarily through financial success. Yet, financial success should not be understood in exclusively "financial" terms; due to the complexity and novelty of the products and services, customers consider profitability a sign of assurance and credibility. Pieced together properly, they create a whole that is bigger than its parts. But if any one of them is flawed, the whole positioning process will falter. This three-stage positioning process has to be considered a *total business activity*, or a value chain. It is certainly not just advertising and public relations. Dynamic positioning pulls a common thread through all parts of the company and then connects them all to the marketplace; it has to affect the corporate headquarters, product planning, marketing, sales, and financial strategy.[40]

Influencing the Infrastructure. To gain a strong market position, McKenna urged companies to understand the workings of the industry infrastructure, the network of retailers, distributors, analysts, journalists, and industry "luminaries" who control the flow of information and opinion in the industry. As Intel's early marketing campaigns proved, it was the influencing and control of the channel structure that would increasingly matter in relationship marketing—and that would head toward a new transformation with the rise of the Web. One of McKenna's greatest contributions in relationship marketing originated from his insistent emphasis on *strategic* relationships. This objective can be broken down into five key elements: using word of mouth, developing the infrastructure, forming strategic relationships, selling to the right customers, and dealing with the press. What, of course, made the task difficult was the fact that although all industries have an infrastructure, it takes a somewhat different form in each case. In general, the infrastructure includes all those people between the manufacturer and the customer who have an influence on the buying process. The infrastructure can be portrayed as an inverted pyramid, with the manufacturer at the bottom and the customers at the top. Each level of the pyramid influences other levels, particularly those above it, as evidenced by two sample industries—personal computers and microprocessors.[41]

While McKenna may have learned these lessons with innovative companies, such as Intel, Apple, and Microsoft, they would become even more critical with the Internet revolution. It was word of mouth that made many early Internet success stories such as Netscape, Hotmail, and Mirabilis. Developing the infrastructure was as critical to Intel as it would be to Microsoft, when both redefined their strategies for the Internet era. Forming strategic relationships (from joint ventures to M&A's)

became the hallmark of the early Web as companies sought early entry while diversifying risk. When and if infrastructure was successfully coupled with strategic relationships (new standards on various levels of the infrastructure), the alliance partners thrived (e.g., the de facto Wintel duopoly of Intel and Microsoft). If these alliances were fragile or weak, the alliances dissolved or never gained the expected momentum (e.g., the Oracle-led NetPC partnerships). Selling to the right customers translated to proper segmentation strategies in marketing (e.g., Dell's direct strategy coupled with effective segmentation); and dealing with press could make or break even the industry leaders in the new real time era (e.g., Intel's handling of the Pentium debacle, Microsoft's high-profile strategic U-turn).

Selling to the Right Customers. While consumers are the key to any business, many companies continue to fail in realizing *which* customers they attract is often more important than how many customers they attract. Just as companies should look to form strategic relationships, they should try to sell to strategic customers. An impressive customer list could give a company a reputation as an innovator or a technological leader or, in general, serve to differentiate its products and services. In other words, McKenna suggested that customers could both make *and* break companies. Moreover, deciding which customers to sell to required creative segmentation of the market, in particular "adaptation sequence." This was McKenna's version of the "technology adoption life cycle." After all, people seem to fit into four categories according to how quickly they adopt new products and beliefs. Some people lead the way; they are the innovators. Next come the early adopters, then the majority. Finally, there are the laggards who are the slowest to adopt new ideas. Building on innovation and diffusion research, McKenna applied the consumer marketing concept into business-to-business marketing (i.e., companies). Instead of companies adopting new technologies, he saw them "adapting" to them. So he arrived to the notion of the "adaptation sequence."[42]

By the end of the 1990s, McKenna had refined the notion of adaptation life cycle, as well as its functions in the business-to-business markets. Now he relied on the concept of "business growth tenets" to illustrate the ideal adaptation sequence—from vision, design, and partnering to launch, growth, and branding (Exhibit 3-5).

The Internet is direct and interactive (i.e., an access medium), and that, argued McKenna, made all the difference.

In the past, most technologies have been broadcast-driven, particularly in marketing. Television, radio, magazines, newspapers are all broadcasting mechanisms. The Internet is an access medium. I choose what I want to see, I access it from different locations, and I can speak back to it. *That* makes it revolutionary.

Exhibit 3-5
Business Growth Tenets

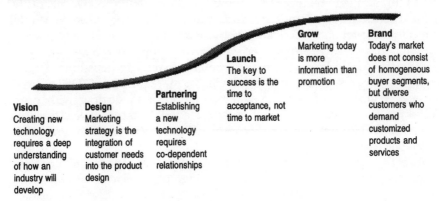

Vision

Creating new technology businesses requires a deep understanding of how an industry will develop

For a diversified technology company, we managed a team that developed a framework used to formulate a "go/no go" decision concerning entry into online information services. The McKenna Group assessed the market opportunity, including trends, size and competitive threats. We developed a strategy for leveraging the company's strengths in the marketplace. We designed feature set and distribution strategy, tested next generation concepts with consumers, modeled required investment and likely return. The McKenna Group created concept positioning in an increasingly crowded marketspace.

Design

Marketing strategy is the integration of customer needs into the product design

For a leading Unix-based workstation manufacturer, we evaluated user requirements for multimedia support in the next generation of workstation products, including audio, video, telephony, and workgroup capabilities. The project included defining a winning strategy and vision to integrate multimedia capabilities into the client's workstation products. The McKenna Group evaluated a multimedia application programmer interface (API) strategy and defined the workstation manufacturer's multimedia program and goals. We conducted an internal asset assessment, market definition, sizing, and market requirements for multimedia-enabled workstation products to help prioritize high potential market opportunities and market capture strategies.

Partnering

Establishing a new technology requires co-dependent relationships

The McKenna Group developed an alliance between a major computer firm and a PBX manufacturer, which provided new outlets for the computer firm's chip technology as well as the opportunity to offer joint marketing programs in emerging markets. At first

Exhibit 3-5 (continued)

glance these firms felt they were competitors, but in fact the technology brought the PBX firm exceptional cost savings in hardware, while the computer architecture enforced new software standards. At the same time, joint marketing reduced overall sales costs for both firms. This was a win/win/win alliance, that was created when an objective third party built a foundation for mutual benefits by responding to the critical needs of each company, as well as the needs of the market.

Launch

The key to success is the time-to-acceptance, not time-to-market

For a developer of an information repository engine, we helped the client to successfully redefine the positioning of its product in the marketplace. The McKenna Group performed an assessment of both customers and non-customers to understand issues critical to the company and the product, developed a positioning strategy, identified and prioritized key target customer segments and developed an infrastructure marketing strategy to re-launch the product and accelerate adoption within the market. In addition, The McKenna Group assisted in identifying and prioritizing strategic alliances for this vendor.

Grow

Marketing today is more information than promotion

For a leading Japanese systems integrator, The McKenna Group reported on developments and trends in home banking within the U.S. The McKenna Group analyzed the business drivers of this market and the competitive, regulatory and technological trends that will influence this market over the next five years. The McKenna Group developed scenarios to assess the impact of the existing market opportunities and threats on the client's business. The study identified specific opportunities for the client, who provides electronic commerce solutions to Japanese banks, to provide home banking services to consumers and small business customers.

Brand

Today's market does not consist of homogenous buyer segments, but diverse customers who demand customized products and services

For an automotive manufacturer, we partnered with a systems integrator to begin to envision how information could be used to establish a direct relationship with this client's customer (to date, this relationship was being relegated through the dealer channel). Through a series of visioneering sessions, we examined the relationship goals for each of their customer segments; we mapped these goals against the purchase process, looking at such critical points in time as regular lease renewals, "building desire" points in time, etc. We examined how information could be delivered in a proactive manner to reinforce the relationship at these critical points in time. The specific technical definition of the system was the responsibility of the systems integrator.

Source: The McKenna Group (1998).

The Internet is *interactive*. The relationship itself is a dialogue. If that dialogue is dynamic, we can both gain, grow, and learn. When I give speeches, my customers give me feedback. That feedback then enables me to change. It can be done in the medical industry, financial services, and other businesses. It is not only important in developing new products and services, it also is important in new ways of thinking about the customer. The Internet makes it possible.[43]

Life Cycles and Chasm

Formerly a partner with Regis McKenna Inc., Geoffrey A. Moore became known in Silicon Valley with his first book, *Crossing the Chasm* (1991), which introduced the idea of the "chasm" that innovative companies and their products must cross in order to reach the lucrative mainstream market (see Exhibit 3-6).[44] Targeted at venture capitalists, product managers, and technology marketers, Moore's book identified what it called a fundamental flaw in the standard technology marketing model. The latter postulated smooth sales growth through a series of well-defined, ever-larger markets. In fact, said Moore, there were really two, fundamentally separate phases in the development of any technology market:

- an early phase that built from a few, highly visible, visionary customers; and
- a mainstream phase, where the buying decisions fell predominantly to pragmatists.

Transitioning between these two phases was anything but smooth. Assuming that success in the early market would translate into mainstream success was a fatal error that caused so many high-flying start-ups to crash into the chasm. "Many companies had great starts, they were having a wonderful launch and then all of a sudden they would fall out of the view," Moore recalls.

The technology adoption life cycle model was a strong one at Regis McKenna. I noticed the presence of this transition after the launch phase. It kept happening at the same place in the life cycle. So I got the idea of a separation. Just as we tend to look at psychographic signs, it became clear to me that there was a kind of repulsion effect between visionaries and pragmatists. The change was not continuous.[45]

By the late 1990s, Moore served as chairman and founder of The Chasm Group, where he continued a full-time consulting practice.[46] He also was a venture partner at Mohr/Davidow Venture Partners. Moore's clients included 3COM, AT&T, Autodesk, BBN Sprint, Cisco, Clarify, Hewlett-Packard, J. D. Edwards, Microsoft, Oracle, as well as numerous venture backed startups. While Moore based his work on the classic "technology

Exhibit 3-6
From the Technology Adoption Life Cycle to Chasm

Formerly a partner with Regis McKenna Inc., Geoffrey A. Moore is chairman and founder of The Chasm Group, where he continues a full time consulting practice. In addition to his full time role at The Chasm Group, he is a venture partner at Mohr/Davidow Venture Partners.

Moore's clients include 3COM, AT&T, Autodesk, BBN Sprint, Cisco, Clarify, Hewlett-Packard, JD Edwards, Microsoft, and Oracle, as well as numerous venture-backed startups.

Published in 1991, Moore's first book, *Crossing the Chasm*, introduced readers to a gap or "chasm" that innovative companies and their products must cross in order to reach the lucrative mainstream market. His second book, *Inside the Tornado*, published in 1995, provided readers with insight into how to capitalize on the potential for hypergrowth beyond the chasm. Both books focus on how the market forces behind the Technology Adoption Life Cycle cause the need for radical shifts in market strategy, and outline appropriate tactics for succeeding in each stage of the cycle.

The Gorilla Game authors are Geoffrey Moore, Paul Johnson and Tom Kippola. Johnson is a Wall Street technology analyst for BancAmerica Robertson Stephens; and Kippola, managing partner of The Chasm Group, is a marketing strategist and private investor.

The Gorilla Game is based partly on the Technology Adoption Life Cycle. It melds Moore's market development models with Johnson's theories of stock market valuation and Kippola's explanation of high-tech competitive advantage to create a unique perspective on the investment value of competitive advantage. The book shows how the significant appreciation in Gorilla stocks is directly linked to the competitive advantage periods that far outreach their competitors.

Source: Chasm Group.

adoption life cycle" model, his approach had two unique emphases. He applied the model in business-to-business *and consumer markets*. He also took seriously the idea of a disruptive and discontinuous technology evolution focusing on the gaps *between* the different (life cycle) markets rather than an externally imposed and linear model of innovation and diffusion. Like McKenna, Moore associated the model with relationship marketing. But unlike McKenna, he applied it primarily in user aggregation, in contrast to business-to-business purposes.[47]

Inside the Tornado (1995) extended Moore's work with the technology adoption life cycle model to incorporate three distinct mainstream market stages—a pre-growth era of niche markets, the mass-market growth, and a post-growth era of mass customization (Exhibit 3-7).

Exhibit 3-7
The Landscape of the Technology Adoption Life Cycle: *Crossing the Chasm* (1991) and *Inside the Tornado* (1995)

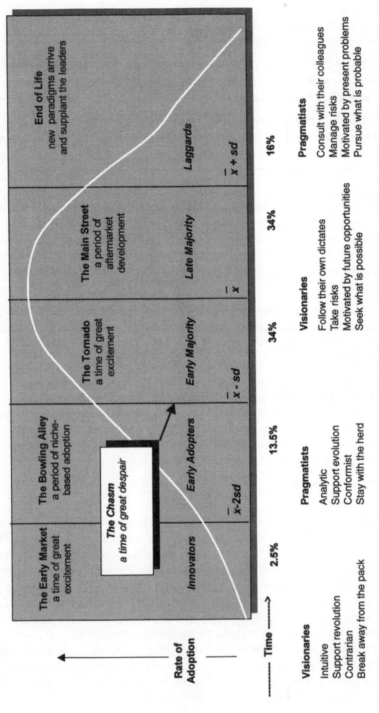

Source: Adapted and modified on the basis of Geoffrey A. Moore's *Crossing the Chasm* (New York: HarperBusiness 1991) and *Inside the Tornado* (New York: HarperBusiness 1995).

These descriptions stemmed from and slightly modified the classic technology adoption life cycle models and the frameworks of classic innovation/diffusion studies. In the traditional models, the innovativeness dimension (as measured by the time at which an individual adopts an innovation/innovations) is regarded as *continuous*. The innovativeness variable is typically partitioned into *five adopter categories* by laying off standard deviation from the average time of adoption. The cumulative number of adopters approaches an S-shaped curve over time, while the frequency distribution of the number of mean adopters per year approaches a normal, bell-shaped curve. The classic literature treats the basic adopter categories as ideal types; they are conceptualizations based on observation of reality that are designed to make comparisons possible. The categories, in turn, imply certain adopter characteristics in the adoption processes:

Innovators: Venturesome
Early Adopters: Respect
Early Majority: Deliberate
Late Majority: Skeptical
Laggards: Traditional

Moore applied these categories to *technology* markets. So he renamed the original categories (technology enthusiasts, visionaries, pragmatists, conservatives, skeptics, and enthusiasts). More importantly, he did not consider the adoption process continuous. He regarded it as *discontinuous*, paying special attention to the transition from visionaries to pragmatists (or, using the original framework, from early adopters to early majority). These two categories were separated by the *chasm*—and Moore's prescriptive guidelines sought to assist the companies in crossing the chasm.

Moore illustrated the dynamics of each market stage with examples from cutting-edge companies such as Hewlett-Packard, Microsoft, Intel, Sybase, PeopleSoft and Lotus. The cases were in technology-enabled or leveraged businesses, where similar market dynamics applied: publishing and broadcasting, banking and finance, health care, as well as entertainment, retail, and so on. In all these markets, industry forces were driving rapid innovation and new leaders were appearing overnight. He then went on to analyze the impact of each stage on strategic partnerships, competitive advantage, positioning, and organizational leadership.

The critical success factor in each of these forms of competition, suggested Moore (the terms anticipated his third book), was to achieve "gorilla status" inside the tornado in order to be the market leader during the growth phase, which resulted in permanent advantages throughout the remainder of the life cycle. Consequently, *timing* was critical to the

tornado strategy. Moore explained how to pool resources and gain sup-
porters during the pre-tornado phase and then how to unleash them
once the tornado hits. Finally, he made note of the post-tornado transition to a maturing market when companies must refocus on winning
additional business from their installed base instead of seeking revenue
growth from new customers. "The biggest challenge for management is
that with each market phase transition, a new business strategy is called
for," he argued, "one that is not only different from their current strategy, but actually contradicts some of its core principles."[48]

Moore developed the chasm model *before* the launch of the Web. "I
was very late in coming into an awareness of the Internet," he acknowledges.[49] Yet, the theory of chasm could be highly illustrative of the crucial business struggles in the transition from the analog to digital
infrastructure.

The early market stage is so crucial in the standard-setting process. In the cellular
rivalry, for instance, the GSM standard is probably a better world standard than
the other existing ones. Initially, the cellular was based on an analog standard
that had to cross the chasm. Following the early adopters, the wealthier, and the
sales people, others began to use the analog cellular. Now the rivals are trying
to implement a digital infrastructure."[50]

In the late 1990s, the United States was not leading the cellular technology rivalry. "If you think the U.S. is a leader in moving from wired
communications to wireless, take a look at Finland," urged The *Wall
Street Journal* in September 1998. "Nearly half of Finns now use wireless
phones, more than double the rate in the U.S., and many . . . have all
their calls forwarded from their wired phones to their mobile lines."[51]
Still, American cellular and telecommunications companies were poised
to follow quickly. Thanks to the same lower calling prices and increased
competition that had driven international wireless growth, some 25% of
U.S. phone users were expected to have wireless phones by century's
end, according to Yankee Group. The number was likely to double by
2006, as wireless providers would offer a broad range of services and
price options. This transition was *not* automatic. The technology alone
would not trigger it; the marketers would have to come up with incentives, rewards, promotions. Argues Moore,

From the *users'* standpoint, you have to pay more, although the new variants
are not that different in practice. In such a competitive situation, the *technology*
is discontinuous but the *user experience* is not that different. It is difficult to introduce an early market technology to a relatively conservative customer base
and the companies are struggling as they deal with it. They have to get the
consumer to pay for it.[52]

Moore's *Inside the Tornado* was followed by *The Gorilla Game* in 1998. It was co-authored with Wall Street technology investment analyst Paul Johnson and private investor and market strategist Tom Kippola. It was based partly on the technology adoption life cycle—the way the market adopts certain kinds of technologies ends up catapulting a single company into an extraordinary, enduring, powerful position ("gorillas"). But the book also melded Moore's market development models with Johnson's theories of stock market valuation and Kippola's explanation of high-tech competitive advantage to create a unique perspective on the investment value of competitive advantage. *The Gorilla Game* purported to show how the significant appreciation in "Gorilla stocks" is directly linked to the competitive advantage periods that far outreach their competitors (compare Exhibit 3-8).[53]

Most gorillas have been and continue to be American IT/Internet companies. Moore's theory of the critical function of the *chasm* may well explain part of the mystery.

Historically, America has enjoyed the advantages of a huge marketplace and competition. As a result, marketing and marketing difficulties have long been explored in the U.S. market. American companies are certainly ahead in marketing effectively in America. U.S. markets tend to be early adopting and much larger than any other national markets. That's given an advantage to American companies in high tech. But if, for example, you send an American company to market in France, we can look pretty damn stupid.

SAP is clearly an exception, but, historically, incumbents have enjoyed huge advantages in the U.S. marketplace. They know how to work the market base to their advantage. American market forms such a great portion of the early adopting world market that standards are often set in the U.S. Once standards are in place, the gorilla has emerged, and the rest of the world comes into the market, they tend to go into the existing market share pattern that has been set in the U.S. So the first entrants have a huge advantage in the *initial* market share battle. Israeli companies have been successful because they have been able to gain access to the early adopting U.S. market. In this regard, Nordic countries, such as Finland, might have certain affinities. The technology alone is not enough. The U.S. incumbents also enjoy the advantage of the whole venture capital infrastructure of Silicon Valley; *that* has not been replicated in other countries.

It is hard to thrive on the shifting ground of the high tech markets. They are in continuing flux. Also, the functional units (e.g., engineering, marketing, sales, customer service) have a different role to play in each stage of the life cycle. The demand on the life cycle is on manufacturing and engineering, sales and marketing and customer service are so different in each of the phases. Organizationally, the life cycle model poses great difficulties to mature companies, just as it provides certain subtle benefits to small and flexible startups. A mature multi-product company is bound to have products in every part of the life cycle; and the same product in different countries may be in different parts of the life cycle.[54]

Exhibit 3-8
Competitive Advantage Period (CAP) Valuation

The conceptual framework of *The Gorilla Game* describes how high-technology markets develop in characteristic ways that differentiate them from other markets. The way the market adopts certain kinds of technologies ends up catapulting a single company "the gorilla" into an extraordinary, enduring, powerful position. Identifying and investing in would be gorillas before their share prices rise dramatically is the basis of Gorilla Game investing strategy.

The Gorilla Game melt Moore's market development models with Johnson's theories of stock market valuation, and Kippola's competitive advantage-based investment philosophy. The book shows how the significant appreciation in Gorilla stocks is directly linked to the lengthy competitive advantage periods that Gorillas enjoy.

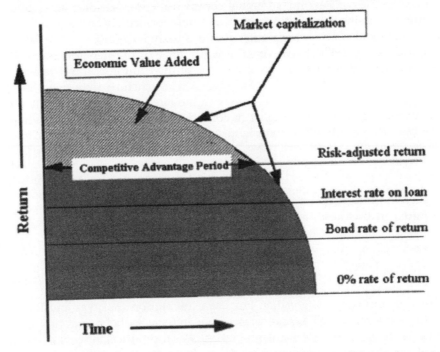

Source: Geoffrey A. Moore, Paul Johnson, and Tom Kippola, *The Gorilla Game: An Investor's Guide to Picking Winners in High Technology* (New York: HarperBusiness 1998). See also the web site at www.gorillagame.com.

Moore suggested that rigid sets of rules often caused mature companies to kill their innovative products or withdraw most of them at just the wrong time. The problem was not one of technology primarily. Instead, determinants in organizational, marketing, and market development did not go hand in hand. Complacent, mature companies end up having product lines that are older and more tired until eventually some marketer comes along and puts them out of business.

THE INTERNET, INTRANETS, AND MARKETING CHANNELS

In the early 1990s, a severe recession gave way to an upturn of the economy and the adoption of new information technology in corporate America. Even toward the close of the 1980s, the manifestoes of "downsizing" and "re-engineering" had precipitated the coming of the electronic enterprises, but with a difference. Prior to the upsurge of the U.S. economy around 1992 and 1993, contemporary business debate lingered in issues of cost-cutting and rationalization rather than actually boosting revenues. It was a reaction to the defeats and losses of U.S. companies and industries to new international competitors, in particular Japan and Germany. As the information revolution transformed corporate America, organizational charts were flattened and horizontalized.[55]

By the early 1990s, however, the entire tone of the debate shifted. It was framed differently, not least because of the Clinton administration's promotion of the National Information Infrastructure initiative (NII). Gone was the "declininist" discourse of the late 1980s.[56] Instead, Silicon Valley emerged as the technology core of the national economy, while optimistic and forward-looking efforts to "embrace change" revived the 1960s "New Frontier" ideas of science and progress.[57]

Information Revolution Causes Business Revolution: The Boom in Business-to-Business Commerce

As the competitive and intellectual environment shifted, so did the course of the national debate on U.S. business. Some of the new bestsellers illustrated the transition. In 1992, William H. Davidow and Michael S. Malone published a business best-seller, *The Virtual Corporation*. It saw America amidst an *information processing* revolution that was causing a *business* revolution. The centerpiece of the latter was the virtual product, a term the authors used to mean both physical products and services. It existed even before it was produced. Its concept, design, and manufacture were stored in the minds of cooperating teams, computers, and flexible production lines.

Building a virtual product will require a company to utterly revise itself, control ever more sophisticated types of information, and master new organizational and production skills. Doing that will change most contemporary firms so completely that what will emerge from the process, a "virtual corporation," will have little in common with what existed before. Again, such a firm in its purest form will never exist. But the advantage will lie with those firms that best pursue such a goal. The closer a corporation gets to cost-effective instantaneous production of mass-customized goods and services, the more competitive and successful it will be.[58]

By February 1993, *Business Week* published a cover story on "The Virtual Corporation." What sounded "like just another bit of management-consultant cyberspeak," argued the magazine, could well be the model for the American business organization in the years ahead. Concurrently, the feature reflected the ongoing change in the framing of the debate: it was moving from products and services to organizational structures.[59] Indeed, as the great U.S. manufacturing organizations were finally "getting" the idea of *mass customization*, much more was involved than a simple catch-up in comparison to international competition. When American business found the terrain of new business competition decidedly different from that of mass production—and, most significantly, *instead of fighting the technological change, embraced it*—these great companies also found out that customers could no longer be lumped together in huge homogeneous markets. "Leading companies have created processes for low-cost, volume production of great variety, and even for individually customized goods and services," argued a perceptive contemporary observer. "They have discovered the new frontier in business competition: Mass Customization."[60]

The compelling new vision of internationally-oriented U.S. business, armed with cutting-edge technologies, emerged amidst the efforts to launch the first interactive television projects and the public debate over the national information infrastructure (NII).[61] Most importantly, it preceded and was bound to instigate the rush to what the contemporary observers called the "electronic information superhighways." In the 1980s, government policies had been poignantly laissez-faire by nature.[62] With the Clinton administration, there were more efforts at a new kind of a partnership between the public and private sector rather than traditional industrial policy. At best, the proponents thought that such initiatives might accelerate free-market competition rather than constrain rivalry. Until the Republican invasion of the Congress in 1994, government policies and initiatives reflected this search for the "third way," especially in the technology sector. By May 1994, for instance, the Office of Technology Assessment (OTA) released a significant report, *Electronic Enterprises: Looking to the Future*, which summarized previous studies from the late 1980s. It saw the nation amidst an extensive information revolution affecting the private and the public sector alike:

Electronic transactions are now commonplace in the U.S. business environment. . . . Businesses, too, rely heavily on electronic technology for record-keeping, accounting, inventory control, production management, and purchasing and sales.

This use of networked information technology barely hints, however, at its full potential for improving U.S. economic performance in the future.[63]

Caught in partisan crossfire, the Congressional Office of Technology Assessment (OTA) was forced to close in September 1995. Prior to that, it did release a slate of reports that reflected the information and the Internet revolution contributing to both.[64]

As these reports documented the emergence and rise of the new economy's information infrastructure, they anticipated (and contributed to) the rise of the Internet and electronic commerce. They would prove particularly important to those managers and marketers seeking ways to understand and exploit the transition from the traditional marketplace to the new marketspace.

With the launch of the Web and the first browser generation, it became the function of Internet marketing to sell the new media to companies (business-to-business markets) and consumers (consumer markets) alike. Since firms could exploit the Web far faster than households, the experiences in the business-to-business marketing would also lead the way in consumer marketing. That reflected a drastic historical change in marketing paradigms. "The largest first use of the Internet is in the business-to-business markets," notes Lester Wunderman, the pioneer of American direct marketing. "Look at the website of Cisco System or Dell Computers. They do not cultivate just slogans; their approach is serious and their designs are meant for adults. Business purchases are based on information. These successful companies know how to use the Internet."[65]

With the old mass production economy, mass marketers like Procter & Gamble had provided the primary paradigms in marketing. With the emerging information economy, business-to-business or direct marketers, such as Federal Express, Dell, and Cisco, would serve as the primary marketing paradigms. In the long term, the Internet would provide the small- and medium-sized enterprises (SMEs) the kind of benefits that used to accrue to the big business. In the past, only the selected few in American big business had been able to enjoy the full benefits of electronic data interchange (EDI)—the intercompany, computer-to-computer transmission of business information in a standard format. Now these systems would have to be upgraded for the Internet era, and they would be seized by big business and SMEs alike. Moreover, the new applications would be built out of competitive necessity, providing little competitive advantage for most users. Instead, they would become a cost of doing business.

The Struggle for the Intranet Markets

As American companies learned about the potential of the Internet in business-to-business marketing, new media firms rushed to assist them in launching the first websites of the big business and the SMEs. "Intranets" evolved in 1994 when Lockheed Martin, NASA, and Amdahl became some of the first to recognize the potential benefits of deploying Internet technology within their own organizations. Amdahl, in particular, took this a step further, recognizing the potential for profits to be pocketed by developing Web-based applications to perform internal business functions. These steps took place almost a year or two *before* the widespread popularization of Netscape Navigator and Microsoft's Internet Explorer.

Intranets: Generic or Proprietary? Between April and May of 1994, Steve Telleen and his colleagues started looking at the intranet as a way of putting an interface on legacy data and making it accessible to others. Telleen was then in charge of what would become known as Amdahl's IntraNet Development Group. He coined the term "intranet" in July 1994.[66] "I had a team of people and we were developing many intranet concepts," he recalls.

I was a strategic marketer for open systems, a sort of a visionary if you will. I tried to get the group to internalize some of these ideas. Talking and doing was insufficient. So I began writing this stuff down for my internal group. The intranet concept of using technology inside the company arose spontaneously. People recognized that this technology could really enhance the resolution of internal problems. Also, we were not alone. Several other companies came upon the concept in a similar manner.[67]

In the past, Telleen and his team had been talking about an "Enterprise Wide Web" or an "Internal Wide Web." "It was around late July 1994 that we started using the term intranet," he recalls. In conjunction with International Data Corp. (IDC), Amdahl sponsored four focus groups with corporations around the country. "We talked to 40 companies about using the intranet for things like the help desk function," Telleen says, and all but one resoundingly endorsed the idea. IDC asked him and his team whether they had a trademark on the intranet concept. They had not.

IDC said we ought to think about it. We did a trademark search and realized we were the only ones using the term. We also talked with our attorneys. We really didn't want a strong trademark because we needed a generic term that everyone could use. If, however, we registered a trademark and tried to enforce it severely, another term might be created. On the other hand, we would have liked to have Amdahl associated with the term. The attorneys told us to use a common-law trademark; we would then defend it. In the process Amdahl would be associated with that term. So, that's what we did. We put out trademark after the intranet.[68]

Between October and November of 1994, Telleen started writing the white paper on the intranets. In January 1995, the paper was put out on the Internet (Exhibit 3-9). Already a month before, Telleen's team had first defended the trademark.

That January, the concept began to snowball. By March, James Barksdale, CEO of Netscape, picked it up and was using it in his presentations. I sent him a letter; he responded and said they weren't going to use the term. By April, he was no longer using the concept in writing, but he was using it in speeches. Since he had been using it and Netscape had gained such visibility, the concept was taking off in a big way—well before Amdahl had been able to achieve a widely known name. A magazine published the term intranet. That was the first time it ever came out in print. Thereafter, the game was over. With the magazine, everyone picked up the term because it was a popular topic. A term was needed; it was found, and "BAM!" it took off. Amdahl, however, still defends its intranet methodology and architecture.[69]

Why Did Amdahl Ignore the Intranet Potential? Understandably, Telleen and his followers at Amdahl got quite excited about the commercial potential of the intranet. Even so, Amdahl ultimately *backed away* from developing an intranet business. Reportedly, Amdahl's withdrawal stemmed from a mainframe-based corporate culture. Founded in 1970 by Gene Amdahl, an IBM veteran, the company had struggled so hard with the burdens of the past that it no longer had the strength to seize the opportunities of the future. In 1994, Amdahl, which manufactured IBM-compatible mainframes, was still among the top 10 makers of large computers. The company also supplied UNIX servers and software, which accounted for its initial interest in the Internet. Yet, its corporate culture was heavily influenced by a conservative mainframe world.

As a critical supplier of IBM, Amdahl's fortunes were intertwined with those of the "Big Blue." Starting in the late 1980s, both had to struggle to survive. After heavy losses in 1993 due to the slow mainframe market, Amdahl rebounded in 1994 and posted its first yearly profit since 1991. In a major reorganization, it cut manufacturing capacity in half and employment by a third and wrote off some $200 million in surplus plant and equipment. When Telleen was pushing for pioneering and ambitious experiments in emergent and volatile growth markets, the Amdahl management may well have been content with the rebound and was not eager to rock the boat. As the company failed to exploit its competitive advantage in the intranets, Telleen left the firm.

Missing the Internet momentum, Amdahl lost an independent future. The story illustrates the fate of many of the old-style IT companies that sought to replicate old business models in a new era. In July 1997, Fujitsu Ltd. unveiled an $850 million offer to take over Amdahl, a deal that

Exhibit 3-9
Steven Telleen: The Intranet White Paper—Framework Overview

IntraNet Methodology (TM)
Concepts and Rationale
(January 1995)

The diagram here provides an overview of the key components of the IntraNet™ information framework. The roof depicts the business goals, which provide the reason for creating the framework. The technical infrastructure at the base provides the necessary foundation for the development, management, and access of the information. It consists of the hardware, software, networks, protocols and standards required to implement the remaining structure. The middle three columns provide the support for the business goals. They include both the publishing and the brokering functions . . . and the additional function of the content approval processes that support the publishing of "official" information. Content approval processes are important for coordination and efficiency and to protect the enterprise and its employees from liability and loss.

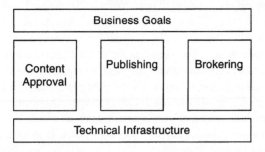

Intranet Organization: Strategies for Managing Change
Steven L. Telleen (June 1997)

Intranet technology makes the creation and publishing of information easy. It also makes the retrieval and viewing of the information easy. What is not easy is finding the relevant information that is created in this independent environment. What Intranet technology cannot provide is the organizational and process infrastructure to support the creation and management of information. Without this infrastructure there is no efficient way for information to be found. Our paper systems have information infrastructures that have been refined over several hundred years. . . . They are inseparable from our concepts of management, because information is the driver of the processes being managed.

The infrastructures that have developed around the management of information on paper have been largely centralized. The characteristics of paper publishing encourage centralization.

Managing distributed systems provides interesting challenges that are not found in centralized environments. The biggest challenge is moving from an attitude of control to an attitude of enabling independent decisions and actions. Without some standards, organizations lose their ability to communicate effectively and coordinate their activities. Without some level of support, domain experts become too involved in low level maintenance activities at the expense of the high leverage functions that most benefit the enterprise. The challenge is meeting the needs for coordination and efficiency without destroying the independence of decision making and action that make enterprises strong and flexible.

Source: Giga Group/Steven Telleen.

ended the company's 27-year run as an independent maker of mainframe computers.[70] Amdahl caught the Internet momentum only in February 1998, when it announced a wide-ranging partnership with Microsoft to help sell Windows NT to large corporations.[71] As Amdahl lost its competitive advantage with the intranets, it would replicate the old imitator business models, in order to survive in the new environment. "Amdahl is a very conservative company with a culture built around following IBM's lead," comments Telleen laconically. "They had no salesforce to deal with the intranet. They were big-iron guys used to huge, one-shot deals, as opposed to selling software and services, so they dropped it."[72]

On a microscopic level, the evolution of the intranets is not only reflective of Amdahl's historical corporate culture and the slowness of big business in a rapidly-growing competitive environment, it also reflects the restructuring of traditional industry clusters. Used to hierarchical and closed information exchange, American big business, initially, was not quite sure what to think of the new intranet models. Most IT companies did not consider the new business segments viable, while the international carriers and local telcos could not enter the industry until after the Telecommunications Act of 1996. *That* left a relative vacuum for tiny and flexible new media firms. By the mid-1990s, these had become the primary suppliers of American media and entertainment, computers and telecommunications, as well as pure Internet plays. As suppliers of American big business and SMEs, these miniscule new media firms became the critical industry drivers.

The Taming of the Intranet: From Netscape to Microsoft. As early as 1994 and 1995, Netscape was quick to pick up the slack. Where Amdahl had been conservative, the Internet firm would be aggressive. In March 1995, Jim Barksdale, CEO of Netscape, first mentioned the intranet to Telleen at a private Silicon Valley breakfast, whereas Marc Andreessen, the co-founder of the company, claims he first recognized the commercial viability of the Net in 1993 at the NCSA. Even then potential clients were calling to use the technology for their business. As the NCSA team took a look at who was doing the buying, 80–90% proved to be businesses, many of whom were eager to deploy Web technology within their companies. By virtually giving away the browser software, Netscape established immediate, widespread visibility with customers and was able to ramp up so fast that within its first 18 months Netscape had nearly 40 million users. The idea was to create a visible, high-profile brand in the consumer markets in order to exploit those features and the ensuing momentum in the *business-to-business* markets.[73]

The market was moving quickly, and by the summer of 1995 Netscape was preparing itself for Microsoft's attacks. Netscape had managed to establish leading market positions with the browsers and servers, but it would no longer have a marketplace on its own. Struggling to stay ahead of the curve, Netscape came out in early 1996 with its SuiteSpot integrated server family, an early effort to provide what it described as full-service intranet capabilities. In October, the company rolled out its latest client-server technologies: Communicator, a new desktop program on the client side that includes Netscape's Navigator browser as a feature; and SuiteSpot 3.0, an integrated server suite that managed communications, sharing, and access to information on the server. With Communicator and SuiteSpot 3.0, Netscape targeted large U.S. corporations. With the new offerings, customers could standardize on one client-server Web-based system that worked with various operating systems, including Macintosh, Unix, and Microsoft's Windows. Unlike Microsoft, Netscape did not have enough products to "extend," but it could "embrace and integrate."

From the start, Netscape had focused on the browser software. Navigator's phenomenal success obscured the fact that the company had long offered a broad range of cross-platform software designed to facilitate the exchange of information and allow users to conduct commerce over the Internet and other TCP/IP-based private intranet networks. In effect, it was the company's intranet software that provided the lion's share of its revenue and profits.[74] While Netscape successfully targeted the enterprise arena with its server software, the intranet market matured rapidly. By late 1995, Hambrecht & Quist (H&Q) analysts were reporting that "the intranet is universally accepted as an integral part of corporations." In particular, the June (1995) quarter marked the mainstreaming of intranet strategies in which corporations looked to benefit from a networked environment that enabled full integration of legacy systems and multiplatform, multioperational systems environments on a single network and in a full solution set. Consequently, the consumer markets' Navigator was only the "surface" of what H&Q projected would grow to be a $10 billion market for enterprise-wide intranet software by the year 2000.[75]

Toward the Full-Service Intranet. What is remarkable is the frantic *pace* of these events. Steve Telleen began writing his white paper in the fall of 1994. By December, his team was already defending the trademark. In January 1995, the paper was posted on the Web. Two months later, James Barksdale was using the concept in his presentations. As Telleen urged the CEO of Netscape not to do that, the notion was snowballing through the PC/Internet press, even while Amdahl was still trying to retain the concept as *its* trademarked property. Although Netscape managed to capture the initial marketplace, Microsoft adopted its "embrace and extend" Internet strategy in the summer of 1995, restructuring the entire company and product line around Internet functionality. By 1996, Netscape expected to capture better than 50% of that market, while H&Q

estimated that Netscape would garner 59%, Microsoft 20%, and Lotus 7%, with the remaining 14% going to other vendors.[76]

When Netscape came up with its revised white paper on the intranets, it noted Navigator and SuiteSpot, used together, formed a complete platform for the Full Service Intranet-based applications described in the previous section (Exhibit 3-10). The *Full Service Intranet* was Netscape's vision of how companies could use standard Internet technologies to deploy a rich, full-function, ubiquitous environment for information sharing, communication, and applications, built on top of open networking technologies and on an open network-based application platform. Netscape opened its vision statement with a telling acknowledgement:

The Full Service Intranet is a concept that Forrester Research first explored in a report of the same title dated March 1, 1996. Simply put, a Full Service Intranet is a TCP/IP network inside a company that links the company's people and information in a way that makes people more productive, information more accessible, and navigation through all the resources and applications of the company's computing environment more seamless than ever before.[77]

Forrester Research had generated intranet-related reports since December 1995. While the firm acknowledged that corporations were deploying intranets rapidly, it also stressed the fact that the contemporary intranets only supported the Web and had an ill-defined relationship with the installed base of proprietary network operating systems. It predicted that such a state of affairs would change: "Over the next four years, the Intranet will be enhanced with new services that will thrust it into the limelight as the key component of corporate networks. The rise of the standards-based 'Full Service Intranet' will come at the expense of proprietary network operating systems (NOS)."[78] It also expected three basic shifts:

- By 2000, the Intranet would grow far beyond a TCP/IP network that just supported the Web. It would have five core standards-based services (i.e., directory, e-mail, file, print, and network management). These would overshadow proprietary NOS solutions from Novell, Microsoft, et al.
- Corporations would migrate from proprietary NOS to Full Service Intranets to get the benefits of easy connections with the outside world, multiple competing suppliers, and lower costs.
- Incumbent vendors like Novell and Microsoft would have the best shot at grabbing leadership positions in the Full Service Intranet market—if they massively overhauled their current products.[79]

Naturally, Netscape rushed to build the full-service intranet, thinking or hoping that Microsoft and Novell would not be ready or willing to

Exhibit 3-10
Netscape and Microsoft: The Intranet Initiatives (1995–96)

	Netscape Navigator	Netscape Navigator Gold	Administration Kit
Universal Client			
Server Platform	*Enterprise Server*	**SuiteSpot**	
	Enterprise Server	*News Server* *Catalog Server*	*Mail Server*
	LiveWire Pro	*Certificate Server* *Proxy Server*	*Directory Server*
Commercial Applications	Publishing System	Community System Merchant System	Live Payment Wallet
Service & Support	Developer Community	Tech Support Training	Consulting

NETSCAPE'S PHILOSOPHY. Our philosophy is that the Internet/intranet revolution has opened the way for companies to embrace open systems and technologies for crafting their network environments without sacrificing any functionality or robustness compared to traditional proprietary alternatives. We build products and systems that make this possible.

100

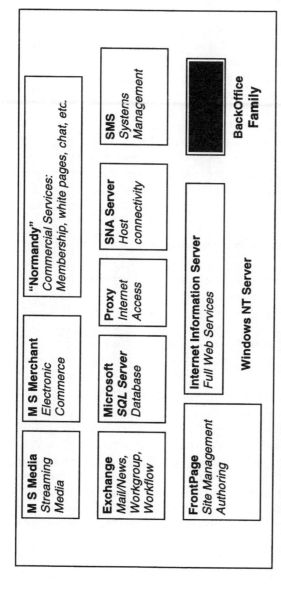

MICROSOFT'S PHILOSOPHY. The term intranet has been used to refer to Internet technology working over a private corporate network. But companies are finding this view too narrow. . . . New business solutions need to integrate with legacy systems expanding the view beyond just Internet technologies. . . . Microsoft's strategy reflects a focus on the integration theme, the completeness theme, and the pervasive use of page and links throughout a system to preserve that simple view for the end-user.

Source: Adapted with minor modifications, see Microsoft (www.microsoft.com) and Netscape Communications (www.netscape.com).

obsolete their existing product lines. Yet, what is equally interesting is the tacit interplay between the independent market research firms (Forrester) and the new entrants (Netscape) in the cyberspace. The former would often serve as kind of strategic assistants for the entrants eager to create a new market rather than to engage in a destructive market share rivalry. Due to their low capitalization, these entrants could afford neither price competition, which all players favored the least, nor advertising competition, which incumbents could afford but entrants could not (Netscape launched the Navigator without ad budget).

Three Stages of Intranet Evolution. While targeting Netscape and to a lesser degree America Online, Microsoft was fully committed to the Internet-intranet market by 1996 when both the software giant and Netscape were already updating their old intranet white papers. These were followed by papers released by major research firms on the expected future outcomes of the marketplace. Since the summer of 1996, for instance, the Yankee Group had paid increasing attention to the intranet phenomena.[80] By mid-1997, the Group expected intranet usage to evolve in three stages:

- A time when businesses used the intranet primarily for internal Web document publication (1995–1997);

- An era of collaborative applications, characterized as "groupware on steroids" by one analyst (1997–1999);

- A period of value chain integration. The Yankee Group defines this as intranet-to-intranet functions, or extranets (i.e., extended Nets), where a business opens a portion of its intranet to suppliers, customers, business partners, and so on (1999–beyond).[81]

The Yankee Group had already found that 87% of the 100 largest U.S. corporations were already developing intranet applications. In addition, more than 30% of European companies had intranets, and the group expected spending on intranet software, including tools, middleware, servers, and applications, to reach nearly $10 billion worldwide by the year 2000. It also generalized intranet adoption to a model to illustrate the intranet evolution and to look at transition points and requirements as large organizations moved from simple Web publishing applications to more complex collaborative and inter-enterprise applications (i.e., extranets) (Exhibit 3-11).

By the turn of 1996 and 1997, however, a number of leading-edge corporations had already graduated to the second stage, and some were moving into the third one. It was during these early years of the Internet that U.S. big business pioneered the use of the Internet for intra- and inter-company purposes.

Exhibit 3-11
The Intranet Evolution: Three Stages

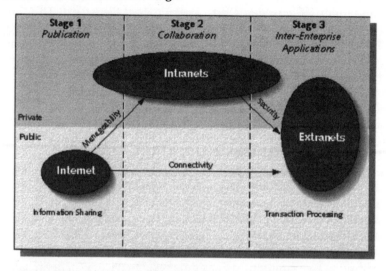

Stage 1 (1995)	Stage 2 (1997)	Stage 3 (1999+)
Internal Web document Publication Address Books Mimic Internet	Collaborative Applications Networked Databases E-mail, Workflow Diverge from Internet	Value-Chain Integration Business Partner Communication and Transactions Reconverge with Internet

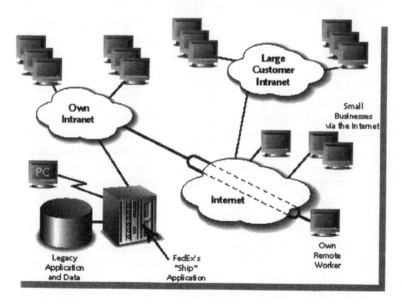

Source: "Intranet Success Stories," *Yankee Watch Internet Computing Strategies* (August 1997).

Fortune 500: The First Web Experiences

By December 1995, research firm International Data Corp. (IDC) began to conduct a census of *Fortune* 500 (F500) companies' websites that illustrated how, and how quickly, the Web was becoming a mainstream channel for major corporations' marketing, communications, and business transactions (Exhibit 3-12).[82]

High Penetration. By June 1996, IDC found that the F500 presence on the Web had increased to 57% (284 of the F500 companies). It forecasted a robust increase to near 80% (more than 390 companies) by the end of the year. The pace of the business-to-business penetration was far faster than that of consumer households: By the end of 1997, "only" 18% of all households were expected to be online, up from 13% in 1996. By the year 2001, that number was thought to rise to 38%—that is, 17.7 million online households in 1996 and 40 million by 2001.[83]

Rising Interactivity. By mid-1996, fully 28% of the F500 on the websites supported some interactive feature(s) on their sites. At first, most had hosted content that was noninteractive "electronic paper". Now sites boasted interactive content, such as database query (65%), financial modeling (19%), communication (9%), and so on. Communication-oriented interactivity was expected to pick up very rapidly as more sites would encourage "content upload"—the contribution of content from site visitors (e.g., collaboration, chat, and so on).

Core Business Transactions. Although nearly one out of five (18%) F500 websites allowed visitors to connect to corporate informational databases, a far smaller percentage (fewer than 5%) let visitors conduct core business transactions (i.e., connect to operational systems) through the site. Among other things, these transactions consisted of online banking (e.g., Wells Fargo), online retailing (e.g., Kroger, Spiegel), online "factory outlet" (e.g., Gateway 2000), online communication services (e.g., MCI), and so on. Another 10% were experimenting with transactions in more peripheral areas to the core product and service offerings of the company. Although only a relatively small number of companies had begun to leverage the new channel in all parts of the value chain, they were the early adopters who were driving the competitors to follow suit.

Product Marketing and Corporate Image Marketing. Most F500 websites were heavily marketing oriented. The largest group (almost 50%) was oriented strongly toward product marketing, whereas the other large contingent (almost one-third of the sites) was strongly oriented toward corporate image marketing. Another 22% attempted to accomplish both. Product marketing took advantage of the Web's capacity to provide for many levels of information.[84]

IDC found certain commonalities among the Top 20 F500 sites—those early entrants of the cyberspace that were soon emulated by their rivals (compare Exhibit 3–11). Three out of four offered some kind of interactive capability. More than half of the sites had support for core business transactions. All but one had marketing focused on products rather than corporate image. Almost one-half of the sites had an entertainment/diversions section. Most had a good mix of interesting graphics and text. Sites with limited graphics generally had exceptionally good performance. These commonalities reflected key attributes that were expected to become widespread in the overall F500 group and the broader business community as Web-based business experience would mature during the next several years.

Interestingly enough, IDC's Top 20 F500 websites were *not* dominated by the information industries. Instead, the industry breakdown consisted of eight information businesses, eight manufacturers, two distribution channels companies, and two transportation companies. The notion that there were two mutually exclusive markets—a physical marketplace ("atoms") and a virtual marketspace ("bits")—had proven untenable in the very first years of Web-driven business-to-business marketing. Those first movers that thrived in the Internet (i.e., made profit rather than "just" market share) saw marketplace and marketspace as *complementary*.

Business-to-Business Markets and Dynamic Trading

In July 1997, Forrester Research published a report on "Sizing Intercompany Commerce." According to the research firm, American big business had begun using the Internet as a kind of a "fourth channel" supplementing face-to-face meetings, mail, and phone with electronic ordering. Exploring the early experiences of businesses using the Internet for intercompany commerce, the report concluded that Internet commerce would grow fortyfold, from $8 billion to $327 billion in goods and services traded between companies, by the year 2002. "Businesses are aggressively adopting intercompany trade over the Internet because they want to cut costs, reduce order processing time, and improve information flow," said Blane Erwin, director of Forrester's Business Trade and Technology Strategies unit, which authored the report. "For most firms, the rise in trade over the Internet also coincides with a marked decrease in phone and fax use, allowing salespeople to concentrate on managing customer accounts" (Exhibit 3-13).[85]

Currently, Forrester saw three distinct types of Internet business trading processes: auction, bid, and catalog. Each of these would evolve as the Internet stripped away days and dollars and added more suppliers and buyers. Dynamic trading was expected to result in accelerated, lower cost, scalable business processes (Exhibit 3-14).

In 1997, intercompany online commerce was dominated by hard-goods manufacturers. But that was expected to change as other industries

Exhibit 3-12
IDC F500 Web Census: Top 20 (June 1996)

Company (in site value rank order)	F500 Rank (1995)	URL	Comments
Wells Fargo	231	www.wellsfargo.com	Online banking via the Web
Wachovia Corp.*	382	www.sfnb.com	Security First National Bank: Wachovia is a shareholder
Kroger*	25	www.foodcoop.com/kroger	Online grocery shopping on the Web, if you live in Columbus, Ohio
Hershey Foods	317	www.hersheys.com	Order Hershey products online in a secure environment
Kelly Services	476	www.kellyservices.com	Create/submit resume online; search job listings, office locations
Spiegel	371	www.spiegel.com	Online catalog, transactions
Sysco	99	www.sysco.com	Online shopping via shopping basket metaphor
UPS	35	www.ups.com	Submit package pickup request; package tracking; cost estimator
Xerox	41	www.xerox.com	Order, purchase products online
Continental Airlines	222	www.flycontinental.com	Query flight schedule database

106

Company		Website	Description
Gateway 2000	421	www.gw2k.com	Online configure, price, purchase
Dell Computer	330	www.dell.com	Online configure, price
Knight-Ridder*	427	www.phillynews.com	Philadelphia OnLine; excellent news source
Norwest	197	www.norwest.com	Hosts an online mall (Godiva, books, etc.); ATM locator
Sprint	75	www.sprint.com	Calculate which services fit you; sign up online
Ford	2	www.ford.com	Attractive; extensive product info; financing calculator
GM	1	www.gm.com	3-D tour of vehicles; extensive product info.; financing calculator
International Paper	60	www.ipaper.com	Enlist visitor input to craft marketing plan for new IP product
MCI	66	www.mci.com	Customized MCI versus AT&T rate comparison; order service online
Time Warner*	159	www.pathfinder.com	Pathfinder electronic newsstand; hyperlinks to many goods, services

*Sites that are not the official Corporate website, but were related sites of note.

Source: International Data Corporation (1996).

Exhibit 3-13
U.S. Internet Commerce Revenues: 1997–2002 ($ Billions)

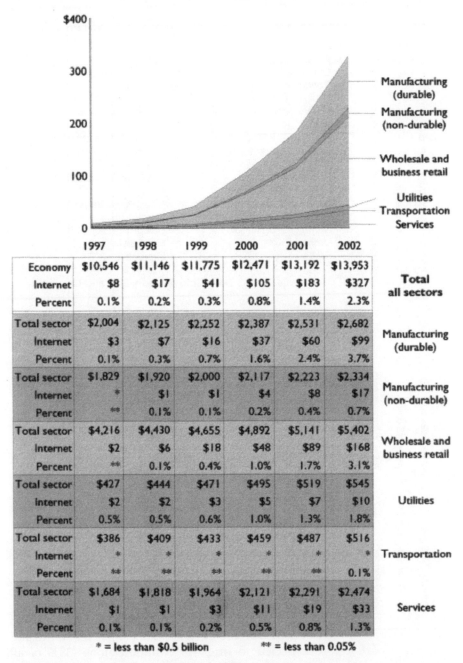

	1997	1998	1999	2000	2001	2002	
Economy	$10,546	$11,146	$11,775	$12,471	$13,192	$13,953	Total all sectors
Internet	$8	$17	$41	$105	$183	$327	
Percent	0.1%	0.2%	0.3%	0.8%	1.4%	2.3%	
Total sector	$2,004	$2,125	$2,252	$2,387	$2,531	$2,682	Manufacturing (durable)
Internet	$3	$7	$16	$37	$60	$99	
Percent	0.1%	0.3%	0.7%	1.6%	2.4%	3.7%	
Total sector	$1,829	$1,920	$2,000	$2,117	$2,223	$2,334	Manufacturing (non-durable)
Internet	*	$1	$1	$4	$8	$17	
Percent	**	0.1%	0.1%	0.2%	0.4%	0.7%	
Total sector	$4,216	$4,430	$4,655	$4,892	$5,141	$5,402	Wholesale and business retail
Internet	$2	$6	$18	$48	$89	$168	
Percent	**	0.1%	0.4%	1.0%	1.7%	3.1%	
Total sector	$427	$444	$471	$495	$519	$545	Utilities
Internet	$2	$2	$3	$5	$7	$10	
Percent	0.5%	0.5%	0.6%	1.0%	1.3%	1.8%	
Total sector	$386	$409	$433	$459	$487	$516	Transportation
Internet	*	*	*	*	*	*	
Percent	**	**	**	**	**	0.1%	
Total sector	$1,684	$1,818	$1,964	$2,121	$2,291	$2,474	Services
Internet	$1	$1	$3	$11	$19	$33	
Percent	0.1%	0.1%	0.2%	0.5%	0.8%	1.3%	

* = less than $0.5 billion   ** = less than 0.05%

Source: Blane Erwin, Mary A. Modahl, and Jesse Johnson, "Sizing Intercompany Commerce," Business Trade & Technology Strategies, 1(1), Forrester Research, Inc., July 1997.

Exhibit 3-14
Dynamic Trading Process—Changes and Breakdown

	Old Process	**Dynamic Trading Process**
Auction	• Phone • Anonymous • Closed offers • Potluck price • Margins hidden • Ad hoc process	• Internet • Anonymous • Open bidding • Best price • Margins known • Standard process
Bid	• Expensive RFP packages • Few bidders are located • Slow process • Rushed response	• Cheap RFP distribution • Broadcast to many bidders • Fast process • Ample lead time for buyers
Catalog	• Expensive paper • Out-of-date price, products • Same catalog for all • Limited SKUs • Static	• Cheap Web pages • Current price, products • Custom catalog • More SKUs • Interactive

How Internet Commerce Breaks Down into Auction, Bid, and Catalog

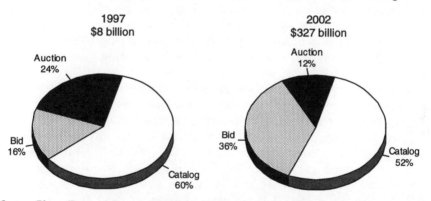

1997
$8 billion

Auction
24%

Bid
16%

Catalog
60%

2002
$327 billion

Auction
12%

Bid
36%

Catalog
52%

Source: Blane Erwin, Mary A. Modahl, and Jesse Johnson, "Sizing Intercompany Commerce," *Business Trade & Technology Strategies*, 1(1), Forrester Research, Inc., July 1997.

sought new ways to cut costs. Forrester saw different strategic groups of companies at the center of the intercompany online commerce: manufacturers, intermediaries, as well as services and utilities.[86]

Manufacturers: First Movers. In 1997, manufacturers, both industry leaders like Cisco and Boeing and small firms like Drabik Tool, kick-started commerce over the Internet. Durable goods makers (e.g., electronics and airplane parts) were expected to ring up $3 billion alone (38% of all Internet business trade that year). Nondurables (e.g., apparel from Lee

Printwear and business forms from Moore) paled in comparison with a total of $182 million.

Cisco Systems: End-to-End Network Connectivity. "You think Amazon.com is big?" asked *Fortune* in August 1998. "The real money online is business-to-business sales, and the king of routers is writing the manual." The feature story was entitled, "How Cisco Mastered the Net."[87] More than any other company, it was selling a gamut of goods and services to other businesses over the Internet. With impressive margins, it also could underwrite a stream of new products. Wall Street liked what it saw: In just three years Cisco's value swelled from $15 billion to *$100 billion.* The booming electronic commerce revenues certainly played a critical role in the valuation. Between the first quarter of fiscal 1997 and the third quarter of 1998, Cisco's revenue segment boomed from $81 million to $960.

By 1998, Cisco was the leading supplier of internetworking products that link LANs and WANs. It had an 85% share of the market for routers and 35% of LAN switches. The company had traditionally targeted the high-end market, but it also provided products for medium-sized and small businesses and was exploring the consumer market. Since it had begun to ride the Internet wave in 1995, it had acquired more than a dozen smaller networking companies. Typically enough, the electronic commerce experiments were not mandated by top management. Instead, a department head would set up a skunkworks, asking a couple of engineers working on a shoestring to see how far a daring idea might take them.

Cisco's first Internet breakthrough came with its Technical Assistance Center, which provided after-sales service. Since networking gear is so complex that after a sale customers remain in continual contact with their supplier, they bought products as much for the quality of after-sales service as for the items' price or features. By 1994 the Technical Assistance Center faced a staffing crisis. The solution was to automate all the routine stuff on the Internet and let buyers serve themselves. Between 1995 and the fall of 1998, Cisco's sales jumped fourfold, while its engineering support staff merely doubled, to 800.[88] Meanwhile, Cisco's customer service was fretting over the company's ordering process. The cause of the delays was the multitude of errors in the orders, which invariably arrived by fax.[89] Putting the sales process on the Internet eliminated mistakes and delays.

Both technical assistance and customer service imply an interface with the buyer. The third and the most critical development in Cisco's Internet momentum came with the realization that through the Internet the company could transform the slow marketplace interface to the fast marketspace points-of-sale. Again, the customer service managers came up with the idea that Cisco should move from selling just *$10* promotional headgear and technical-support services to pushing its *$1.5 million* routers;

marketing managers took the idea to the senior executives. Between mid-1996 and the fall of 1998, the company moved 57% of its sales (around $1.3 billion in the third quarter of 1998) in routers, switches, and other gear onto the Web. The goal for 1998 was 80%. The electronic commerce activities had a critical impact on profits.[90]

Intermediaries: Leveraging Manufacturer Links. With the flow of manufacturers' Internet trade pointed purposely at their wholesalers, middlemen were expected to thrive to the tune of $2 billion in Internet-based resales in 1997. Given Dell's and 3Com's strength in Internet trade, the presence of distributors like MicroAge and Tech Data was not considered surprising. But distributors like BT and Boise Cascade led the arrival of office supplies into the fourth channel as well.

The Dell Direct Model. According to Dell Computers Corp., one of the nation's leading direct computer systems companies, its "award-winning customer service, industry-leading growth and financial performance" differentiates the company from competitors. The company attributed the source of the differentiation to its unique direct-to-customer business model. By "direct," it referred to the relationships with its customers—from home-PC users to the world's largest corporations. There were *no* retailers or other resellers "adding unnecessary time and cost, or diminishing Dell's understanding of customer expectations." Insofar as the *company* was concerned, computer systems customers and investors were increasingly turning to Dell and its unique direct model for five specific reasons:

- *Price for Performance.* By eliminating resellers, retailers, and other costly intermediary steps together with the industry's most efficient procurement, manufacturing, and distribution process, Dell offered its customers more powerful and richly configured systems for the money than competitors.

- *Customization.* Every Dell system was built to order. Customers got exactly what they wanted.

- *Service and Support.* Dell used knowledge gained from direct contact before and after the sale to provide award-winning, tailored customer service.

- *Latest Technology.* Dell's efficient model meant the latest relevant technology is introduced in its product lines much more quickly than through slow-moving indirect distribution channels. Inventory was turned over every ten (or fewer) days, on average, keeping related costs low.

- *Superior Shareholder Value.* During the fiscal 1997, the value of Dell common stock more than doubled. In 1996 and 1997, Dell was the top-performing stock on the Standard & Poor's 500 and NASDAQ 100, and represented the top-performing U.S. stock on the Dow Jones World Stock Index.[91]

As Dell continuously refined its direct approach to manufacturing, selling and servicing personal-computing systems, it was committed to extending the advantages inherent in its efficient business model. The

Dell initiatives included moving even greater volumes of product sales, service and support to the Internet, and further expanding an already broad range of value-added services. The company considered the Internet, "the purest and most efficient form of the direct model," to provide greater convenience and efficiency to customers and, in turn, to Dell. After all, Dell services were focused on enhancing computing solutions for, and simplifying the system buying decisions of, current and potential customers.

By taking its direct business model to even higher levels through the Internet and value-added services, Dell intended to continue to grow its business at a multiple of the high-growth rate anticipated for the computer systems industry as a whole. The company thought it had significant opportunity for expansion in all parts of the world—especially in markets outside of the United States, in all customer segments, and in all product categories, ranging from home PCs to enterprise products such as network servers and workstations. In September 1998, for instance, Dell announced its ConnectDirect (SM), a wide-ranging technology initiative to provide Dell customers with easy, fast and personalized access to the Internet. The initiative included agreements with AT&T World Net Service, Excite, Inc., and SBC Communications, Inc. to provide services to Dell customers.[92]

Services and Utilities: Niches. Other industry sectors—utilities, transportation, and services—were expected to tally up $3 billion of fourth channel trade in 1997. The bulk of the Internet commerce came from utilities, where $2 billion of natural gas and crude oil was spot traded through firms like Altra Energy and QuickTrade. Services, which included software, were expected to reach $1 billion by year-end. Despite trailblazers like FedEx and Ryder, transportation was not thought to exceed $30 million in Internet sales. Forrester expected nothing short of growth, with total Internet sales shooting to $327 billion in 2002. Companies were in for a wild ride as suppliers, distributors, and customers would pile online.

FedEx: Transportation Model. Formed in 1988 when Federal Express bought trucking company Caliber System, FDX Corporation had half a dozen subsidiaries that were led by FedEx, the world's leading express transportation company, with 44,700 drop-off locations, more than 600 aircraft, and 40,900 vehicles. Since the mid-1990s, FedEx has internationalized rapidly, from China to Latin America. Fedex.com was launched prior to many other Internet businesses in November 1994. It also gained rave reviews because it allowed customers to track packages all over the world. Four years later, it was receiving 1.7 million tracking requests per month, saving the company the cost of handling those requests through phone calls. With "FedEx interNetShip," launched in July 1996, the shipper's customers can arrange for deliveries through the Web by filling out an electronic airbill and printing out their own label.

In addition to allowing users to print their own shipping labels, interNetShip lets customers communicate with recipients via e-mail and use a software package called BusinessLink, which allows businesses to sell goods over the Internet that would then be delivered by FedEx. As a Web pioneer in customer service, FedEx also played a significant role in helping customers move their businesses online. With its strong brand name and technological lead, FedEx was poised to take a larger share of the delivery business than competitors UPS and Airborne Freight (ABF).

In the early years of the Internet, the sales focus was on digital intangibles, but "at some point, all those bits turn into boxes," said Mike Janes, FedEx's vice president for electronic commerce and logistics marketing, in mid-1998. And when consumer markets joined the business-to-business Web rush and people started ordering online en masse, Janes thought people would want those goods to arrive as fast as possible: "The Internet is about instant gratification. You want the thing now, and FedEx plays right into that."[93]

FedEx's online retail accounts included L. L. Bean and Williams-Sonoma, but those shipments were only a fraction of its business. In 1998, the vast majority of shipments processed online remained business-to-business transactions (e.g., Cisco, Dell, and Insight Direct). FedEx processed two-thirds of its 3 million shipments each business day through electronic networks, including its private networks and website. FedEx's e-commerce strategy formed an inherent part of its overall business strategy. Even before it expected to generate more volume, FedEx's e-commerce strategy aimed to cut costs. Toward the end of the decade, some analysts were monitoring the company as a "closet Internet stock," even if many considered electronic commerce prospects highly inflated and insignificant in the short term. Still, value investors bought into FedEx early because of its embrace of electronic commerce; they anticipated the strategy to pay off in long term.

The Convergence of IT and Intranet/Extranet Markets. While the public debate focused on the browsers, the intranet movement swept through corporate America. In general terms, it meant a simple extension of the long-lasting corporate mission to increase the reach of information systems throughout the enterprise. Historically, the intranet opportunity could be viewed as a logical extension of the past fifteen years.[94] At first sight, then, one was tempted to craft intranet products and services within the old business model: designing products aimed at the same end users, requiring the same distribution channels, the same support strategies, and the same pricing models and therefore product costs. But as the IDC noted, the new era would be *different*. It was being driven by the creation of a "wired marketplace," with corporations using the Internet (and its successors) to reach out and connect to hundreds of millions to billions of wired consumers. In corporate America, the late 1990s were driven by the *externally focused application of the Internet*, instead of the internally focused, EDI-like intranets. As intranets were rapidly becoming an integral part of the emerging wired marketplace, the suppliers would have to exploit two business models simultaneously.[95]

Even as the buzz over the extranets (whether one chose to call them extended intranets, intercompany commerce, etc.) surpassed that of the intranets around 1996 and 1997, the convergence of stand-alone and Web-driven markets blurred traditional industry boundaries. From the standpoint of Internet marketing and long-term strategy, it would be crucial to view extranets as new and more cost-effective forms of channel management. According to Steve Telleen,

The term "extranet" did not originate from us. It seems to have been developed more as a marketing term. I had always envisioned the concept of an extranet. Basically, it was an issue of a protective set of contents and where to draw the boundaries. . . . But I'm not convinced that extranet is a useful term. It tends to connote electronic commerce applications. I find it more valuable to look at it as supply chain management and distributor chain content—as content, processes, or even from the standpoint of "what can a distributor do?" In other words, what types of practices are good for suppliers, and what are good practices for consumers?[96]

If intranets and extranets were rapidly evolving into extended points-of-sale, how should one exploit their business potential in marketing? For years, the most perceptive observers had advocated the notion of "relationship marketing" in Silicon Valley. When that concept would be coupled with the Internet momentum, the consequences were bound to reverberate through the entire U.S. economy. As the lessons of business-to-business marketing began to spill over to consumer marketing, *that* is precisely what happened in the second half of the 1990s.

NOTES

1. Daniel Bell [1973], "Foreword," in *The Coming of Post-Industrial Society: A Venture in Social Forecasting* (New York: Basic Books 1976), p. xv.

2. Ibid.

3. Annalee Saxenian, *Regional Advantage: Culture and Competition in Silicon Valley and Route 128* (Cambridge, MA: Harvard University Press 1994), pp. 2–3. On the general industrial organization and business strategies of geographic clustering, see in particular Michael E. Porter, *The Competitive Advantage of Nations* (New York: The Free Press 1990).

4. The following account of relationship management follows the classic

study: Theodor Levitt, "Relationship Management," *Harvard Business Review*, September–October 1983.

5. Dan Steinbock, Interview with Theodor Levitt, Professor Emeritus, Department of Marketing, Harvard Business School, September 18, 1998.

6. On the evolution of Intel and its microprocessors, Silicon Valley, and the business economics of the cluster, see, e.g., Annalee Saxenian, *Regional Advantage*; Michael S. Malone, *The Microprocessor: A Biography* (New York: Telos [Springer-Verlag] 1995); Charles H. Ferguson and Charles R. Morris, *Computer Wars: The Fall of IBM and the Future of Global Technology* (New York: Random House 1993); Rosabeth Moss Kanter, *World Class: Thriving Locally in the Global Economy* (New York: Simon & Schuster 1995).

7. See "From Relationship Marketing to Real Time" in this chapter.

8. Regis McKenna, *The Regis Touch: New Marketing Strategies for Uncertain Times* (New York: Addison-Wesley Publishing 1985), pp. 21–25.

9. See "Toward Global Markets" in chapter 6 of this book.

10. See Marco Iansiti and A. MacCormack, "Developing Products on Internet Time," Harvard Business School Working Paper #97–027.

11. "The emergence of new technologies can provide dramatic opportunities in dynamic environments," argued Marco Iansiti. "But to be used effectively, new technological possibilities must be carefully matched to their application context." See Marco Iansiti, *Technology Integration: Making Critical Choices in a Dynamic World* (Boston: Harvard Business School Press 1998), p. x.

12. This account on Intel's marketing campaigns is indebted to Albert Yu, who has played a critical role as manager of the company's microprocessor products from the 1970s to the close of the 1990s. See Dan Steinbock, Interview with Albert Yu, Senior VP and General Manager, Microprocessor Products Group, Intel Corp., October 12, 1998. The account also relies on Albert Yu, *Creating the Digital Future: The Secrets of Consistent Innovation at Intel* (New York: The Free Press 1998), chapter 5.

13. In a sense, the theory of co-opetition repackaged some of the fundamental notions on competitive advantage. "Most industries are affected in some way by complementary products—that is, products that are used jointly with their product by the buyer," Michael Porter had noted in his influential *Competitive Advantage* (1998). "Computer software and computer hardware, for example, are complements. Complements are the opposite of substitutes because the sale of one promotes the sale of another. Sometimes a number of complements are part of a firm's product line, while in other cases complements are supplied by other industries." See Michael E. Porter, *Competitive Advantage* (New York: The Free Press 1998), especially chapter 12.

14. See Adam M. Brandenburger and Barry J. Nalebuff, *Co-opetition* (New York: Current/Doubleday 1996), pp. 12. The book abounds with Intel-inspired examples and applications of co-opetition.

15. Andrew S. Grove, *Only the Paranoid Survive: How to Exploit the Crisis Points That Challenge Every Company and Career* (New York: Doubleday 1996), p. 29.

16. Yu, *Creating the Digital Future*, chapter 5.

17. Grove, *Only the Paranoid Survive*, p. 29.

18. Yu, *Creating the Digital Future*, chapter 5.

19. Steinbock, Interview with Yu; Yu, *Creating the Digital Future*, chapter 5.

20. After the mid-1990s, the Pentium debacle triggered a veritable cottage industry of case studies. See in particular *The Intel Pentium Chip Controversy (A)*, Harvard Business School 9–196–091, Rev. March 6, 1996; *The Intel Pentium Chip Controversy (B)*, Harvard Business School 9–196–092, September 18, 1995). In *Only the Paranoid Survive*, Grove portrayed the affair as a metaphor of an underlying structural industry change—and as a lesson of how to exploit the strategic inflection point.

21. Grove, *Only the Paranoid Survive*, p. 19.

22. Ibid, pp. 3–5.

23. Tom Quinlan, "Having Bested Other Chip Vendors, Intel Corp. Is Ready to Take on a Real Challenge: Beanie Babies," *San Jose Mercury News*, August 29, 1997.

24. Dean Takahashi, "Intel's Grove to Give an Earful on Battle for Viewers' Hearts," *Wall Street Journal*, November 18, 1996. See also "Intel CEO Andy Grove Tells Comdex Attendees the Microprocessor Revolution Is Still in Progress," Intel Press Release, Santa Clara, CA, November 18, 1996.

25. Regis McKenna, *The Regis Touch*, p. 3.

26. Dan Steinbock, Interview with Regis McKenna, Chairman, The McKenna Group, September 18, 1998.

27. The McKenna Group (www.mckenna-group.com) has offices in Cambridge, Massachusetts, and Tokyo, with affiliate offices in London, Paris, and Dusseldorf.

28. McKenna's *The Regis Touch* (later *Relationship Marketing*) originated from the first years of the 1980s PC revolution, whereas *Real Time* was published amidst the early years of the Internet revolution. The subtitles reflect the times and the approaches. Where the former was subtitled, "New Marketing Strategies for Uncertain Times," the latter was called, "Preparing for the Age of the Never Satisfied Customer." McKenna himself sees a strong continuity between the two. "The *Relationship Marketing* really did touch well upon real time and the influences of technology on people and the marketplace. In *Real Time*, I argued that because things are moving so fast and are driven by the nature of digital technology, you have to be prepared for the eventuality of anything. How do you do that? Well, again, you rely on the technology and you also rely on this constant presence with your customer." Steinbock, Interview with Regis McKenna.

29. Steinbock, Interview with Regis McKenna.

30. The implications of such an "integration" of the marketing concept and competitive strategy was first really explored by Regis McKenna in a now classic study, "Marketing Is Everything," *Harvard Business Review*, January–February 1991.

31. McKenna, *The Regis Touch*, p. 4.

32. For McKenna's views on the increasing product/service diversity, see "Marketing in an Age of Diversity," *Harvard Business Review*, September–October 1988; and on the new product development, Regis McKenna, "Why High Tech Products Fail," *The International High Technology Marketing Review*, 1987.

33. McKenna, *The Regis Touch*, pp. 5–7. On the context of the new marketing concept, see Steven P. Schnaars, *Marketing Strategy: Customers & Competition*, 2d ed. (New York: The Free Press 1998); Frederick E. Webster, Jr., *Market-Driven*

Management: Using the New Marketing Concept to Create a Customer-Oriented Company (New York: John Wiley & Sons 1994).

34. McKenna, *The Regis Touch*; see chapter 2 on "Dynamic Positioning: The Cornerstones of the New Marketing."

35. Steinbock, Interview with Regis McKenna.

36. "I was talking about the right of choice and that you had to build the relationships with your customers because they had more choices. If there was a relationship between the marketers and the consumer, then that would be the only thing that would keep the consumers from selecting the competitor." The work assignments, of course, anticipated these developments even in the 1970s. In his lectures and consulting, McKenna began to build, develop, and implement these ideas in the early 1980s. See, e.g., Regis McKenna, "Marketing in an Age of Diversity."

37. "Even *In Search of Excellence* by Tom Peters and his co-authors gave examples of companies treating their customers in an intimate way that reflected relationship marketing. The labeling isn't important. What is important is what companies are practicing. When my book came out, relationship marketing people thought this is one of those fuzzy West Coast concepts that everybody is supposed to be friendly. . . . Of course, the book was about the use of technology, and how it enables you to manage lots of customers, whether that's self service or interactive service or call centers or ATM machines. Those are all embodiments of relationship marketing." Ibid.

38. Steinbock, Interview with Regis McKenna.

39. Ibid.

40. Ibid.

41. Ibid.

42. McKenna, *The Regis Touch*; see chapter 6 on "Developing a Strategy: Three Steps to Success." Later, of course, Geoffrey A. Moore developed his notion of "chasm" on the basis of the life cycle analysis. Indeed, the technology adoption life cycle would inspire an entirely new generation of researchers, practitioners, and consultants. While some would use the framework to analyze problems of marketing and shareholder value (e.g., Moore, Slywotzky), others would seize its explanatory potential in technology strategy (e.g., Tushman, Utterback). See, e.g., Adrian J. Slywotzky, *Value Migration: How to Think Several Moves Ahead of the Competition* (Boston: Harvard Business School Press 1996); Slywotzky and David J. Morrison, with Bob Andelman, *The Profit Zone: How Strategic Business Design Will Lead You to Tomorrow's Profits* (New York: Random House 1997); James M. Utterback, *Mastering the Dynamics of Innovation* (Boston: Harvard Business School Press 1996); and Michael L. Tushman and Charles A. O'Reilly III, *Winning through Innovation: A Practical Guide to Leading Organizational Change and Renewal* (Boston: Harvard Business School Press 1998).

43. Ibid.

44. Geoffrey A. Moore, *Crossing the Chasm: Marketing and Selling High-Tech Products to Mainstream Customers* (New York: HarperBusiness 1991), pp. 6–7.

45. Dan Steinbock, Interview with Geoffrey A. Moore, Chairman, The Chasm Group, May 18, 1998.

46. Prior to founding TCG in 1992, Moore was a principal and partner at Regis

McKenna, Inc., a leading high-tech marketing and communications company. He held a bachelor's degree from Stanford University and a Ph.D. from the University of Washington, both in literature, and served as an English professor at Olivet College. "In 1978, I was an English professor until I decided to return to business. Initially, I joined a software company to work in training and education. In a couple of years, I got involved in Sales and Marketing. Over the next ten years I was involved in Sales and Marketing in over three software companies. One of them was a client of Regis McKenna. When I left the third company in 1987, I joined McKenna, which was transitioning from PR to a consulting firm." Steinbock, Interview with Geoffrey A. Moore.

47. *"The Regis Touch* came out in 1984. It was the first great book about high tech marketing. Although the life cycle model is 50 years old, the application to high tech really started with Regis McKenna's work in the mid-1980's. In that sense, this kind of relationship marketing is probably fifteen years old." Steinbock, Interview with Moore.

48. Promotional materials. See Geoffrey A. Moore, *Inside the Tornado: Marketing Strategies from Silicon Valley's Cutting Edge* (New York: HarperBusiness 1995).

49. "I knew about it as a technology only around 1993 or 1994. But like a lot of people I just didn't get it at the time. And although *Inside the Tornado* came out in the fall of 1995, there are only one or two mentions of the Internet. At the time, I thought that proprietary networks, such as the Microsoft Network, would win the rivalry. The Internet was something that took me by surprise." See Steinbock, Interview with Moore.

50. Steinbock, Interview with Geoffrey A. Moore.

51. "Many American manufacturers and service providers see a day when, as in Finland, the wires in our homes and under our streets serve primarily as data-hauling networks, while much of the talk moves over the airwaves. Even in markets where wired phones remain dominant, experts say, U.S. phone companies may see the wired/wireless distinction disappear in customers' minds. Companies will sell a pervasive dial tone in various forms geared to consumer needs." See Quentin Hardy, "For a Glimpse of the U.S.'s Cordless Future, Just Set Your Sights Overseas," *Wall Street Journal*, September 21, 1998.

52. Steinbock, Interview with Geoffrey A. Moore.

53. *The Gorilla Game* differed from general growth investment books because it focused exclusively on high-tech and specifically on product-oriented companies that sold into mass markets undergoing hypergrowth. Another differentiator was that consolidation, not diversification, was used as its primary risk-reduction strategy for long-term holds. The third unique characteristic lay in the effort to couple competitive strategy with valuation strategy—an objective Paul Johnson and his colleagues had explored in their pioneering papers on competitive advantage periods (CAP). See Geoffrey A. Moore, Paul Johnson, and Tom Kippola, *The Gorilla Game: An Investor's Guide to Picking Winners in High Technology* (New York: HarperBusiness 1998). See also the Web site at www.gorillagame.com.

54. Steinbock, Interview with Geoffrey A. Moore. *The Gorilla Game* was part of a two-book contract. The second book is tentatively called *Living on the Frontline*—Moore's effort to analyze what a mature organization can do to accommodate multiple business strategies within a single organizational structure.

55. See, e.g., John A. Byrne, "The Horizontal Corporation," *Business Week*, December 20, 1993.

56. For a concise introduction to the debate on "declinism," see Michael Prowse, "Is America in Decline," *Harvard Business Review*, July–August 1992.

57. The slate of the publications by the Clinton administration in the early 1990s is a living testimony for the reframing of national agenda. What started as the nation's new economic policy soon led to the nation's new technology policy, the National Information Infrastructure (NII) initiative, the Global Information Infrastructure (GII) initiative, the electronic commerce initiative, the science and education initiatives, and so on. These developments were in sync and, to significant extent, triggered by the administration's conversion program—that is, a massive national effort to push the U.S. economy from the Cold War to the era of global competition.

58. William H. Davidow and Michael S. Malone, *The Virtual Corporation* (New York: HarperCollins 1992); see chapter 1 on "A New Kind of Business."

59. "The virtual corporation is a temporary network of independent companies—suppliers, customers, even erstwhile rivals—linked by information technology to share skills, costs, and access to one another's markets. It will have neither central office nor organization chart. It will have no hierarchy, no vertical integration. Instead, proponents say this new, evolving corporate model will be fluid and flexible—a group of collaborators that quickly unite to exploit a specific opportunity. Once the opportunity is met, the venture will, more often than not, disband." See John A. Byrne, with Richard Brandt and Otis Port, "The Virtual Corporation," *Business Week*, February 2, 1993.

60. B. Joseph Pine II, *Mass Customization: The New Competition in Business Competition* (Boston: Harvard Business School Press 1993), pp. 6–7.

61. See "From Mass Marketing to Internet Dynamics" in Chapter 2 of this book.

62. On the evolution of the U.S. de facto industrial policy, see Otis L. Graham, Jr., *Losing Time. The Industrial Policy Debate* (Cambridge, MA: Harvard University Press 1992).

63. See U.S. Congress, Office of Technology Assessment, *Electronic Enterprises: Looking to the Future*, OTA-TCT-600 (Washington, DC: U.S. Government Printing Office, May 1994).

64. During its 23-year history, the Congressional Office of Technology Assessment (OTA) provided Congressional members and committees with objective and authoritative analysis of the complex scientific and technical issues of the late 20th century. On the history and the end of OTA, see "The Debate Over Assessing Technology," *Business Week*, April 8, 1972; Colin Norman, "OTA Caught in Partisan Crossfire," *Technology Review*, October–November 1977; Gregory C. Kunkle, "New Challenge or Past Revisited? The Office of Technology Assessment in Historical Context," *Technology in Society*, 17(2), 1995, pp. 175–196; Warren E. Leary, "Congress's Science Agency Prepares to Close Its Doors," *New York Times*, September 24, 1995.

65. Dan Steinboek, interview with Lester Wunderman, chairman of Wunderman Cato Johnson, senior adviser to the board of directors of Young & Rubicam, and director of Dentsu Wunderman Direct in Japan, August 17, 1998.

66. For a journalistic account on the genesis of the first intranet models and

Telleen's role among the pioneers, see Laton McCartney, "Intranet Business Follows Race for Cyberspace," *Upside*, December 1996.

67. Dan Steinbock, Interview with Steven Telleen, Consultant, Giga Group, September 4, 1998.

68. Ibid.

69. Ibid.

70. After the deal, both suppliers of mainframe computers that were compatible with those sold by IBM were owned by Japanese firms. Amdahl's rival for the No. 2 spot in that $8 billion-a-year worldwide market was Hitachi Data Systems, which was owned by Hitachi Ltd. and Electronic Data Systems Corp. and which entered the market in 1989 after buying a mainframe line from National Semiconductor Corp. Between them, Hitachi and Amdahl controlled about 25% of the IBM-compatible market, according to market researcher International Data Corp. The rest was held by IBM. As it relegated hardware operations to Fujitsu, Amdahl laid off thousands of workers. But success in services was not enough to offset losses from Amdahl's core mainframe business, where it had steadily lost ground. On Fujitsu's acquisition, see Lee Gomes, "Amdahl's Autonomy Fades as Fujitsu Makes Offer," *Wall Street Journal*, July 31, 1997.

71. On Amdahl's Microsoft deal, see Saul Hansell, "Maker of IBM Clones Teams with Microsoft," *Wall Street Journal*, February 2, 1998.

72. Ibid.

73. Bob Flanagan, director of the Internet unit at The Yankee Group, called the tactic "the warm puppy approach." The way to get customers into a pet store is to put a puppy (Navigator) in the window. The strategy worked brilliantly, and Netscape became the fastest-growing software company in history. See Laton McCartney, "Intranet Business Follows Race for Cyberspace."

74. By late 1995, reportedly some 50% of Netscape's sales were for software used in the development of corporate intranets. That software played a key role in Netscape's strong third-quarter 1996 results (revenue rose 329% over the same quarter in 1995, to $100 million, while the company earned $7.7 million, up from $175,000). By 1996, about 80% of the company's revenue came from intranet products and services. See Netscape's 10-K's and management discussions.

75. See McCartney, "Intranet Business Follows Race to Cyberspace."

76. These market share estimates were quoted in McCartney, "Intranet Business Follows Race to Cyberspace."

77. Marc Andreessen and The Netscape Product Team, "The Netscape Intranet Vision and Product Roadmap," Version 1.2, Netscape Communications Corp., July 16, 1996.

78. Thomas J. Pincince, David Goodtree, and Carolyn Barth, "The Full Service Intranet," Forrester Research, March 1, 1996.

79. Ibid.

80. On the Yankee Group releases, see, e.g., "Carpe Intranetum: Seize the Power of Intranets," *Yankee Watch Internet Computing Strategies*, 1(11), July 1996; "A New Framework for Business-to-Business on the Internet," *Yankee Watch Internet Computing Strategies*, 1(14), November 1996; "Netscape's AppFoundry Promotes Intranet Building Blocks," *Yankee Watch Internet Computing Strategies*, 2(1), January 1997; "What's So Hot About Domino?" *Yankee Watch Internet Computing Strategies*, 2(4), March 1997; "Ten Lessons from the Internet," *Yankee Watch In-*

ternet Computing Strategies, 2(6), April 1997; "Enterprise Electronic Commerce '97: EDI Meets the Internet," *Yankee Watch Enterprise Applications*, 2(9), May 1997; "Internet Computing in Europe," *Yankee Watch Internet Computing Strategies*, 2(7), May 1997; "Rapid Intranet Roll-out: Inventa's LightSpeed Implementation Framework," *Yankee Watch Internet Computing Strategies*, 2(10), July 1997.

81. See "Intranet Success Stories," *Yankee Watch Internet Computing Strategies*, August 1997.

82. The following paragraphs on the U.S. big business and the Web rely on Frank Gens, "What Are the *Fortune* 500 Doing on the Web?" IDC, June 1996.

83. Janet Kornblum, "Study: Net Reaching Mass Market," CNET, December 15, 1997. The CNET report relied on research by International Data Corporation (IDC) which, in turn, based its numbers and projections on an annual survey of 2,500 households as well as other research.

84. Surprisingly, a large group of companies used their Web sites for marketing company image. Still, many research firms considered using a Web site primarily as a channel for supporting corporate image not to be a particularly effective use of the medium, at least using traditional print-oriented marketing content. Instead, in order to deepen customers' identification with company image, they would advise firms to take advantage of the interactive capabilities of the Web.

85. See Blane Erwin, Mary A. Modahl, and Jesse Johnson, "Sizing Intercompany Commerce," *Business Trade & Technology Strategies*, 1(1), Forrester Research, Inc., July 1997.

86. The Forrester study (see the previous note) provides the framework for the following brief cases.

87. Shawn Tully, "How Cisco Mastered the Net," *Fortune*, August 17, 1998.

88. Without automated sales support, Cisco estimated it would need well over 1,000 additional engineers. Estimated savings amounted to $75 million a year, plus another $250 million it kept by distributing support software over the Internet rather than transferring it to disks and mailing them to customers. Finally, the company might have foregone the billions in sales if it had not been able to find those 1,000 extra engineers.

89. Cisco's products are complex and custom-built. It also offered dozens of choices for each, but many of the combinations do not work together. Making matters worse, customers found the prices for 13,000 parts in often out-of-date catalogs as thick as phone books. When Cisco received orders with the wrong prices or configurations (40% of the time), it simply faxed them back to the customers.

90. At many technology companies, profitability shrank as sales took off. Prices fell as new players entered the market. Unlike many of its rivals, Cisco managed to keep its selling and servicing costs far lower than its competitors'. Including savings harvested from manufacturing, the Internet was saving Cisco about $360 million a year and helping preserve its 32% operating margins.

91. Dell Computer Corp. (1998).

92. The initiative offered customers an easy Internet sign-on process, the freedom to choose Internet access from leading Internet Service Providers (ISPs), and personalized Web start pages that offer customizable news content and direct links to Dell services, support, and registration. See "Dell Introduces the

'ConnectDirect' Initiative for Easy, Fast and Personalized Access to the Internet," Dell Computers Corp., September 23, 1998

93. Amey Stone, "FedEx: An Internet Stock," *Business Week*, June 22, 1998.

94. Or what IDC called the second era of IT growth (i.e. the PC, LAN, and client/server software had been the chief tools IT suppliers offered to support this mission). It was easy for an IT supplier to see the browsers, Web servers, development tools, TCP/IP software, firewalls, and the hardware and services that enabled them as simply the latest tools in this same market environment. See also *Intranets and Virtual Private Networks: A Data Communications Perspective*, Data Communications, Yankee Group, December 1996.

95. The successful IT suppliers were the ones that would manage to "compete today in the second-era market model while preparing their products and companies for the very different market model just beginning to take shape." See Frank Gens, "The Intranet in Perspective: Opportunity and Risk," International Data Corporation, August 1996.

96. Steinbock, Interview with Steven Telleen.

4

Consumer Marketing on the Web

As the Web took off, so did the first experiments in Web-driven direct marketing. The *technology* of digital marketing communications may have emerged only in the 1990s, but its first viable *commercial models* were developed in the post–World War II era—just as its potential was first seen in the late 1950s and the early 1960s.

THE PROMISE OF INTERACTIVE MARKETING

When Edwin Artzt, chief executive of Procter & Gamble, gave his famous crisis address in 1994, one observer who paid attention was Lester Wunderman, the pioneer of direct marketing to whom America owes the ubiquity of the American Express card, the creation of the Columbia Record Club, and the high profile of L. L. Bean. Unlike others in Madison Avenue, Wunderman was not that impressed.

Artzt did not know what he was talking about. He was not a man who was brought up to believe that his company should respond to the consumer, even if he knew advertising would have to become accountable. A lot of people know that, yet go with the religion, "Let's build a brand!" They're talking about holy sausage.[1]

In the post–World War II era, Lester Wunderman conceived and perfected many visionary marketing techniques that transformed the advertising industry and would shape the interactive marketplace of the future. Through direct marketing, he has sought to put manufacturers *directly* in touch with consumers. He became aware of the direct potential of the Internet at a very early stage, as a member of a select group set up by the National Research Council. "The Internet seemed like what I had been looking for all my life," he recalls. "Even the 800 number had to be publicized. Prior to the Web, there was no real medium for the public. Whatever the advertisers choose to do, the Internet is the consumer's media."[2]

Wunderman expects the intensity of rivalry and new entrants to prevent the sellers from locking in the buyers.

Consumers have bargaining power, and they are beginning to exercise it. They purchase cars on the Internet. They begin to exercise the right to know what the price should be. Consumers cannot be locked against their own interest. If I am a steady customer of a particular supplier, he can make me a better purchase arrangement as a result of my repurchasing. Such repurchases would serve the interest of each side. Moreover, we don't really know about the durability of online communities or the business of brand communities. True, there are virtual communities that are like affinity groups, but they have preexisted the Internet that simply provides an easier means to create such communities.[3]

When Wunderman published his celebrated *Being Direct* in 1996, he subtitled the autobiography, "Making Advertising Pay." Along with disintermediation, *accountability* penetrates the very principles of the sort of direct relationship marketing he has advocated through his career that spans the rise and rejuvenation of the U.S. advertising industry. As an enabling infrastructure, however, the Internet came decades later than its interactive promise. The idea preceded its technological manifestation.

The First Virtual Store: Being Direct

In the 1950s and 1960s, when other ad agencies still disdained what was then called mail-order selling, Lester Wunderman revolutionized the industry by introducing the first bound-in subscription cards for magazines and preprinted newspaper inserts. He also persuaded Time Inc. to use an 800 number to sell its magazines. These discoveries are part of his legend. What is less known is that he also developed the notion of a "virtual store." In 1949, Wunderman notes in his autobiographical *Being Direct*, one of his clients at Sackheim was the John Blye Shop for Men.

There were three Blye shops, one on Broadway, one in White Plains, and a "Fifth Avenue" shop. . . . They sold chic, expensive men's wear to young executives. Arnold Blye, the owner, was an ambitious merchant who wanted his business to grow faster. . . .

I asked what he would do if I showed him a street where almost a million young, fashion-conscious, affluent men shopped every month. He said he would open a store there in a minute. I told him there was such a place. "Where is it?" he asked. "*Esquire* magazine," I replied.

I proposed that we approach *Esquire* and offer it not an advertising contract but a "lease" for what would now be called a "virtual store."[4]

The problem with the single-page John Blye store in print was that it was only a store window. To succeed, Wunderman thought, they should have been able to show the entire inventory, which was not cost-efficient prior to the Internet.[5]

For Wunderman, the moral of the story is that

there were but so many people that passed by that corner of the store and yet he had a very specific target audience. There were more people in the target population than in the area where he was paying very high rent. Now, he did not object to his rent, but he sure objected to the rates of *Esquire* magazine. He didn't understand that they were going to pass by *his* store window because he didn't think of the ad as the store window.[6]

The MIT Speech on Direct Marketing: Revolution in Selling

During the 1960s, Wunderman was among the first to conceive of and define the dimensions of interactive marketing. Wunderman first used the term "direct marketing" publicly on October 1, 1961, in a speech to the Hundred Million Club of New York, an organization of leaders in the direct mail business. Describing his discontent with "mail-order advertising" and its lack of creative thinking and forward planning, he presented direct marketing as the "new frontier" of the Kennedy era:

The next ten years will see a continuing decline of the mail-order business as it has been defined in the past. It will be replaced by Direct Marketing—a new and more efficient method of selling, based on scientific advertising principles and serviced by increasingly more automated warehousing, shipping and collection techniques.[7]

In 1967, a quarter of a century prior to the launch of the Web, the pioneer of direct response delivered a famous speech at MIT on "Direct Marketing—The New Revolution in Selling."[8] He described the sales relationship of the future as "interactive." In tomorrow's electronic marketplace, the interactive techniques he pioneered would account for the great majority of sales worldwide.

Theoretically, the prediction was accurate, but the complacency of the big manufacturers and mass marketers made it irrelevant. Wunderman could not foresee the strategic moves of the retail intermediaries, which made information a source of competitive advantage and, thereby, not only retained their channel function but also broadened their bargaining power. On the other hand, he did foresee the instrumental use values of computing power in marketing management; these extensions of man would make the whole marketing process more human in the "post-industrial society." Unlike the prophets of mass marketing, standardization and high volume, he already saw a very different kind of a future. He saw Americans living in an "age of repersonalization and individuation."

A computer can know and remember as much marketing detail about 200,000,000 consumers as did the owner of a crossroads general store about his handful of customers. It can know and select such personal details as who prefers strong coffee, imported beer, new fashions, bright colors.... New marketing forms which will link these facts to advertising and selling must evolve—and this can be done in only one way—Direct Marketing, where the advertising and buying become a single action. Those marketers who ignore the implications of our new individualized information society will be left behind in what may well come to be known as the age of mass production and marketing ignorance.[9]

Instead of peddling mass-produced commodities, Wunderman argued that advertising was going to become a personal service of each individual—that is, completely individualized, volume direct mail, which he believed "will soon create personalized advertising opportunities we never dreamed of."[10] A quarter of a century later, this vision would become familiar as "mass customization" and the Internet promised to extend its impact by integrating old and new forms of advertising and direct response.

Wunderman conceived the interactive notion of mass customization in parallel with the publication of *Nineteen Eighty-Four* (1949). He spoke for "repersonalization and individuation" in the late 1950s and early 1960s—that is amidst the Cold War and the popular metaphors and images of *mass* village (Marshall McLuhan), and the *organization* man (William W. Whyte). "It *was* very contrary to the mainstream at the time," acknowledges Wunderman. "In the past, our societies and economies were based on the idea of mass production, mass distribution, mass marketing, and mass advertising. When I spoke out for a different view, it was not always well accepted."[11]

Direct and Dialogue Marketing

To Lester Wunderman, marketing is an ongoing process: "The minute it deals with the past it becomes less effective." Insofar as he is concerned, direct is a far more inclusive notion than many academics or some practitioners presume.

Direct marketing includes database marketing and relationship marketing. If one talks about direct marketing as a kind of a relationship between a seller and a buyer and if one defines that relationship as direct and based on information, then that definition has to include database marketing because otherwise how would one person identify another? Direct also involves a relationship. What is the object of two people being in dialogue with each other, if not to have some kind of a relationship? What is the object of any dialogue except to grow beyond the dialogue? At least partially, direct marketing intends to have a constructive and ongoing relationship between a seller and a buyer, ideally a producer and a consumer, based on what they know about each other. So, direct marketing includes database and relationship marketing. . . .

People seize words without understanding. A bunch of technicians have their buzzwords: Let's make a database, relationship marketing, loyalty. . . . There are three things I would be loyal to and risk my life for my country, family, and church or faith. How loyal would I be to a company? What would I risk? Nothing! Loyalty. . . . they really mean purchase. Even I often use the word incorrectly. . . . Direct mail, for example, is like shooting: set up a target and the advertisers are going to hit them right in the bull's eye. The targets are all the paragons and algorithms you can list. I was after something different. I wanted *a medium where the advertiser would become the target and the consumer would become the shooter.* That's what's happening. It is a profoundly different marketplace.[12]

The idea of direct marketing is not "just" a tactic; it is a strategy—a way of dealing with the consumer without mediations, interactively, through an ongoing dialogue. This is the cornerstone of Wunderman's approach.

Since, as a consumer, I am the one who consumes, eventually you can't make or sell anything unless I use it. Therein lies the power. I finally have a medium that begins to use the advertiser as *my* database, instead of me being *his* database. Direct marketing is an information-based dialogue and it has to serve both parties. It has to serve the consumer. It has to help the consumer get the service or products he/she wants. It has to serve the vendor or manufacturer to provide the things that this individual consumer wants and that call for other forms of promotion and distribution. You can't add relationship marketing to old-fashioned businesses. It just cannot be done! People have a relationship with other people, not with the factory. We are now beyond the industrial revolution and in an information age. Well, that changes everything. For advertising and marketing management, this means changes in everything. I do not have a lot of respect for trying to modify old systems with new ideas. Banner advertising on the Internet is not working; [those practitioners] think the Internet is television, just as the catalogue companies think it is direct mail.

For the moment, the idea of banners has taken the small minds because it is the most comfortable replica of television. After all, a one-line banner is similar to a one-line-TV commercial. . . . We're talking about dialogues and relationships, as well as an intent to move them to a more informational plane. We have to grow up. Only children talk to each other in these simplistic terms. Get a group of 5-year-olds and they sound like a bunch of national advertisers. It is ridiculous that the economies of the world should be based on baby talk.[13]

For Wunderman, banner advertising, or direct forms of current Internet advertising may represent merely intermediary forms of Web-based relationship marketing.

For a long time, I, for example, thought that Amazon.com would disappear. The economics are against them. More recently, I've begun to see their grand strategic design. They want to be a *general vendor and a major retailer* source to many things. True, they started with books, but some of the other items have a higher margin than books. Amazon.com had a different idea. Let's get the order *first*, and only *then* the product. That makes an interesting financing theory. Suddenly, you have the use of other people's money and then you get the merchandise and you don't have to pay someone for another 60 days. That effort is successful because of a good strategic intent, based on an idea of a virtual store. Finally, there's the use of the database that consists of millions of people of whom Amazon knows a lot.[14]

When Wunderman talks about relationship marketing, he does not speak of scientific database experiments, but about a personal, individual dialogue, something that will change both sides of the interaction through learning. In that regard, relationship or dialogue marketing goes beyond direct marketing.[15]

DIRECT RESPONSE AND ONE-TO-ONE MARKETING

What became known as one-to-one marketing in the early 1990s evolved from frustration with traditional rules, tactics, and strategies that had proved ineffective in the late 1980s. The discipline stemmed from a chance meeting with a marketing practitioner and a marketing professor at Toledo in early 1990.[16]

At the time, Don Peppers was working in New York at Lintas: USA, a large, multinational advertising agency with clients like Coca-Cola, General Motors, Unilever, and IBM. He directed Lintas's business development efforts in the United States. While the issue of the increasing fractionalization of mass media was being debated intensely in the business, he had begun to suspect that communications and information technologies on the near horizon would eliminate the underlying basis for mass marketing itself. A new era would need new rules, tactics, and competitive strategies.

Peppers had always been interested in economics and entrepreneurial issues. In a sense, he had been practicing one-to-one marketing at Lintas, where he had a dual function. He had to win new clients for the agency and develop relationships with them.

To understand advertising, one has to understand mass marketing. It's really all about creating an image, a brand, and so forth. However, to win clients for the agency it's all about relationship marketing—that is, to create relationships with potential new clients, meet them for dinner, try to remember the problems of their companies, modes of conversation and so forth.[17]

In the summer of 1989, the American Advertising Federation asked him to speak on the topic of "the future of media." Peppers says he prepared for the speech by asking himself, What will Kellogg's do when a kid can talk back to a corn flakes commercial? "The answer is that they won't do anything with that feedback," he says. "How will they change their marketing strategy? That feedback is only useful to a mass marketer if it is represents a broader population. If it doesn't represent some kind of manageable niche population of customers, then it's not useful to the marketer." He began to develop the idea that, with the rise of interactivity, more companies would have to become relationship marketers and win new clients one at a time. In the process, the computers would substitute human interactivity.[18]

At the time, Martha Rogers, a marketing professor at Toledo's Bowling Green State University, taught college students about the disciplines of mass marketing and advertising. Lecturing on the importance of the classic "4Ps" of marketing (product, place, price, promotion), she taught product positioning and coached her students in how to develop creative advertising to break through the burgeoning clutter of mass media commercial messages. But, like Peppers, she had become less comfortable with teaching mass marketing to students who would not be practicing it. Of course, she had tried teaching the "new developments" (niche marketing, micromarketing, database marketing, geodemographic statistical analysis), as well as hot new topics such as integrated marketing communications. Yet, she found it increasingly difficult to expect her students to develop any understanding of real mass marketing when she herself severely doubted the effectiveness and long-term use of the mass marketing models that still dominated most of the scholarly literature.

After the speech, Martha Rogers introduced herself to Peppers and suggested writing a book about the topic. The two began working on *The One to One Future* in January 1990. While they already were envisioning a new marketing paradigm based on mass customization, its technological vehicle did not exist yet. "At the time, the Internet was used only by the military, government people, and some college professors," recalls Peppers.

The World Wide Web did not even exist as word. Through those three years, we developed our thoughts considerably. The Web became popular only after our book was published. In 1995 and in 1996, the book sold more copies than in

1993 and 1994, when it was primarily bought by website operators, even though the Web was not even mentioned in the first edition of *The One to One Future* in the fall of 1993. As we wrote, it was still a work of science fiction. We tried to imagine what life would be like if you could interact with customers.[19]

Both Peppers and Rogers had become convinced that individualized media would not only make individualized marketing possible, but would *require* it. There would not be just customized news and entertainment, but customized products, individually addressable commercial messaging, and two-way, one-to-one dialogues between marketers and consumers as well. And all of these would be managed with the increasingly efficient information technology. So the two began to outline a new frame of reference for marketing:

Today we are passing through a technological discontinuity of epic proportions, and most of us are not even remotely prepared. The old paradigm, a system of mass production, mass media, and mass marketing, is being replaced by a totally new paradigm, a one-to-one economic system.

The 1:1 future will be characterized by customized production, individually addressable media, and 1:1 marketing, totally changing the rules of business competition and growth. Instead of market share, the goal of most business competition will be share of customer—one customer at a time.[20]

The new marketing paradigm, argued the authors, would have severe implications for customer management:

Products will be increasingly tailored to individual tastes, electronic media will be inexpensively addressed to individual consumers, and many products ordered over the phone will be delivered to the home in eight hours or less.

In the 1:1 future businesses will focus less on short-term profits derived from quarterly or annual transaction volumes, and more on the kind of profits that can be realized from long-term customer retention and lifetime values.[21]

In time, *The One to One Future* would result in two sequels: *Enterprise One to One* (1997) and *The One to One Fieldbook* (1998).[22]

Essentially, one-to-one marketers argue that, by the 1980s, American marketers were facing a "paradigm shift of epic proportions" from the industrial era to the information age. The nation was witnessing a meltdown of the mass-marketing paradigm that had governed business competition throughout the 20th century. The new paradigm would be one-to-one—mandated by cheaper and faster data management, interactive media, and increasing capabilities for mass customization. Insofar as one-to-one marketers were concerned, the paradigm had half a dozen fundamental rules.[23]

Definition of One-to-One (1:1) Marketing. The basis for one-to-one marketing is share of customer, not just market share. Instead of selling as many products as possible over the next sales period to whomever will buy them, the goal of the one-to-one marketers is to sell one customer at a time as many products as possible over the lifetime of that customer's patronage. Mass marketers developed a product and tried to find customers for that product. One-to-one marketers would develop a customer and try to find products for that customer. Historically, the transition of emphasis from the product to the customer meant a reversal of focus. While information technology made it possible, distributed computing (the Internet and other interactive forms of Web-driven digital computing) would make it cost-efficient.

Share of Customer. The ability to identify each customer makes it possible to calculate *share of customer* (i.e., the company's share of all the business this customer does), as well as *lifetime value* (LTV) of each customer. One-to-one marketers can differentiate customers, not just products, in order to ascertain and predict which customers are worth more than others and how to meet each one's individual needs. Historically and today, as mass marketers look at the market rather than the individual customer, they concentrate on getting a greater number of transactions during a particular time period or in a given geographic area. From the marketer's perspective, these transactions are all *independent* of one another. Instead, one-to-one marketers see a single customer not as a one-time transaction, but as a series of transactions *over time* (or, as Peppers and Rogers would say, "not as an on-off switch, but as a volume dial"). They think of the task of generating a greater share of the customer's business as maximizing an individual's lifetime value to the firm. The true, current value of the customer is a function of the customer's future purchases, across all the product lines, brands, and services offered by the firm.[24] Without such knowledge of the amount of these purchases, one has to rely on statistical modeling techniques, based on information about that individual's past *behavior*.

As an empirical objective, the lifetime value is hardly a new one. Since the 1980s, direct response and data marketing had utilized similar tactics. But, again, distributed computing made it possible for even individual marketers to exploit the kind of marketing databases that used to belong to *Fortune* 500 giants only. Direct and database marketers had familiarized American marketing with the notion of lifetime value; one-to-one marketers would popularize the notion in new applications.

Customer Management. Mass marketing companies know how to manage products, and reward their successful product managers for *selling more product and winning more market share*. But customer managers at one-to-one organizations know how to *manage and grow their customers' value* and are rewarded for increasing the share of customers and the lifetime value for each customer one at a time. One-to-one marketers focus on the critical importance of actual past behavior (i.e., transactional databases). Or as the authors put it, "The 1:1 marketer doesn't want information *about* customers. He wants information *from* customers, one at a time."[25]

Direct-response and database marketers had long known that not every customer had equal value to the marketer. Even some brand strategists had embraced the challenge to develop new research methodologies (e.g., the rise of differential marketing).[26] They all would have to identify the most valuable customers; the customers that gave the firm more business through referrals; the customers who were not worth catering to at all; the prospects the firm would like to convert to customers; and the types of consumers the firm would consider real prospects. Direct-response and database marketing gave the one-to-one marketers the Pareto Principle—roughly put, the idea that 80% of any company's business comes from 20% of its customers. Just like frequent flyer programs provided a means for differentiating an airline's most valuable customers from its less valuable customers, one-to-one marketers would use such programs *to differentiate customers, not just products.* Peppers and Rogers emphasized the significance of programs that could be used to "loyalize" the firm's customers (i.e., to make loyal customers *more* loyal).[27]

Marketer/Customer Dialogue. Mass marketing is *adversarial.* One-to-one marketing is *collaborative.* Customer acquisition is far more costly than customer retention. However, since mass marketing still ruled in most American companies, most firms were overspending on customer acquisition and underspending on customer retention. As mass marketers rely on nonaddressable mass media, they tend to treat both new *and current* customers as *new* customers, argue Peppers and Rogers. "This irrational devotion to customer acquisition leads directly to a contest of wills between marketer and customer."[28]

Customers and marketers are perceived as adversaries, as if they were enemies in a battlefield.[29] This stress on customer acquisition has contributed to the so-called hypercompetition by conditioning consumers to switch brands in response to discounts and price breaks. One-to-one marketers did not advocate "more" incentives and promotions, or "more" branding. They bespoke for collaborative marketing in which the marketer listened to the customer and invited the customer to participate in actually making the product, even before asking the customer to take it. If and when they used frequency-marketing programs, they preferred to use them as collaborative tools rather than just marketing promotions. While the objective of mass-media advertising is to acquire new customers, one-to-one marketers want to build dialogues with individual customers and establish relationships based on mutual learning.

Manufacturer vs. Retailer. In *The One to One Future,* the authors argued, quite presciently and anticipating the rapid rise of electronic commerce, that the store of the future will transcend geography by separating the information-exchange function and the inventory function of the traditional retailer. Channels will emerge as one of the most compelling management issues of the one-to-one future. Ultimately, the question: Who will "own" the customer relationship? (i.e., the manufacturer or the retailer) is an empirical question.

According to Peppers, one-to-one marketing does cause problems but instead of technology, these stem from the culture and corporate organization of mass marketers.

If you're a successful product marketer, you have a good product that people like, and you probably have developed a good brand name for that product. This brand has value and you don't want to risk that value. You have an advertising manager, marketing managers, and product managers and you have a business you care for. We don't encourage companies to throw everything aside and try something entirely new. The change can be implemented through incremental progress.[30]

One-to-One Marketing in the History of Marketing. But how should one-to-one marketing be conceptualized in terms of the existing marketing approaches? Ultimately, it is the customer differentiation matrix that provides the solution. Let us determine differentiation according to two fundamental criteria: *customer valuations* and *customer needs*. Then let us assign customers three different kinds of values (according to their valuations and/or needs): *high, medium,* and *low*. These basic procedures result in a matrix that aggregates customers into four fundamental quadruples: mass marketing, niche marketing, loyalty marketing, and one-to-one marketing (Exhibit 4-1).

- In mass marketing, differentiation by customer valuations and by customer needs tends to be low.
- In niche marketing, differentiation by customer valuations remains low, but differentiation by customer needs may be high.
- In loyalty marketing (which can be considered the mirror image of niche marketing), the positions are reversed: now differentiation by customer valuations can be quite high, but differentiation by customer needs can be relatively low.
- Finally, in one-to-one marketing proper, both differentiation by customer valuations and customer needs can be quite high.

Each quadruple conforms to certain *historical eras of marketing*. While mass marketing, of course, reflects the traditional mass marketing concept, niche marketing is more descriptive of various segmentation approaches. While loyalty marketing appears to emphasize and require the

Exhibit 4-1
Customer Differentiation Matrix: Marketing Concepts

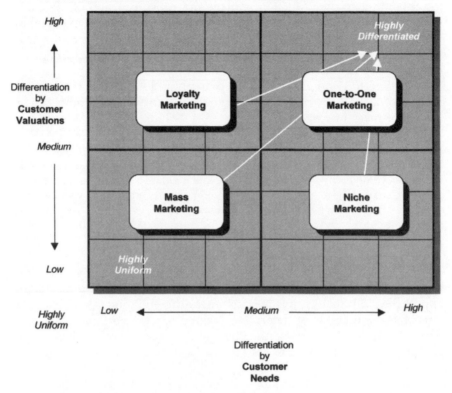

more recent approaches in direct marketing and database marketing, one-to-one marketing is far more demanding in concept and technology—it additionally requires real time interactivity *and* customization. These *marketing concepts*, in turn, enable the one-to-one marketer to build on the historical marketing knowledge while applying it in the new present. In order to implement this nascent marketing concept, the one-to-one marketer has to proceed in four stages:

- *Identify*: Marketers have to identify customers individually, where they are, and how to reach them.
- *Differentiate*: They must know how to differentiate customers by their needs and values, and then address those needs individually.
- *Interact*: They make customer interaction an important part of the growth strategy, in a fairly cost-efficient manner. Knowing what their customers have bought in the past (the "actual value" of the customer), they explore the incremental business that they might get from this customer (the "strategic value" of the customer) by asking more.

Exhibit 4-2
Customer Differentiation Matrix: Implementing Marketing Concepts

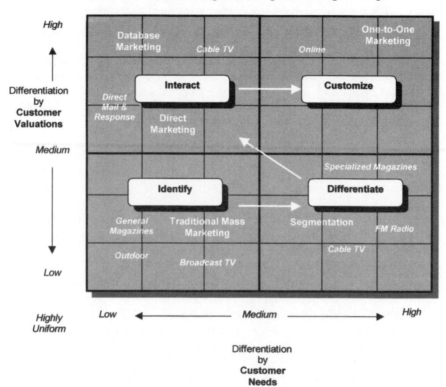

• *Customize*: A customer has to be able to define the parameters of his own product or service, based on his/her needs and values. The firm must be willing and able to customize some aspects of its value chain.[31]

Like frequent flyer programs, these principles aim toward creating loyal customers. Historically, however, far more is involved.

   In each case, the one-to-one marketer is not, strictly speaking, engaging in something entirely new, but building on the past historical concepts and knowledge. While identification of customers requires mass marketing, customer differentiation would be impossible without segmentation techniques. While customer interaction presumes the use of direct marketing technologies, customization would not be cost-effective without the use of web-driven marketing techniques. This historical zigzag—from mass marketing to niche marketing to loyalty marketing to one-to-one marketing—is predicated on technology evolution which, in turn, has made possible the use of certain dominant (media) advertising and promotion approaches (Exhibit 4-2).

Due to its reliance on real time interactivity *and* exploitation of customization, one-to-one marketing *does* represent a qualitatively new phase in the history of marketing. It is a revolutionary stage. Now customers *can* respond (and, as any website manager could readily acknowledge, they do). That is bound to accelerate the shift of bargaining power from the sellers to the buyers. Still, even this marketing phase should not be understood as autonomous, just as the past marketing approaches should not be seen as irrelevant for the purposes of the one-to-one marketer. On the contrary, even the most highly differentiated web-driven one-to-one marketing should be understood as a new historical layer in the ongoing evolution of the marketing concept.

The Hewlett-Packard Experience. By 1998, Hewlett-Packard, had in place some 100 different one-to-one marketing initiatives that were being tracked around the world in different divisions. Each initiative focused on a specific customer, selected customers, or the business units implementing the initiative. The latter would have to generate adequate return on investment. "H-P's goal," said Peppers, "was to structure each initiative so that it would be more or less self-funding and had a measurable set of results."[32] In mass marketing, brands had managers watching out for them, but customers did not. Pursuing a share-of-customer strategy required a customer management organization.

By 1998, Richard J. Justice, director of American sales and marketing for Hewlett-Packard, was a 20-year H-P veteran responsible for the company's recent sales force reorganization toward a more share-of-customer orientation. In 1991, Hewlett-Packard changed its regional sales approach and created a structure in which salespeople concentrated on businesses within specific industries. This modification was perhaps the most visible part of the overhaul of H-P's Computer Systems Organization sales approach. A year after the reorganization, the H-P division successfully identified its key customers and the industries with the highest growth potential. The payoff came in 1994: revenues expanded from $20.3 billion to $25 billion while earnings grew from $298 million to $476 million ($1.18/share to $1.83/share).[33]

Privacy and One-to-One Marketing. Privacy issues have different levels of sensitivity in different cultures. Readiness to implement one-to-one programs is dependent not just on technological skills but also on the level of regulation: the stricter the privacy rules (e.g., Scandinavian countries) or the more extensive the regulatory regimes (e.g., Germany), the more interference with the principles of one-to-one marketing.[34] According to Peppers,

"If regulation will make it illegal for a grocery store to maintain information on the groceries that the customer wants, does that mean that every time the customer goes to order groceries online that he/she would have to redo the grocery list? Why shouldn't the firm be allowed to do it and update it weekly? After all, such a program provides tremendous customer convenience. Eventually privacy regulations will catch up with the reality of one-to-one marketing. But in the short term, any business enterprise has an obligation to have thought through the implications of the privacy issue with respect to their customers and to come up with a policy to protect their customers that still allows them to do business.[35]

In general, says Peppers, one-to-one marketing had far more affinities with direct marketing than with traditional mass marketing.

In mass marketing—or niche marketing, which is just a little more sophisticated form of mass marketing—I carve a mass of population into smaller and smaller little segments. Then I try to find a medium that is right for each segment, but I still don't know who my customers are. I don't have their identities. I can't have a marketing relationship with them if I don't know who they are.[36]

Still, direct marketing and one-to-one marketing were *not* identical.

Traditional direct marketing uses a customer database that I can use to actually identify my customers, individually. *But* the traditional database marketer still is a product-driven marketer. He starts with the product and looks for the customer that is right for that product. So I've got a program manager or a product manager. In other words, I'm not starting with *the customer looking for the product* which is what one-to-one marketing is all about.
One-to-one marketing is really traditional marketing in reverse. I start with the customer and become interactive with that customer. I try to get the customer to tell me something about what he wants. Then I tailor my behavior to the customer, based on that customer's individual needs. This is much closer to direct marketing than to traditional nondirect marketing. But it is still one step beyond the direct marketer's product-driven marketing program.[37]

The basic tenets of one-to-one marketing evolved before the birth of the Web. The fundamentals of direct response were discovered in the post-World War II era. In consumer marketing, their Web-related applications emerged after the launch of the browsers around 1993 and 1994—including the first and legendary online consumer marketing campaign. Modem Media's Zima site provided a model for others to come. Instead of low-cost solutions, this interactive ad agency opted for strategic positioning; it chose *value* for *price*. Where others provided similar offerings at declining prices, Modem would ceaselessly differentiate its offerings: the first tried to do the same thing *better* (low-cost solutions), the second would do things *differently* (differentiation). These efforts were rewarded when Modem redesigned the Zima website.

THE STORY OF ZIMA: FROM HOME PAGES TO WEBSITES

"Zima was the first consumer marketing campaign on the Internet, period," says Robert "Bob" Allen, president of Modem Media.

Certainly, we had done a lot of consumer marketing through other electronic vehicles, through Prodigy or America Online or using interactive telephone systems, and so on. But Zima was truly the first consumer campaign on the Web. In effect, a lot of it was on instinct as opposed to research. It was a brand new product that was being introduced by Coors Brewing Co. They wanted to associate the product with things that were cool and cutting edge. At that time, the Internet was just right around the corner, the focus of a lot of press, in every newscast, and so on. Yes, it was more of a timing issue than anything else: *we* were looking for some sort of a vehicle to promote this new medium. Zima became the vehicle; the Internet provided the media. The Web campaign featured a lot of original content; that was something new. The content also was heavily branded. I see it as an online brand extension, as opposed to trying to replicate the product online.[38]

A Different Marketing Campaign, Really . . .

The story of Zima began in 1991, when Coors put together a team drawn from production, marketing, public relations, and the company's ad agency Foote, Cone & Belding. The mission was to create an "alternative" to beer, starting from scratch. Hoping to ride two trends—consumer experimentation and New Age beverages—the Z team conducted hundreds of focus groups, testing everything from the taste to the name, taken from the Russian word for winter. The concept: create something different, appeal to young adults, and minimize cannibalization of existing business. While the competitors were also concocting new brews, most products died fast. Miller Brewing Co.'s Qube clear malt, for instance, generated a lot of curiosity and trial, but the vast majority gave up the brand after just one try.[39]

When Zima was tested in three markets in the fall of 1992, it scored high, almost like with the introduction of Coors Light. True, some team members felt that the repeat sales were not encouraging, and that the business was drifting toward women, who drank far less beer. Yet, most doubts were overcome by the publicity that accompanied the national rollout of Zima in early 1994: the fluted-glass bottles, the eye-catching in-store displays, and one of the first consumer-product websites. In 1994 alone, Coors lavished a staggering $38 million on Zima, *some 38% of its entire ad budget*. Much more was spent on packaging, merchandising, and product development. Rivals Miller Lite and Budweiser were beginning to falter, but Coors, certain that it had a gusher, bet on Zima rather than exploit their weaknesses.[40]

As the first and one of the most influential consumer marketing campaigns on the Web, the Zima activities provided a powerful model for Modem's rivals and incumbent agency networks.[41] Undoubtedly, the Zima website did manage to crystallize the "best practices" of Internet marketing communications by the mid-1990s, just as it held forth the future ad potential of the Web. Soon Modem's ingenious Internet campaign would be emulated from Silicon Valley to Madison Avenue.[42]

Internet Media Plan, and Objectives. As Modem's account director for consumer products, John C. Nardone managed the overall strategic direction for all consumer-oriented business. Having established his career as a product marketing strategist at such leading consumer product companies as Procter & Gamble and PepsiCo, Nardone emphasized the overall objectives of the marketing program, even prior to thinking about a given project's Web media strategy:

• Are we trying to build awareness?
• Change consumer perceptions?
• Drive traffic to a website?
• Is it a "direct response" program, in which we are asking consumers to take immediate action?
• Or is it a "branding" assignment, in which we want to build a certain image or association with the product?[43]

These objectives were not seen as mutually exclusive. In the Zima case, the purpose of the integrated marketing communications campaign was certainly to build awareness. It sought to utilize rather than change consumer perceptions. Non-Internet media vehicles (TV commercials) were used to drive traffic to Zima's website. The program did seek to "loyalize" the consumer through various direct-response initiatives, including e-mail responses, relationship marketing, and active dialogue between the consumer and the vendor.

Consumer Use of the Web: From Site-Centric to Needs-Based Solutions. For Modem, the design and launch of the website was *not* the objective; rather, it was a means to an end. The function of the Zima site was to serve the *advertiser*. In the early "site-centric" Web advertising efforts, the advertiser owned a piece of Web real estate, and tried to herd consumers to it. According to the theory, the consumer had a specific information need and the goal was to fulfill it. Unlike most early Web advertising efforts that were "site-centric" in approach, Modem favored a "user-centric" approach. In this case, the consumer is thought to be online to pursue an interest. He/she might start with a search or directory, but is likely to follow links from one site to the next, pursuing items that catch his/her attention. This sort of classic "surfing" behavior is much less goal oriented. Skeptical about the site-centric approach, Modem focused on a user-centric approach, which recognized the consumer and his/her individual session as the main point of the strategy.[44]

Targeting. Traditional media is targeted at consumers based on demographic information. For instance, media buyers purchase TV or radio spots based on a broad range of age and gender breaks. In the mid-1990s, only few Web properties had such demographic information on their users. So the very first buyers used two basic methods of targeting. They relied on "psychographics" rather than demographics. In practice, this translated to targeting by interest and related environments. And the buyers might target specific search words on the search engines and directories. Say, a consumer sought the word "stocks," the buyer could show him/her an ad for online brokerage services.[45]

After the mid-1990s, several sites began to use more sophisticated methods in targeting. Now they relied on users' technical characteristics (e.g., operating system, browser type, ISP, etc.); time of day; intelligent agents to dynamically match ads to the users; the reach and frequency of ad delivery to ensure that identical consumer groups would not have to view the same ad over and over.

In 1994, Coors had identified the early adopters of the Internet as the potential users of Zima Clearmalt, an alcoholic beverage. The company recruited Modem Media to design and launch the Zima website, which targeted consumers who were 21–34 years old, opinion leaders, relatively upscale, and skewing heavily male (i.e., a typical Internet early-adopter segment). Prior to the mid-1990s, the penetration of the Web remained too low for extensive consumer marketing, but it did allow efforts to attract certain specific user segments. Zima's demographics coincided with those of the early Internet—youthful male cohorts, higher social-economic strata, higher education, and lifestyle orientation.

Launched nationally in 1994 into the thick of the New Age beverage craze, Zima was sold as something different, defined mostly by what it was *not*: not a beer, not a wine cooler, and without even a color. Early TV ads featuring Z-speak contributed to a decidedly offbeat image. "What'z in it?" asked a barkeep. "It'z a zecret. It'z zomething different," replied the mysterious pitchman in his white suit and black hat. Lured by a quirky ad campaign, twenty-somethings rushed to try the strange new brew. The first results were stunning. Eager to try the new brand, Generation Xers propelled Zima to a 1.2% share of the beer market, almost overnight.

The First Online Consumer Campaign

In general, any media plan on the Web can either bring consumers to the interactive message (pull), or bring the message to interactive consumers (push). The first provided a "herding" model of driving consumers to a website, while the second reflected a wider view of the Web as a flexible communications vehicle (e.g., the emergence of Web-driven direct marketing). In the Zima.com case, the herding model was used in cross-promotion (e.g., TV commercials as traffic builders for the website), while the second one exploited the Internet's more inherent capabilities— especially e-mail

Use E-Mail to Trigger Interest and Establish Dialogue. The Zima campaign originated from an e-mail address printed on the inside label of the bottle, "youcan@zima.com." The idea to use such "bottle mail" to approach potential buyers was bold at a time when Internet penetration was still very low and most Americans did not even know what e-mail addresses meant. Still, the brand received thousands of e-mail messages from curious consumers across the nation. It served as a true *marketing channel*, whose function was to make potential users aware and interested in a new brand. Soon after the e-mail launch, the advertiser set up a home page on the burgeoning World Wide Web (www.zima.com). Zima had become one of the first, if not *the* first, national consumer packaged goods to have its own dedicated server.

Graphic Statement: The Home Page as a Brand Interface. Zima also exploited the notion of a home page as a kind of a brand interface. Since it was the first thing that the users saw upon entering the website, it also was the most critical aspect on the site. Or as Marrelli put it: "Within seconds, the consumer should get an idea of what the site is all about and where to go within the site. If the opportunity is missed, the surfer may never return, given the wide array of choices at his/her disposal."[46]

If the rivalry was already evident, it would get far more intense in the coming years. After all, the Zima site was developed in parallel with the launch of the commercial browsers. In June 1994, there were more than 2,700 websites; almost 14% of them were commercial (.com). By June 1996, just two years later, the number of websites had boomed to an estimated 230,000, of which 68% were commercial. No previous marketing channel in history had had to deal with such a drastic proliferation of distribution pipelines. *This* was the challenge of the interactive media that Edwin Artzt, former chief executive of Procter & Gamble, had just declared the primary threat for all mass marketers in the new era. But it was no longer in the future; it was becoming reality. Interactive ad agencies would have to find ways to deal with the challenge and the opportunity.

Cross-Promotions: Leveraging through Familiarity. In Zima's case, the de-

Exhibit 4-3
Modem Media: The Graphic Statement

The corporate logo of Modem Media reflects its efforts to express things through graphic statements:

"Puzzled? Turn to Modem."

The message targeted America's big business and mass marketers, in particular incumbent brand leaders who did not know what to do in a new competitive environment. They had a problem. Modem provided the solution.

In the case of Zima, the design team created a banner graphic that leveraged imagery directly from the television commercials.

A message directly accessible by clicking on the main banner advises consumers that Zima is for "Adult Humanz Only," and that "21 Means 21." By placing the message directly on the banner, Zima is making a statement to younger members of the audience that the site (and more importantly, the beverage) is not for them.

Source: Modem Media, www.zima.com.

sign team created a banner graphic that leveraged imagery from the TV commercials. "It's a good example of integrated marketing communications, where high familiarity with the television spots was used to the brand's advantage in cyberspace," notes Marrelli (compare Exhibit 4-3).[47] Technology, however, entailed inherent constraints in cross-promotions.

In the early days of Internet marketing, most marketers stressed that the graphic elements on a home page should be as small as possible (in kilobytes), without compromising the visual strategy. After all, in 1994, most consumers still surfed the Web at the slow 14.4 baud rate. With rapidly-increasing access speeds, the significance of this "technical" limitation was bound to lessen in time. Typically, the most astute user-friendly online providers, such as America Online, designed web pages assuming the use of the least fast modems, (i.e., avoiding highly elaborate visual schemes and favoring instrumental yet expressive graphics). Because large and visually bold graphics were time consuming and often troublesome to download, many users were more willing to stop the process and abandon the page. The website was inherently instrumental and not merely expressive. All graphic elements had to serve a purpose—to solidify the direct relationship between the consumer and the brand.

To an Internet marketer, however, the access speed was only a part of the problem that really involved the entire graphic statement of the site. The web pages simply had to be integrated with the overall marketing communications. Internet companies and interactive ad agencies were the first to grasp the full significance of cross-promotions. The advantage of a known brand favored aggressive first movers, including search engines (Yahoo!), online service providers (America Online) and Internet retail companies (E*Trade, Amazon). They all were eager and willing to build brand rapidly. It also seemed to benefit those incumbents that saw their opportunity quite early in the game, including media companies (Time Warner's Pathfinder), newspapers (*Wall Street Journal, New York Times*), international carriers (MCI, AT&T), computer magazines (*ZDNet*) and so on. Hybrid operations sought to develop online and offline capabilities simultaneously (e.g., CNET's online and cable news services). In each case, the objective was identical: to leverage a new brand through the familiarity associated with the old brand. Such a brand extension diversified risk and could optimize audience—by, say, directing TV audiences to websites and user traffic to TV services.[48]

Navigation Structure: From Billboards to Interactivity. When American corporations launched their first home pages, some tried too hard (Levi-Straus's highly complex multimedia experiments), while most tried too little (the gray one-way websites with recycled newsletters and abbreviated annual reports). As users did not rush to the sites, companies gained a better understanding of the importance of the navigation structure. If the website's graphic statement should go hand in hand with proper access speed and leverage on existing brand equity, navigation structure refers to the inherent properties of the site's interactive capabilities.

Toward the end of the 1990s, most major websites (advertisers, Web publishers, corporations) had a primary statement consisting of complex

Exhibit 4-4
The Zima Fridge

For Zima, the decided navigation structure was a combination of buttons and an image map. The various buttons were clearly evident on the top of the home page.

The image map utilized in Zima.com was branded "The Fridge." It pointed to ten discrete areas (other pages) within Zima. com.

"The reason for utilizing a virtual refrigerator as a navigation structure should be obvious. A refrigerator is an excellent real-world metaphor for virtual beverage to be located. Where can one get real Zima? In a refrigerator, of course. Where does one access Zima digital content? Naturally, in 'The Fridge'."
—Charles Marrelli, Senior Copy Writer, Modern Media

Source: Modern Media.

and visually rich image maps, and a text-based clickable table of contents. However, it was the Zima fridge that played a critical role in the popularization of the image map (i.e., a single graphic with multiple hotspots programmed into it). Most often, these hotspots hyperlinked internally to the site, even if the web pages also included a list of preferred links (Hot Links). Zima's navigation structure was a combination of an image map and buttons. The image map itself was branded ("The Fridge") and pointed to some ten different areas within the website. The refrigerator served as a useful metaphor to locate a virtual beverage (Exhibit 4-4).

In the long term, the *concept* of the navigation structure would prove more important than the specifics of its *execution*, which were subject to the Internet dynamics. As the users navigated toward the Zima Fridge and opened its door, it actually squeaked. At the time, the use of Web-driven *audio* was still a relatively new experience with a regular PC. Certainly, CD-ROMs and multimedia had familiarized many users with stand-alone audio and video, but *networked* audio and video represented a new experience. For a novice Internet user, it was as exciting as if the Little Tramp of Chaplin's early silent movies had shaken the moviegoers by bursting into talk with loud sound, clear voice, and transparent audio.

Product Information: The Use of Hyperlinked Web Pages. To the creators of Zima, *information* was not only a means of marketing but also the most inherent determinant of customer relationship management. At CUC International, the founders of Modem Media had learned about electronic catalogs. As students of direct marketing, they knew that information was the common denominator of the Web and classic direct mail. And as advertising practitioners they strongly believed in the potential of the Web in brand building. Unlike any other historical media, the Web could provide massive amounts of information through hyperlinked web pages. The interactive ad agency could frame product information, but its specific use depended on the surfer.

In the mid-1990s, the technologies were still primitive but, ultimately, Internet marketing would transcend the existing types of advertising (i.e., media advertising, direct marketing, and promotions). Like TV and cable, the Internet would eventually optimize the "visual look" of traditional media. Like newspapers and magazines (but even more so), it could provide massive amounts of product information; unlike both, it also could offer an interactive feedback loop. Like sales promotion, the Internet made possible cross-promotions, which had become familiar since the late 1980s with industry leaders (e.g., networks, studios, and fast-food chains). And like direct marketing, the Internet could both trigger a response *and* provide means for fullfilment; but unlike direct, it could provide both in real time—instantly and far more cost-efficiently.

For Zima, the website provided an excellent possibility to publish product information. Since Zima was introduced nationwide in 1994 and sought to define an entire category of alcoholic beverages, the product was bound to give rise to a number of questions in the marketplace. Emulating the popular Internet convention of the FAQ (Frequently Asked Questions), the creators developed "Re: Zima" which would address the most obvious consumer questions, albeit in an entertaining and slightly offbeat manner. The function of the style was to make the responses more palatable to the target audience (Exhibit 4-5).

The Feedback Loop: Proactive Contact. To use an interactive medium without using its interactive capabilities sounds contradictory. Yet, this is precisely what happened in consumer marketing in the early days of the Internet. Unfamiliar with the conventions and potential of the Web, many consumer marketers sought to impose a broadcast model onto the Internet. Initially, such mistakes were forgiven. But as the enabling technologies got more complex, the number of industry rivals accelerated, the higher-speed access solutions moved from test markets to mass markets, and the consumers themselves became increasingly sophisticated with the ways of the Web, the absence of interactivity would no longer be acceptable.

In the Zima case, the creators of the website utilized the e-mail com-

Exhibit 4-5
"Welcome to Interrogative Heaven. Re: Zima"

It is a repository of the most relevant and burning questions you might have about Zima Clearmalt. To expedite things, all of the questions have been indexed at the top of this page. So raise your hand. Hopefully there will be a Zima in it. What?

- What is Zima?
- What are the ingredients in Zima?
- Where is Zima available?
- What is the alcohol content of Zima?
- How many calories are in Zima?
- Who owns Zima Beverage Company?
- How is Coors stock listed?
- Does Zima Clearmalt show up on a breathalyzer?
- What is the sugar content?
- What kind of alcohol is in Zima Clearmalt?
- When and where was Zima introduced?
- Where did the name Zima come from?
- Who is the advertising agency for Zima?
- How is Zima priced?
- Is Zima pasteurized?
- How do I contact Zima?

What is Zima?
Zima just is. Why question it. Go with the flow. For those of you who absolutely have to know, Zima is a malt-based alcohol beverage that is light, clean and refreshing. It has the same alcohol content as beer. . . . Zima is a refreshing alternative to beer, wine, wine coolers or mixed drinks.

What are the ingredients in Zima?
Most of the ingredients are zecret. But, here are a few hints. Do the words barley malt, natural carbohydrates, hops, water and yeast sound familiar? There's also a bit of class, a touch of self-respect and a smidgen of general happiness in Zima. Can you taste it? And, of course, we would be remiss if we didn't mention the proprietary flavor formulation of #$%@ and *%$$!. Thanks for asking!

Where is Zima available?
Zima was initially introduced in three test markets in September, 1992 and was rolled out nationwide in February, 1994. Zima is presently only available in the United States (if you're 21, that is).

What is the alcohol content of Zima?
Zima has about the same alcohol content as a premium beer . . . 3.7% by weight (4.6% by volume).

How many calories are in Zima?
There are 148 calories per 12 ounces . . . that's 12.34 calories per ounce.

When and where was Zima introduced?
Zima was first introduced on Earth in September, 1992 in three test markets: Syracuse, NY; Sacramento, CA; and Nashville, TN. Strangely enough, one gentleman, Paul Douglass, was the first individual to drink the beverage in all three markets. He subsequently changed his name to Paul Zouglass.

Source: Modem Media.

ponent, "the most basic, yet crucial aspect of online advertising."[49] For years, even decades, advocates of direct and relationship marketing had spoken for the kind of interactivity that the Web was about to make possible—and that the proliferation of marketing channels and the ensuing noise had made vital. Even before the rise of Internet marketing, relationship marketers like Regis McKenna had associated the reality of channel multiplication with the need for interactivity:

[advertising's dirtly little secret is that] it serves no useful purpose. In today's market, advertising simply misses the fundamental point of marketing—adaptability, flexibility, and responsiveness. The new marketing requires a feedback loop; it is this element that is missing from the monologue of advertising but that is built into the dialogue of marketing. The feedback loop, connecting company and customer, is central to the operating definition of a truly market-driven company: a company that adapts in a timely way to the changing needs of the customer.[50]

By adding an e-mail feedback loop (a "write to us" web page), the creators of the Zima campaign allowed and encouraged their audience to interact. The feedback loop had two significant functions: First, active interactivity anticipated equally active transactions that were expected to accelerate with electronic commerce. Second, the concept of the feedback loop is more important than its particular execution. While the Zima campaign relied on e-mail, other interactive methods would become available with the development of the enabling technologies.

As the creators of the Zima campaign soon found out, most comments were rather innocuous ("Keep up the good work!"). In other cases, the comments could expose problems that the brand management needed to know ("I've had a difficult time finding Zima on the shelves in my area."). In order to maintain a quality relationship, the advertiser had to reply to all e-mail correspondence. With Zima and other consumer marketers, the volume of incoming e-mail necessitated a program that automatically sent a reply back to the consumer. These mailbots, or infobots, simply acknowledged the message and thanked the consumer for the feedback. Thereafter, the Zima responses were individually scanned by the brand's customer service department. When and if a second level of response was deemed necessary (". . . sorry you've had trouble finding Zima," for example), a more personal correspondence was sent out. Relying on the emergent one-to-one dialogue, the brand management also had all e-mail bundled monthly and delivered to key members of the team. The responses served the purpose of consumer research. By scanning the aggregate feedback, the brand team could qualitatively assess the performance of the brand, the effectiveness of the website, and the psychographics of the consumer.[51]

Finally, the feedback loop used a proactive Zima e-mail method that broadcasted messages to the "Tribe Z" affinity club on roughly a monthly basis. In the coming years, this concept became quite popular from Web publishers like the *Wall Street Journal Interactive Edition* to the emergent Internet retail operations like Amazon.com. The proactive feedback loop evolved from a *mutual* agreement between the website and the consumer: once the latter *voluntarily* placed himself/herself on the list, he/she could expect various kinds of Zima-related newsletters, late-breaking product news, site enhancements, and so on. From the marketer's standpoint, the proactive method allowed consumers to self-segment themselves for the purposes of the product marketing, and thereby to contribute to the quality and frequency of the dialogue.

Ideally, the more valuable the consumer segments were for the purposes of Zima, the more personal, intensive, and extensive correspondence they received. The personal tone of the Zima authority, the frequency of interactive communications, and the intensive use of the feedback loop depended on the attractiveness of the customer segment ("heavy users," "light users," etc.) and whether the attractiveness was defined in terms of desirable demographics or on the basis of actual purchase behavior.

Simulated Demonstrations. In an online environment, software marketers can make samples of their product available online. While these "digital intangibles" can be distributed directly to the consumers via the Internet, the delivery of consumer packaged goods requires physical distribution and is far more complex logistically. Still, marketers could use the new medium to portray benefits through product demonstration. The early broadcast television provided a precedent. In the 1950s, the first generation of TV commercials sought purposefully to visualize the "unique selling proposition" of Rosser Reeves. Ted Bates & Co., for instance, positioned Anacin as a "tension headache" remedy by diagramming a tension headache. In time, the concept found more sophisticated portrayals, including Bulova's watch torture test. From the Chevrolet spots to Speedy Alka-Seltzer, TV commercials all relied on the clever use of graphic and visual elements to demonstrate the product benefits.

Relying on this rich heritage of American TV advertising, Modem developed the Zima Gold virtual sipping demonstration when the brand, in the spring of 1995, introduced a new product. The advertiser sought the agency's assistance in driving consumers to sample Zima Gold. Modem used creative copy and visuals to simulate a consumer trying Zima Gold for the first time. Each time the viewer clicked on the Zima Gold bottle, less beverage appeared in the bottle. While such an execution was theoretically possible in traditional print or broadcast media, it would not have been cost-effective (print) and not nearly as interactive (print or broadcast).

Frequently Updated Content. Prior to the launch of HotWired, most web-sites (mass marketers, Web publishers, corporations) relied on repur-posed or recycled content. For cost reasons, the use of original content was considered neither profitable nor useful. Relying on a "site-centric" approach, many of the first Web advertisers presumed that a mere pres-ence would guarantee user traffic. The reality was different. Like a diner, a website is open 24 hours, but to keep "regulars" coming back for more, it must occasionally change the menu. Without *frequently updated content*, a website leaves users cold.

In order to provide freshness to the Zima site, the creators developed a character named Duncan to deliver a biweekly journal that kept the site interesting for the online audience. Duncan was the ultimate Zima drinker, the stereotypical and regular Zima guy. While he was never actually seen by the online audience, his journal installments appeared on the site. The creative idea was to put the "cool" character in a number of different situations for drinking or purchasing the product, whether Duncan was mountain biking, paying taxes, or dating his virtual girl-friend, Alexandria. The idea was not only to launch a new brand, but a new brand that encouraged purchase behavior. Similarly, multimedia elements (e.g., images, icons, sounds, links) were woven into the copy not only to exploit the Web as a medium but also to enhance and main-tain the interactive relationship in the brand environment.

The addition of frequently updated content was crucial in the early days of Internet marketing; it served to accelerate interest in the new medium. Similarly, basic cable did not really take off among advertisers until aggressive early entrants like Turner began to invest heavily in original content.[52] In the mid-1990s, the Duncan installments were Mo-dem's version of cable's original content in the late 1980s.

Consumer Research and Development on the Web. The designers of the Zima site understood that the Internet was well suited for the purposes of consumer research, even better than direct mail or telephone voice response (TVR). Even a successful direct mail campaign often generates only a 1–2% response rate. The click rate of Web campaigns was not dissimilar. Unlike direct mail, however, a Web questionnaire was far more cost-efficient and user-friendly; and it did not carry the burden of the relatively high-cost postal service. Like telephone voice response, the Web questionnaires offered multiple choice environments. But unlike au-tomated phone surveys, such questionnaires were far less cumbersome to conduct.

In a sense, consumer research and development on the Web could be regarded as a mere instance of the feedback loop. However, systematic, consistent, and reliable Web questionnaires provided continuous infor-mation that could greatly benefit both the Web developers and the site managers.

Interlinked Communities. "One of the most fascinating things about Zima.com is that you get to *leave* it," writes Modem's Marrelli on the brand's pointers to other websites. The entire World Wide Web is built largely upon the notion of *hyperlinking*, whereby a Web surfer jumps from one site to the next like digital hopscotch."[53]

What makes the Web unique and so dynamic is the idea of an inter-linked community—or, as we might say today, an "online community." The creators of the *World Wide* Web certainly were motivated by a McLuhanian vision of a globally interlinked community. Yet, the first Internet marketers may have been more perceptive. If global marketing was so hard and the privilege of only a few multinational corporations in the offline world, it might be quite unrealistic to expect that the mere presence of the Web would suddenly change things. Even more impor-tantly, if the U.S. marketplace had only recently gone through a severe fragmentation as a result of channel proliferation, it was almost inevi-table that the Internet, through its accelerating channel multiplication, would dramatically contribute to channel multiplication. It would cer-tainly not reduce but rather accelerate the growth of distribution pipe-lines.

In order to survive, the websites would have to accomplish profita-bility. Global visions were nice and fine but irrelevant to an advertiser who was interested in the fate of a specific brand in a specific online community. In the Zima case, a major component of the site was to point to other websites that offered interesting and relevant content for the target market. Labeled "Z-Spots" (and discernible in The Fridge), the purpose of this web page was to give consumers an index to other com-pelling sites on the Web. It was only natural to assume that the Zima segment would be interested in Zima-related directories. Therefore, the showpiece of Z-Spots was the Zima Bar and Restaurant Guide, a kind of a preliminary Zagat or a "directory of directories" for users looking for local nightspots across the country.[54]

In addition to the Z-Spots, the Zima.com also retained users within the site by offering downloadable multimedia files, including digital im-agery ("Views"), shareware video games ("Diversions"), desktop icons ("Icons"), and others. Certainly, the offerings were not new and unique. CNET, for instance, was providing entire lists of downloadable files. Still, the fact that these offerings were provided by an *advertiser* was a new development. In both cases, such activities served as transaction exper-iments preparing for the coming of electronic commerce. In the Zima case, the idea of Z-Spots was narrow; it would allow the advertiser to direct traffic to brand-related sites that did not pose competitive threat to Zima. While Internet-based directories had long thrived in military, research and academic online communities, *Web*-driven lists like Yahoo! were emerging hand in hand with the launch of Zima.com whose Z-

Spots served as a miniature version of a typical search engine. At the time, however, these engines were driven by the building of their directories rather than the user audiences that used the lists.

As such, Z-Spots anticipated the business concept of the first search engines, the transition to the idea of destination sites and later portals. By 1997 and 1998, several strategic groups of content/aggregators struggled to serve as *the* intermediary between the users and the World Wide Web. *If*, instead, advertisers would try succeed in serving as *direct* gatekeepers of content, the intermediary role of the strategic content/aggregator service providers would become suspect, even obsolete. *That* was the dream of direct marketers and electronic commerce companies and the nightmare of the online intermediaries—or "infomediaries" as they would soon be called.

Affinity Clubs, Distinction and Exclusivity: Toward Portal Strategies. In order to fight channel proliferation and build strong customer loyalty, relationship marketers, in the 1980s, learned to add financial benefits into the offerings, in particular frequency marketing and club marketing programs. Based on the acknowledgement that only 20% of a company's customers could account for 80% of its business, frequency marketing was designed to provide rewards to customers who bought frequently and/or in substantial amounts—from airlines like American Airlines to hotels like Marriott. In the process, many companies also created *affinity* groups, or clubs, among their customers to bond them closer to the company. Some club memberships were offered upon purchase or promised purchase of a certain amount, or by paying a fee.[55] Due to the Internet dynamic, *inter*activity would proceed, anticipate, and encourage *trans*actions. While the mere presence of such clubs would ensure distinction, the active participation of the user could be rewarded by exclusivity. The Zima site was not an exception; on the contrary, it offered means of bonding that both reflected existing efforts by the online service providers (especially America Online) to create virtual communities, but also provided new and original ideas for the Web and online community developers of the OSPs.

Early in the Zima online initiative, the creators developed "Tribe Z," an online affinity group to enrich a better communication channel between the Zima brand and self-selected Zima drinkers. The product itself ruled out those members of the online audience who were below the legal age limit to consume the product (hence the main banner texts, "Adult Humanz Only," and "21 Means 21").[56] After they filled out an online survey, the Tribe Z members gained access to an exclusive area of Zima.com (i.e., The Freezer). The Zima creators thought that "[The Freezer] gave high affinity consumers a sense of exclusivity in their own *private* online environment. For the advertiser, it provided an extra level of data collection. Since each consumer was given a unique password, unobtrusively tracking the consumer within the environment was possible."[57]

But the site developers were also after something far more ambitious. Their objective was to enable the members to inhabit the brand space that, ultimately, would turn them into a "cohort with the brand." By allowing the Tribe Z members to obtain personalized home pages, they would also brand the members for the purpose of the advertiser and data gathering.[58]

The Zima campaign did not rely on consumer responses only. As Modem would later be assigned to develop "beyond the banner" experiences for iVillage's *ParentSoup* and *About Work* online communities, the latter would rely on the experiences of the Zima campaign to enhance customer loyalty and branded online communities.

Although the online vision and execution were new and pioneering, their concept went back to the historical first efforts to create club marketing in America. Just as, for instance, iVillage's *ParentSoup* and *About Work* online communities, not to speak of their *Book Club* or *Money* and *Relationships* areas, tended to attract somewhat different user segments, the first club marketing developers soon realized that different clubs represented different degrees of segmentation. When Lester Wunderman, in the mid-1950s, developed a "department store" of record clubs, its departments were called divisions ("Classical Music," "Broadway Shows," "Jazz," "Listening and Dancing," while others would be added as needed). Similarly, online communities like iVillage.com would evolve from a basic concept ("The Women's Network") which, in time, would generate spinoff communities ("Parent Soup," "Work from Home," "Relationships," etc.). When Wunderman conceived of the concept of a *multidivision* club, he considered it "a revolutionary change in club design. I was certain that a club that appealed to diverse tastes would attract millions of members."[59]

In 1997, the idea of branded online communities eventually took off. But its *concept* had been dormant for quite a few years. It was the Zima site's Freezer that bespoke for the idea of allowing consumers to "move-in" and place their own home pages within an exclusive realm of the online community (The Freezer). A simple graphic icon concealed the future evolution of branded communities, as well as the "portal mania" of 1997.

Starting in 1994, Modem Media's Zima campaign pioneered the use of the Web in consumer marketing. In the coming years, the basic characteristics of the campaign would be emulated by America's leading mass marketers, Web publishers, and corporations. The most important ones can be condensed into the following:

- Determination of the Internet media plan and objectives;
- Focus on needs-based solutions in the consumer use of the Web;
- The use of e-mail to trigger interest and establish dialogue;
- The graphic statement, or the use of the home page as a brand interface;
- The use of cross-promotions (i.e., leveraging through familiarity);
- The use of navigation structure, from billboards to interactivity;
- The availability of product information (i.e., the use of hyperlinked web pages);
- Focus on the feedback loop and proactive contact;
- Availability of creative, simulated demonstrations;
- The use of frequently updated content to keep the site content fresh;
- The reliance on Web-driven consumer market R&D;
- The availability of interlinked communities with the right strategic partners;
- The use of affinity clubs, distinction, and exclusivity to solidify brand loyalty.

After these characteristics had proliferated in the U.S.-driven market-space, they soon emerged in foreign markets. After the mid-1990s, Zima.com was widely copied, cloned, replicated, and imitated as a model best practice in Web-driven consumer marketing. Charles Marrelli, senior copy writer of Modem Media, had reason to see the future of the Zima site bright. After all, it was *the* first mover, *the* precedent, *the* source—and it would only get better with new and futuristic bells and whistles:

The Zima brand has made a clear investment in cyberspace and Web advertising. The site will continue to be maintained, with major interface overhauls occurring on an annual basis . . . With a medium like the Web being constantly in development, the only way to maintain an advantage is to continue to stay on the edge of the technology curve.[60]

A few months later, the Zima.com was gone. Instead, the user who happened to stumble onto the site found a bare screen with a thin explanation: "Zima. A few degrees cooler."

The Site and the Campaign: Triumph and Failure

Undoubtedly, it was Zima that made Modem Media famous and a source of emulation on Madison Avenue. "What makes Modem Media unique is the fact that they put strategy before technology," said Mark Lee, brand manager on Zima.[61] Yet, if a Tribe Z member tried to find his online community in late 1997, he would have discovered a simple web page with no buttons.

In 1994, the Zima campaign propelled the Zima share of the beer market rapidly, but within a year, sales fell by half from 1.3 million barrels to 650,000. In 1996, they dropped an additional estimated 38%. In 1995, Coors was still touting Zima as having great potential, but in a 1996 year-end release, the beverage barely merited a word: the company's 39% earnings rebound, to $47.3 million on sales of $1.7 billion, was achieved by cost-cutting and gains by stalwarts, Original Coors and Coors Light. Abandoning its hope for a powerhouse new product to levitate its market share, the No. 3 brewer was once again staking its future on its flagship brands. In October 1997, *Business Week* published a feature story on "The tale of Zima's extraordinary rise and fall," which the magazine labeled "one of the more embarrassing marketing miscalculations of the decade."[62]

In retrospect, the dazzling early success led to a false sense of strength and complacency. The marketing had created a huge amount of visibility, and Zima became "cool." In the process, the marketers took their own myth for reality, which set up the expectation of a growing, long-term business. Within just months of the rollout, Zima started to go flat. Perhaps, Coors could have retrenched sooner if the marketers had listened to the marketplace. Early on, distributors alerted them that Zima drinkers were mixing the beverage with fruit juice; even the website's consumer research indicated that flavors should have been added. Still, Coors resisted changes, fearing that a flavored product would downgrade Zima to the has-been status of a wine cooler.

Moreover, even though the consumer profile was largely female, Coors stuck to the belief that the brand appealed to men as well. That led to two more critical errors. Convinced that Zima sales could at least hold steady in 1995, Coors experimented with "male" Zimas, settling on a high-octane Zima Gold with a slight taste of bourbon. Rushed into national rollout in the spring of 1995, Gold lasted just six weeks. After the Gold debacle, Coors saw the light and, in 1996, ad spending fell to an estimated $6.5 million. The once hot website became a virtual desert, its games and other interactive features were gone. A much-diminished Zima made money on an operating basis, but Coors was still far from recouping the estimated $180 million it had poured into the launch. The marketing management was more than eager to put the embarrassing Zima affair behind it.

Simply put, the users loved the campaign, but not the taste. In the early 1950s, Alka-Seltzer and Anacin had used broadcast TV, a new medium, for their unique selling proposition, but they *delivered* the promise. The first provided "fast relief"; the second got rid of "tension headaches." Zima, instead, offered a proposition without delivery, which triggered a massive wave of tryouts, but little *repeat* use. The original mystique was not revived by a second wave of ads in 1994. Instead, the once hip drink had become the butt of David Letterman jokes. On Madison Avenue, many who had little faith in Internet marketing considered the Zima debacle the prophecy of their most nightmarish dreams. After all, the debacle coincided with the "market correction" in the Internet and technology stocks.

In retrospect, however, one should distinguish the *campaign* from its *unique selling proposition*. The first delivered, the second did not. Just as Zima.com had demonstrated its creative and technological superiority to other contemporary sites, the debacle only proved the age-old wisdom that no matter how good the campaign, if the product is not worth buying, it will not be sold.

Zima failed. Zima.com triumphed.

THE STORY OF BANNER ADVERTISING: BANNERS, DIRECT, AND STANDARDIZATION

With the launch of the browsers, the privatization of the Internet gained new momentum. After mid-1994, the number of Internet sites or "domains" identified with the ".com" suffix designating commercial sites exceeded the number of education sites represented by the ".edu" suffix.[63] The Internet community of academic and scientific researchers entered a frantic period of change. With the commercialization of the Web, mass marketers had to redefine their offline brands online. After HotWired, banner advertising picked up. After Pathfinder, autonomous sites proved their superiority over umbrella concepts. Yet, the industry had been born and industry standards did not exist yet. How should mass marketers redefine offline brands in an online world? Should one consider the brands web pages within a site? Or should one regard them as domains? And if the latter were true, how could the marketer protect the brand in online flux?

Mass Marketers, Brands, and Domain Names

In August 1995, after the onset of the browser wars, Kraft and Procter & Gamble registered a combined 184 domain names on the Internet (ranging from hotdogconstructionco.com to luvs.com, crisco.com, badbreath.com and dentures.com). It was a significant strategic move. The registration was based on the perceived value of the domain as a generic brand asset—an insight boosted by the soaring valuations of the new Web-driven category killers, from Amazon.com in 1997 to Drugstore.com in 1998.

America's greatest mass marketers were claiming "real estate" in the cyberspace. Having monitored the commercialization of banner advertising for almost a year now, mass marketers concluded that they needed to occupy valuable real estate to secure their brand names in cyberspace. When Donald Trump and Manhattan's powerful realtors paid for air space, they did not buy air. They bought potentially valuable real estate. It would be the same with cyberspace, concluded the mass marketers. Virtual or air—if there was a market, there would be buyers and sellers, and the early entrants would enjoy first-mover benefits.

As the Internet grew and the search engines and other "hubs" were able to direct increasing user traffic to and from certain popular websites, mass marketers had little faith in brand umbrellas. If Pathfinder, despite the muscle of the world's most powerful media and entertainment corporation, had failed, why should lesser known mass marketers fare any better? If Disney, the master of strategic synergy, opted for several websites instead of a single one, why should mass marketers choose differently? And if direct marketers were right in their long-term predictions and a significant portion of transactions were about to migrate to the Web, could marketers wait any longer? By the fall of 1995, mass marketers had drawn their conclusions: The positioning of brands required autonomous websites for each product/brand.

P&G and Kraft dominated their segments in the physical marketplace; now they and other major marketers began to position their brands in the virtual marketspace. After the registrations of the leading global marketers accelerated, regional and national marketers followed suit. Many had little faith in the positive utopias of the Internet pundits; they were driven by negative motivations. If *they* did not build "brand sites," in due time the competition might. When Amazon.com and E*Trade rushed to the cyberspace, bookstore chains and financial services hardly noticed. By the mid-1990s, Amazon was rapidly evolving into a global brand as well as diversifying into other retail segments, while incumbent chains (Barnes & Noble, Borders) were busy trying to understand the new rules of the game. Meanwhile, E*Trade kept cutting prices and brokerages had no alternative but follow the suit and rush to the marketspace—belatedly.

Determined not to repeat the mistakes of bookstore chains and financial services, mass marketers began to mark their territory in the cyberspace. Still, they understood that negative concerns were not synonymous with strategic guidelines. They knew what they should *not* do; they were far less certain about what they *should* do. They did not "discover" brand sites; they "invented" them—through trial and error.

HotWired: The First Sponsored Banner Deals

From its beginnings in the early 1990s, San Francisco-based Wired Ventures, Inc. perceived itself as "a new kind of global, diversified media company engaged in creating compelling, branded content with attitude for print, online, and television."[64] Wired aimed to create a "smart media for smart people around the world"—high quality information and entertainment products aimed at a well-educated, affluent, technologically savvy, and influential consumer group. The Internet made possible a cost-efficient way to reach *globally* the demographic cream advertisers despaired for. Wired took seriously the notion of the *World Wide* Web.

By the mid-1990s, the Wired's business segments included publishing *Wired* magazine and programming original content on the Web through the company's HotWired network of online content sites. In just a few years, the company had developed *Wired* and HotWired into strong brands that widely symbolized the new media and the digital age. With its creative, research, technological, sales, and management expertise, and its established brands, Wired Ventures believed it had created an extensive *platform* from which to launch additional brands across multiple media.

Rather than its 1960s' precedent *Rolling Stone*, *Wired*'s splashy graphic style, fluorescent colors, and flashy feature stories were reminiscent of the trendy and glossy urban magazines *Details* and *Interview*. It was launched to cover the profound changes caused by the convergence of the computer, communications, and telecommunications industries. The magazine made convergence "sexy." Still, the first issue did not feature a word on the Internet, which gained public momentum only a few months later. At the end of April 1996, the paid circulation had grown to an estimated 300,000 in the United States. Clearly, its magazine model was working, from the very beginning. Then it went online.

Wired coined the concept of "digital generation." Still, it was less about "youth culture" and more about those *early adopter* segments attracted by the fashionable issues of the "culture of technology." Through its focus strategy, the magazine carved a profitable niche in the advertising market. The concept of *Wired* was to deliver to the advertisers

the top 10% of creators, managers, and professionals in the information industries, business, government, design, entertainment, the media and education. . . . Before *Wired*, you couldn't efficiently reach the Digital Generation. . . . That's why we created *Wired* and its unique advertising environment. . . . There are a lot of *magazines* the Digital Generation has to read. Now there's one it wants to read.[65]

When the website was launched on the Web on October 27, 1994, it pioneered the most explosive new ad medium since the start of the cable. With 14 charter sponsors and the hip attitude of its parent, Wired Ventures, the site went down in history as the first showcase for Web banner advertising.[66]

Developing an Ad Market for Online Media. The emerging market for online media was not something inevitable, necessary, or automatic. It

OUACHITA TECHNICAL COLLEGE

was a *created* process; it was not discovered, it was invented. It was something that had to be conceived, researched, and developed, often against financial obstacles, prevailing ad practices, and powerful incumbents in media and publishing. During the emergent stage of the Internet media, *risk* and *uncertainty* were the operative concerns, not reward and certainty.[67]

A few agencies had already placed ads on Prodigy; others were building sites for brands like Coors' Zima and networkMCI. "I remember sitting on a plane with Andrew Anker [president of HotWired]," recalls Mark Kvamme, president of CKS Group. "He said, 'We threw up a price, and it was mindboggling that we were getting 10 advertisers.'" Messner Vetere Berger McNamee Schmetterer/Euro RSCG committed four clients to the launch, while Modem Media bought space for AT&T before it even told the client. "There was no guarantee, and we didn't care," acknowledged agency partner G. M. O'Connell. "It was the worst economic buying decision probably ever made." In 1996, most industry observers were looking to advertising not merely to sustain the medium but to save it. Without advertising, Web publishers and all the infrastructure companies were expected to go out of business.[68]

The online advertisers ranged from consumer products companies (e.g., Toyota, VISA) to technology and telecommunications companies (e.g., Silicon Graphics, AT&T). After HotWired discovered that visitors considered registration too inhibiting, the company decided against charging usage fees for its services. Unlike "mainstream" magazines and newspapers, HotWired did not merely repurpose existing feature stories. It featured topics such as politics, travel, arts, entertainment, health, careers, and lifestyle, as well as content based on *Wired* magazine. In a year, it grew to 235,000 subscribers. Relying on *original* content, it raised expectations, intensified competition, and contributed to rising entry barriers.

Historically, it was HotWired that made possible the first marketing efforts on the Web. According to Louis Rossetto, the then-CEO and editorial director of Wired Ventures,

We just felt that we needed some way to advertise in our pages. I don't know why, but from the beginning, I had this image on my mind of a stripe that went across the top of the browser. I didn't even realize that we were inventing it in the process. It just felt so obvious a thing to do, but in fact we were the first. . . . It was much harder to launch *Wired* magazine and get advertisers, even though HotWired was a far bigger risk for an advertiser.[69]

In the process of developing an ad market for its new online media, Wired Ventures encountered many of the obstacles that would later become familiar to the early Internet firms which would try to replicate

Wired's advertising model. As Wired diversified into the online products and distribution channels, it also explored a multitude of new methods of deriving and increasing revenue, including

- long-term advertising contracts and frequency discounts,
- cross-publication advertising packages,
- co-branding of program content,
- user-customized online advertising,
- use of detailed demographic data of online and print consumers,
- relationships with online services for the delivery of online content in exchange for royalties based on user fees.[70]

Between 1994 and 1996, an entire infrastructure sprung up to support the nascent online advertising industry. In the long term, however, even Rossetto did not consider advertising the only viable revenue model. Since few Internet users exhibited any willingness to pay for the medium, he expected increasing competition among publishers in general and newspaper publishers in particular. In order to provide a superior offering, Wired Ventures aspired to offer both content and context (i.e., a virtual community that would eventually serve as "critical mass" for transaction business).

With very few exceptions, people don't want to pay for the medium, at least not in the U.S. . . . . But this business is not just about content, which is what America Online is saying. It's also about the fact that you've got such a large community that you can put things in front of them. Regardless of whether they'll be reading a newspaper or talking to somebody else, you have their attention and you can sell some of it to the advertisers. . . . There's a clear benefit to interactive advertising. More and more advertisers are realizing that. For instance, America Online has eight million people. That's almost the size of a Top-25 TV show in the U.S. It's 50% more than *Life* magazine was at its height. I don't see any reason why they shouldn't sell a significant amount of advertising.[71]

By April 1996, HotWired received 25,000–30,000 visitors per weekday, up from 12,000–19,000 visitors in September 1995. Between 1993 and 1997, Wired's revenues increased from $2.9 million to $47 million, but it continued to generate net losses. In August 1998, the company was bought by Conde Nast Publications (Advance Publications) for an estimated $75 to $80 million. A little while later, Lycos, a major portal, agreed to buy the company for $83 million. The voice of the "digital revolution" continued to exist, but its original owners were gone.

What gave Wired Ventures its place in the history of Internet marketing ensured the company's financial turmoil: Wired's ventures outside magazine publishing proved less than successful, hurting overall profits.

Like so many new online ventures, it caused a lot of initial motion, but proved a money pit.

The Sponsor Model. Insofar as Robert Allen, president of Modem Media, is concerned, HotWired's sponsored Web advertising triggered the birth of Internet advertising. "That was a *defining moment*, that was the first-paid advertising on the Internet," he recalls.

We could see the rise of Web advertising, even prior to the HotWired initiative. In effect, we were selling the Internet as a kind of a coming attraction or something that was right around the corner. We spent a lot of time going to our clients trying to educate them. We also had many clients working with AT&T that was, by its very nature, highly technology-driven. Finally, our clients were looking for means to test those technologies very early on. One of these instruments proved to be HotWired. So we became the first advertising agency in the United States to purchase online media through a Web publisher and then developed the first commercial advertising campaigns that ran in it. The launch of HotWired was the defining moment not only for that company but also for Modem Media and the entire advertising online industry.[72]

Even if HotWired was the first to develop and implement successfully a sponsored banner model for the *Web*, it was not the first to initiate *Internet* advertising. After all, there had been other pioneering companies that had launched operational ad models for the nascent medium, such as Prodigy and CUC International (see Chapter 2). Also, some pioneering Internet marketers think that, historically, the driver of the funding stemmed from the *sponsor* model rather than the sponsored *banner* model. In that sense, the first browsers may have been the first to transfer the marketplace ad model into the marketspace.

"Internet advertising really began with Netscape Navigator, Wired and sponsored banner advertisers came in only *after* sponsored browsers," argues Fergus O'Daly, Jr., former CEO of Poppe Tyson, a critical interactive agency pioneer, and former president of CKS Partners.

At the time, we were working in Silicon Valley with the team that had done Navigator 1.0. A meeting was held between Jim Clark, CEO of Netscape, and David Carlick, my business partner at Poppe. The question came up as to whether they could sell advertising on the Netscape home page that was getting some 20 million visits. At the time, it was the only browser out there. We had our media director call Vick Martin [senior VP of public relations] of AT&T. We offered to sell a banner on the Netscape site for $40,000 for three months. That price was pulled out of thin air. Martin bought the banner on Netscape. Immediately, thereafter, we formed DoubleClick, which got into the business of selling banners to Yahoo! and Excite, whereas we did some work for advertising and publishing sites. The first ad ever to sell on the Web was AT&T's, and it appeared on the Netscape home page. I doubt HotWired had the same effect as the browser. If HotWired was getting a million hits, they were lucky. Netscape got as many as 20 to 25 million unique visitors.[73]

In the long term, the issue of whether Web advertising began with the websites or browsers may not be as significant as that of the evolving structure of bargaining power in the nascent industry. Initially, advertisers, lacking the experience in interactivity, presumed that a mere home site would be enough to attract traffic. When HotWired began to deliver original content, it gained momentum. Still, individual single-content sites would never prove as attractive to user masses as browsers, search engines, and other "portals." As these sites began to invest into their "destination sites," they were able to garner a major portion of ad revenues. And they would continue to dominate ad revenues—but only as long as they served as gatekeepers in access and navigation.

The example of HotWired inspired other publishing houses to join the bandwagon. In November 1994, CMP Publications launched TechWeb with ads from AT&T, MCI, and Tandem Computers. In December 1994, Microsoft began to reevaluate its strategy and licensed Spyglass technology to help it quickly develop a Web browser. The Internet had entered a dramatic growth stage. It was rapidly transcending more traditional and proprietary browser technologies, which had fueled the growth of the online service providers in the early 1990s.

Not everyone adopted HotWired's model, however. In the majority of the new services, companies built different services for different products. Brands were "re-launched" on the Web as distinct and autonomous sites. What would become known as "offline brands" were redefined, redesigned, and repurposed as "online brands." That was the regular course of things. Even while HotWired was launching its site in October 1994, Time Warner had far more ambitious plans. What if one were to reject the concept of a product or service brand site in favor of a far wider notion of a corporate brand that would serve as a kind of an umbrella site?

Pathfinder's Brand Umbrella

Instead of launching autonomous websites for its portfolio of brand properties, Time Warner created a single website, Pathfinder, through which the Web users could access the home pages of distinct brands. These individual brands comprised news weeklies (*Time*), human interest magazines (*People*), movie studios (Warner Bros.), music and record industry (Warner Music), and other properties of the world's greatest media and entertainment company. The function of Pathfinder was to serve as a sort of a "brand umbrella" for the parent's properties. Like HotWired, Time Warner opened the Pathfinder service with test ads from

AT&T. Soon thereafter, it was followed by Ziff Davis's ZD Net on the Web.

After its launch in October 1994, Pathfinder became one of the most visited content sites on the Web. To surfers it connoted not just one or two, but an entire slate of great and longstanding brands. Yet, after only two years of operations, Pathfinder was facing increasing losses (reportedly, at least $8 million annually with no end in sight). It also suffered from seemingly constant management turmoil (with the departure of James Kinsella, the founding editor, and the resignation of Paul Sagan, Time's new media president, the rate of turnover was unusual even on the Web). With the merger of Time Warner and Turner Broadcasting, Pathfinder was often compared to CNN Interactive and CNN Sports Illustrated. The two were among the few profitable Web properties, which was only likely to add to the pressure for profitability.

By October 1996, Forrester Research suggested that Pathfinder had been "marching down the wrong road." The mishmash of content was united only by its common Time Warner ownership, spawning an unwieldy site that was wide-ranging but lacked depth. While popular weekly and monthly magazines provided the core of the content, the site had been forced to spend huge sums for additional staff to provide daily updates. Forrester suggested Time Warner "should blow Pathfinder apart and rebuild the pieces as content networks—deep sites focused on special interests. These focused properties would provide a better user experience while commanding a higher CPM. With the acquisition of Turner, Time Warner has the content stream to land four sites in the top ten rather than rely on the single Pathfinder site." Forrester recommended Time Warner license out any leftover content that did not fit into one of the following categories: news (a combination of CNN.com and *Time* magazine into a single news and analysis site), business and finance (a melding of CNNfn, *Fortune*, and *Money*), sports (a combined CNN/Sports Illustrated offering), and entertainment (the integration of CNN's celebrity coverage with *People* and *Entertainment Weekly*).[74]

Such suggestions bespoke for a focused strategy patterned on the basis of distinct brands, which embraced the Internet as a distributed medium. It would take another two years until Time Warner would really begin to redefine Pathfinder's brand model.

By October 1998, Time Warner removed its digital version of *People* magazine from the Web, making it available only to America Online subscribers. The deal was part of an expanded content alliance that made Time.com, Entertainment Weekly Online, ParentTime and Money.com "anchor tenants" on AOL. Not only did the alliance indicate resignation, but the strategic decision to take People off the Web was still another sign that Time Warner's Time New Media unit was focusing on marketing individual magazines online. Linda McCutcheon, president of

Time New Media, acknowledged that the company's Pathfinder name would eventually fade away in favor of unique brand names for its individual magazines. "Consumers don't go online to find Pathfinder. They think that's a car," she said.[75] The Pathfinder hub approach had failed, and some observers did not spare Time Warner of criticism:

By basically selling the online rights to *People* magazine to America Online for chump change, and by its gradual widespread retreat from the ambitions of Pathfinder, Time Warner is admitting defeat. It is admitting that it cannot compete with upstarts like Yahoo!, Excite, Amazon, and the like. It is admitting that it has no idea how to find an audience on the Web, placing the company's bets behind delivery, not programming. And the heirs to the once-mighty publishing barons at Time Inc. are conceding that while they still sit atop the print magazine mountaintop, they are not prepared for the volcanic changes in media and information that will sweep them from that perch in a few short years.[76]

While the criticism may not have been entirely displaced, the idea of a corporate home page as a brand umbrella has its advantages.

The Potential Advantages of Leveraging Corporate Brand Online. In the *physical* marketplace, many classic companies, from Sony to General Electric, had proved the approach could not only work, but might result in a multiplier effect on financial performance. As a result, one might justify an online brand umbrella through recourse to leveraging the corporate brand. In fact, that precisely had been the original raison d'être of several thriving websites, including the online versions of ESPN and CNN. Similarly, cross-promotion would prove very effective on the Web, from entire sites (CNET) to individual TV shows (the *E.R.* pilot episode of the fall of 1997); it, too, would often use the corporate brand (or other properties) as a source of leverage. Such leveraging often achieved its task through careful crafting of the brand, establishing a key message, integrating communications to reach corporate goals, and seeking a multiplier effect on key audiences. Skillfully implemented, such campaigns had resulted in gaining recognition for the spin-off, and boosting corporate branding on a global scale.[77]

Corporate brands often stem from solid and strong corporations that have been around for quite a while. In other words, they reflect "brand strategies over time."

Corporate Brand Strategies over Time. In his *Building Strong Brands*, David A. Aaker uses real brand-building cases from America's greatest corporations to demonstrate how strong brands have been created and managed. A key issue in managing brands over time—including long-standing corporate brands—is the decision to change an identity, position, or execution. Changing any of these three, argues Aaker, can be expensive and potentially damaging. While an identity change is more fundamental, a change in position and execution can be disruptive as well. In general, the goal should be to create an effective identity whose position and execution will endure and not become obsolete or tired. While there are legitimate rationales to make a change in identity, position or execution appropriate or even necessary, Aaker urges maintaining a consistent identity.[78]

In the Pathfinder case, there was nothing wrong with the theory, but Time Warner may not have been the best possible candidate. In addition, the case demonstrates a "nightmare scenario" of an optimal implementation.

The Actual Disadvantages of the Pathfinder Concept. At Pathfinder, the original plan was an ambitious one. As so often, the intent was noble—to improve the competitive situation of Time Warner's new media unit. However, the preferred objective—changing one of the drivers of brand equity—was not warranted. Time Warner's brands had loyal readers and viewers in the physical marketplace, but these were seldom enamored by the *corporate* brand. A person who read *Fortune, Time,* or *People* enjoyed the features but knew little about Time Inc., and less about Time Warner. A loyal viewer of CNN or CNNfn was interested in current affairs or financial news, but had little regard for Time Warner, which was often seen as a distant, portfolio parent. In other words, the parent was known for its *products and services*, not as a parent. It was not a Disney or a Sony. As such, the transition from marketplace to marketspace was bound to constrain the power of the brand properties. Instead of experimenting with the transition, Pathfinder should have ridden the transition. Yet, for all the right motives, the service, initially, did make all the wrong decisions that may have served to further erode the power of the offline brands.

Strategically, Pathfinder did right by absorbing speedily the "best practices" of the Web; but strategically, it committed a serious mistake by relying on a corporate brand umbrella that had little *offline* justification. For example, the teens who enjoyed rap or grunge were not into the music because of the suits at Time Warner's corporate headquarters. The idea of a corporate home page as a brand umbrella has its advantages, but it presumes highly effective synergies. The latter were rhetorically evoked with the merger of Time Inc. and Warner Communications Inc. in 1989 and, again, with the merger of Time Warner and Turner Broadcasting in 1995. Moreover, these takeover struggles had put the parent under severe profitability attrition struggle to manage massive debt reduction and engage in strategic alliances.[79] Officially, of course, Time Warner executives argued that the company's organizational chart was the model for future media conglomerates. Yet, industry observers often criticized Time Warner for a *lack of synergy* resulting in intradivision roughhousing. Hence, for instance, the publication of *Variety's* critical cover story on Time Warner in March 1994: "SYNERGY, SCHMYN-ERGY!"[80]

Historically, Time Warner had perhaps the most freewheeling, entrepreneurial and highly-decentralized corporate culture of all Hollywood studios. That had been its strength and asset. Yet, by its organization, Pathfinder presumed that it had a highly synergic corporate culture; that the existing offline brand strategy was ineffective (it was not, and it was based on a portfolio of thriving brand properties, not on the parent as a property); that the online paradigm required a new identity or execution (it did not; just because the Web *was* new, an old-style but competitive identity or execution would have done just fine); that a superior identity or execution could be found (it was not, not even after half a decade of financial losses); and that customers were bored with a tired identity and execution (they were not, they just wanted to use the Web as a new means to "meet" that identity). As a result, Pathfinder faced change pressures but was not capable of responding to them. Trying to do things differently was an admirable strategic objective, but it presumed the capability to deliver. Even if Pathfinder had had all the adequate technical skills, it still could not have implemented a consistent corporate brand identity online because it lacked one offline. Consequently, Pathfinder did not generate benefits of consistency, but rather disadvantages of inconsistency—the position eroded, identity symbols suffered, and cost efficiencies turned into lost investment expenditures.

While the theory of a corporate brand umbrella site had its undeniable theoretical advantages, Time Warner was not effectively positioned to implement such vision, either offline or online. Indeed, it may be instructive that even Disney, arguably the most synergistic of all the studios, avoided such a site strategy in its early Internet marketing efforts.

In retrospect, Pathfinder's mistaken strategic assumptions seem obvious. In the mid-1990s, however, it was difficult to see the forest from the trees. Both autonomous and umbrella sites were dependent on banners. What complicated all valuations was the fact that there were *no* industry standards for the banners. While creatives were having a field day testing different formats, salespeople got weary trying to make media deals without numbers, or with numbers that were not comparable. As a result, advertisers waited—they needed reliable and valid numbers. The banners would have to be standardized for industry purposes.

After HotWired introduced sponsored banner advertising, it would take another year and a half before CASIE (The Coalition for Advertsing Supported Information & Entertainment) and the Internet Advertising Bureau agreed to a standard set of banner sizes. The process proved even more interesting than the result. It also set a precedent for the promotion of industry standards.

Banners and Industry Standards

In June 1996, Internet Advertising Bureau (IAB) held its inaugural meeting, with attendees listening to presentations on the mission and organization of the body, which was set up to promote the interests of Web publishers with the advertising community. The bureau's goal was "making the Internet a credible medium for advertisers," said Rich LeFurgy, acting chairman of the organization's steering committee and vice president at Starwave. Other members of the committee included ad executives from Infoseek, Juno Online Services, Microsoft, Prodigy, Softbank Interactive, Time Incorporated New Media, Turner Interactive Marketing & Sales, and CNET: The Computer Network. The steering committee was dominated by members of Microsoft, software companies, and a single Hollywood studio (Time Warner).

IAB's newsletter saw the meeting as historical:

Internet Advertising Bureau: Web publishers get down to business.
Things move fast on the Web and as if to prove the point the IAB (nee Internet Advertising Council) had already managed to undergo a name change before the start of its inaugural meeting, which took place in New York on June 21st. This gathering had the feel of a defining moment as 319 attendees, representing a fair proportion of the Web publishing industry, listened to presentations on the mission and organization of the body which has been set up to promote their interests with the advertising community. The meeting was notable for the fact that at least three-fourths of the attendees were wearing suits—surely a record for a large Web-related gathering, and an indicator of a theme that recurred throughout, which was the Web's need to become more businesslike.[81]

What the newsletter did not mention was a sign of things to come: The very industry that had created television as a commercial medium was nowhere to be found. A new medium was being born, faster than any of its historical predecessors. And, yet, there were no ad agencies in the steering committee. Of course, that would not continue. Ad agencies were counting on external growth (e.g., mergers and acquisitions, strategic partnerships). If they had been unable to develop and nurture interactive and new media skills and capabilities in-house, they would buy them. Between the fall of 1996 and summer of 1997, most leading new media enterprises and interactive ad agencies were acquired, merged, or partnered with the world's leading agency networks, directly or indirectly. But even amidst the M&A waves these ad giants were not sure what they were buying—ad agencies? contemporary direct marketers? or new age software houses? As the industry was changing at sight, the boundaries were seemingly redrawn with each new acquisition.[82]

The IAB favored all developments that were likely to make the Internet a *credible medium* to advertisers. Consequently, the Bureau saw the concentration of bargaining power as positive evolution to the extent that it might facilitate industry practices (e.g., standardization of banners, ad networks to enable high-scale media buys in fragmented markets). Prior to the ad networks, for instance, a simple test of mass marketing in the Internet could require separate negotiations on 125 advertisements. Advertisers often rotated simultaneous campaigns in many different websites. Without jointly-agreed standard banner sizes, however, they lost time and resources from creative content development, at the expense of banner sizing and fitting.[83]

The industry evolution required standards which were promoted not only by IAB but also by CASIE and a joint program of IAB and American ad agencies (American Association of Advertising Agencies, AAAA), as well as advertisers (Association of National Advertisers, ANA). As long as banners on various websites relied on 100–250 different sizes, heterogeneous industry practices held up industry evolution. Consequently, IAB and CASIE decided to replace the diversity of different standards with just half a dozen standard ad types (Exhibit 4-6). Of course, they could only make recommendations and could not force member organizations to agree to the joint rules of the game. Yet, the majority of players did and would adapt to new practices, which served the interest of the entire industry and its individual players.

MASS MARKETERS LAUNCH WEBSITES

About half a year prior to Netscape's historical IPO in August 1995, the Internet valuations began to climb. It was time for the Web publishers (media and entertainment, newspapers, magazines, books) to join the game.

In February 1995, CBS launched its website, while ESPN started pitching advertisers on $1 million charter sponsorship of its upcoming website and other online properties. If marketers, ad agencies, and media and entertainment companies had been slow to react initially, now they were launching sites in droves. In April 1995, Time Warner's Pathfinder signed its first advertisers, AT&T and Saturn, with ads costing $30,000 per quarter. Following the suite, ZD Net started taking ads, while ESPN launched ESPNET SportsZone via Starwave Corp. Soon Interactive Imaginations launched Riddler, a gaming site that incorporated marketer sites as clues. Through the 1980s, Conde Nast had been the trendsetter of magazine business (*Vanity Fair, New Yorker, ym.*), but, unlike many other magazine houses, it did not simply launch websites, but formed its own CondeNet new-media unit.

The fall of 1995 witnessed the building of the first sites of many global brands. CNN launched a website, while Hachette opened Web versions

Exhibit 4-6
Banner Advertising: Standard Ad Types*

In response to requests from the advertising community, the Standards and Practices Committee of the IAB, with input from CASIE, has used market data to examine the full range of banner types: for example, vertical, horizontal, half and button, and sizes currently in use. The Committee has identified the following as the most commonly accepted:

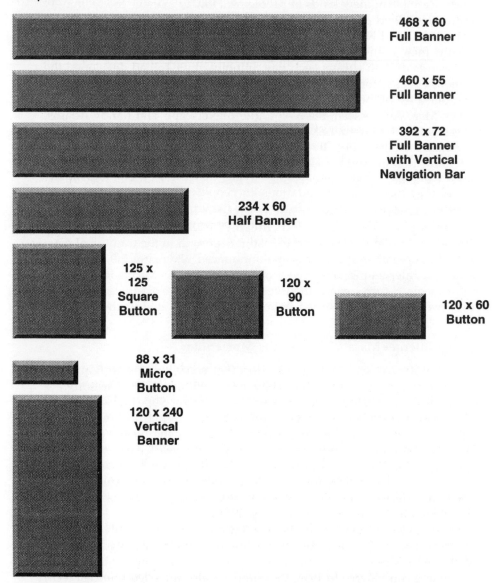

*Pixel Size.
Source: "CASIE & IAB Voluntary Guidelines for Banner Advertising" (IAB, CASIE), 1996.

of *Elle* and *Car and Driver*. One of the Web's most expensive sites at $100,000 per quarter, ESPNET SportsZone signed eight advertisers to contracts totaling more than $1 million. And CondeNet managed to contract eight charter advertisers for Epicurious and Conde Nast Traveler websites, including AT&T, American Airlines, and Westin.

The Surge of Yahoo! With increasing traffic, the most active Internet users were facing new kinds of problems: How to manage the seemingly bottomless flood of information? Back in 1994, two graduate students at Stanford, David Filo and Jerry Yang, had faced a similar problem as they set up their own Web index site, which was soon being accessed by thousands of Web surfers each day. Initially, the two had developed the Yahoo! ("Yet Another Hierarchical Officious Oracle") search engine to compile a list of their favorite Internet sites. Things changed dramatically when Marc Andresseen, the co-founder of Netscape, and Randy Adams, president of the Internet Shopping Network, helped Filo and Yang commercialize their service. By March 1995, the two students gave up their doctorate dreams and focused on Yahoo!, which soon became the leading search engine. In just three years, it would have a driver role in the "portal mania."

With the rapid increase of Internet-related IPO's, traditional IT companies began reformulating and redeploying their strategies in order to gain expertise on the Web and to instigate growth in the traditional markets. In September 1995, Netscape announced Navigator 2.0, which accelerated Internet marketing and user navigation. As Microsoft launched its strategic U-turn toward the Internet, the software giant also triggered the "browser wars." That led to an intense market momentum.

The Internet Mass Market Gains Momentum

It was Microsoft's strategic decision that contributed significantly to the first boom of Internet IPOs between 1995 and 1996. The software giant even paid $200,000 to sponsor the historical Super Bowl website. If Microsoft was willing to bet its future on the Internet, so would others. The newspaper publishers entered a new era as the New York Times launched on the Web with ads from $120,000-per-year "partners" Toyota and Chemical Bank. Two to three months later, it was followed by the Wall Street Interactive Journal. Even Sony Corp. of America, the consumer-electronics giant, said it was seeking partners for its upcoming Sony Station website, for a price of $500,000 to $1 million.

Meanwhile, Intel instigated the market momentum not only with new microprocessors but also by increasing investment activity in Silicon Valley and Madison Avenue and funding new and innovative online marketing campaigns. In 1996, the company also unveiled Intercast technology to deliver Web content and TV programming *simultaneously*. Intel developed and commercialized new hybrid technologies in order to expand the marketplace for its core products—the microprocessors. "My vision is that, in the course of the next five to ten years, a billion PCs will go online worldwide," said Craig C. Barrett, Intel's new CEO and president in July 1998. "I'd like to see Intel's microprocessors in all of them. *Growth* is Intel's first, second, and third objective."[84]

As the advertisers and Web publishers rushed to the Internet, the demand for reliable and valid audience numbers soared. By October 1995, the Audit Bureau of Circulations started testing audits of websites. As measurement, media placement, and auditing firms flocked in the nascent industry to position themselves strategically, uncertainty would continue to reign for years. In February 1996, NetGravity introduced the AdServer ad management system for websites, while Focalink Communications was pushing SmartBanner media planning services (just a few months later, the company would introduce Market Match Web media planning tool). PointCast launched an offline news and information network featuring animated ads.

Only a few months after the launch of HotWired, there followed the first efforts to use the Internet in direct response. In January 1995, five major advertisers—MCI, Saturn, Timex, Jim Beam, and AirWalk—joined Vibe Online in deals ranging from $20,000 to $60,000 for 6 months. In November 1994, Roy Schwedelson had delivered a pioneering speech at the Direct Marketing Association (DMA) conference in Toronto urging direct marketers to get involved. Returning from Comdex, he and his brother, Jay Schwedelson, came up with an initial concept of a banner ad placement service. The WebConnect advertising media kit was placed on the Web. It offered a direct response marketing model. By the mid-1990s, the momentum toward direct response in Internet marketing accelerated.

From WebConnect to Internet Direct Response

Founded in 1994 by Roy Schwedelson and Jay Schwedelson, WebConnect provided the combined knowledge, experience, and methodologies of targeted direct response marketing and broad-reaching advertising media placement. Billing itself as the "first and most innovative media placement service of the Internet," the company delivered highly targeted ad coverage in a variety of market areas on the Web (e.g., consumer, home office, business-to-business, financial, electronic). It tracked and reported the actions of the prospects through the entire sales process, from the first impression to an actual purchase or inquiry. WebConnect sought to provide the accountability that the advertisers needed to build successful online advertising campaigns. It also provided the clients an opportunity to obtain immediate feedback on the campaigns, in order to determine just how effective each site had been in delivering the most responsive customers.[85]

By mid-1995, the momentum toward direct response in Internet marketing accelerated. When WebConnect was introduced to catalogers at the summer Catalog Conference in Chicago, that meant an offering of over 60 business, consumer, and high-tech market categories from a base of over 500 member sites. Even though direct marketers were now intensively exploring the options of Internet-based direct marketing, many veteran practitioners of leading ad agencies and media buyers were somewhat weary of these ambitious visions. They had not forgotten the historical precedents. In the 1970s and 1980s, the advocates of direct marketing had inflated the potential of direct marketing with unrealistic hopes. Due to intense rivalry, the mighty dreams crashed on thin margins.

As direct marketers were considering their strategic options, publishers began to measure and appraise Web-driven direct marketers. In mid-August 1996, publishing company CMP Media and Worldata announced a joint venture in which CMP invested a major stake—reportedly $20 million—in Worldata's WebConnect service. The investment was considered an "interesting" one for CMP, which also owned a stake in Focalink Communications.[86] Two years later, Worldata, a major direct marketing services organization for over 23 years and the originator of Web-Connect, repurchased CMP Media's 50% interest in WebConnect. "By reuniting WebConnect with Worldata, we've reaffirmed our commitment to the new and expanding role that the World Wide Web is playing in the direct marketing sector," commented Roy Schwedelson, CEO of Worldata.[87]

After the fate of WebConnect, direct marketers got concerned for their future. By October 1998, The Direct Marketing Association announced it was taking over the Association of Interactive Media (AIM), one of the leading Internet-business trade groups.[88] The DMA's members included more than 4,100 businesses in interactive and database marketing from the United States and 53 other nations, including such companies as IBM, Dell Computer, L. L. Bean, J. Crew, AT&T, MCI, Time Inc., Microsoft, The McGraw-Hill Company, Rodale Press, AOL, and Lucent Technologies. AIM was a non-profit association that represented some 250 Web-driven organizations, including MindSpring, Yoyodyne, Hotmail, Bloomberg LP, Citicorp, Nielsen Media Research, SportsLine USA, Universal Studios, and MTV Interactive. AIM would operate as a subsidiary of DMA, based in New York.

Representing bulk mailers and telemarketers nationwide, the DMA was eager to adapt its bulk-mailing techniques for the Internet. The association did not intend to be a bystander on the Web; it hoped the alliances would enable its members to target consumers, via the Web.

Unlike traditional direct marketing, the Internet offered instant access to millions of users worldwide at a fraction of the cost. Under the traditional model, mass marketers pay for the paper, printing, and postage of every piece of mail they send. In the Internet, bulk e-mailings could be launched to millions at virtually no cost. While most DMA members were already using the Internet, they had only begun to integrate the new medium with classic direct staple. "They certainly have an interest in finding out how to do things effectively," said Robert Wientzen, president and chief executive officer of the DMA. "This acquisition is going to provide for a technology exchange between two groups."[89]

The acquisition *was* historical.

CPMs versus Direct Response: How to Price the Internet?

According to a report from CommerceNet and Nielsen Media Research, some 24 million adults in the United States and Canada now had access to the Internet. That triggered the arrival of the first free e-mailers in April 1996, such as Juno Online Services and Freemark Communications. In May, content developer iVillage netted $800,000 in ad commitments on an ad model that intermingled editorial with marketing. The model focused activities to targeted online communities, drawing from a corporate philosophy of humanizing cyberspace. In June 1996, Microsoft's *Slate* debuted on the Web, while HotWired tapped Levi's Dockers for one-year sponsorship of the Dream Jobs channel.

In July 1996, AT&T broke its "intermercial" ad campaign, featuring animated banners and emulating TV commercials. By September 1996, even General Motors doubled its website content to more than 38,000 pages, making it one of the largest marketer sites. Meanwhile, BackWeb Technologies introduced a private online broadcast system, with GM as one of the first users. GM was seeking increasing efficiencies in internal operations (intranets); but it also aspired to solidify supplier chains (extranets) and was eager to experiment with transactive business models.

Most Internet users were still dependent on 28.8 kbps modems. The performance of microprocessors continued to grow exponentially, but slow-speed modems prevented users from enjoying the full benefits of "Moore's Law." By the end of summer 1996, @Home Corp. became the first U.S. company to provide an alternative to slow-speed modems. It started to pitch marketers on the @Home high-speed online network. While the strategic objective would take longer than many contemporaries suspected, the implementation of a high-speed network was a matter of time (by late 1998 both cable modems and DSL were targeting mass markets).

By 1996, mass marketers were proliferating on the Web. They sought to retain the old offline customers while gaining new ones through the

Internet. In order to fund their investments, they needed advertising revenue; in order to garner advertisers, they had to be able to manage, measure, and compare audiences. How should they price the Internet?

If Edwin Artzt, chairman and CEO of P&G, had awakened Madison Avenue to the challenge of interactive advertising in 1994, it was John Pepper, P&G's new chairman and chief executive, who, starting in the fall of 1995, would have to implement the mass marketer's emergent Internet strategy. The Internet was not exempt from the new rule of financial discipline at P&G. In effect, the company was willing to extend the pay-for-performance principle into cyberspace. Rather than clicks (an Internet version of ratings in measured media advertising), it wanted to make click-rate (an Internet version of response rate in direct marketing) the basic criteria of compensation in Internet advertising.

By the fall of 1996, Procter & Gamble had ten websites, seven for products. As it fostered growth of interactive media, P&G moved quickly to establish pay-for-performance measurement principles with vendors. P&G wanted more impact per dollar from measured-media spending. When it comes to making media buys, it had always been a tough negotiator.

Initially, the use of a CPM (cost per thousand viewers) model on the Internet indicated a willingness to seize the pricing models of *traditional* media and to impose them onto the *new* media. The model benefited most the firms that enjoyed the highest user traffic and least those companies whose websites attracted relatively low traffic.[90] At the end of April 1996, Procter & Gamble struck a deal with Yahoo! that aspired to set a new standard for Internet advertising. The deal called for P&G to pay when users would "click-through" its ads rather than when they only "eyeballed" the images. In the past, companies advertising online paid rates based on the number of people who (presumably) saw their ads. In this arrangement, the cost per thousand viewers ranged from $5 to $80, depending on the target audience. Generally, the price increased significantly, when advertisers were guaranteed a target audience. Following the debate of the P&G/Yahoo! model, the measurement industry gradually defined more precise definitions for crucial terms like "ad clicks" (clicks) and "ad click rates" (click rates) (see Exhibit 4-7):

- *Ad click*: user clicks on ad.
- *Ad click rate*: ratio of ad clicks to ad views.
- *Ad view*: the ad is actually seen by the user.

When P&G chose click rate as the primary criteria of Internet media purchases, it selected a direct rather than a media model of pricing. Implicitly, that model meant that the pricing of Internet media would no

Exhibit 4-7
Internet Measurement Guidelines: User-Related Terms (CASIE)

Founded in May 1994, the mission of CASIE was to create an environment where consumers would have the broadest possible array of high-quality media options at the lowest possible cost. Therefore, one of CASIE's key projects would be the development of proper media measurement guidelines, in order to:

- Determine what to measure
- Encourage comparability between trackers
- Define standard interactive advertising terms
- Share research findings.

Ad click—when user clicks on ad.

Ad click rate—ratio of ad clicks to ad views.

Ad display/Ad delivered—when an ad is successfully displayed on the user's computer screen.

Ad download—when an ad is downloaded by a user. Ads can be downloaded but aborted before actually being displayed on the user's screen.

Ad request—the request for an advertisement as a direct result of a visitor's action and as recorded by the ad server.

Ad transfers—the successful arrival of a user at the advertiser's web site. When a user clicks on an advertisement, a click-through is recorded and re-directs or "transfers" the user's browser to an advertiser's web site. If the user successfully arrives at the advertiser's web site, an ad transfer is recorded. In some cases, the click-through may fail to produce an ad transfer due to an overload of traffic on the advertiser's server or a user's slow Internet connection.

Ad view—when the ad is actually seen by the user. Note this is not measurable.

Cost-per-transfer—cost of advertising on a web page divided by the number of transfers the ad received.

Hit (also Request)—1. A single request for a resource via a web server or any entry in a web server log. A hit can result in the successful delivery of content to the user or an error. A successful hit to a page containing an advertisement is counted as an impression for that advertisement. Nearly all web servers log each hit to an access log file. 2. When visitors reach a web site, their computer sends a request to the site's computer (server) to begin displaying pages. Each element of a requested page (including graphics, text, interactive items) is recorded by the site's web server log file as a "hit." Because page designs and visit patterns vary from site to site, the number of hits bears no relationship to the number of pages viewed or visits to a site.

Impression—1. A single viewing of a page. Viewing the page assumes that the user also viewed the ads on that page. 2. The presence of an ad on a web page that may leave an impression on a user. An impression is recorded whether the user acts on the ad or not. Also called "ad view."

Inference—one way to measure a visitor's unique identity. This measure uses deduction or inference based on time spent as logged by the server. If a server receives a new request from the same client within 30 minutes, it is inferred that a new request comes from the same visitor and the time since the last page request was spent viewing the last page.

174

Exhibit 4-7 (continued)

Non-registered user—a user who visits a web site and elects not to, or is not required to, provide certain information, and hence may be denied access to part(s) of the site.

Page—a single cohesive container of information presented to a user on a web site. A page may contain text, images, and other in-line elements. It may be static or dynamically generated. A page count is roughly comparable to a vehicle circular estimate.

Page Request—the opportunity for an HTML document to appear in a browser window as a direct result of a visitor's interaction with a web site.

Page Views—number of times a user requests a page which may contain a particular ad. Indicative of the number of times an ad was potentially seen, or "gross impressions." Page views overstate ad impressions when users turn "Auto Load Images" off to speed browsing.

Referral Link—the referring page, or referral link, is a place from which the visitor clicked to get to the current page. In other words, since a hyperlink connects one URL to another, in clicking on a link the browser moves from the referring URL to the destination URL.

Return visits—the average number of times a visitor returns to a site over a period of time.

Session—a sequence of hits made by one user at one site. If a user makes no request from a site during a predetermined (and discretionary) period of time, the next hit would constitute the beginning of a new visit. A series of transactions performed by a user that can be tracked across successive web sites. For example, in a single session, a user may start on a publisher's web site, click on an advertisement and then go to an advertiser's web site and make a purchase. See *visit.*

Transfer—the successful response to a page request; also when a browser receives a complete page of content from a web server. Note: Streamed content (such as RealAudio) is measured differently and does not require a complete download in order to be considered successfully transferred.

Unique users—the number of different individuals who visit a site within a specific time period are called unique users. To identify unique users, web sites rely on some form of user registration or an identification system such as I/CODE.

User registration—information contributed by a visitor which usually includes characteristics such as visitor's age, gender, zip code and often much more. Registration system is usually based on an ID code or password to allow the site to determine the number of unique visitors and to track a visitor's behavior within that site.

Visit—a series of page requests by a visitor without 30 consecutive minutes of inactivity.

Visit duration—the time between the first and last request of a visit. This time doesn't include how long users viewed the last request of a visit. Visit duration is only relevant if you are talking about a series of consecutive requests. If you measure visits with cookies, the requests don't have to be consecutive.

Yield—the percentage of clicks vs. impressions on an ad within a specific page. Also called "ad click rate."

Source: Glossary of Internet Advertising Terms and Interactive Measurement Guidelines, Coalition for Advertising Supported Information and Entertainment [CASIE] (New York: AAA, ANA 1998).

longer be based on ad clicks, but on the consequent activity on the part of the *viewer* (a click of the advertiser's banners, a call to an 800-number, etc.). Like in direct mail, the response rates in the Internet were very low, varying around 1–4%. Unlike direct mailers who, in theory, could target all Americans, the Web direct marketers began their activities in a nascent industry where the penetration hardly exceeded 5–10%.

The first Internet CPM debate did not result in an industry solution, but led to a temporary truce. As various players did not want to choose one (CPM) or another exclusive solution (direct model), they began to favor each for different reasons and in different mixtures (hybrid models). By the spring of 1997, Forrester Research reported that only 23% of the advertisers they spoke with wanted pricing to be based on cost per thousand impressions (CPMs), whereas 39% favored click-throughs, 18% cost per lead/order, and 16% various hybrids. In other words, three of four advertisers wanted pricing to be based on results (direct response model) rather than CPMs (media advertising model).[91]

So the old opposition between brand advertising and direct marketing moved from the marketplace to the marketspace. The deal between Procter & Gamble and Yahoo! illustrated the bargaining power of the mass marketers, and the adaptability of the Internet players. But more than anything else, it reflected the uncertainty about the rules of the game on the Web.

NOTES

1. Dan Steinbock, Interview with Lester Wunderman, chairman of Wunderman Cato Johnson, senior adviser to the board of directors of Young & Rubicam, and director of Dentsu Wunderman Direct in Japan, August 17, 1998.

2. "Wunderman uses his pioneer's license and remarkable storytelling ability to teach the reader about advertising of a very different kind—a communication medium which puts the consumer increasingly in control," notes Nicholas Negroponte, an author of an Internet bestseller (*Being Digital*) which Wunderman himself (*Being Direct*) may have emulated. See the cover of Lester Wunderman, *Being Direct. Making Advertising Pay* (New York: Random House 1996).

3. Steinbock, Interview with Lester Wunderman.

4. Lester Wunderman, *Being Direct*, see chapter 8, "The Virtual Store That Opened in *Esquire* Magazine."

5. Ibid.

6. Steinbock, Interview with Lester Wunderman.

7. Wunderman, *Being Direct*, especially chapter 17, "How I Discovered Direct Marketing."

8. Ibid.

9. Ibid.

10. Ibid.

11. Wunderman attributes his way of thinking to his studies. He attended

Brooklyn College, The New York School for Social Research, and Columbia University where he did graduate work in cultural anthropology and art history. See Steinbock, Interview with Lester Wunderman.

12. Ibid.

13. Ibid.

14. Ibid.

15. See Wunderman, *Being Direct*, chapter 18.

16. For an account of this meeting and its context, see Don Peppers and Martha Rogers [1993], Preface to *The One to One Future: Building Relationships One Customer at a Time* (New York: Currency/Doubleday 1996).

17. Dan Steinbock, Interview with Don Peppers, Partner, Peppers and Rogers Group, May 4, 1998.

18. Ibid.

19. Ibid.

20. Peppers and Rogers, *The One to One Future*, pp. 4–5.

21. Ibid., p. 5.

22. See Don Peppers and Martha Rogers, *Enterprise One to One: Tools for Competing in the Interactive Age* (New York: Currency/Doubleday 1997); Don Peppers and Martha Rogers, *The One to One Fieldbook: The Complete Toolkit for Implementing a 1 to 1 Marketing Program* (New York: Currency/Doubleday 1998).

23. For more details on the following defining characteristics of one-to-one marketing, see Peppers and Rogers, *The One to One Future*, "User's Guide."

24. As Peppers and Rogers note, *if* the amount of these purchases were known, it would be easy to calculate the customer's value to the firm over that period. The marketer would look at the products that the customer would be buying and calculate the incremental profit to the firm of each future sale, generating a stream of future profit. Then the marketer would apply a discount rate to that profit stream to derive its current value to him/her, just as one would with any net present value calculation. See Peppers and Rogers, *The One to One Future*, p. 41.

25. Ibid., p. 102.

26. On differential marketing, see, e.g., Garth Hallberg, *All Consumers Are Not Created Equal: The Differential Marketing Strategy for Brand Loyalty and Profits* (New York: John Wiley & Sons 1995).

27. Again, direct marketing provided the objective of loyalization, whose principles Peppers and Rogers adopted from Lester Wunderman. While recognizing the value of the principle, the latter, however, was less sanguine of its sustained force (see "The Promise of Interactive Marketing" earlier in this chapter).

28. Peppers and Rogers, *The One to One Future*, p. 54.

29. "Marketers 'aim' at 'target' markets (or use 'precision targeting'). They measure media effectiveness 'against' the target which they 'segment.' And if they are not fighting with customers, they are fighting over them in market-share 'battles' with their competitors, or 'share wars.' " Ibid., p. 54.

30. "For example, we might suggest that you take a small selection of customers as a test group and appoint that customer manager for those customer relationships. Then you insulate this test group from routine solicitations, phone calls and mailing pieces that all other customers get. The customer manager will be in charge of the addressable communication with these customers. His job is to

set the strategy for these customers and measure your success against the control group (similar customers, no customer managers). You can prove the effectiveness of the program in the short term." Steinbock, Interview with Don Peppers.

31. On the implementation of one-to-one marketing programs, see Peppers and Rogers, *The One to One Fieldbook*.

32. Ibid.

33. Daniel S. Levine, "Justice Served," *Sales & Marketing Management*, May 1995, pp. 52–61.

34. "In Scandinavia, for instance, people are more concerned about the privacy issue than I think is worth talking about. Irrespective of the culture, it's best to start with an explicit privacy policy for your customer. It needs four basic points. First, I need to tell the customer what are the benefits to having and using this information. For example, do I get to fit the product better to the customer, or do I remember his/her groceries so that he/she doesn't have to remember them. Second, I need to outline the things I would never do with the customer information. Most importantly, I need to tell to the customer that I will not sell the information to another marketer. Thirdly, I need to give the customer some control to provide options to the customer. Fourthly, I need to tell the customer what event would require me to notify him/her. If I start my program with this four part privacy policy, at least my heart will be in the right place with respect to protecting the customer's privacy and in most regulatory regimes, I will be protected in violation of the privacy policy being implemented." Steinbock, Interview with Don Peppers.

35. Steinbock, Interview with Don Peppers.

36. Ibid.

37. Ibid.

38. Dan Steinbock, Interview with Robert Allen, president of Modem Media, May 25, 1998.

39. See Richard A. Melcher, "Why Zima Faded So Fast," *Business Week*, March 10, 1997.

40. Ibid.

41. While the published statements of the creators of marketing campaigns may coincide with real audience reactions, they also may reflect ex post facto rationalizations. Any study of Web marketing campaigns should include the analyses of *all* available primary sources, including the websites. Since, however, the creators play such a crucial role in the design and launch of any website, it would be foolish to ignore their objectives, which are often based on pragmatic "trial and error" experiences.

42. The following sections are based on the author's analysis of the now-defunct Zima website and on the account by Charles Marrelli, a senior copywriter at Modem Media, "Anatomy of a Web Advertisement: A Case Study of Zima.com." See also John C. Nardone, "Measuring the Effectiveness of Interactive Media: Internet Media Evaluation and Buying Strategy," in Edward Forrest and Richard Mizerski (eds.), *Interactive Marketing: The Future Present* (Chicago: AMA 1996), pp. 241–258, 259–264. Interestingly enough, the softcover edition of this essay collection, *Cybermarketing*, edited by Regina Brady, Edward Forrest, and Richard Mizerski (Chicago: NTC 1997), includes most of the very same

essays. Yet, Nardone's essay, while carrying an identical title, is now a different one.

43. See Nardone, "Measuring the Effectiveness of Interactive Media: Internet Media Evaluation and Buying Strategy," *Cybermarketing*, pp. 247–256.

44. Nardone, "Measuring the Effectiveness of Interactive Media."

45. See Chapter 5 in this book, the section on "context-based keywords."

46. Marrelli, "Anatomy of a Web Advertisement."

47. Ibid.

48. On the joint launch of the *E.R.* pilot episode and its website in the fall of 1997, see chapter 5: "Cross-Promotion."

49. Marrelli, "Anatomy of a Web Advertisement."

50. Regis McKenna, "Marketing Is Everything," *Harvard Business Review*, January–February 1991. See also McKenna, *Relationship Marketing: Successful Strategies for the Age of the Customer* (Reading, MA: Addison-Wesley Publishing Co. 1991), chapter 1.

51. Marrelli, "Anatomy of a Web Advertisement."

52. By the late 1980s, the mere presence of new marketing channels was no longer enough; penetration alone did not automatically guarantee advertiser support. It was original content that "legitimized" the new medium as a vehicle, but that meant expensive and often risky investments. In 1983, for instance, cable networks spent only $153 million of their $255 million programming budgets on original programs, whereas, by 1990, the corresponding figure had boomed to $1.3 billion (more than half on original shows). On the rise of cable, see Dan Steinbock, *Triumph and Erosion in the American Media and Entertainment Industries* (Westport, CT: Quorum Books 1995), pp. 63–78.

53. Marrelli, "Anatomy of a Web Advertisement."

54. Ibid.

55. In the early 1980s, American Airlines became one of the first companies to pioneer a frequency marketing program when it began to offer free mileage credit to its customers. Soon thereafter, others followed the suit: hotels adopted frequency marketing (e.g., Marriott's Honored Guest Program), credit-card companies offered points based on their cards' usage level, supermarket chains provided "price club cards" offering member customers unadvertised discounts on particular items. On the rise of marketing management methods to build satisfaction through quality, service, and value, see Philip Kotler, *Marketing Management. Analysis, Planning, Implementation, and Control*, 9th ed. (Upper Saddle River, NJ: Prentice Hall 1997), chapter 2.

56. In the Zima case, online demographics matched up with the brand's target market. But some members of the online audience were below the legal age limit. To control club membership, Zima relied on banner advertising and membership limits, but it also limited Tribe Z membership to individuals to 21 and over. Age disclosure was a necessary component of the Tribe Z survey. Any individuals citing their age as younger than 21 were forbidden membership in the affinity club. Still, the Zima site had no effective means to confirm the validity of the age disclosure. This problem had little to do with the technology; it was intertwined with issues of free speech and regulation (local, regional, national, international).

57. Marrelli, "Anatomy of a Web Advertisement."

58. Ibid.

59. See Lester Wunderman, *Being Direct: Making Advertising Pay* (New York: Random House 1997), p. 106.

60. Marrelli, "Anatomy of a Web Advertisement."

61. See "From A(T&T) to Z(ima), Modem Makes Its Mark—Interactive Shop Develops Winning Formula," Modem Media, Sept. 18, 1995.

62. Melcher, "Why Zima Faded So Fast."

63. *See* Anthony M. Rutkowski, *Internet Trends,* http://www.genmagic.com/internet/trends/ sld001.htm.

64. See Wired Ventures, Inc., Prospectus, as filed with the Securities and Exchange Commission on May 30, 1996.

65. Wired Venture's media kits (1997).

66. See Debra Aho Williamson, "Web Ads Mark 2nd Birthday with Decisive Issues Ahead," *Advertising Age,* October 21, 1996.

67. See Wired Ventures, Inc., Prospectus. Especially sections on "Fluctuations in Operating Results," and "Developing Market for Online Media; Uncertain Acceptance of the Internet As an Advertising Medium."

68. See Williamson, "Web Ads Mark 2nd Birthday."

69. Dan Steinbock, Interview with Louis Rossetto, then-CEO and editorial director of Wired Ventures, February 28, 1997.

70. Wired Ventures, Inc., Prospectus.

71. Steinbock, Interview with Louis Rossetto.

72. Steinbock, Interview with Robert Allen.

73. Dan Steinbock, Interview with Fergus O'Daly, August 3, 1998. In effect, AT&T and Netscape would have a unique relationship. Having served on Netscape's board since October 1994, Jim Barksdale joined Netscape in January 1995. Prior to Netscape, Barksdale served as CEO of AT&T Wireless Services, following the merger of AT&T and McCaw Cellular Communications. From January 1992 until the merger in September 1994, he held the positions of president and COO of McCaw.

74. Bill Bass, "What Time Warner Should Do with Pathfinder," *Media & Technology Strategies,* Forrester Research, Inc., 1(2), October 30, 1996.

75. Nick Wingfield, "Time's Deal with AOL Takes *People* Magazine Off the Web," *Wall Street Journal,* October 19, 1998.

76. Tom Watson, "The Portal That Never Was," *@NY,* October 23, 1998.

77. See, e.g., James R. Gregory, with Jack G. Wiechmann, *Leveraging the Corporate Brand* (Lincolnwood, IL: NTC 1997).

78. David A. Aaker, *Building Strong Brands* (New York: The Free Press 1996), see chapter 7.

79. See Dan Steinbock, *Triumph and Erosion in the American Media and Entertainment Industries,* especially the section on "Time Warner: Struggle for Control," pp. 161–171.

80. Ibid.

81. IAB, June 1996.

82. I intend to explore the rise of the new media and interactive ad agency clusters in a forthcoming companion piece. It will focus on the competitive strategies of these highly enterpreneurial firms, from the late 1980s to the end of the 1990s.

83. See IAB reports.

84. Dan Steinbock, Interview with Craig C. Barrett, CEO and President, Intel Corporation, July 24, 1998.

85. WebConnect (1998).

86. "CMP Media, Worldata to invest in WebConnect," *Advertising Age*, August 16, 1996. Focalink was currently testing a service called MarketMatch that offered information on appropriate Web markets for different ad agencies' clients.

87. Web Connect, Press Releases.

88. "The DMA Acquires Association for Interactive Media to Create the world's Largest Trade Association of Business on the Net," Association for Interactive Media, October 12, 1998.

89. See Rebecca Quick, "Direct Marketing Association to Merge with Association of Interactive Media," *Wall Street Journal*, October 12, 1998.

90. Typically, magazine publishers (e.g., HotWired, Pathfinder, and ZD Net), which made specific publications to highly-segmented audiences, were most vocal against the CPM model and resisted the change.

91. Mary A. Modahl and Ruth MacQuiddy, "Internet Advertising," *Media & Technology Strategies*, 1(1), Forrester Research, September 1, 1996.

5

Ad Banners and Online Communities

"Is Advertising Finally Dead?" asked *Wired* magazine in February 1994, amidst the browser frenzy. First the remote, then the cable revolution, and now—the Internet?

Written by the advocates of one-to-one marketing, the authors were convinced that the world of 21st-century telecommunications, with its bumper crop of marketing opportunities for everything from greeting cards to room fresheners, would spawn new and myriad ways to sell products and learn about consumers. "Advertising isn't dead," they argued, "it's been reborn."[1]

But exactly *how* will it be reborn?

PROBLEMS OF ONLINE BRANDING

Easier said than done. Some direct marketers have long suspected that the reliance of media advertising on attitudinal factors, instead of behavioral ones, has resulted in "much ado about nothing." Moreover, they consider the Internet an *information* media and therefore antithetical to media advertising. If television exemplifies the physical marketplace and the Internet the virtual marketspace, Lester Wunderman, a pioneer direct marketer, sees them as polar opposites. "The intent of the Internet is information, whereas that of television is entertainment. The brand will be built more easily by information than by superficiality."

Lester Wunderman: Building Brand on Information

"If the advertiser wants my business, he has to understand what I want," argues Lester Wunderman, the pioneer of direct marketing.

"Branding starts with identifying a product with the name of the manufacturer. Branding is not information; it is empty information. The brand is not just the product. Brands are but a shorthand for information gone out of a product. Will it be as important in the next society? I'm not that sure."

The End of the Marlboro Man. "In a way, the brand is the opposite of information. The cowboy, for example, had nothing to do with the Marlboro, but with virility, outdoors and so on. That's *not* information. Information is about the level of nicotine and tar. As the Web begins to offer comparative product information, branding will become a different proposition. A brand is the absence of information. I can tell you very little in just 30 seconds; things will become quite different when everyone has access to information media. And that's what the Web is all about. It is an information media."[2]

The Shallow Ambition of the Green Giant. "It wasn't until David Ogilvy and Raymond Rubicam that ad practitioners conceived of a brand personality. They began to invent these hypothetical, virtual personalities. It was easier to sell a personality. They didn't want to tell you how small green peas were picked and grown. On television, there is no time for that. Instead, they looked for easy identifiers. Hence, the Green Giant. Psychologically, however, a brand is a very shallow ambition. A brand has no deep penetration into the psyche. So, the brands are going to be in big trouble."[3]

Build Brand on Information, Not Baby Talk! "Really, billions are invested in superficiality. If people spoke in terms of the punch lines in commercials, you'd think we're all idiots. It would be baby talk: 'A pause that refreshes' . . . 'IBM, here's a solution for a small planet' . . . In reality, people want to know what the hell this computer *does*! We've persuaded ourselves to think that there is a second language out there, TV speak. It is a language invented for television, and other media. Yet, it's not the way people speak to each other; it's not dialogue. So when we talk about dialogue and human relationships, ad practitioners cannot continue to do it on the childish basis they've done. Read any magazine, see what they say and try to repeat it to me. I'd laugh at you. You wouldn't buy a product based on it. So the requirement to *re-brand* is going to be severe. The Internet will cause rethinking of brands."[4]

Fergus O'Daly, Jr.: Category Positionings Are Coming . . .

Fergus O'Daly, Jr., another pioneer marketer, sees no easy answer to the question whether Internet marketing represents media advertising, direct response, or both. "The Internet works both ways. You can build brand using the Web as a medium. You also can sell a lot of products using it as a direct marketing channel or as a direct sales channel. However, selling directly may never be in the best interest of some companies. For others, trying to build a brand online with advertising would probably be much better done from a promotional standpoint; instead of their big websites, they could do couponing, promotion and contests."[5]

Instead of Fancy Websites, Build Functional Promotions. "The focus of Procter & Gamble, for instance, should be more in what they can do on the Web than to promote their brand in the traditional sense. Another problem stems from the users shopping through these virtual stores; P&G must protect its brand equity in the Web environment. They should not invest more in the website, but promotions and contests. Also, they must work very closely with the online stores so that, just as they get good exposure at the supermarket, they will get the same treatment on the online supermarkets and virtual markets."[6]

The Relative Absence of Pure Online Brands. "Whether traditional or online, the branding scenario is the same. In the traditional physical marketplace, things are a lot simpler in terms of competition, establishing the positioning, and so on. If I want to come out with a new soap powder, I can look at the past 40 years of history to see who did what, what worked and what didn't work. However, if you want to build a *virtual* brand, there is not a lot to go on. When, for instance, Amazon.com came out with the idea that they would sell books online, there was nothing for them to base that on. There was *no online history* [of "best practices"]. Now it is starting to occur in certain business segments where you have companies, such as Borders, Amazon, and Barnes & Noble. Maybe a Ford guy will come in now that he's got something to look at; and perhaps he gets some lessons that he gleans information from. Now he can look at his positioning a little differently: " 'The online bookstores did this-and-that, and I don't want to be in that position. So I need to differentiate myself, and then I want to brand myself.' "[7]

Category Positioning. "The positioning *is* tougher online. I've seen it with all the sites that I've worked and watched online. I would say that 75% of their original positioning has been wrong. The firms have had to change them about three-quarters of the way into all their money. *All of them,* including Amazon and the search engines. The original positionings of Yahoo! and Excite are ancient. What they initially thought was going to happen did not happen. What's happening for them now may be more profound and better, but still it is not what they planned. Positioning and creating a virtual brand is hard on the Web. The ones that seem to work are the ones that stay *within their categories,* such as books, cars, jobs, and the like. They are clearer and easy enough to do. Durable goods is a category, so is home decorating. There will be a lot of people with money that will invest and try to use this-and-that category, whether it's about furniture or washing machines, air conditioners or books and CD. Some of them have gone very well and are quite successful. But even the categories are going to disappear very quickly because they are still very *broad* as categories."[8]

"The question is how do you position yourself within these categories when there are three to four competitors already in there. If there are three CD distributors already in there, will there be three or four top ones and the ones below will never make a buck? In marketing, that has, historically, been the case. As the old expression says, 'Number #1 makes pretty good money. Number #2 manages to keep its head above worry. And number #3 is always struggling.' That scenario is going to play out on the Internet. You *are* going to see #1 and #2. You will see strong leaders in each one of these categories and an awful lot of people behind trying to figure out how to get it done and take that lead away from them. But, clearly, if you have a strong brand that's recognizable in the traditional sense, if you then enter the virtual markets and spend enough money and make the investment, *then* you are going to get strong imagination on the part of the public. That's what Barnes & Noble has done. Will Amazon.com eventually win? I actually think that Barnes & Noble will eventually beat Amazon.com at their game. But it will take some time. B&N has 3,000 stores and they know how to store and buy books. They know how to ship and deliver. Even if Amazon.com has done an extraordinary job of picking up on all that stuff, they are still years and years of experience behind them. Initially, B&N missed a tremendous opportunity to capture the online world. They let a new entrant occupy the real estate over them. Now the companies are learning that lesson the hard way. But in the long run, B&N does have a long history and business relationships. They have no bad baggage with the consumer. If they do things right, if they are smarter in technology and from relationship building, they will succeed over Amazon. They will be the stronger player."[9]

For years, brand analysts had argued that the most important assets of companies are *intangible*. These assets, which comprise brand equity, are a primary source of competitive advantage and future earnings, contends professor David Aaker.

Online Brands: Ubiquity, Integration, and Interactivity

In 1998, David A. Aaker, the E. T. Grether Professor of Marketing Strategy at the University of California at Berkeley, was the author of 10 books and more than 80 articles on branding, advertising, and business strategy. One of the most cited and quoted authors in the field of marketing, Aaker consulted and lectured extensively throughout the world on brand strategy. "I was stimulated to study branding because of my work in strategy in the 1980's," he recalls. "I came to the conclusion that you need to manage and build assets. The three main assets that have to be managed are brands, people, and information technology. My main focus has been on brands: *What is brand equity?* That became my first book and the second was on *how do you manage brand equity.*"[10]

Although Aaker began to explore the Internet more seriously only in the late 1990s, his work in technology marketing illustrates some affinities. Like the Internet, technology changes rapidly.

In some industries, you get the branding strategy set up and you are there forever. But in high technology you're there for perhaps four months, and things may change again. As a result, you need to have a kind of a dynamic and living process. It can't consist of just a beginning and an end. It has to be an ongoing process. That also means that you have to project into the future. You must have a future-oriented brand strategy. You have got to have flexibility and an ability to change.[11]

Managing Brand Equity (1991). In *Managing Brand Equity*, Aaker presented the value of a brand as a strategic asset and a company's primary source of competitive advantage. The most important assets of any business, Aaker argued, are *intangible*: its company name, brand, symbols, and slogans, and their underlying associations, perceived quality, name awareness, customer base, and proprietary resources such as patents, trademarks, and channel relationships.[12]

These assets, which comprise brand equity, are a primary source of competitive advantage and future earnings, contends Aaker. Yet, research shows that managers cannot identify with confidence their brand associations, levels of consumer awareness, or degree of customer loyalty. Moreover, since the 1980s, managers desperate for short-term financial results have often unwittingly damaged their brands through price promotions and unwise brand extensions, causing irreversible deterioration of the value of the brand name. Although several companies, such as Canada Dry and Colgate-Palmolive, created an equity management position to be guardian of the value of brand names, far too few managers, Aaker concluded, really understood the concept of brand equity and how it must be implemented.[13]

Building Strong Brands (1995). In *Building Strong Brands*, Aaker used brand-building cases from Saturn, General Electric, Kodak, Healthy Choice, McDonald's, and others to demonstrate how strong brands were created and managed.[14] A common pitfall of brand strategists is to focus on brand attributes. Aaker showed how to break out of the box by considering emotional and self-expressive benefits and by introducing the brand-as-person, brand-as-organization, and brand-as-symbol perspectives. The twin concepts of brand identity (the brand image that brand strategists aspire to create or maintain) and brand position (that part of the brand identity that is to be actively communicated) play a key role in managing the "out-of-the-box" brand. A second pitfall is to ignore the fact that individual brands are part of a larger system consisting of many intertwined and overlapping brands and sub-brands. Aaker showed how to manage the "brand system" to achieve clarity and synergy, to adapt to a changing environment, and to leverage brand assets into new markets and products.

As executives in a wide range of industries sought to prevent their products and services from becoming commodities, many were recommitting themselves to brands as a foundation of business strategy. With the transition from the physical marketplace to the virtual marketspace, this recommitment became a necessity. As industries turned increasingly hostile to brands, strong brand-building skills were needed to survive and prosper. Still, Aaker did not see the Internet impact as so extensive in the short term as the Internet visionaries might have it.

One can't generalize. It all depends on the content. For the automobiles, stocks, and books—perhaps even for clothing—the distribution already *has* changed. The Web is a factor on all those areas. But it's really a kind of an augmentation of the existing channel structures; it's just one more channel. But that channel is very threatening in automobiles, for example. It's the same in the insurance and the banking and financial services. In those segments, some companies are really paralyzed because they have channel conflicts. Certainly, everything is going to change. But in some other industries, such as packaged goods and certain services, it doesn't really change the channel.[15]

Managing Brand Equity and *Building Strong Brands* tell nothing about the Internet, or online brands. Nor does the notion of the Internet or the Web appear in the indexes. Still, the absence of online examples in no way refutes the applicability of Aaker's framework on branding in the virtual marketspace. Also, many of his celebrated case studies involve companies that have been pioneering websites and Internet retail, online branding, as well as the extension of offline branding into cyberspace, including Procter & Gamble, Intel, Nissan, Levi Strauss, Ford, Saturn, Kodak, General Electric, Body Shop, and many others. In physical and online branding, Aaker thought that "the fundamentals are the same— brand strategy, brand equity, and so on. What is different is how you get there. *Implementation* is different. This is so important in interactive business."[16] "With marketing in particular, he emphasized three factors, which might be called ubiquity, integration, and interactivity.

- *Ubiquity.* "While one can have a great stand-alone site, that will only work for firms that own some kind of application or benefit and are extremely well known. Most firms, however, must be all over the Internet. They have to be where the people go; they just can't have the illusion that people will come to them."

- *Integration.* "The Internet has to be tied into all the other communications vehicles. It can't be a stand-alone entity only."
- *Interactivity.* "The Internet is interactive. Firms have to use that capability to provide links to their customers. They really can't do it any other way. If, for example, you compare the Internet to mass advertising, mass marketing comes out looking pretty pathetic because it's just not interactive."

"The Internet has changed the world of brand building," says Aaker. "There is no question about it."[17]

By the late 1990s, some relationship marketers were already trying to embrace the change by making information technology serve brand building.

Regis McKenna: Toward Information-Rich Brands

"Through relationship marketing, the companies are saying that you, as a customer, are interesting," argues Regis McKenna, a pioneer of relationship marketing in Silicon Valley.

With real time, however, the pressure is on the *sales* in relationship marketing. We no longer have time; we have to adjust and adapt. We must be competitive and technologically attuned. We live now in the age of the "never satisfied customer." How do you build a relationship in such an age? You have to have a constant presence. Starbucks has done a great job accomplishing such presence. They're everywhere. Today, anyone can be a broadcaster. Anyone can be a receiver. On the Internet we can have millions of channels. With access to browsers and search engines, we have found a technology to filter and help us make choices and access those things that we want or need. That will change the way we brand and that will change the way we deal with customers.[18]

McKenna urged companies to embrace *interactive information technology*. It gave consumers the power to choose and shape brand relationships with suppliers. New brands would (have to) be information rich. He illustrated the idea with three core dimensions:

- Products and services are information dependent, and customer loyalty is enhanced by dialogue.
- The complexity of purchase decisions can be low to high.
- The risk in these relationships and transactions may also be low to high.

At the low end of the scale, products such as Pepsi or Coke are interchangeable and disposable. The purchase decision is simple and low risk and does not necessarily require rich dialogue. A heart surgery, however, necessitates intense information-rich dialogue with care providers; it is complex and may be high risk. Brands should be seen as *relationships*, and, as such, their development is different for different categories of producers.[19]

With products that are more costly, complicated, and subtly differentiated, the customer has more at stake. In these cases, the producers must build sustaining presence and relationships with the customer that extend well beyond the point of sale. Conversely, with products that are less costly, simple, and relatively undifferentiated, the customer has less at stake. In these cases, "commoditization" may proceed far faster than expected, especially as price competition will increase with the expansion of the Internet. Just like Intel in the 1970s, producers must become more service-like, including commodity producers such as soap and soft drinks. "Detergent makers, using databases, the Internet, and 800 numbers, can offer consumers advice on cleaning and stain problems," says McKenna. "Soft drink suppliers might plan parties or offer nutrition and diet counsel. Driven by the need to maintain customer loyalty and grasping the great advantage of the new information and communication tools, every product company will, in some way, become a service company."[20]

In the past, some skeptics had ridiculed such ideas. Still, these ideas were spreading rapidly, even among the "commodity producers." The Internet, in particular, provided a direct, interactive, and feedback loop-enhanced media for the purpose. Take, for instance, The Pampers Parenting Institute, founded in late 1996. The mission of the PPI was to build on the equity of the Pampers brand and inspire loyalty of Pampers customers by providing this resource.[21]

Brand, Traffic, and Transactions

Sponsored Internet advertising originates from the early years of Prodigy at the turn of the 1990s. Sponsored Web advertising stems from the first months of Netscape's Navigator, just as sponsored banner advertising began with the launch of HotWired in late 1994. While each event boosted the Net momentum, the consolidation of the business *really* began with the consolidation of the players (viable business models, rising entry barrier), the first M&A waves (acquisitions of interactive agencies and new media enterprises by leading ad agency networks), and organization of the industry (trade associations)—in particular the standardization of banner advertising in late 1996. Despite the emergence of the market, it could not serve as a nodal point for supply and demand unless both sides could come to an agreement on unit categories (banner sizes), valid measurement and auditing procedures, as well as comparative yardsticks.

Advertisers, typically, define objectives for their campaigns and then overlay the particular strengths and weaknesses of each medium to decide which and how much of each medium to buy. While television, for example, is considered useful in image advertising (strong audio and video) and brand awareness (extensive reach), other media are more effective in educating and disseminating information about a new product (such as print) or generating direct user response (direct mail). Moreover, in a campaign, different forms of advertising may be used to support one another. Finally, to accomplish the particular objectives of each campaign, advertisers must consider the appropriate level of reach (the percentage of an audience exposed to at least one ad impression over a given period of time) and frequency (how often each person or home is exposed to a message). In the mid-1990s, with limited Internet penetration (relative to TV, radio, and so forth), Internet advertising could not yet provide the reach of these other media. Also, the proliferation of websites made such reach very difficult to achieve. However, the Internet could deliver a high degree of frequency, especially on sites with repeat/ habitual users.[22]

Undoubtedly, these tools, methods and standards were rapidly maturing. Indeed, the consolidation of the measurement and auditing business between 1997 and 1998 indicated that the state of flux would gradually diminish. In time, that would translate to revenue growth in the Internet advertising and various related and supporting media. As important as these developments were and as much as they bespoke of the coming maturing of the Web, they still neglected its *potential*. At best, it is naïve to assume that one could apply the tools, methods, and standards of the past broadcast era (centralized, top-down, one-way, packaged communications) to measure progress of a quite different era of dialogue and interactivity (distributed, bottom-up, two-way, real-time communications).

How *should* one conceptualize the dynamics in the Internet advertising? Think of a three-layer process that starts from awareness creation, which may proceed to traffic-generation, which may result in transactions. One leads to another.

Create Awareness. Think of the primary task as that of *creating awareness*. That is the classic goal of branding and most typical of traditional media advertising. The objectives may comprise launching a product or service, branding, and promotions; generation of new leads, announcements of special events or products; establishing online presence (home page, website). Measurements tend to focus on the maximization of the number of exposures of the target group to the banner.

Generate Traffic. Think of the primary task as that of generating traffic. That is the classic goal of direct response and most typical of direct marketing. The objective may consist of traffic generation into a given website; reinforcement of product benefits, special offers; significance of positive visit experience; use of the brand as leverage (banner logos). Measurements focus on the click rate, which is evaluated on the basis of proper criteria.

Transactions. Think of the primary task as that of sales promotion. This is the classic goal of conversion building and most typical of sales promotions. The objective may comprise sales promotion in a given website; banners supporting sales and convincing to action; the use of teaser banners. Note that the website must deliver the banner's promise. Measurements focus on conversion rate, which is evaluated on the basis of the determinants used with the click rate.

Interactive Dialogue. Think of the primary task as that of dialogue facilitation. This is the classic goal in relationship marketing, and a customer database enables a marketer to mass customize such dialogue with mass audiences.

Assume, for instance, that the user is browsing the stories on the CNET site. Most probably, he/she is not there by chance; the user wants to see "what's going on," and he/she knows the site, or about the site. Next the user notices a banner for "the new Microsoft Windows Media Player" (awareness creation). He/she is curious, clicks the mouse and arrives in the new web page where an animated button suggests, "Click here to download" (traffic generation). The user is still interested, clicks the mouse again and arrives in a still new web page where he/she can download the item (transaction), free of charge or for a fee (Exhibit 5-1).

Technically, site managers, designers, and developers can facilitate the progress (e.g., the use of particular banners or banner elements, web page hierarchies, aesthetic solutions, etc.). Similarly, each new pattern of request and response should be archived in the customer database, whose knowledge of the user shall increase dialogue by dialogue. But, ultimately, the *sequence* remains. To engage in a transaction, the user must be on the site; to arrive in the site, the user must be interested in it; and, most importantly, the entire sequence starts from a given site— it is these high-traffic sites, "portals," whose bottleneck position virtually ensures their popularity and/or profitability.

Brand, traffic, transactions . . . Media advertising, direct marketing, sales promotions . . . In the Internet, these formerly separate worlds may come together, support and reinforce one another. But it would take years before marketers would gain the necessary skills and knowledge to achieve proper integration and balance between marketing disciplines and technological instruments.

Even a decade before the rise of the Internet, American mass advertising had come to an end. After deregulation, market segmentation, new technology, and alternative media outlets and ad options, mass marketing was simply a thing of the past, as evidenced by the rapid erosion of

Exhibit 5-1
Internet Advertising—Objectives and Measurement Alternatives

Objective	Measurement Alternatives
Create Awareness *Branding* *(Media Advertising)* Launch of product or service, branding, promotions; generation of new leads; announcement of special events or products; establishing online presence (home page, web site)	Instead of estimates of gross impressions based on a publication's circulation or a projected number of TV viewers, maximize the number of exposures of the target group to the banner
Generate Traffic *Direct Response* *(Direct Marketing)* Traffic generation into a given web site; reinforcement of product benefits, special offers; significance of positive visit experience; use of brand as leverage (i.e., banner logos)	Evaluate click rate; evaluate the results on the basis of what (product/service), how (the banner quality) and where (web sites, ad networks, etc.) Internet marketing is being used; the number of web pages visited by the surfers, the average duration of the visit (e.g., cookies)
Transactions *Build Conversion* *(Sales Promotions)* Sales promotion in a given web site; banners support sales and convince to action (i.e., purchase, filling an online form, etc.); use of teaser banners; the web site must deliver the banner's promise	Conversion rate; evaluation of results on the basis of the determinants used with the click rate

Interactive Dialogue

←——————————————————→

Monitor banners and clicks; click rates; and conversion rates; optimal use of banner and other Internet advertising on the basis of results brand loyalty and the equally rapid proliferation of promotions. The Web would merely aggravate the fragmentation—or provide the last nail for the coffin (see Chapter 1).

Moreover, the emergence of database and relationship marketing—first in business-to-business markets, later in consumer markets—had been transforming the traditional "rules of game" since the 1970s and 1980s. And the impact of direct marketing originated from the 1950s and 1960s. All of these disciplines questioned the very ground of traditional media advertising, from inaccuracy to accountability. If, as most Internet marketers argued, the Web represented a powerful drive of technology integration, they did *not* mean that this integration would take place on the terms of Internet *advertising* (at best, a small segment of all actual and *potential* Internet applications). Instead, such integration would have to proceed on the terms of a *new marketing concept*—one that the pioneering marketers, such as Regis McKenna and others, had been developing for years (see Chapter 2).[23]

Prior to that integration, marketers would have to get familiar with their new online instruments. That process began with the Web and the arrival of the first browsers around 1993 and 1994. It peaked around 1997 and 1998 when the online budgets became an inherent part of the media plan.

ONLINE AND OFFLINE ADVERTISING

After the mid-1990s, the emergence of the Internet media and the consolidation of interactive ad agency business coincided; the two went hand in hand. To increase profitability, the market leaders had to be able to raise entry barriers and switching costs. In order to raise entry barriers and switching costs, they engaged in waves of M&A activities. In the process, the stronger companies grew stronger, the smaller focused on niche markets, and the fragile ones were restructured, sliced in pieces, sold off, or liquidated.

In the late 1990s, Internet began to come to its own as a "media." *Technologically*, this process accelerated rapidly with the launch of the World Wide Web and Mosaic, the commercial browsers (Netscape Navigator, Microsoft's Internet Explorer), the fusion of traditional analog TV and networked PCs (the rise of NetPC's and Web TV Networks), as well as many other convergence developments. *Commercially*, viable business and marketing models played a critical role—not just, for instance, the creation of banner advertising, but the standardization of banners for the purposes of media selling, buying, and planning.

Most methods and techniques of Internet marketing communications evolved during the first five years after the launch of the Web. In the summer of 1997, Jupiter Communications, the leading Internet consumer market research company, published an influential research report on Internet advertising models. Specializing in emerging consumer online and interactive technologies, the New York City–based research, consulting, and publishing firm identified several distinct models for creative online advertising: banners, sponsorships, nested ad content, interstitials, product placement, advertorials, and incentive advertising.

Jupiter's report analyzed the effectiveness of each form in achieving specific goals—whether targeting an audience, branding a product, driving traffic to one's site, executing point-of-purchase sales, or providing easy accessibility for mainstream consumers.[24] The model provided an adequate framework for Internet marketers, in particular consumer marketers and Web publishers. In the long term, it was necessary, but not sufficient.[25]

The models of Internet marketing communications can also be differentiated according to their chronological dominance (Exhibit 5-2).

Early Internet Techniques from E-Mail to Home Pages. The first phase (e.g., chat groups, e-mail) preceded the emergence of the World Wide Web and the first generation of browsers, but adjusted quite rapidly to the new developments (e.g., the first home pages, advertisers' websites, nested ad content).

Banners and Extended Variations. The evolution of Internet marketing communications ensued with sponsored banners (banner advertising, i.e., banners, buttons, keywords, hot corners, etc.). It became possible with the first browsers and evolved into extended variations (cross-branded content, interstitials).

Online Direct Models. If banner advertising represents efforts to apply the traditional broadcast ad model on the Web, online direct reflect attempts by direct marketers to exploit their ad model in the cyberspace (e.g., direct response, advertising networks, etc.). (On the first direct models, see Chapter 4.)

Offline Advertising (e.g., Push). Starting in the mid-1990s, push validated the idea that even *off-line* marketing communications could be based on effective business models. Historically, this phase accompanied extended banner variations. Still, it should be appraised separately because it involves far more than the incremental development of banners, banner variations or extensions, or other *on-line* marketing communications.

Hybrid Access Technologies. If push extended Internet marketing communications from online to offline advertising, WebTV networks reflected and accelerated the convergence of the traditional television set and the contemporary PC. Providing a form of hybrid access into the Web, it also gave rise to new opportunities in Internet marketing communications.

Virtual Communities: Portals. This phase is partly autonomous, but it is also *based* on all the previous phases and represents their continuation

Exhibit 5-2
Evolution of Internet Marketing Communications: From the 1980s to the Late 1990s

Time Periods	Internet Marketing Communications	Dominant Techniques	Some Yardsticks
1980s-1994: Prior to Browser Wars →	1. I-techniques from e-mail to home pages • Chat • E-Mail • Advertisers' web sites • Nested Ad Content	• Electronic billboard • Non-profit online communities • Newsletters • Corporate web sites • Web sites of distinct brands • Micro web sites within the banner	• EDI (big business) • Failure of interactive TV • The first generation of browsers • First home pages • First web sites • One-to-one marketing
1995-1996 Peak of Browser Wars →	2. Online banners/extensions • Banners – and Buttons, Keywords, Portals, Hot Corners, and so on • Cross-Branded Content • Interstitials 3. Online Direct Models • Direct services; ad nets 4. Offline Advertising • Push 5. Online Communities • Destination sites; free e-mailers; ICQ; portals	• Static • Animated • Sponsored • Product placements • Animated (intermercials) • Customized mass marketing (DoubleClick, Link Exchange, • Content sites/mass reach (AOL Digital City, MS Sidewalk, etc.) • Mediation of content producers	• Launch of HotWired • From non-profit banners to sponsored banners • Netscape IPO triggers 1st Internet IPO wave • B-to-b builds web sites (intranets, extranets) • I-ad agencies: from test budgets to profit centers • Rise and failure of Pathfinder • Rise of new media business • Industry organization (IAB, CASIE, NYNMA) • Consolidation of new media by int'l ad agency networks
1997 - Consolidation and convergence →	6. Hybrids • WebTV Networks 7. Internet retail and Models of E-Commerce 8. New/Discontinuous Platforms • 3-D Browsers, etc.	• Increasingly complex marketing communications • First Filters (PICS) • Breakdown/ differentiation of banner models	• 2nd Internet IPO wave (Amazon, E*Trade, etc.) • Rise of e-commerce stocks • "Portal mania"; stock market's highest valuations • Rise of high-speed access (e.g., cable modems, DSL, etc.)

as *virtual communities*. These online communities—or "destination sites," as they were called at the time—evolved through the integration of various Internet marketing techniques into extended websites. By 1997 and 1998, when they became known as "portals," most had adopted and absorbed Web-driven direct response to accelerate the expansion of their installed bases (e.g., Microsoft's acquisition of Hotmail, America Online's purchase of Mirabilis and its ICQ, Yahoo's buy of the online game and sweepstake powerhouse Yoyodyne, etc.). Certain models of electronic commerce were reminiscent of high-traffic portals (e.g., Amazon.com, E*Trade, etc.), but their focus on transactions went far beyond the modified broadcast ad model—and gave rise to new kinds of auction companies (e.g., Price.com, eBay, etc.), which some observers saw as precedents of online category killers.

New and/or Discontinuous Platforms. By definition, this phase relies on new techniques, which require increasing bandwidth and high access speed. This phase can be inferred, but its specifics cannot be determined *a priori*. These products, services, and technologies may serve as both substitutes or complements of the existing Internet activities and ad models (e.g., 3D browsers).

In the following, the emphasis will be on those forms of Internet marketing communications that currently serve as the drivers of the business. Practical considerations dictate this focus. However exciting or interesting the banners and their variations as techniques or creative products, they are useful only if they serve the markets.

By 1997, Jupiter analysts could conclude that online advertising was well on its way to becoming a highly significant segment of the advertising industry and that traditional advertising agencies and advertisers were taking notice. As late as 1995, the Web ad revenues had amounted to just $60 million. In its *The 1998 Online Advertising Report*, Jupiter forecasted Web ad revenues to increase to $9 billion by the year 2002.[26] Most of this advertising stemmed from banner advertising.

Banner Advertising

Between 1993 and 1994, when Mosaic dominated the market and Netscape Navigator began its explosive expansion, the first Web advertisers found their business models by trial and error. By the mid-1990s, banners emerged as the most common advertising product sold on the Web. It was the ad unit of choice for the majority of the advertisers. The evolution of banner ads went hand in hand with the dynamics of the Internet. Between 1993 and the late 1990s, the surfers got used to faster modems (from 14,4 and 28.8-kbps to 56.6-kbps). By 1998, both telcos and cable companies were launching higher-speed solutions in test and established markets.

Banners

In the past, "heavy users" had relied on ISDN, but now MSOs were pushing cable modems while telcos relied on DSL. The development of the technology and the decline of price went hand in hand with more sophisticated banner advertising: the faster the pace of the convergence, the faster the transition from the static banners to dynamic banners. Instead of the "old" and passive banner ads, the idea was to use more animation, color, sound, and complexity to attract users' attention more effectively. These techniques helped to deliver some of the advantages TV and radio advertising currently had over print-like banners.

In the future, most of these intermediary phases—e.g., animated, sound, and real-time banners—may well be forgotten. But in the second half of the 1990s, each yardstick served a function in the justification of banners and Internet advertising as a legitimate form of advertising. Nothing happened automatically. No transition took place just because it made sense technologically. Each had to be justified in terms of the entire ad budget, integrated marketing communications, or return on invested capital (ROI). In the long run, however, many companies (especially in Silicon Valley) had a significant interest in the expansion of the Internet marketplace. They would often attempt to ease the competitive pressures by trying to accelerate the development of online ad models. In August 1997, for instance, chip-making giant Intel was overhauling its cooperative-advertising program with customers in a way that could singlehandedly boost overall ad spending on the Internet annually by more than 40%, or about $166 million.[27] Research firm Dataquest estimated that, in 1998, Intel would bring in $13.9 billion from sales of chips to manufacturers.[28]

Static Banners. In the early phase of their evolution, the banner ads were relatively static. In retrospect, these banners look "primitive" in their design and appeal, a little like the relatively unsophisticated black and white commercials of American television in the early 1950s. The concept of the banner is clear, but the execution is simplistic. The technology and slow access speed constrained a more sophisticated unique selling proposal.

Animated Banners. After the mid-1990s, a typical banner ad was a horizontal, rectangular graphic image appearing at the top of a web page, and often using GIF, Java, or Shockwave animations. The banner usually included some text (i.e., a phrase or slogan and the advertiser's name and Internet address). If the user found the ad intriguing enough, he/she would click on the ad, which activated an embedded link, to visit the advertiser's website.[29]

Sound Banners. Until the fall of 1997, Web surfers had seen mainly static and animated banners. In early September, they encountered ads that not only blinked and danced for attention but also banged and yelled at users. AT&T launched a two-week ad campaign on about a half-dozen sites featuring a little girl who knocked on the door and plead, "Hey, let me in." The ad debuted on popular sites such as USA Today, Lycos, GeoCities, and CBS Sportsline. The surfers found the experience as exciting as perhaps the first movie viewers who heard Al Jolson sing in a "talkie." Sound was hardly new to Internet advertising, but, in the AT&T campaign, an advertiser used it in a broad-based ad program. Unlike most sound-based ads that required the user to download applications or players, this ad worked across platforms without plug-ins.[30] Modem Media, a pioneer interactive ad agency, developed the ad for AT&T. Joshua Sacks, the agency's account director, said that Modem was aiming to bring the characters developed in AT&T's television commercials to the Web. "We're really trying to press the envelope."[31]

Real-Time Banners. In March 1998, Darwin Digital, a division of advertising giant Saatchi & Saatchi, introduced a Java-based product, NOW (for "news on the Web") that allowed its client, Time New Media, to deliver up-to-date information via banners. That contrasted with a two-day to two-week wait that Time and Darwin Digital said was the current lag for updating banners. The ads were launched on Yahoo!, Lycos, and Time New Media. The new advertising technique allowed the advertisers themselves to update the ads.[32] "This is the first service to really place the power to change real-time content and put it into the advertiser's hands," said Darwin Digital chief technology officer Daniel Reznick. "Up until now, the whole process of buying media online has been a very offline process. Buying media space and placing the creative content has been slow and cumbersome."[33]

Transactive Banners. Until the spring of 1998, online advertisers would often use click-through to measure their ad message and media buy, which did not always account for impulse buying. In April, however, two products were announced to spark impulse buying online. Narrative's Enliven/Impulse service allowed customers to place orders and enter major credit card data *directly into a banner*. Narrative's partners for the Enliven/Impulse service were 1–800–Flowers, Eddie Bauer Inc., and Godiva Chocolatier. In a few animated screens, the new banner let the customer place an order in about a minute. Also, Narrative's Enliven/ HardCopy service allowed marketers to distribute literature on demand printed through banners. This service was the result of a collaborative design effort with Hewlett-Packard Co.; it allowed advertisers to design sales literature for the Internet that more closely resembled their branding and corporate identity image. Both Java-based services simplified the sales process, made banners more interactive, and avoided drawing visitors off of a hosting website.[34]

Exhibit 5-3
Banner Effectiveness Tips (1996)

Lesson 1: Target, Target, Target
. . . Taking advantage of the Web's ability to deliver highly targeted audiences will help you generate leads and sales and create the one-to-one relationships which will extend and build your brand.

Lesson 2: Pose Questions
Don't just make statements or show pretty pictures. Use questions ("Looking for free software?" "Have you seen?"). They initiate an interaction with the banner by acting as a teaser. They entice people to click on your banner. More importantly, they can raise click-through by 16% over average.

Lesson 3: Bright Colors
Colors affect the eye differently. Using bright colors can help attract a user's eye, contributing to higher response rates. Research has shown that blue, green and yellow work best, while white, red, and black are less effective.

Lesson 4: Home Is Not Always Sweet
While the home page often performs very well, a site may have other pages that outperform it. . . . By carefully analyzing these pages, you can increase your response by placing your banner on a page that better attracts your target audience.

Lesson 5: Location, Location, Location
According to research, banners that appear on first page load are more likely to be clicked on. Negotiate ad placement on the top of page when buying space. The best possible scenario is having banners placed both on the top and on the bottom of a page.

Lesson 6: Use Animation
Animation can help catch a user's eye. Strategic use of movement grabs attention more effectively than static banners. Using simple Java or .gif animation can increase response rates by up to 25%.

Lesson 7: Use Cryptic Messages
. . . Cryptic ad banners can help involve a user in the message. Because the "sponsor" of the message is not revealed, cryptic messages can be very intriguing. But there is a downside. Branding is forfeited on the ad. This may not be an issue if branding is not your main objective. Cryptic messages typically increase click-through 18%.

Lesson 8: Call to Action
As in traditional direct response, a call to action is known to raise response rates. Simple phrases such as "Click Here," "Visit Now" and "Enter Here" tend to improve response rates by 15%. These phrases should be strategically placed in the ad, preferably on the right side. This is where the eye will be drawn.

Lesson 9: Avoid Banner Burnout
. . . After the fourth impression, average response rates typically dropped to under 1%. We call this banner burnout, the point at which a banner stops delivering a good Return on Investment. . . . Controlling your frequency extends your reach and maximizes your ad dollar.

Lesson 10: Measure Beyond the Click
Click-through is not always the best measurement of campaign effectiveness. It depends on your objectives.

Exhibit 5-3 (continued)

If you are simply trying to drive traffic, the click-through is great. If you are trying to gather leads, the best measurement is the number of people who clicked through and filled out a lead form. 3% click-through and 80% lead fulfillment is better than 10% click-through and 20% fulfillment. If you are trying to measure brand impact, conduct an online brand awareness study, or measure user interaction with your site.

Source: DoubleClick (1996).

Banner Effectiveness. By 1996, DoubleClick/I/Pro research showed that banner effectiveness was influenced by some ten basic determinants, which ranged from the general objectives of the campaign to the details of the design. To be effective, for instance, banners had to be properly targeted; strategic use of animation grabbed attention far more effectively than static banners, and so on (Exhibit 5-3). The DoubleClick/I/PRO research also questioned traditional industry wisdom, arguing that there was a "sweet-spot" for user response; after the fourth impression, average response rates tended to drop to under 1%. This is what the researchers called banner burnout, the point at which a banner stops delivering a good return on investment (ROI).[35]

Even these research results must be seen against a moving target (i.e., the rapidly-expanding Web demographics and Internet dynamics). *When* DoubleClick/I/PRO research was conducted in 1996, the Internet penetration was relatively low. In *such* an early Web environment, animations, among other things, still *differed* from the majority of banners. But when the rest of the banners caught up, even animated banners became part of the general "noise" in cyberspace. New technological innovations could provide only fleeting advantages. The process was inescapable, and similar developments had been seen in the evolution (and decreased length) of American TV commercials (compare Exhibit 2-1). With the Internet, however, the compression of time and pace was overwhelming. What took two to three decades in television advertising took just two to three years in banner advertising.

Buttons

"Buttons" soon emerged as some of the smallest ad units on the Web. As miniature banners, they often served as selling vehicles for Web publishers. On CNET, for example, these buttons were advertisements for various software products (Exhibit 5-4). The companies paid the Web publisher (here CNET) a royalty for placing its button on a home page or web pages. If and when the user clicked on the button, it took the user to the company's download site. That site featured a more or less detailed description of the product, other information and access links

Exhibit 5-4
Buttons, Keywords, and Interstitials

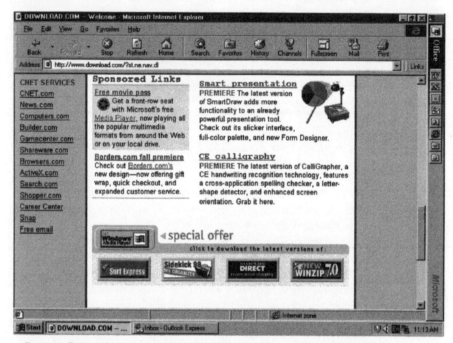

Buttons. Buttons soon emerged as some of the smallest ad units on the Web. As miniature banners, *buttons* often serve as selling vehicles for Web publishers. On CNET, for example, these buttons are advertisements for various software products (here Windows Media Player, Surf Express, Sidekick 98, Surplus Direct, and New Winzip 7.0).

www.download.com

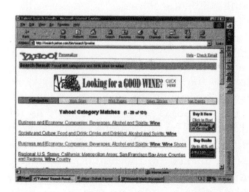

Context-Based Keywords. If, in October 1998, one would have conducted a context-based keyword search for "wine" on Yahoo, it would have yielded 101 categories and 3,416 sites, but also an advertisement for Wine Spectator's "Looking for a Good Wine?"

www.yahoo.com

Exhibit 5-4 (continued)

Interstitials. Berkeley Systems used a full-color, full-sound, animated spot to begin the online version of its "You Don't Know Jack" game show (for which a user had to download a separate application).

www.bezerk.com

to download a digital intangible (e.g., software products) directly or to order a more tangible product (e.g., an Amazon book). On their miniature level, buttons reflect the integration of media advertising *and* direct response through the Internet as the medium. Unlike both advertising and direct, however, these buttons provided a direct *point-of-sales* interface. Consequently, their role would be critical in the emerging electronic commerce.

Context-Based Keywords

With text input by their users, search engines conduct searches of relevant content on the Web or in more narrow content categories offered to the user. Along with the search results, search companies typically display ads. In order to enhance their revenue sources, the engines allow advertisers to buy context-based key words, which display the advertiser's banner when a user searches for the word purchased. Usually, the word or words purchased are in some relevant way related to the advertiser's products, services, and/or company. In the first years of the Internet, for instance, sexually-related content proved to be a powerful driver of usage, just as it had served the same function in the early home video era. In October 1996, Mark Grimes obtained the Yahoo! Top 200 list from a banner placement company and displayed it; 60% of the top 20 keywords were sexual in nature.[36] If, in October 1998, one would have conducted a search for a commercially useful, context-based keyword (here "wine"), the search would have yielded a typical list of categories and sites (here 101 categories and 3,416 sites), but also netted an advertisement for an advertiser (here Wine Spectator's "Looking for a Good Wine?") (Exhibit 5-4).

Between 1996 and 1997, Infoseek and Yahoo! charged some $1,000 per month per keyword, and based on a target of 20,000 impressions, this yielded a CPM of $50. In its fiscal 1997, for instance, Yahoo! structured its advertising pricing on the basis of three kinds of advertising: banner ads, premium positions on the top page of Yahoo! properties that typically were used in connection with promotions and special events (promotions, special events), and context-based keyword advertising. Keyword advertising permitted advertisers to target users based upon specified keywords that a user enters when searching within Yahoo! For example, if a user enters the term "automobile" or "car," an automobile manufacturer's advertisement could appear on pages displaying the results of such a search.[37]

Interstitials

The Internet Advertising Bureau (IAB) declared 1997 a "break-through year." In 1997, Internet ad spending reached $906 million, up 240% from 1996. What may have been as, or even more, important in the long term was the changing composition of the Web ad units. While ad banners remained the dominant form of Internet advertising, interstitials—ads that appeared on the screen while Web pages downloaded—were growing in popularity.[38] The shifts had come quite abruptly; they reflected the Internet dynamic, in particular the increasing efficiency of the microprocessors and growing bandwidth.

The cumbersome word "interstitial" connotes the space that intervenes between things. Many contemporary interstitials were simply full-screen ads that occasionally popped up between pages on cutting-edge sites (compare Exhibit 5-4). The term was also applied to splash screen ads, which consisted of static ad pages that the user had to click to get to the next page. As a phenomenon, the interstitials became more widely known in first half of the year 1996. CNET was among the first to observe the *commercial significance* of the interstitials. Calling them "Billboards on the Infobahn," the online publication considered the new web ad units a TV trend infiltrating the Internet:

They can sing, they can dance, and they're always in your face. Welcome to the latest trend in online advertising. They go well beyond the usual "banner" ads—those ribbons of information that sit atop your screen, begging you to click on them while you go about your business. Instead, these new inventions come to your screen quite uninvited and unannounced and they take over. For the most part, they either sit there in the middle of your screen long enough for you to read their message, or they perform a little jig to a digitized tune. In the advertising trade, they're called "interstitials."[39]

When HotWired was launched with its sponsored banner advertising, banner ads proliferated rapidly in the Internet, usually sitting at the top of Web pages. The more familiar they became as a mode of advertising, the easier it was for the users to ignore them. Some advertisers resorted to animated Java applets to catch attention, whereas others experimented with designs that had more depth (e.g. more information instead of "just" taking the user to a referring page). Unlike the traditional one-way TV screen which allowed little information (viewers sit too far to absorb complex text information), the interactive PC screen allowed more complex text information loads (users sit in front of the PC). But after the basic format of the banner ads had been standardized, the ad unit did not exactly encourage dramatic graphic, data, or audio innovations.

The comparisons between the interstitial advertisements and television spots were obvious. A far cry from the staid, oft-maligned banner ads ubiquitous to the Web, these mini-commercials were thought to represent the next wave—an imitation of the immersive, more creatively flexible pitches found on TV. Interstitials popped up to snare the user's attention in a more active, TV-like manner. This type of ad came in various forms, including a "cover page" of ads that a user had to click through to get to a home, the quick "billboards" flashed between a site's pages, or a full-color, full-sound, animated spot.[40] Essentially, the interstitials provided the advertisers and Web publishers a way to go "beyond the banners." These ads appeared on the screen *while* the users were still surfing, often when they were entering a site. Most interstitials took two basic forms: static or animated.

Static Interstitials. The first interstitials were static. Most commonly, a static picture filled the screen with text about the advertised product or service. Sometimes, the picture disappeared after a certain amount of time or allowed one to click it away. The classic example was Women's Wire, which provided an ad-driven interstitial "cover page"; it would pop up before the official home page loaded onto the screen. In these first interstitials, the static solution was necessitated by primitive technology and slow access speed. The downside involved a backlash in which frustrated users might leave a site: if users would have to wait too long for the interstitial cover page to fade away and the official home page to load onto the screen, they would surf away. With accelerating digitalization and increasing access speed and bandwidth, static interstitials were soon replaced by animated interstitials.

Animated Interstitials. Heavy on multimedia, animated interstitial ads included sound and simple animation. Indeed, some observers considered "true" interstitials animated ones lasting 5–15 seconds. Due to the technology, they also required the users to download players and content before viewing. At best, they did look like TV commercials, but few users would download additional software merely to view them; such obstacles constrained their use in the latter half of the 1990s. They were not useful in an Internet media whose reach was still, and would long remain, far behind that of broadcast or cable TV. If, however, the users were already loyal to or had a relationship with a given website, they could enhance frequency.

The classic animated interstitials consisted of online games, which had a highly loyal niche market. The best known example may well have been the "You Don't Know Jack—The Netshow" (Exhibit 5–4). Berkeley Systems' irreverent quiz game became a hit when it went online in December 1996, registering more than 100,000 players. The interactive game was designed to mimic a television game show. After every five or six questions, a mini-commercial popped onto the monitor, taking up the entire screen with animation and music. "It's an Up Thing," rang the familiar jingle imploring players to drink Seven Up. In another ad, for a popular search engine, a pitch man asked "Do You Yahoo!?" The concept of these TV-like spots got a key endorsement in April 1997, when MSNBC launched an experiment with online commercials, a two-week trial for a five-second, animated commercial on its "Life" page. The commercials allowed advertisers to convey a brand message without having to rely on a visitor to click on a banner (i.e., the company was looking for the equivalent of 30-second spot).[41] Known primarily for its push-technology leadership, PointCast was also an interstitial pioneer. In the second half of 1996, it began running little animated advertisements in its screensaver and newsreader.

By mid-1997, Jupiter Communications concluded that while banners had dominated online advertising so far, several other creative possibilities were now emerging, including interstitials. Jupiter forecasted that by the year 2001, a quarter of all online ad spending would go to interstitials.[42] Many observers and industry practitioners considered the estimate far too optimistic, including Fergus O'Daly, Jr., former chief executive of Poppe Tyson and later CKS Partners (Eastern Region) (Exhibit 5-5).

Sponsorships

During the early days of the Internet, the advertisers launched their first home pages. The mission and the objectives of these pioneering web pages was seldom carefully thought through. Oftentimes, the idea was to launch a site quickly, in order to position the company or brand "where the action is" and to benefit from learning experience. Some home pages featured the corporate image, the business mission, and the

Exhibit 5-5
It's the Marketplace, Stupid . . .

"From the very beginning, I haven't thought that the interstitials would make it on the Web," argues Fergus O'Daly, Jr., a seasoned ad agency veteran and former executive of Poppe Tyson and CKS Partners (Eastern). "Interstitials have a very small share in the market. It's one of those things that occasionally pop up on the Web. Initially, it may have seemed like a great idea that got everyone excited. But it is not a real business."

O'Daly suggests that the proponents of the interstitials were enamored by technology, at the expense of the marketplace. "True, as the bandwidth increases, the cable and the telephone companies will come together. But even with the ability to deliver more video capability, the Web will never be a TV set. By the year 2000, most web users will be female consumers. If that is the case, then the firms should look what it is that *women* like."

Of course, certain forms of Internet advertising and user segments were not mutually exclusive. If, generally speaking, the Internet entailed a shift of bargaining power to the buyer, developing this medium on the terms of the technology was precisely the wrong thing to do. Hence, O'Daly's emphasis on the Internet as a promotional *sales* medium. "Instead of straightforward brand advertising on the Internet, the companies should use promotional banners and animation. Users love to see and react to messages, such as 'FREE' or 'DISCOUNT.' Rather than do something just for the sake of technology, it is better to use banners. If my rowboat changes six different colors on the banner, it won't be getting hits. The smart thing is to show product differentiation that can be demonstrated in a banner. If, for instance, there is an umbrella that opens in a different way, you could show that in a fast banner and attract someone's attention. That stuff should go *into* the banners.

"Similarly, being able to buy products in the banner and not having to go to a web site is a great idea. That way you can acquire, within a banner, a coupon of a product that you are familiar with. 'Total toothpaste!' 'Look here!' 'Fill out the X and we'll give you 25 cents off'—they are all good ideas if that's what people want.

"Banners are here to stay. Still, what you do *within* the banner will change and video will be part of that change. It will become far more prevalent in consumer marketing; it will replace jumping through a web site where you can get easily lost. In the business-to-business, companies such as IBM will have to advertise specific products. It is wrong to expect the users to click on IBM.com and go into the firm's web site to spend three-to-four minutes finding out where the product is. If things are done properly with a splash page, they will get more traffic from clicking on a proper banner."

Source: Dan Steinbock, interview with Fergus O'Daly, formerly President, CKS Partners, Inc., August 3, 1998.

annual report. These companies saw the Internet as an electronic bill-board—a one-way venue of corporate communications. At the opposite end, companies invested heavily on high-profile web pages that featured, along with the corporate image, the business mission, and the annual report, other information on the company, its services and products, games, links, and so on. These companies saw the then-Internet as an embodiment of the Web visionaries' visions. Both efforts missed the point. The former regarded the Web as just another marketing channel, a sort of a cost-efficient but one-way cable; the latter mistook the then-slow Internet for the future high-bandwidth medium. The former did not exploit the technologies endogeneous to the medium; the latter thought too much of them.

At the time, most nontechnology advertisers were launching minimal sites with just the basic functions. Those companies that went further (e.g., Levi Strauss's first home page) were far fewer and often exploited the web pages for the purposes of event marketing. Historically, the relaunch of the first home pages by both advertisers and Web publishers coincided with the Internet market correction between late May and August 1996. The new web pages were often designed more pragmatically and cost-efficiently. Mass marketers also began to explore new Web-driven business models. When, for instance, Levi Strauss coupled the concept of website with mass customization, it came up with the idea of Levi's Original Spin (i.e., customers creating their own jeans).

Sponsorships proliferated rapidly in the Web, and in a variety of forms. Oftentimes, the boundaries between online editorials and marketing grew blurry. Many first entrants felt they had to "stretch" the old distinctions, if only to survive financially and justify the presence of an autonomous Web profit unit. Many incumbents were "forgiven" for such conduct. After the players understood that profitability through subscriber revenues was a myth, most sought to accelerate advertiser revenues. The situation was far more difficult for those entrenched players, such as newspaper houses, whose branded product rode on the idea of neutrality and objectivity (e.g., the occasional debates over the database marketing programs of New York Times Electronic Media).[43]

*Sponsorship Types.*Both advertisers and Web publishers encouraged the users to click through to the sponsor's site. Due to the low penetration of the early Internet (and the ensuing low click-through rates), most players exploited their early web pages mainly for learning and long-term brand building. For that purpose, the Internet was not as useful as, say, broadcast or cable television, even if it did provide critical learning experience to the first entrants. The definitions of sponsorship on the Web were far from clear. Still, one might divide them into several basic categories: branded content, advertorials, microsites, portals, product placements, and event promotions—the latter would play a critical role in bringing the Web to American households and accelerating the convergence momentum.[44]

Sponsored and Branded Content

When HotWired, in October 1994, ran the first Web ad, it offered a 12-week sponsorship for a flat rate of $30,000 to AT&T and ran an ad for "The Virtual Museum," along with ads from Sprint, MCI, Volvo, and others. Since no precedents existed, HotWired's arrangement became an early model for others to follow and even two to three years later many sites still sold flat-rate sponsorships. Unlike the HotWired website, however, they were compelled to guarantee a minimum number of impressions. While the *sponsored content* appeared in a new medium, its pricing applied a variation on the CPM theme.

In the *branded content* model, a more specific version of sponsored content, the advertiser usually had no role in creating or shaping the content. The Web publisher assumed responsibility for editorial control, whereas the brand benefited from the association with the quality content. These strategic "partnerships" could bring synergic benefits to each. As deals, these partnerships had to be negotiated as longer-term contracts or exclusive arrangements so that other advertisers would not be associated with the content. An advertiser could sponsor a regular section of a site (e.g., Oldmobile's sponsorship of CBS SportLine's Auto Racing section) or, in some cases, the entire site (e.g., Toyota's underwritten ad budget of Time Warner's Cars and Culture site). In July 1998, for instance, Toyota appeared in several sections of New York Times on the Web.

Advertorials

Advertorials could be considered specific instances of sponsored content. They also blurred the line between ad and editorial content on the Web. Originating in print journalism, they were usually isolated as paid advertisements (e.g., distinct font, surrounding border, "Paid Advertisement" label, and so on). Unlike web publishing, however, newspaper industry had long been a mature industry. Small Web publishers stretched boundaries to survive, but entrenched media companies were quick to follow them. As advertising designed to blend with editorials, advertorials were more akin to infomercials and would, in the long term, fulfill a somewhat identical role as direct sale instruments. In certain cases, the Web publisher created the advertiser's editorial, which helped it fuse with the rest of the site. For instance, Microsoft Expedia's Mungo Park, the famed online adventure magazine, offered marketers a unique opportunity to use the Web to reach a highly valued niche audience. As the website put it, "The technology behind Mungo Park allowed armchair travelers to explore the world interactively—without getting their feet wet!"[45]

Portals, Portal Sponsorships

As a vehicle of Internet advertising, a portal sponsorship, or portal (not to be confused with a portal *site*), represented one of the murkiest categories of sponsorship. As a hybrid, a portal had a dual function: it was an arrangement in which one site agreed to integrate the content of another site as a service to users and a branding value to the content provider. In the mid-1990s, it was widely used by CNET's site pages; it referred to a linkable graphic that resided within the tool bar of these pages.[46]

In many portal arrangements, the exchange stemmed on barter rather than money. Through such arrangements, an entrenched player could exploit its entrenched positions through links with various business segments. Such deals were natural playground for synergic plays. In the late 1990s, a typical example involved the the cross-promotional portal arrangements of ABCNews.com and Mr. Showbiz which were owned by Capital Cities/ABC, which in turn was owned by Walt Disney Corp., which had legendary expertise in the exploitation of cross-promotional synergies. In other kind of portal sponsorships, exclusive portals could direct high user traffic (e.g., America Online's exclusive link deals with certain category sites). In still other arrangements, rival websites battled ferociously to secure exclusive linking arrangements (e.g., the rivalry of Amazon and Barnes & Noble for the preferred online bookstore).

*Hot Corners.*Hot corners were CNET's linkable graphics that resided in the upper-right corner of the DOWNLOAD.COM pages. The ad was linked to a hot-corner ad area, where the company could display corporate and product information.[47]

Product Placements (Brand Placements)

In general, product placements are just another of the many tools that marketers can use to enhance the visibility of a brand and support the advertising process. Often referred to as brand placement, product placement was long considered a means to brand exposure. Marketers and advertisers thought product placements affected only consumers' perceptions of a brand (i.e., attitudinal rather than behavioral factors). With the immediate sales impact of many successful campaigns, however, product placement can be situated along more traditional sales promotion tactics, such as coupons, sampling, and sweepstakes. After E.T. gobbled up Reese's Pieces in 1982, big consumer-products companies began to include placement in their marketing arsenal. Getting a business or product into the plot or onto the set of a movie or TV show can help catapult a company out of obscurity. When Tom Cruise prominently sipped the Jamaican brew Red Stripe in *The Firm*, for example, sales increased 50%.[48]

By the fall of 1996, major marketers were getting into product placements by allowing content sites to link to sites where certain products were sold. This type of advertising, barely in its infancy, ranged from linking a seemingly unrelated content site directly to a product site where goods were sold or vice versa. As we already have seen, Microsoft Network's online travel agency Expedia linked directly with the online service's Mungo Park, a site featuring multimedia-rich reporting about world exhibitions. Banner ads were being enhanced so that they flashed or "morphed" to grab the surfer's attention. Companies were experimenting with layering banner ads so that readers could click on them for more information without going to the advertiser's home page.[49]

With the passage of time, product placements got more extensive, sophisticated, complex, and attractive. In August 1998, for instance, America Online announced a marketing agreement with *Baywatch*, a popular and internationally syndicated TV show. The online service would receive product placement and be written into the plot of a Baywatch episode in the spring of 1999. In addition, the two parties sponsored a race car that competed in the Ford Los Angeles Street Race. "One of the reasons for '*Baywatch's* long-term success has been its cutting-edge partnerships with progressive companies like AOL," remarked Joe Scotti, VP of Marketing and Sales for Pearson Television. *Baywatch* producer Kevin Beggs added, "The opportunity to partner with AOL, with its 12.5 million online members, is a perfect creative and strategic fit for *Baywatch*. Finding high-tech ways to enhance our program and to reach new viewers is extremely important to *Baywatch* and our parent company, Pearson Television."[50] In such marketing agreements, the right strategic alliances benefited all parties.

Microsites

Having first familiarized advertisers and Web publishers with sponsored content, HotWired also took it further by rolling out "microsites" sponsored by its advertisers. Less intrusive than banners, sponsored sites attracted many advertisers who hoped the users would associate the content with the advertiser's company, product, or service. One of the earliest examples was HotWired's site called Dream Jobs, which was sponsored by Dockers. Designed to promote the idea that, in one's dream job, one could wear Dockers at work, the microsite exploited lifestyle marketing. Many microsites expanded the advertorials to multiple ad/ content pages and were reminiscent of special ad supplements to magazines and newspapers. A pioneer in sponsorships, New York Times Electronic Media let advertisers obtain personal profile information from users, which allowed ads to be highly targeted. It also provided microsites to major corporations like Delta, Visa, and Dunkin' Donuts, which leveraged the New York Times' material to create microsites. The newspaper house's Web unit considered these sites "branding plays that position the corporate message with The Times' content."

Like Dream Jobs, these sites strove to maintain a thematic consistency with the Web publisher's content *while* allowing the advertiser to familiarize the visitor with the brand. The idea was not to draw the visitor away from the editorial site to the advertiser's corporate site; rather, it was to augment the editorial content with advertising content. At best, the de facto strategic partnership allowed both to realize their objectives (journalism, brand-building/online sales); at worst, the joint pages compromised objectivity in journalism, led to incongruities between editorial and ad content, or permitted editorials that might be considered harmful from the standpoint of the brand.

Many analysts considered the best example of a mutually useful online service using Web technology to be Physicians' Online Network. As the world's leading medical information and communication network, it connected a growing base of physician members with the largest online community of their peers. It offered the most up-to-date medical resources, Web access, and direct links to associations, health plans, pharmaceutical sponsors, and healthcare organizations. The service could be accessed only by registered physicians. It had in excess of 130,000 members, or almost 25% of practicing physicians in North America.[51]

Reflecting a more general concept, this "online community" of professionals offered a targeted demographic, which created a compelling market for advertisers in the industry (medical field). It was an intriguing Web model providing a precedent for *many other* trade and industry associations that harbored both profit-oriented and nonprofit objectives.

Event Promotions

Unlike longer-term sponsored or branded content, event promotions were short-term arrangements, typically a few weeks, highlighting a special offer, contest, or event. They required a closer integration of publisher and advertiser content. Serving the goals of short-term campaigns, they sought great visibility. With the emergence of pay-per-view cable, for instance, the media and entertainment industry had tried to sell the attractiveness of the delivery channel with high-profile, big-name PPV events, including rock concerts, professional wrestling, prize fights, movie premieres, and Broadway shows. Even prior to the PPV, Warner had offered the Larry Holmes–Gerry Cooney heavy-weight title fight on its QUBE systems in 1982.[52] Unsurprisingly, the technique became quite familiar as the lines between the TV and the PC began to get blurry.

Even prior to the mid-1990s, the Web publishers often posted event promotions at the top of the home page. In the era of slow access speeds, that part of the screen would the first to be downloaded; it had to be attractive. With its high-traffic navigation hub, Yahoo! served many clients in such contest sponsorship. In fact, it was this focus on promotions and the customer databases that prompted the destination site to acquire Yoyodyne in the fall of 1998.[53] Often integrated into the Yahoo! logos and icons, such promotions had a relatively constant function in the website. The near-permanent role of promotional partners like VISA, for instance, anticipated the coming of electronic commerce. Unlike television or cable, however, the Internet had not yet been sold to the critical mass of Americans.

Cross-Promotion

Selling the Internet Media: Cross-Promotion. After the mid-1990s, event promotion *also* served to sell the new media to American households. In this sense, it functioned as an instrument of cross-promotion (i.e., promotion of a product to the buyers of another product sold by the same seller). The expansion of the Web, for instance, resulted in promotional efforts in several emerging categories, including music. Already in December 1996, *Rolling Stone* and America Online had teamed up to offer Rolling Stone Online, featuring music news, reviews, features, and live interviews. Not to be outdone, Microsoft Network launched an online serialization of former *Rolling Stone* writer Fred Goldman's book, *The Mansion on the Hill: Dylan, Young, Geffen, Springsteen, and the Head-On Collision of Rock and Commerce.* Capitalizing on its brand popularity, Sony Online, in March 1997, launched a site that included an online music channel dubbed Siren. By mid-July, MTV Networks and Yahoo! rolled out their online music guide, dubbed Unfurled, heating up competition in the online music market.[54] In turn, sports events were being updated regularly on their respective websites (e.g., the Giants' website), which allowed the fans to follow scores, receive audio clips and game rosters— as well as get used to the medium.

As event- and cross-promotion accelerated, online TV listings increasingly were at the center of TV and PC convergence. In January 1997, WebTV and Rupert Murdoch's TV Guide, for instance, launched an alliance to link editorial content. The service, which would be renamed the TV Guide Entertainment Network, was about to offer more than 200,000 pages of content, including a movie database, quizzes, and soap opera news as well as chat sites featuring entertainment and sports figures. The objective of the website was defensive, to protect the turf.[55] By the end of 1997, clickTV said its TV listings included more than 11,000 cable, broadcast, and DBS (direct broadcast satellite) lineups. Concurrently, the rivalry was heating up as new providers entered the marketplace, including Gist which partnered with the Internet Movie Database (IMDb) to provide TV listings and movie-related information. These services posed still another threat to print media, especially metropolitan daily newspapers, which considered TV listings *their* stable.

The phenomenon was not limited to sports, music, online and other major categories. It extended to drama, which some observers saw as the promotional locomotive for the new Internet media. In September 1997,

NBC pulled an excellent season opening with a live Webcast and chat surrounding the season premiere of its top rated drama, *ER*. The *ER* cast performed the episode twice in order to give TV audiences on both coasts the chance to see it live. The rebroadcast switched the two versions, showing the East Coast version to West Coast audiences and vice versa. The network also took advantage of all of its media outlets in publicizing the premiere. NBC used Astrovision, its large-screen Times Square television screen, to promote the cybercast, and links from the NBC, Warner Bros., and Talk City sites were also set up to funnel additional traffic to the site. Mary Devincenzi, a spokeswoman for Talk City, believed that this had been the first time the Internet had been used so extensively to hype a television program: "Bringing it [TV] to the Internet is very new. We think it will be huge."[56] It *was*. The season premiere attracted in record numbers *both* Internet users *and* TV viewers. The *ER* pilot garnered a record audience of some 42.7 million American TV viewers. The ERLive.com project on the Net attracted nearly 2 million page views of chat, trivia games, and 3-D set tours. Users received more than 60,000 ERLive.com streaming video feeds related to the show's premiere, and users logged 293,950 chat minutes while watching the video feeds.[57]

This success and others of similar kind had a significant function in the history of the Internet *adoption*. It inspired other companies to exploit event promotion to sell products and services, and the Internet to the Americans. In growth markets, success bred success. But it was *event-* and *cross*-promotion that often served to make the success real. At first, firms tried to create and exploit new and pure online brands. But they soon got a bitter lesson on the complexity of building strong brands on the Internet.

The Creation of Pure Online Brands: The Rise and Decline of Cybersoaps. In June 1995, American Cybercast emerged from a Los Angeles advertising agency that, while experimenting with ways to advertise on-line, created a website with a daily story about five young adults living in a trendy beach-area neighborhood. The agency hired actors to depict the characters, weaved in sound and downloadable video and answered e-mail from people who visited the site, which was called The Spot. It quickly drew a following and became a model for other episodic websites.[58] Thematically, The Spot was modeled after the contemporary sitcom favorite *Friends*; the financial model emulated the 1950s' "Golden Years" of American television when the sponsor dominated the networks.

American Cybercast, run by cable TV and ad executives, was trying to replicate Procter & Gamble's success with daytime TV soap operas. "There's a real race on for gaining market dominance quickly," said Sheri Herman, president of American Cybercast and formerly senior vice president of marketing for E! Entertainment Television. She believed broadcast and cable networks would eventually add episodic programs to their websites. "There's been a dawning recognition that they need to have an Internet presence. The cable industry started as solving a reception problem and the traditional players in broadcast industry were not aggressive in cable initially. I don't think that's going to happen again."[59]

American Cybercast wanted to develop a name brand in cyberspace for entertainment episodes the way TV networks have. But building strong online brands would not prove easy. Trying to accomplish such a feat when the Internet penetration was still relatively low, with low access speed and a broadcast business model was a heroic but doomed enterprise. By January 1997, CNET reported on the demise of the nascent genre:

Once touted as the perfect marriage of television and the Internet, cybersoaps promised to provide all the thrills of traditional TV soap operas—alien abduction, marital betrayal, family secrets—with the interactivity and community that only the Web could provide. But despite promises of glory, Web soaps have been unable to make ends meet. Unlike TV soaps, Web-sodics appealed to "20-somethings" with little disposable income, not exactly prime targets for potential advertisers. And as the 100-plus soaps on the Web were not able to generate enough traffic to stand on their own, they would have to be produced with counterparts on television and even films to survive.[60]

The timing was crucial. As cybersoaps eclipsed, event- and cross-promotions began to proliferate. Being able to exploit existing assets, the incumbent broadcast and cable leaders enjoyed a competitive advantage against the new entrants who had no strong offline brands to leverage in cyberspace. Most of these players were either entrenched media and entertainment leaders (e.g., ESPN/ESPNET SportsZone, MSNBC of Microsoft and NBC), or new and early entrants (e.g., CNET, Wired Ventures) which had quickly diversified to exploit first-mover benefits. They all sought to drive user traffic and thereby advertising revenues by cross-promoting a given site or several sites through different media. CNET was a classic example: as a producer of cable and network TV programming, it drove traffic onto its websites. The approach also typified sites with a cross-media presence, such as ESPNET SportsZone, MSNBC, and ZDNet. As long as the new Internet media had not become a mainstream item in American households, there was a natural tendency in a new medium to exploit the pre-Internet business models which were perceived as safer and less risky.

Of course, there were some examples of pure online brands, even if, as a whole, these were marginal and cult phenomena rather than staple in average households. As exceptions, they confirmed the rule. One of the most instructive ones was the Dancing Baby (see Exhibit 5-6).

Exhibit 5-6
Dancing Baby

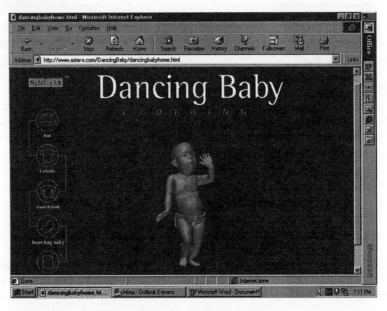

http://www.aster-x.com/DancingBaby/dancingbabyhome.html

Kinetix, the independent, multimedia business unit of Autodesk, Inc., is devoted to revolutionizing 3D computing with powerful graphics software for Microsoft® Windows NT workstations and Windows 95.

In 1998, Kinetix became even more widely known around the world due to its close association with the Dancing Baby phenomenon. Dancing Baby became a cult hero on the World Wide Web, with dozens of Dancing Baby Web sites attracting growing legions of online fans. The undulating infant also claimed an expanding television audience, with recurring appearances on David E. Kelley Productions' hit series *Ally McBeal*.

http://www.aster-x.com/DancingBaby/tshirts.html

Source: Kinetix. © Copyright 1996–99 Unreal Pictures, Inc./Autodesk, Inc.

A Success Story in Merchandising and Licensing: Ally McBeal's *Dancing Baby*. In early January 1998, American TV viewers fell in love with the Dancing Baby, originally known as "Baby Cha Cha," who made its television debut on the hit Fox TV series *Ally McBeal*. It had received as much attention as the September Webcast of the live season premiere of NBC's hit show *ER*. Now the convergence took a step still further, with the actual content being influenced by an Internet phenomenon. Typically, the success arrived by accident: the Dancing Baby appeared on the Fox show as a hallucination of title character Ally McBeal, serving as a reminder that her biological clock was ticking.[61]

The gyrating computer infant began its life in 1997 as a demonstration of Kinetix's animation Character Studio software (Exhibit 5-6). Dancing to a 1970s tune, "Hooked on a Feeling" by Blue Swede, the Web fad popped up on e-mail and home pages. Originally created for Kinetix by Unreal Pictures as a sample file for Kinetix's award-winning Character Studio software, Dancing Baby became a Web cult hero, with dozens of Dancing Baby websites attracting growing legions of online fans. In the process, the original Net baby was branded, cloned, replicated, and leveraged: new versions of Baby Cha Cha cropped up, including Kickboxing Baby, Rasta Baby, Retro Baby, and Psycho Baby.

With worldwide headquarters in San Francisco's hip SOMA neighborhood, Kinetix was a division of Autodesk, the fourth largest PC software company in the world, with three million customers in 150 countries. With more than 100 employees in over 60 sales and support offices worldwide, Kinetix reached customers on six continents through more than 200 authorized multimedia resellers and distributors. It created modeling and animation software. Interestingly enough, nearly half of Kinetix's revenues (48%) came from outside North America.[62] Unlike American Cybercast, it was far better positioned to meld together media and software—and to accomplish the task in the *World Wide* Web.

By 1998, the undulating infant also claimed an expanding television audience, with recurring appearances on *Ally McBeal* and Blockbuster Video advertisements, with special guest appearances on *The Rosie O'Donnell Show*, the American Comedy Awards, and David Letterman's coveted Top 10 list. As an online brand, the gyrating blockbuster baby attracted numerous licensing deals that resulted in a wide variety of Dancing Baby merchandise, from T-shirts to dancing dolls.[63] The digital toddler was fast becoming a retail hit in a dozen countries *worldwide*, including Australia, New Zealand, Mexico, the United Kingdom, and in countries throughout the Middle East, Europe, and Scandinavia.

BROADCAST HYBRIDS

The gyrating Dancing Baby could become a temporary licensing and merchandising blockbuster. But more enduring success required the leverage of existing assets, faster access speed, higher penetration, as well as utilization of a *distributed* medium, not the traditional broadcast model—a lesson that was learned only with the failure of the push technology.

Push and Offline Advertising

In March 1997, *Wired* magazine published a widely quoted cover story: "PUSH! Kiss Your Browser Goodbye: The Radical Future of Media Beyond the Web." The oracle of the digital generation declared the browser wars over; they had become irrelevant. The future belonged to push:

A new medium is arising, surging across the Web in the preferred, many-to-many way: anything flows from anyone to anyone—from anywhere to anywhere—anytime. . . . This new medium doesn't wait for clicks. It doesn't need computers. It means personalized experiences not bound by a page. . . . The buzz phrase for this convergence is "push media."[64]

By the summer of 1997, Jupiter predicted that "push technology solutions will become ubiquitous among leading websites, and that a significant portion of publishers' revenue will be derived from these services."[65] The first part of the sentence did come true, even if the reality was somewhat more prosaic than the hype. Many incumbents and new entrants did embrace push, but as just *one* of the many promising Internet technologies. The second part of the sentence did not reflect the reality of the Internet. Push services did not resolve the problem of profitability on the Web. On the contrary, they may have been part of the problem.

Until the emergence of the push services, Internet advertising was widely perceived as synonymous with *online* advertising. What was truly subversive in the rapid growth of the push providers was the fact that they offered *off*line advertising for tailored information delivery. The innovation spawned several software and service companies that implemented the push framework by delivering user-configured content to subscribers. PointCast was the pioneering and best-known example, but the category also included rival providers, such as IFusion Com. Moreover, the leading browsers were eager to slice a cut in the market. Netscape's Inbox Direct for Navigator 3.0, for instance, offered a new content delivery service that bundled content supplied by more than 40 content providers, from the *New York Times* and CMP Media to Gartner Group and HotWired. Similar offerings included My Yahoo! and Individual's NewsPage Direct, as well as Juno Online Services.

In retrospect, *offline* advertising was hyped beyond recognition. Perhaps, the timing was not irrelevant. The hopes coincided with a competitive environment that emerged *after* the market correction in the Internet stocks in the second half of 1996. As advertising became the primary revenue source for most Web companies, many saw their future dependent on advertisers and media and entertainment conglomerates. Instead of a highly distributed, bottom-up Web, these content producers had a natural interest in a highly centralized, top-down Internet. Initially, they were expected to invest heavily in the push services, as opposed to various forms of online advertising. Such expectations were based on the assumption that the sellers held the bargaining power on the Web, whereas, in reality, that power had drastically shifted toward the buyers. The push technology did reveal an exciting, neglected, and potentially profitable offline dimension of Internet advertising, but despite the magnificent hype, it could never deliver the inflated expectations that so many observers attached to it.

With push, the content producers sought to turn the Internet into a TV set. It was not the only available option. One might reverse the framework. That is what WebTV aspired to accomplish. It aspired to turn the TV into the Internet. It took seriously the notion of *distributed* computing. Therefore, it would have more enduring power.

The WebTV Story

The high-profile browser wars presumed that the *browsers* would continue to play their gatekeeper function in channeling the Web traffic. Yet, the browsers certainly were not the only available option. By the mid-1990s, the browsers extended from Netscape's Navigator to Microsoft's Internet Explorer and a slate of niche alternatives (e.g., Apache, Opera and so on). By the spring of 1997, *Wired* magazine touted push, (i.e., a centralized *off*line media), as the access solution for the distributed Web. There also were the former advocates of interactive television who believed in new kinds of hybrids, such as WebTV, which by late 1996 was set up to deliver the Internet to a mass-market audience.

A pioneer in the fusion of multimedia, video, and telecommunications technologies, Steve Perlman was the original developer of the WebTV concept of bringing the Internet into the homes of families worldwide directly through their TV sets.[66] He spent the first half of the 1990s trying to develop and produce the new hybrid. After the mid-decade, the founders of WebTV Networks, Inc.—Steve Perlman, Bruce Leak, and Phil Goldman (all former colleagues at Apple)—were ready to commercialize their product (Exhibit 5-7). "WebTV Networks to Offer Internet Link Over TV Set," reported the *Wall Street Journal* in September 1996.[67] By November 1996, the little black box was Net ready for prime time. "On first viewing, Web TV's plug-in unit for turning a television set into a World Wide Web browser appears to be the most benign new piece of consumer electronic gear since the cable TV box," reported the *New York Times*.

But don't be fooled . . . the United States Government has classified this $300 device as "munitions" that can't be exported because of the sophisticated data-

Exhibit 5-7
The WebTV Story, or Mozart and Salieris

As a liberal arts student at Columbia University, Perlman created numerous graphics systems, modems, and speech and music programs in his spare time, which he sold under contract to Atari, Inc., and Dun and Bradstreet. He established his reputation as a technology guru during a six-year tenure at Apple Computer, Inc., where he was instrumental in the development of much of the essential multimedia and video technology in the world-renowned Macintosh computer.

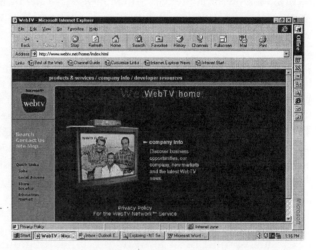

Box shot reprinted with permission from Microsoft Corporation.

Perlman's story is typical of many innovative researchers and enterpreneurs who, instead of being rewarded for their drive, were often punished for not conforming to the bureaucracy, more or less subtly. Perlman advocated his often-spurned ideas for new products so relentlessly that managers banished him to a distant cubicle in the company's research operations. At Apple, Perlman wrote a paper entitled *Keeping Innovation at Apple: Growing Up Without Growing Old*, which warned of corporate mediocrities. Comparing them to Salieri, the composer rival to Mozart portrayed in the film "Amadeus," Perlman said "Apple was taken down by Salieris."

Perlman's reputation as a fountain of ingenious ideas about new ways of using computers, not to speak of his willingness to push those ideas despite perceived management indifference, made him a "problem," not an asset to the company.

Next Perlman spent four innovative years at General Magic, Inc., where, as managing director of advanced products, he designed the company's second-generation computer system, Magic TV. Despite the support of great technologists, it took five more years to get the product out the door; and it sold for $1,000. So he left again, this time to cofound Catapult, a multiuser online game network that developed an excellent product in only six months and made revenue as an online service provider. Catapult was acquired in July 1995 by its competitor Mpath.

Again, Perlman left dissatisfied. He called Catapult investor Marvin Davis, who promptly handed over a seed-round check. The company went underground for a year, calling itself Artemis Research. Perlman says he did not want to operate under the WebTV moniker early on for fear of intrusive attention from the press and competitors. Instead, Artemis's Web site, which described research on small animals, drew concerned responses from animal-rights activists. In June 1996, Artemis became WebTV.

Source: For the early history of WebTV Networks, see Jonathan Burke, "Internet for the Masses," *The Red Herring,* October 1996; Lee Gomes, "WebTV's Steve Perlman, Microsoft Deal Is Vindication," the *Wall Street Journal,* April 9, 1997. See also WebTV's home page: www.webtv.net.My WebTV.

scrambling it uses when connecting to the Internet via a standard telephone line. ... And government weirdness aside, this black box is indeed a formidable marketing weapon for supremacy in the melding of the personal computer and the television in the American living room. Hanging on the outcome are the destinies of electronics firms around the world.[68]

The precursor to a wave of Net computers, add-on boxes, and TVs with built-in surfing capability, the WebTV design introduced by Philips Magnavox and Sony solved many of the technical problems inherent in turning a TV screen into a computer display.[69] Despite a promotional blitz in which Philips alone spent an estimated $50 million on TV and print ads, WebTV was not the hot product of Christmas 1996. Retailers and industry executives suggested that Sony and Philips together may have sold some 30,000 of the 100,000 WebTV devices they distributed in time for Christmas. Despite the praise lavished by reviewers and early purchasers, 93% of those surveyed by Dataquest Inc. said they do not plan to purchase a Web television system at any point. "The Internet television in its current form does not have significant market potential in Dataquest's view," said Van Baker, director and principal analyst of Dataquest's The Digital Consumer program. "The interface and usability of the device leaves a lot of room for improvement, and the value to the consumer—especially the non-PC household—is questionable." WebTV considered the study flawed.[70]

Founded in 1971, Dataquest served as a global market research and consulting company serving the high-technology and financial communities. Owned by the highly regarded Gartner Group, Dataquest provided worldwide market coverage on the semiconductor, computer systems and peripherals, communications, document management, software, and services sectors of the information technology industry. Its primary clientele consisted of *incumbent* U.S. and worldwide leaders of these technologies. Similarly, in the late 1940s and early 1950s, market research firms, assigned by the then-dominant print and radio businesses, had explored the commercial viability of television in America. And, similarly, on the basis of market surveys they had concluded that, aside from the early adopters and techno hobbyists, American listeners were not interested in compelling audiovisual novelties. A few years later, many print and radio firms were struggling for survival and seeking proper audience segments, the TV production had moved from New York to Hollywood, and the majority of Americans owned a TV set. The moral of the story is not that the extrapolation of history serves as a means to predict the future. Rather, the lesson is that while surveys may provide useful information on *existing* markets that the users are familiar with, their use is not always justified with *potential* markets that the users, by definition, are not familiar with.

Moreover, the parallel with the early adopter markets in the 1950s and the 1990s should not be stretched thin. When the broadcasters introduced television, the number of proper mass marketing vehicles was low. Regulation, high entry barriers, low level of rivalry, few competitors, absence of substitutes—all these determinants virtually ensured the effortless triumph of broadcast television. Toward the late 1990s, the founders of WebTV Networks and their rivals were faced with an entirely different competitive environment. In addition to the already segmented marketplace and a multitude of marketing channels, many other determinants virtually guaranteed the difficulties in the introduction of WebTV—including deregulation, low entry barriers, highly intense rivalry, the high numbers of competitors, the presence of an increasing number of potential substitutes, and so on.

By early 1997, some 15 million U.S. homes had PCs capable of tapping the Internet, but 97 million homes had TV sets. Moreover, WebTV was an entirely new category of product, and consumers are slow to respond to such innovations. The videocassette recorder and direct broadcast satellite TV both had slow starts. By April 1997, a study by Forrester Research concluded that WebTV and similar devices would not reach 1 million U.S. households until the year 2000. "Web browsing is simply not compelling enough to attract today's TV viewers," says Josh Bernoff, a senior analyst at Forrester and author of the report. The emphasis of *today's* market is crucial. Forrester expected that the widespread availability of televisions delivering relevant interactive experiences and Internet screen phones with features like instant white pages, weather, and take-out ordering would finally drive 14.7 million households to connect their TVs to the Internet in 2002, while 9.2 million would have Internet-connected screen phones. "These changes will challenge TV networks to broaden their interactive competency and put pressure on computer makers to simplify their interfaces," concluded Bernoff. "New interactive service providers will rise up to serve consumers with Net-enhanced TVs and telephones, challenging traditional online powers like America Online."[71]

As the long-term prospects began to look more positive, incumbent market innovators started to seek entry. In April 1997, WebTV Networks agreed to be bought by Microsoft for $425 million in stock and cash. Since the three co-founders had equal ownership stakes in WebTV, they were now worth tens of millions of dollars in Microsoft stock. The purchase was a vindication for the 36-year-old Perlman, the sort he said he often didn't receive at Apple, where he worked from 1984 to 1990.

By October 1998, the global market for information appliances was expected to balloon from 3 million units in 1997 and a projected 5.9 million in 1998 to about 55.7 million units in 2002, according to a new study by International Data Corp. The strongest growth in this business was in Internet gaming consoles, smart handheld devices and, most importantly, the "Net-TV" devices—cable set-top boxes and Microsoft Corp.'s WebTV Networks service. Network computers, on the other hand, would see weaker growth because of the emergence of low-cost PCs. Now the screen phone market also was facing a lot of competition from Net-TV devices, he said. According to another new study from IDC, the Net-TV market should grow from 900,000 units in 1997 and a projected 1.4 million units in 1998 to about 11.5 million units worldwide in 2002. IDC saw the Net-TV market breaking out into three segments.

- At the low end will be the one-way delivery of information such as news, stock quotes, movie lists, and electronic programming guides to users.
- The midrange part of the Net-TV market will feature services such as surveys, polls, and basic electronic commerce.
- At the high end, consumers will be able to browse the Web and send e-mail from their TVs.[72]

IDC expected Internet-ready television sets, which will no longer require set-top boxes, to become available in 2004 to 2006.

Only two years before, another research firm had argued that "The Internet television in its current form does not have significant market potential." Of course, WebTV had refined its product line since the fall of 1996, but neither the concept nor the implementation had drastically changed. The *users*, however, had become a little more familiar with the product, through marketing, advertising, press, PR, and promotions. That made the difference—not the technology as such.

ONLINE ACCESS AND COMMUNITY PROVIDERS

After the mid-1980s, both e-mail and chat—these "pre-Web modes of communications—had been redefined by WELL, a nonprofit pioneer of virtual communities. The Internet's early military and research communities no longer held monopoly to electronic communications. By the turn of the 1990s, the privatization of the Internet prompted online service providers (OSPs) to provide simplified access to cyberspace. Emulating the pioneering example of WELL, America Online extended the model to commercial virtual communities. The Internet was not just about context or content, it was about *communication*. At the time, the capital-intensive local telcos and international carriers did not provide Internet access. That became possible only with the new Telecommunications Act of 1996.

Though the numbers of the Internet and online service users cannot be measured with certainty, Morgan Stanley Research, in the mid-1990s, estimated that there were about 9 million interactive Internet users and about three times that number who used e-mail. The number of Internet/ Web users was expected to grow to about 150 million by the year 2000. By then, most users would have real-time graphical user interface access. The number of Internet users grew explosively, at a historical sustained rate of approximately 100% per year. Similar growth occurred in the online services market. In the second half of the 1990s, the growth in the Internet (i.e., more connected computers) was expected to correlate with the rate of growth in the installed base of PCs. Concurrently, the transition from "heavy users" to "critical mass" was expected to coincide with qualitative changes in the *use* of the Web. Morgan Stanley thought that the Internet market growth had hardly been born, and that it would prove to be big.[73]

In the mid-1990s, there were several degrees of Internet connectivity, from the least expensive to the most expensive: e-mail and Usenet news only; partial Internet access; Internet service providers (ISPs); OSPs; online/hybrid service providers. The first two were not fully interactive, and did not offer exhaustive Web Internet access—the latter ones did.

- *E-Mail Service Providers.* By the end of 1994, there were about 10 times as many e-mail users as Web users. This large group consisted of e-mail users, who were defined as having the capability of obtaining Internet e-mail (and Usenet information) only. Initially, many corporate networks had this degree of connectivity. Similarly, the FidoNet network was used frequently by bulletin board services (BBSs). After the very first years of the Web, several companies began to offer e-mail services. If corporate e-mail drove this cluster in the beginning of the Web, free e-mail services accelerated its dramatic growth after the mid-1990s.

- *Partial Internet Access Providers.* Initially, partial Internet access comprised a class of users who had real-time access (in contrast to the delayed batch-feed method) to other Internet hosts, but lacked the degree of graphics capability or connectivity needed to interact on the Web. After the launch of Netscape's and Microsoft's first browser generation, the significance of these providers diminished rapidly. Most often, they were simply integrated with the other service providers.

Full Web access implies that the user is working primarily on an IP-enabled computer that has graphics capabilities, such as Mosaic-type Web software. Once this type of connection was established, full Web access was achieved and users could run Web browser software.

Internet Service Providers (ISPs). From the beginning, Internet service providers, such as Netcom, PSINet, UUNET, and BBN Planet, offered full Web access to their users. With the new Telecommunications Act of 1996, local telcos (Baby Bells) and international carriers (AT&T, MCI, Sprint) got into the industry. Price competition harvested the smallest and weakest ISPs. ISPs perceived themselves as distributors of Internet access primarily. By the turn of the millennium, analysts expected to see more than 190 million surfers using Internet access services.

Online/Hybrid Service Providers (OSPs). Many online service providers, such as America Online, CompuServe and Prodigy did not initially offer full Web access; competition forced them to do so after the mid-1990s. Still, only 20% or 30% of OSP subscribers used it. Some OSPs, such as AOL engaged in aggressive growth strategies, in order to position themselves prior to the rise of challengers, especially the leading browsers (Netscape's Navigator in 1994, Microsoft's MSN in 1995). In 1995, these providers had less than 10 million subscribers. By the year 2000, they were expected to double, mainly because of AOL.

The Internet preceded its graphic user interface. Some Internet technologies that were integrated with the Web offerings still serve a significant function in Internet marketing. These practices could be called *offline* advertising as opposed to online advertising or *non-Web* advertising in contrast to Web advertising. Among other things, these alternatives include e-mail, chat, push, and ICQ. The full capabilities of targeted and interactive one-to-one marketing can be realized *only with full demographic information on the users.* This fact makes non-Web advertising so attractive to the advertisers. Unlike the Web with its anonymity, these services offer users highly personalized services that, *in return*, require the users to register their age, gender, geographic location, and other relevant demographic and lifestyle data.

The inflated hopes and costly failures of subscription-driven Web publishers had proved that even popular and branded websites would easily lose nine of their ten users, when and if they would require a payment and registration for services. By vertically integrating non-Web services into their existing websites, many entrenched companies hoped to exploit these services as hooks that would first accelerate the traffic on the website and, ultimately, direct a significant segment of this traffic to the site's other offerings, especially ones involving electronic commerce.

In the early days of the Internet, most users originated from academic and research communities. Due to their nonprofit objectives, they had a negative view of commercial advertising. With the expansion of the Internet, most users came to have a more malleable view of the netiquette. Direct e-mail is perceived as a tradeoff: if it is delivered without an explicit request, it saves in transaction costs.

From Direct E-Mail to Spamming. Unlike the "junk e-mailers," the leading direct e-mailers acknowledged and continued to recognize the reciprocity inherent in the tradeoff. They did not and would not distribute e-mail updates, without asking users first if they are willing to receive such content. Junk e-mailers, however, did and would push unsolicited e-mail. Consequently, the fragile boundaries of legitimate free e-mail could grow quite blurry during the early Internet years. One of the more notorious cases involved two greencard lawyers, Laurence A. Canter and Martha S. Siegel, who in 1994 repeatedly sent out a message offering their services in helping to enter the U.S. greencard lottery to almost all usenet newsgroups. The two went on to write a book, *How to Make a Fortune on the Information Superhighway* (1995) and founded an Internet advertising company, Cybersell.[74] Still, it was Sanford Wallace whose case would cast a long shadow on the reputable direct e-mailers and industry practices.[75] After unsolicited junk fax submissions were outlawed by the U.S. Congress, Wallace turned his attention to the junk e-mail industry. In 1997, his CyberPromotions estimated that it would gross more than $3 million, quadrupling the $800,000 in revenues his corporation had reported the previous year. A year later, the one-time spam king was being charged $2 million to settle the last outstanding lawsuit against his company.[76]

Perhaps better than any other strategic group of pure Internet companies, the free e-mail services reflect the Internet's tradeoff between privacy and convenience. In return for highly personalized services, these firms required the users to register their age, gender, geographic location, and other relevant demographic and lifestyle data—but only in return of the consumer's explicit acceptance.

Explosion of Free E-Mail Services

Initially, e-mail had been developed in the early 1970s to serve military and research communications, but the applications multiplied rapidly with the expansion of the Web. At the peak of the browser wars, industry analysts observed a surge in the demand for free e-mail. In addition to cost-efficiency, the incumbent players and especially new entrants were intrigued by the high switching costs inherent to e-mail systems. Such characteristics could provide aggregators significant subscriber bases and raise entry barriers. In addition to the consolidation potential, the timing was not irrelevant. By the mid-1990s, the Internet was moving rapidly toward mass penetration. E-mail was becoming attractive to ordinary Americans. It looked more and more like a "killer app."

The communications function evolved with the emergence and mass adoption of online communities and the rapid saturation of the U.S. markets by the leading OSPs, ISPs, international carriers, and local telcos. In 1996, Four11, an Internet "white pages" directory of e-mail addresses, started experimenting with free e-mail, only to launch its RocketMail site in the following March. By July 1997, Excite, a web search engine, followed suit with an advertiser-supported e-mail service called MailExcite. In October 1997, Yahoo! acquired the closely held Four11 in a $92 million stock swap. The deal gave Yahoo! access to several directory services, including phone and e-mail listings; it also began offering Four11's free RocketMail e-mail service. In December 1997, Qualcomm's Eudora division announced that it planned to offer free e-mail (at the time, Eudora was used by 18 million people).[77] By the fall of 1997, a handful of free e-mail companies dominated the industry.

Juno. Providing free Internet e-mail service to its subscribers, Juno Online Services was one of the first among the free e-mailers seeking to generate revenues through selling the space to advertisers for direct product sales or for the provision of optional billable services. In exchange, Juno required users to fill out a registration form that allowed it to target very specific and well-defined demographic groups. As an early entrant, Juno had to struggle to differentiate itself from junk e-mailers. Supported by New York investment banker D. E. Shaw & Co.,[78] it was not a Web-based operation. With a membership estimated at 3 million and some 2.5 million daily messages, Juno, unlike its rivals, required the use of special PC software. Still, in less than one and a half years, the number of its advertisers grew from 25 to 80.

MailExcite. Relying on the Web muscle of its search engine parent, Excite, MailExcite did not disclose membership numbers, which were estimated at close to 100,000 members. It had in excess of 2 million daily visitors, although the unit had been in operation a little longer than one month.

Four11. Initially an on-line "white pages" directory, Four11 had more than 10 million names, e-mail addresses, and 700,000 telephones numbers. As RocketMail was plugged into Four11, members could easily find others and e-mail them. In addition to RocketMail, Yahoo! owned Yahoo! Mail, a free Web-based e-mail that featured a customizable personal address book, automatic mail filtering, spellchecking, message searching, and more.

Hotmail. With its 6.5 million members, Hotmail was the fastest-growing service, adding 40,000 new members daily and handling about 10 million messages daily. It was considered very attractive by some 35 advertisers.

AOL NetMail. By December 1997, America Online expanded its Web presence with new AOL.com products, including AOL NetMail. In the long run, the latter was to enable AOL members to send and receive AOL e-mail from any computer with Web access. NetMail was currently in its beta phase. At first, it had only limited compatibility with various operating systems and browsers. Unlike other Web-based e-mail services such as Hotmail and GeoCities, NetMail was not written in HTML which could not provide users with the AOL features, look, and feel to which users are accustomed. Also, unlike its rivals, NetMail was not a free e-mail service.[79]

In 1996, more than 40 million American e-mail users were sending in excess of 100 messages a day. By 2005, Forrester Research expected the user base to reach more than 170 million users, creating a staggering 5 billion messages a day on the public Internet and private intranets.[80] Still, with intense rivalry, the number of competitors rose and free e-mail providers had to expand and differentiate their subscriber bases to increase their attractiveness to the advertisers. With their search engine, free e-mail, chat services, and "instant message" capabilities, Excite, Yahoo!, and some other rivals saw free e-mail as a critical component of their portal strategy.

The problem with the business model was that even the largest and fastest-expanding providers found it hard to stay afloat. Even if they got close to profitability, acquisition offers from larger players proved more tempting. By the late 1990s, *all* major free e-mailers were vertically integrated with capital-intensive parent companies, including MailExcite (Excite), Four11 (Yahoo!), Hotmail (Microsoft), Juno (D. E. Shaw & Co.), and AOL NetMail (America Online). From the standpoint of the players, the acquisition of Hotmail Corp. by Microsoft offered a model paradigm that exemplified both the perceived threats and the opportunities.

HotMail—The World's Largest Free E-Mailer

On the Independence Day of 1996, Hotmail Corp. launched Hotmail, "the world's first Web-based free e-mail service." It gave away fully featured free e-mail accounts at its home site. Upon registration a user instantly got an e-mail account with an address such as "user@Hotmail.com." Users could start using this e-mail account over the Web immediately and as often as they chose to. With Hotmail they could access their e-mail from any computer or platform via the World Wide Web. Unlike other major e-mail systems or online providers, Hotmail did not require any software other than a browser. In other words, Hotmail users could securely check their personal e-mail from any Internet connection, anywhere in the world.[81] It was an exciting concept, but was it an actionable business model? That issue would cause a lot of debate *and* division among industry observers.

The facts, however, were indisputable: Hotmail's growth was explosive. In early January 1997, only half a year after the launch of Hotmail, the service had 1 million registered subscribers. More than 12,000 new subscribers were registering each day. By the end of the year, Hotmail's subscriber base exceeded 9 million subscribers. When the company had been launched on July 4, 1996 with the spirit and hope associated with Independence Day, the theme was "to become independent from your corporate e-mail or of your ISP or even your PC." People should be able to get to their e-mail from *any* Web device. The insight into giving its members a free, personal e-mail account, coupled with a commitment to being customer driven, resulted in a loyal membership. The e-mail service was intuitive for the novice and supported advanced features like filtering for the experienced user.

The service grew almost twice as fast as forecasted optimistically by Sabeer Bhatia, president and CEO of Hotmail. Over a period of just fifteen months, the company zoomed from nothing to nearly ten million subscribers—about the same number that AOL has enlisted after thirteen years in the business.

Microsoft Buys Hotmail. After two months of protracted courtship, Hotmail agreed on the last day of 1997 to be swallowed up for an estimated price of $385 million. It would become a subsidiary of Microsoft and its ten million subscribers would come under the umbrella of Microsoft Network (MSN). Microsoft wanted Hotmail. In fact, when venture capitalist Tim Draper, one of the startup's backers and directors, spurned Microsoft's original offer, the software giant came back with a sweetened deal. As Microsoft bought the leader, more than one-quarter of Hotmail's 60 employees became instant paper millionaires.[82] According to Shirish Nadkarni, director of product planning for the Microsoft Network, the company had been intending for some time either to create or acquire a free e-mail service.[83]

Under the arrangement, Hotmail would continue to operate under its name and as a wholly owned subsidiary of Microsoft. It had between 50 and 60 advertisers, but declined to specify its advertising revenue or whether it was making a profit. While Hotmail had 9.5 million active accounts, its regular user base was not that high: some 5.5 million subscribers used the service at least once a month—it had twice as many e-mail accounts as Microsoft (2 million, spring 1997). Hotmail booked less than $4 million in its 1997 sales, despite its huge customer base. As the data gathered from Hotmail's questionnaires let advertisers target likely buyers, the bonanza would come from selling over the Internet. Electronic commerce was the strategic objective of the buyout. Over the coming months, Hotmail would be integrated into sites on the Microsoft Network, such as MSN.com, travel site Expedia, and car-buying site CarPoint.[84]

The Hotmail buy posed a challenge to MSN.com's main rival, America Online (AOL). The deal also left the few remaining startup "freemailers" looking for partners. Rival RocketMail had been sold out to Yahoo! in October. The acquisition revived concern over Microsoft's dominant market position in operating systems *and* application software. The Hotmail acquisition capped a year in which Microsoft spent an estimated $1.5–$2 billion on buyouts and invested heavily in at least seventeen technology companies.[85]

The MSN-Hotmail deal illustrated how the line between online services and search directories was blurring rapidly. The addition of features,

Exhibit 5-8
Jarkko Oikarinen on IRC: "Don't Shoot the Messenger"

The Function of Chat—IRC came up because there was a clear need for it. It was not to replace talk. . . . The purpose of talk is different. The original purpose of IRC was more to provide similar features that existed on BITNET and DECNET (i.e., bitnet chat system and the DECNET phone).

Anonymity—What makes IRC special is the sense of anonymity. The only things that you often know of the other person are those that you can conclude from the discussions.

Integration with the WWW—The structure of the Web is much more scalable than IRC. I believe IRC will be integrated into the Web, or at least the functionality of IRC.

Chat Communities and Their Discontents—[In addition to real time chat, did you ever imagine IRC also to become a place for flooders, stalkers, harassers, and disturbed people to congregate as well?] These things are in the nature of people and I think it is inevitable to some extent. IRC is just one media for these activities. [What is your opinion on the use of the DCC feature to distribute and promote illegal activities such as child pornography and software piracy?] I do not accept these illegal activities. However, I do not think IRC is to blame. If there were no IRC, these activities would take place somewhere else. Any useful tool can be used for good and bad. Don't shoot the messenger.

The Next Big Thing?—[What do you envision as the next step beyond IRC in network communications?] It can already be seen in the VRLM worlds, with people being represented as avatars, live audio and live video communications. Another step towards cyberspace.

Source: www.user-com.undernet.org/promotions/interview.html. The Undernet Public Relations Committee, The Undernet Internet Relay Chat Network, April 19, 1997. [Slightly modified for the purpose of abbreviation.]

such as free Web-based e-mail, made them all the more alike. By April and June 1998, this homogenization of ISPs, OSPs, search engines, international carriers, local telcos, and Hollywood studios would lead to still new M&A waves ("portal mania").

Internet Relay Chat (IRC)

By the late 1990s, Internet Relay Chat (IRC) meant an Internet Protocol that allowed one to have real-time, text-based conversations with other people around the world, similar to the chat rooms found on AOL and Compuserve. Essentially, it was a decentralized multi-user chat system, designed in 1988 by Jarkko Oikarinen, a Finnish engineering student (Exhibit 5-8). IRC is based on text messages sent on a line-by-line basis to all other users who are linked to the same channel. The conversation, which can be saved in file form, is like online play script writing or word-by-word minutes recording. The system has been applied in many ways, from small-scale instant meetings to reporting global-scale events in real time. It has become especially popular as a chat box among students. IRC was designed as a replacement for the "talk" program but soon became much more than that.[86]

Since its start in Finland, chat has been used in over 60 countries around the world. With the privatization of the Internet, businesses embraced chat for use in customer service, online business meetings, and many other applications. The driving force behind the medium, however, remained the instant real-time communication and flirtation as well as sexually-oriented dialogue. By late 1996, chat also was becoming a *measurable* advertising medium. Ichat Inc., a maker of chat software, partnered with I/Pro and NetGravity to provide sites with traffic analysis of chat rooms and targeted advertising in them. Under an agreement with NetGravity, the "ichat Rooms" server let sites target ads to specific chat content and participating users. Indeed, it had become conceivable that if a person would type "thirsty" in an ichat software created chat room, he/she could be presented with an advertising message about a soft drink, said Harry Pape, marketing manager for ichat, which boasted more than 200 customers and 45 employees.[87]

ichat faced a broad range of competition from Microsoft, The Palace, Chatware, and at least a dozen others. Still, like what Lotus did to collaborative computing, ichat was turning chat sessions into more of a productivity tool than a conversation mechanism.

Until well in the mid-1990s, advertisers ignored online "chat" or poked fun at the phenomenon. For instance, a print advertisement for Sauza Tequila mockingly chided: "You have a great sex life. On the Internet." And a print ad for Dewar's Scotch confided, "It's not so much the 'chat room' as it is the sitting-home-alone-by-yourself part that concerns us." Things began to change only in November 1996, when a study by two divisions of Cordiant PLC suggested that marketers ought to take more seriously the emerging online communities. "The explosive growth of this area, and the passion consumers bring to it, made it clear this is the most powerful, most intense form of activity on line," said Myra Stark of Saatchi & Saatchi Advertising. A principal reason for the study, said Greg Smith, VP and manager for nontraditional media at Zenith, the co-sponsor, was that chat accounted for 26% of all time spent on commercial online services.[88] The study offered several suggestions for advertisers interested in approaching the chatting classes among computer users, while respecting the integrity of these communities. For instance:

- Chat rooms could be designed as part of corporate websites, noted Betsy Frank, executive VP and director for strategic media resources at Zenith. Such a solution, she argued, could help "create and build brands and brand affinity. . . . That demands a pretty courageous marketer," she added, "to let consumers talk to each other about his or her product."

- Chat could be sponsored or underwritten in the same way that advertisers affiliated with public broadcasting. "You announce at the door, 'This is brought to you by,' " Smith said, "and then you get out of the way."

- Relationship marketing programs could be developed. For instance, a baby-products company could create a multipurpose website featuring chats with baby-care experts.[89]

By early 1997, America Online took the lead in chat advertising, enabling marketers to display ads to the millions of users of its more than 15,000 chat rooms. That year also witnessed the rise of Web-based chat software. By late October, real-time chat was no longer a phenomenon of the early adopters, the first advertising experiments, or even AOL's legendary chat rooms. "Was yesterday a worldwide crash or a U.S. correction?" asked a worried *investor* in an online chat room, the day after the Dow Jones Industrial Average plunged more than 550 points. The sponsor of the carefully moderated event was Merrill Lynch and the chat was led by John Steffens, its brokerage chief. The financial giant was just one of the many companies experimenting with chat. Often the idea was to compete more effectively and cut costs.[90]

By the summer of 1998, chat no longer triggered associations of "cybersex" only. Chat was changing, maturing, diversifying. It was being used in business, education, and consumer service. It offered an instrument to promote television and movie stars and to provide a forum for authors to talk to their readers. It was also being renamed "real-time customer interaction" and labeled an "Internet collaboration tool."

"Right now, chat is the easiest and most reliable way to communicate over the Internet in real time," said James P. Tito, president and chief executive of Eshare Technologies, a major provider of chat technology to companies like Merrill Lynch, 1–800-Flowers, Mail Boxes Etc., and AT&T Worldnet Services. He estimated that of the 107 million people who used the Internet worldwide, at least 40 million to 50 million used chat in some fashion, including the more recent innovations of one-on-one chat pioneered by AOL's Buddy List and Instant Messenger systems. With its 12 million users, AOL, the largest online service in the United States, found that its users spent 19% of their time in online chat rooms, 2% more than the time they spent combing the Internet. Similarly, Yahoo! scheduled at least 100 chat events a month. At The Globe, an Internet site that encouraged its users to build online communities, about 30% of the more than five million users chatted online.[91]

Still, the results were mixed for advertisers. On the one hand, the audiences could be quite loyal, and most chat sites were able to collect basic demographic information about users that could be used in ad targeting. On the other hand, chat did not really drive traffic because users relied on chat sites to converse, not to click through to advertisers' home pages. Also, online discussions could not be controlled, which brand managers perceived as a risk to their products.

Mirabilis: From Word of Mouth to Word of Mouse

ICQ Inc., the successor of Mirablis Ltd., was created when America Online acquired all Mirabilis's assets. Launched in November 1996, ICQ was the creation of three twentysomethings from Tel Aviv, Israel. Pronounced "I Seek You," the product was an Internet-based pager that let users know when their friends were online. The Web-based communications system then allowed the users to exchange text-based messages instantaneously. ICQ also gave its users the ability to play games and exchange files and URLs. Like AOL's Instant Messenger service, formerly ICQ's biggest rival, ICQ allowed users to communicate with each other while logged on to the Internet and could be accessed on any platform.

From Connected to Interconnected Users. Mirabilis was founded in July 1996 when twentysomething Israeli avid-computer users Yair Goldfinger (Chief Technology Officer), Arik Vardi (Chief Executive Officer), and Sefi Vigiser (President) created the company in order to introduce a new way of *communication* over the Internet.[92] In 1996, the three founding partners visited Silicon Valley. Millions of people had been connected to one huge worldwide network—the Internet. Those people were connected—*but not interconnected*. They realized that if one missing component could be added, all these people, in addition to interacting with Web servers, would be able to interact *with each other*. The missing link was the technology that would enable the Internet users to locate each other online on the Internet and create peer-to-peer communication channels in a straightforward, easy, and simple manner. The three saw themselves as the first movers. They would pioneer this technology, opening a whole new industry.

Word of Mouse. By February 1998, more than 40,000 copies of ICQ were being downloaded every day. Since its release in November 1996, Mirabilis had registered some 7.5 million ICQ subscribers. Without any marketing presence in the United States, or any real marketing budget either, the company had attracted more than 2 million people who used it daily, mainly by word of mouth—or mouse. And linking directly to the ICQ panel, the company's website served as a guide to lists of users who shared common interests and to thousands of user-created online chat rooms on various topics. The product had become the Web's chat software of choice *without a single advertisement*.

Unlike the current market leaders like AOL and Microsoft, Mirabilis also exploited focus strategies. Its segments were younger than those of the incumbent rivals. The user interface reflected underlying differences. AOL's Instant Messenger, for instance, offered a simple TV style screen, and if the user scrolled down for more, he/she would have seen perhaps three more screens of similar offerings. In terms of screen space, Mirabilis's offering consisted of some ten screen-filled spaces; in terms of intrascreen content, it had perhaps half a dozen more offerings than its rivals.

At first sight, the interface was almost incomprehensible. It had a toolbar of newly added lists, newly added ICQ groups, a ICQ greeting gallery, ICQ for PalmPilot, and Open ICQ chat rooms; it had a gallery of download options; it had an entire hierarchy of items for ICQ users by topics and interests (e.g., "What Is ICQ?" "Using This Site," "Find Friends," "Site Builders"), a list of networks (e.g., Home Pages Gallery, Science and Technology, Cities in U.S. & Canada), various activity segments from chat and sports to women and students; it had an entire slate of ICQ services, from chat request and birthday center to message boards and communications center. These were augmented by different support options and several search directories. This mosaic of products and services included advertisers' buttons, registration help, and home page alternatives. All of these made up only the first full screen for the user; if the user scrolled down for more, he/she saw nine or ten screens full of similar products and services.

Segment characteristics determine user impressions. The older surfers who were less experienced with the ways of the Web were likely to reject the Mirabilis offering for its rivals. Also, more was involved than a simple match between the interface and the user segment. Whereas AOL's web page, for instance, had been designed to fulfill the requirements of traditional branding (e.g., composition, colors, style, elements), Mirabilis paid less attention to visual design and far more to instrumentality (e.g., use values, easy-to-find elements, simple hiearchies, and so on). AOL's model stemmed from traditional TV-style broadcasting, whereas Mirabilis may have felt closer to the example of Yahoo!

AOL's Acquisition: From Mirabilis Ltd. to ICQ Inc. Between 1996 and June 1998, Mirabilis amassed one of the Internet's largest audiences, counting more than 11 million subscribers worldwide, nearly as many as AOL. Moreover, ICQ's market was younger and more Net-savvy than AOL's base: 60% of all users registered to ICQ resided outside the United States, with 40% of them living in Europe. Meanwhile, ICQ had some 500,000 simultaneous users and was growing at the rate of 1 million new subscribers every 22 days. Just as Microsoft had eyed the rise of Hotmail with suspicion and admiration, AOL monitored closely the explosive growth of Mirabilis—until it decided to acquire its largest potential rival. On June 8, 1998, America Online acquired Mirabilis for $287 million in cash. The deal did not come out of the blue; to ensure the long-term growth of the service, Mirabilis already had begun to look for a partner for ICQ.[93]

Mirabilis continued to be based in Tel Aviv and operated by its founding team as a free Web-based service with its own brand identity. In other words, AOL was adapting to acquisitions that essentially translated to multiple-brand strategies.[94] This was a new but perhaps inevitable strategic decision at AOL: the more it grew, the more it would have to diversify. Through the acquisition, AOL also gained exclusive possession of Mirabilis's ICQ software that, coupled with the customer base, could open more distribution channels for AOL to broker between product vendors and ICQ users.[95]

The Rise of Portals

"Take cyberspace's newest catch phrase and a long-awaited prediction, ram them together, and you get a reordering of the rules of the Internet game—as well as a huge amount of money changing hands in a very brief period of time," reported The Wall Street Journal Interactive Edition in the early summer of 1998. "That's what happened in the spring of 1998, as 'portal sites' became the talk of cyberspace and media and communications giants finally moved to turn their online ambitions into reality, leading to a flurry of dealmaking and the prospect of profound changes for the Web."[96] Indeed, even the very word, "portal," had been relatively unfamiliar until the latter half of 1997, when it had become something of a catch-phrase in industry and trade events.[97]

In the early 1990s, the rise of the Web and the launch of Mosaic and Netscape Navigator left Web surfers lost in a vast sea of data. To find their way, the users turned to a number of sites known then as search engines or Internet directories. Initially, most had served as support vehicles in academia or as personal hobbies of individual Internet (*pre-Web*) surfers. Things changed with the rapid privatization of the Internet. The launch of the Web was followed by the birth of the great information access tools, such as InfoSeek, Yahoo!, Lycos, and Web-Crawler.[98]

Available free of charge on the Web, these massive databases had lots of information available and the browsers made them more user-friendly and easier to access. While search engines evolved from directories, online service providers focused on communication. In concept, however, the function of an online service interface and a Web database site was not that dissimilar. Both allowed quick retrieval of vast amounts of information. The difference stemmed from *pricing*. OSPs were paid for their service on a per hour and/or monthly charge, whereas a Web database service was usually paid for by ad revenue. When this pricing principle no longer operated (i.e., the new Telecommunications Act of 1996), the differences between the search engines and the OSPs blurred accordingly. The former added OSP features and functions into the offerings, while the latter built search engines and directories of their own. Now both focused on ad revenue streams and sought to position themselves as "destination sites" in the nascent electronic commerce. They would not channel the traffic elsewhere; they would try to attract, retain, and nurture it—within the site.

In order to become destination sites, the search engines in particular rushed to offer a vast number of services—free e-mail, free home pages, message boards, personalized news, chat services, electronic shopping, and Internet access. Unlike Netscape Navigator or Microsoft Internet Explorer, these search engines had neither developed the first commercial browser nor could they benefit from an extensive subscriber base controlled by a corporate parent. Still, they were becoming the starting points of choice for Web users. In their new incarnation, the battling Internet directories became known as "portal sites."[99]

As leading media and telecommunications giants eventually began to understand the crucial driver role of the portals in the Internet mass traffic, they realized they could no longer remain bystanders. Media giants could strike deals to guide more traffic to their Web outposts, and telecommunications giants could use the online world as a marketing lever for their other products. The mergers began in May 1998, when Excite struck a deal with Netscape, whose Netcenter site was one of the Web's most-visited destinations. Then AT&T struck deals with Lycos, Excite, and Infoseek to couple its Internet access with the three companies' sites. A few weeks later, General Electric's NBC unit paid $32 million for a minority stake in new-media player CNET to acquire a majority of Snap!, CNET's struggling Internet portal. NBC signaled the kind of Internet commitment that anticipated the rush of TV networks into cyberspace and the fusion of the PC and the TV. A week later, Disney acquired 43% of Infoseek and the right to build a majority stake.[100] In retrospect, the marketing concept of Yahoo! and American Online proved highly successful.

"Do You Yahoo!"

By 1998, the Santa Clara, California–based Yahoo! was the most popular site on the Web, with the surfers calling on Yahoo! to view an estimated 95 million pages of electronic data a day. It was second only to Netscape in terms of online advertising revenue. Founded by two doctoral students, David Filo and Jerry Yang, Yahoo! saw itself as a global Internet media company that offered a network of branded Web programming. As the first online navigational guide to the Web, it was the single largest guide in terms of traffic, advertising, household, and business user reach. It provided targeted Internet resources and communications services for a broad range of audiences, based on demographic, key-subject, and geographic interests. It was one of the most recognized brands associated with the Internet.[101]

From Searches to Services. Yahoo! defined the category. In 1993, it had not existed. After the mid-1990s, the irreverent TV commercials, "Do You Yahoo!", made the company a household word. With more features and functions, Yahoo! acquired the role of a portal and sought to reposition itself as a global Internet media player as it moved into the Internet access market. By March 1998, Yahoo!'s market share was twice as high as that of its closest rival. Meanwhile, consumers were changing the way they used these sites. On Yahoo!, only one out of three users came to search. Most were interested in other Yahoo! features, like e-mail or chat services or Yahoo! Finance, which had become one of the most popular financial sites on the Web. "We certainly are becoming more online service-like," Jerry Yang said in early 1998. "But that doesn't make our navigation service any less important."[102]

By 1998, Yahoo!'s principal offering was its website, Yahoo! In addition, the company had solidified its position in the Internet through various geographic and targeted online properties. The comprehensive subject-based, demographic and geographic listings in Yahoo! provided a platform for the company to develop and offer a multitude of targeted online properties. The company worked with strategic partners who developed localized or targeted content and, in some cases, promoted and sold advertising. The company also developed Web-based media properties that allowed the user to personalize and tailor the presentation of information and navigational resources. If implemented successfully, the company believed that these services could strengthen customer loyalty to the Yahoo! brand and create additional revenue opportunities through broader end user and advertiser base and increasingly targeted advertising opportunities. By the same token, they would also add to buyers' switching costs and marginalize rivals through higher entry barriers.

In the longer term, advertising sales and electronic commerce were expected to make or break Yahoo! Until 1998, the company derived substantially all of its revenues from the sale of banner advertisements, while minor revenue sources included placement fees, promotions, and transactions on Yahoo! properties. As the electronic commerce was expected to pick up toward the end of the 1990s, Yahoo!, like so many other Internet companies, was rushing toward the Internet retail, hoping to cash its share. In the short-term, however, Yahoo! was a new brand;

transactions also had a brand-building function. By developing an extended family of Yahoo!-branded properties, the company sought to offer advertisers a wide range of placement options.

The Brand-Building Strategy: Building Awareness through Irreverence. After 1996, the goal became to keep surfers on Yahoo!'s site instead of sending them elsewhere, thus ensuring that ad dollars continue to flow into the company coffers. The portal strategy meant significant investments in marketing and advertising. In order to reach new users, Yahoo! would have to exploit traditional venues of media advertising. It would have to become far more visible, familiar, and ubiquitous. In January 1996, Karen Edwards, who had worked on the Apple account at advertising agency BBDO, became Yahoo!'s director of brand advertising. She would have a crucial role in the branding of Yahoo! Joining the company at nearly its inception, she had seen the company grow from about 20 employees to about 230. She also witnessed and influenced the Yahoo! brand to blossom from an amorphous Internet technology to one of new media's most recognized and emulated Web brands.[103]

Soon after Edwards arrived, Yahoo! launched $5 million worth of television commercials. The ads were directed at people who had heard about the Web but had not yet logged on. In a survey it conducted before the first ad, the company asked a cross section of Americans, "What is Yahoo!?" Only 8% correctly identified the company. Edwards moved into "guerrilla marketing" mode. She pushed the brand into sports events, rock concerts, magazines, and other conventional channels, as well as some strange ones—she gave free paint jobs to any employee who would splatter the logo over his or her car.[104]

During 1996 and 1997, American TV audiences began to get an idea of Yahoo! The new search engine relied on irreverent advertising to make its presence more visible in traditional media. By February 1997, the *New York Times* associated Yahoo!'s new media strategy with that of leading consumer-product marketers. "Thanks to those clown-size fish in the company's TV ads, or the hillbilly yodel in the radio spots, even investors who have never surfed cyberspace have likely heard of Yahoo!—a leader in the market for services that help users search for information on the World Wide Web. Following the example of McDonald's and other consumer-product marketers, Yahoo!, like its closest competitors, Lycos, Excite and Infoseek, has been building brand awareness through sizable television and radio advertising campaigns."[105] Still, this particular strategy was dictated by the impact of the Telecommunications Act on the revenue sources of Yahoo! and many other Internet firms. Branding was not a value as such; it was instrumental as a means of the redefined strategy.

Toward the end of 1997, advertisers started to make Yahoo! their online buy. By December, Yahoo! had 1,700 paying advertisers, up from just 112 in early 1996. Revenues tripled, to $67 million. Without the one-time charge for buying Four11, the company would have recorded a profit of $2.5 million for the year instead of a $23 million loss. Advertisers were signing up for relationships that brought in more cash. In the spring of 1997, Yahoo! was the first of the four publicly held search engines to post a profit. It also was about to spend between $10 and $15 million on advertising that year, including a spot during the January Super Bowl. Concurrently, the number of advertisers on Yahoo!'s websites rose from 340 in the third quarter to 550. Yahoo!'s marketing approach generated strong results and high visibility.[106]

Under the Yahoo! brand, the company provided intuitive, context-based guides to online content, Web search capabilities, aggregated third-party content, e-mail, and community and personalization features. For advertisers, the lure of Yahoo! was precisely the target audiences defined by its demographically or geographically focused sites. Of course, Yahoo! was not only developing new product lines and brand extensions in order to expand. Building the awareness served to increase entry barriers. The more extensively Yahoo! could invade and capture "shelf-space" in the Internet, (i.e., the users' mind-share), the harder it would be for imitators and late entrants to enter this industry segment and mark their territory in it.

Branding America Online

The surge of online communities of computer-linked online communities was predicted a year before the first man walked on the moon. In 1968, three influential researchers with close ties to ARPA (Department of Defense) launched the research program that resulted in the creation of the first such community, the ARPANET, the predecessor of the Internet. "What will on-line interactive communities be like?" Licklider and Taylor wrote in 1968. "In most fields they will consist of geographically separated members, sometimes grouped in small clusters and sometimes working individually. They will be communities not of common location, but of common interest."[107] In the mid-1980s, that dream assumed a more concrete and virtual form in WELL (Whole Earth 'Lectronic Link)—a nonprofit computer conferencing system that enabled people around the world to carry on public conversations and exchange private electronic mail. "Millions of people on every continent also participate in the computer-mediated social groups known as virtual communities," noted Howard Rheingold, a pioneer of WELL before the first browsers, "and this population is growing fast."[108]

Few people had any idea about the frantic pace of this growth. Few except, perhaps, for Steven Case, CEO of America Online. The online experience was a hard-sell in the aftermath of the 1990–1991 recession;

but when the business began to pick up, it soared. From 200,000 members in 1992, AOL surged to some 11–12 million in late 1997. As the online service provider shot up, it passed CompuServe and Prodigy on the way down.

By the late 1990s, AOL's mission was

to become the recognized brand leader in the development of an interactive medium that transcends traditional boundaries between people and places to create an interactive global community that holds the potential to change the way people communicate, stay informed, learn, shop and do business. To accomplish this mission, the company's strategy is to . . . establish America Online and AOL as recognized brand names and to build customer loyalty as a foundation for growth in subscribers and revenues.[109]

By 1998, the Dulles, Virginia–based America Online (AOL) was the world's leading online service, with 12 million members. In the fall of 1997, the acquisition of CompuServe, its main rival, gave the company some 2.5 million more subscribers, putting it far ahead of Microsoft Network and giving it a 60% market share.[110] The acquisition also strengthened AOL's position in Europe, where AOL, German-based media company Bertelsmann, and French utility Vivendi operated CompuServe Europe's and AOL France's online business.

By the spring of 1998, AOL reached about as many homes as cable operators Time Warner or Tele-Communications. Unlike the MSOs, however, it was adding more than 10,000 users a day. It had more subscribers than *Time, Newsweek,* and *U.S. News & World Report* combined. During weekday prime time, the number of people logged on to AOL peaked at around 650,000, which was not that different from the ratings of such cable networks as MTV and CNN. In 1996, users had spent an average of 14 minutes a day plugged into AOL; by 1998, the visitors stayed for an average of 51 minutes. Nielsen ratings confirmed the online giant's dreams and the TV networks' nightmare: users were watching less TV. Most importantly, AOL subscribers were not nerds or techies. Instead, they were slightly upscale users who owned PCs, and 52% of them were women. The audience was AOL's most valuable asset, more valuable than its infrastructure or technology. The online giant was not really a content aggregator, as Wall Street's analysts thought; it was primarily an audience aggregator or, even better, an audience segmentor. It bought and sold eyeballs. It managed audiences primarily, programming secondarily—but, unlike the TV networks or cable MSOs, it was capable of one-to-one marketing.

By summer 1997, America Online had become the global leader in the interactive communications and services medium, with over $1.6 billion in revenue. AOL generated revenues principally through membership and usage fees, as well as increasingly from other sources, including electronic commerce and ad revenues. The company offered its online services in the United States, Austria, Canada, France, Germany, Japan, Sweden, Switzerland, and the United Kingdom. It also offered access to its AOL service in over 100 countries. With flat-rate pricing and thousands of competitors offering Internet access, AOL was working to tap other revenue sources, particularly advertising. Through such venues as Entertainment Asylum, the company was developing the content to attract a mass audience so that it could compete with TV networks for advertisers. Other growing sources of revenues included marketing agreements with companies such as Amazon.com, Intuit, and 1–800-FLOWERS, which paid AOL for promotion on AOL's website and fees to AOL on subscriber purchases. Far better than its initial online rivals, America Online saw its mission in marketing terms—highly user-friendly online services for as many Americans as possible.

Marketing and Distribution. After AOL went public in 1992, Steve Case and Jan Brandt, AOL's CEO and marketing director, respectively, devised a harder sell than any ever tried by an online service. They would send out software disks by direct mail to millions of computer owners, offering them free trials of AOL (Exhibit 5-9). The tactic had worked for Brandt in her previous job, where she had recruited new members to My Weekly Reader book club by sending them a free book rather than a pitch letter. Just like AT&T and America's largest consumer marketers, AOL wanted to be anywhere, anytime, any place; as American and as much present as Coca-Cola. "My job," says Brandt, "was to give new meaning to the word ubiquity." According to the legend, Brandt's wall features a couple of framed disks, captioned WE COME IN PEACE and RESISTANCE IS FUTILE.[111]

As a result of the direct marketing campaign, AOL's membership soared, from 155,000 at the time of the IPO to 4.6 million at the start of 1996. It was not easy to handle the explosive growth. Yet it may have been a necessity. To compete with the entrenched media and entertainment companies, computing giants, and telcos, AOL had to grow explosively, by any means necessary. What many critics considered irresponsible overspending was merely AOL's tactic to reap first-mover benefits sooner rather than later. It was a risky growth strategy, but the accounting methods were hardly new or unique.[112] In the 1980s, Wayne Huizenga's Blockbuster had resorted to somewhat similar accounting devices, for near-identical motivations, and against the same incumbent media and entertainment conglomerates.[113]

Transformations in Marketing Mix. During the 1990s, America Online changed its marketing mix several times, often abruptly and drastically. These changes were dictated by the dynamics of the Internet evolution. They were made possible by AOL's enterpreneurial business and mar-

Exhibit 5-9
Branding America Online: Make It Ubiquitous

Through the first half of the 1990s, Steve Case, CEO of America Online, formulated the online service provider's mission and strategy. In the second half of the 1980s, Robert Pittman served as AOL's missionary and evangelist; he was a marketing whiz who had co-founded MTV and helped create the brilliant "I want my MTV" ad campaign. Avoiding short-sighted cost-cutting, he forged a slate of profitable deals and exploited branding to increase switching costs and minimize churn.

But it was Jan Brandt, AOL's marketing director, who came up with the direct marketing plan to proliferate America with millions of AOL disks. The marketing strategy was simple and risky—to make America Online as ubiquitous as AT&T, Coca-Cola, General Motors. Brandt was named AOL's President of Marketing in September 1997. Prior to this, she had been Senior Vice President of Acquisition Marketing and responsible for member acquisitions and growth and merchandise sales.

"When people in the industry saw us giving away the software, they could not believe that we would do it," Brandt says. The plan to proliferate America with AOL disks "was so expensive. No one had done something like this before. The industry thought that we were crazy for spending so much money. They forgot the other side of the story. They were so focused on the unit cost of a disk or mailing or promotion piece that they neglected the dramatic increases in responses that we were getting from people."

In effect, there *was* something of a precedent.

Brandt had an extensive background in product marketing, magazine circulation, publishing, insurance and book clubs. From November 1988 to April 1993, Brandt was Vice President of Advertising for Newfield Publications Publishing (formerly Field Publications). "We were selling children's books and book clubs in competition against some *Time Life* book clubs and so forth. Our books were the least expensive. They were intended for middle-class families; yet it was very difficult to tell parents, the predominant purchasers of these children's books, about the high quality of these books. I was so convinced that if people could hold these books in their hands and they would see the quality for themselves, they would sign up for our book club. So we conducted an expensive campaign. We sent out a full, unabridged children's full-color, hardcover book to parents enticing them to join the book club with a very simple promotion from the president of the company."

"It was a phenomenally successful program," Brandt recalls. "That experience enabled me to take the leap with a product like AOL that defied description. There was really very little in the product category at the time. That's why it was exactly the correct strategy to put these disks into the hands of millions of Americans."

Source: Dan Steinbock, interview with Janice Brandt, President of Marketing, America Online, October 8, 1998.

keting strategies. Far faster and more flexibly than its rivals, AOL would review and remold its product portfolio; rebuild and rechannel its distribution avenues; reconsider and reposition its promotional tactics; reprice its products; and restructure its organization. Rapid changes in the direction did not take place without a debate. As the leading online service provider, AOL would often be the first to break traditional ways of doing business. As the new Telecommunications Act of 1996 popularized a fixed-fee for Internet access providers, it also made ad revenues critical to the expansion of the Internet. Soon thereafter, AOL began to serve as a matchmaker between its audiences and advertisers. In the early 1990s, the Internet community would hardly have welcomed such developments; even in the spring of 1997, they gave rise to ambivalent reactions (e.g., AOL's decision to open chat rooms to online advertisements).[114]

As consumers were increasingly annoyed with the proliferation of advertising messages and the ensuing "noise," a consumer backlash was perceived as a real possibility. Yet, AOL's growth strategy left few alternatives. The strategic decision came at a time when the company desperately needed new sources of revenue. Insofar as advertisers were concerned, AOL's pricing decisions did not make their experiments any easier. AOL planned to charge $5 to $15 per thousand "impressions," or sightings, rivaling the $7 to $28 CPM (cost-per-thousand viewers) of network television, which boasted a far larger audience, run ads in living color, and was a much more conservative forum. So why did many advertisers *still* invest in chat room ads? Around 1997 and 1998, AOL, like rival OSPs and ISPs, could boast with *targeted* and desirable upperbrow user demographics.[115]

Toward 1:1 Marketing: Issues of Privacy and Targeting. To provide highly focused targeting opportunities, AOL made use of its new demographic ad server. It allowed marketers to target ads with precision by matching users' personal information with data from offline direct marketing companies such as Polk and MetroMail. The process could reveal more than 200 variables about an individual that could be layered to paint rich consumer portraits. For instance, a car company could direct an ad at 40-year-old males with $100,000-plus incomes who haven't purchased a car in the last five years. So far, GTE Wireless, Tropicana Dole Beverages North America, and Ameritech Corp. have signed up for the targeting. While providing unprecedented targeting opportunities with its new demographic ad server, America Online was coming under fire from privacy advocates.[116] According to AOL, the service not only brought value to advertisers but enabled them to reach the online members with ads that the latter were more interested in. The company compared the service to the common selective binding that news magazines like *Time* used to create issues customized for people living in specific ZIP codes. The difference was that while one could not customize newsstand editions, AOL could target all of its members.[117]

Despite debates over privacy issues, it seemed inevitable that, in one form or another, targeting had come to stay. By 1998, other companies were quickly getting into the act.[118]

Brand Building Programs and Strategies. AOL built its brand name through a broad array of programs and strategies, including broadcast advertising campaigns, direct mail, magazine inserts, and increasingly from co-marketing, cross-promotion, and bundling agreements. It entered into co-marketing agreements with its media partners and with affinity groups and associations to market directly to and cater to the needs of specific audiences. It pursued cross-promotional opportunities through expanding existing, and establishing new, partnerships. Examples included agreements with ABC Sports, CBS SportsLine, CUC International, Tel-Save Holdings, and 1–800–Flowers that allowed the company and its partners to jointly market, promote, and advertise their products and services. Additionally, AOL had been preinstalled on nearly all leading PCs for the consumer market, and could be accessed through an icon on the Windows 95 and Apple Macintosh desktops and through ISPs such as the AT&T WorldNet service. AOL's marketing strategy was expected to place a greater emphasis on these cost-effective bundling agreements. Although the company would continue to market its products via direct mail programs, such programs were expected to be more cost-efficient, as they will be directed to more narrowly targeted consumer groups.

Retention Programs and Flat-Rate Pricing. America Online utilized specialized retention programs that were designed to increase customer loyalty and satisfaction and to maximize customer subscription life. These retention programs included regularly scheduled online events and conferences; the regular addition of new content, services, and software programs; and online promotions of upcoming online events and new features.[119]

The goal of AOL's marketing program was to attract and retain members. Like the cable MSOs of the early 1980s, most OSPs suffered from churn. Attracting new subscribers was expensive and relatively futile, if the company would not be able to hold onto its existing clientele. AOL sought to build brand recognition and member loyalty and to make it easy for consumers to try, and subscribe to, the AOL service. In 1997 alone, AOL added roughly 2.9 million members, and had to invest $700 million in its access network and in customer service.

A "marketing whiz kid," Robert Pittman had co-founded MTV and helped create the "I want my MTV" advertising campaign that forced reluctant cable operators to carry the channel. When Pittman assumed his duties at AOL and took charge of the online giant's operations, that was widely interpreted as just another proof that the company was now competing with the nation's largest media conglomerates. He did not simply attack the costs. That was something "everybody" was doing. It was not a strategy; it was part of the game, necessary but not adequate. In the spring of 1998, he laid off 500 people from CompuServe and another 200 from AOL Studios, a money-losing content unit, as both were brought under his control. Pittman also used AOL's scale to drive hard deals with backbone providers like WorldCom, gradually pushing AOL's cost of connect time down from 95 cents an hour to less than 50 cents an hour. But most importantly, as the AOL brand built strength, he was able to spend less on marketing. Between March 1996 and March 1998, AOL's cost of acquiring a new subscriber dropped from $375 to $90.[120]

Just as MTV, in the first half of the 1980s, had been able to cut costs of acquiring new subscribers through heavy branding, AOL would do the same. It cut significantly the acquisition costs of new subscribers, spent less on marketing by leveraging the brand, and avoided high churn and retained more subscribers through both cost-cutting and branding measures. As rivals drifted to price competition, AOL restructured operations to cut costs but invested in branding to loyalize its old, new, and potential clients. While many of its rivals saw only short-term and fleeting gains, AOL was positioning strategically—for longer-term and more solid gains.

Brand strength proved particularly useful with the emergence of Internet retail. The key was to leverage AOL's massive subscriber base for all it was worth. Pittman would have to squeeze big dollars out of retailers, advertisers, publishers, programmers, and anyone else looking to reach the millions of eyeballs on AOL. In that regard, the key role belonged to Dan Borislow and his long-distance company Tel-Save. Relying on Tel-Save's infrastructure, AOL would attract a growing share of Internet retail business.[121] A flurry of deals followed. CUC International paid $50 million for AOL to carry its online discount-shopping service. Preview Travel paid $32 million to become the service's online travel agent; 1–800–Flowers bought the flower concession for $25 million; and N2K paid $18 million to become the sole music retailer. In most cases, bidders were also pitted against one another. In February 1998, Intuit agreed to pay $30 million to sell financial services. Ahead were deals with sellers of insurance, office supplies, groceries, and most intriguingly, digital imaging. Once families put pictures in their AOL Photo Album to share with relatives and friends, switching to another online provider might be less frequent.

AOL positioned itself strategically between the suppliers and the end consumer. As an intermediary, it was tough, shrewd, and skillful in cutting into the bargaining power of the suppliers and playing them against one another. Since it controlled the "last mile" to consumer homes, it could even afford to make deals with rival players. After Amazon.com paid $19 million to become the bookseller on AOL's website, Barnes & Noble agreed to a $40 million deal to be the exclusive book retailer inside

AOL. As commerce deals accelerated, advertising proved less lucrative. The momentum was moving toward Internet retail.

From Commissions to Rent. By July 1997, however, AOL was questioning the cherished model for online commerce and overhauled its approach to online shopping. Instead of relying mainly on a cut of their sales, AOL would collect rent from its electronic retailers. Even prior to the commercialization of the Internet, the proponents of interactive television and the home-shopping cablers had touted snaring even a tiny percentage of every electronic transaction as a sure-fire route to profits. Accordingly, most of AOL's initial agreements with merchants emphasized commissions over flat-rate payments. But, by the summer of 1997, AOL had become weary of what it perceived as a one-sided business model: the problem with commissions was a lack of risk for retailers. The change in the online shopping model followed the recent demise of World Avenue, an Internet-based shopping mall launched by IBM Corp. in 1996.[122] There was no penalty for failing to generate sales, so merchants could afford to treat their online storefronts as experiments only. For all practical purposes, online sales at AOL and elsewhere had fallen short of the expectations. By August 1998, AOL launched its redesigned Shopping Channel and award its prime "real estate" to retailers willing to pay upfront rental fees.[123] Prior to mid-1998, brokerage firms like DLJdirect and E*Trade paid nearly $500,000 a year for space on AOL's Personal Finance channel. When a new customer opened an account as a result of an ad, AOL got a slice of all future commissions. Both DLJdirect and E*Trade paid AOL on every single trade. By June 1998, however, occupying space on America Online Inc.'s popular personal-finance site got a lot more expensive for the nation's biggest online brokerage firms.[124]

In online services and Internet retail, AOL had not yet faced a serious competitive challenge. In the past, prospective rivals like IBM, CBS, Sears, AT&T, and Microsoft had all fallen short. Still, the biggest telecommunications players had not given up. The telcos and cable companies were coming after AOL's customers to cut into its market dominance.

TOWARD AD NETWORKS

The infrastructure of media buying and planning in the Internet evolved only a few months after October 1994 when HotWired launched with its 14 corporate sponsors. Following the Telecommunications Act of 1996, advertising emerged as the primary revenue source for many websites and the primary driver on Internet economics, first in the United States and soon thereafter internationally. Meanwhile, the Web pioneers moved from the design and launch of distinct websites to the management of entire ad networks. Such networks provided scale benefits that were impossible to reach with distinct web pages. In the process, these first movers moved bargaining power from individual websites toward ad network management.

Initially, the top sites, especially those launched by media, sought to make *content* the basis of the revenue model. Advertiser needs, however, upped the ante for content sites, which soon proved to be only one form of sites. As the Internet meant even greater audience fragmentation than the cable in the 1980s, ad practitioners soon began to aggregate disaggregated sites with affinities.

To fulfill its promise, the Internet needed ad networks. According to Forrester, single sites, even large ones, did not hold the key to Web advertising, for several reasons:

- *Diffuse viewer traffic.* The top sites had masses of visitors compared with the smallest ones. Still, the Web had hundreds of thousands of commercial sites. To reach people, advertisers had to get beyond the few top names, out to at least several hundred sites. They had to be able to consolidate the fragmented.

- *Content churn.* New content producers launched home pages daily. Word of mouth could make or break a new site. Of the top 100 sites listed at 100hot.com in 1996, 15% were new each month.

- *Following users.* The most popular sites were search engines. But once their query was filled, people dispersed to the content sites. To be in tune with the medium, ads had to follow people.

- *Ads expire.* DoubleClick's ad tests implied that once a person had seen a banner twice, there was no point in showing it again. To be effective, advertisers had to rotate ads and reach new people. Such a requirement was tough on single sites, which focused on building repeat visitors.[125]

In the late 1980s, most multiple system operators (MSOs) had suffered from relatively high levels of churn until they paid more attention to customer service. Indeed, the Internet revolution of the mid-1990s had some affinities with the cable revolution a decade before.

Channel Proliferation. In the course of the 1980s, broadcast TV advertising had suffered a drastic erosion with the rise of cable, as well as the growth of independent TV stations and syndication. In the early 1980s, the "Three Big" networks controlled more than 90% of the prime time and therefore a similar proportion of broadcast advertising; by the end of the decade, they had less than 60% left. Concurrently, the new marketing channels (cable) acquired significant collective bargaining power, while the attractiveness of individual cable channels proved far weaker than those of the "Big Three" networks. Something similar happened with the Internet's top sites, or "portals," as they became known in the spring of 1997. Even though their users were not that loyal, they did command the highest traffic volumes and therefore the highest CPMs.

From Mass Ratings to Focused Segments. With the cable revolution, even the ratings of the most favorite cable channels (e.g., MTV's highest audiences garnered less than 1% ratings) were far behind those of the most popular network TV shows (15–25%). Still, cable advertising thrived because it could provide blocks of targeted demographic segments (e.g., MTV's teen viewers), instead of mass TV's large audience blocks (e.g., 18–49-year-old viewers). As the first Internet ratings became available, it was hardly a surprise that they proved far smaller than those of cable networks. It was left to the advertisers and Web publishers alike to find ways to consolidate the (Web) segments of (TV and cable) audience segments, in order to achieve proper scale economies.

In this sense, the Internet merely accelerated a kind of evolution that had arrived with the cable revolution. While ad budgets grew very slowly, the channel proliferation was explosive. As the size of the pie remained nearly identical and as the increasing number of slices caused a fragmentation of the pie, each slice proved to be smaller than ever before. But the Internet revolution also went far further than the cable revolution. It was not just about channel multiplication; the faster interactivity proliferated, the more rapid was the shift of the bargaining power from the sellers to the buyers. Of course, the remote control that became popular in the late 1970s and early 1980s had heralded such changes. But even with a remote control, an individual viewer could only choose from a small set (from a dozen to less than 100) of available channel options, whereas the Web multiplied the set of choice options to hundreds, thousands, or more. Moreover, through the hyperlinks, the Web programming, unlike traditional TV or cable programming, was geared to interactivity.

The result? *A highly distributed medium, with highly segmented audiences.* Consequently, advertisers could not acknowledge single and distinct websites as the exclusive or ultimate drivers of the new industry. If the Internet's competitive advantages lay in network economies and interactivity, advertisers would have to find ways to exploit both. Double-Click was one of the pioneer·ng companies to provide a viable business model on *how* to accomplish both objectives. It demonstrated how to achieve the kind of frequency and reach that mass marketers required for their brands. It assisted micromarketers to implement the kind of interactive one-to-one marketing that they required for their brands. In both cases, DoubleClick had to question, rethink, and reformulate the traditional industry wisdom on the development of new brands or building and extending old ones.

Indeed, the Internet's evolutionary dynamics, coupled with the advertisers' needs in media advertising and sales promotion, favored aggregating distinct sites into networks of sites on the basis of relevant criteria.

Relying on the procedures and discoveries of DoubleClick and other pioneering Web agencies, advertisers, and Web publishers, Forrester Research sought to deduce proactively the new advertising practices (i.e., as and even before they would emerge on the Web). Like distinct content providers, these networks would package the Web's dispersed content and traffic for advertisers. From the advertisers' standpoint, however, the two were not of equal practical significance. Compared with single content sites, networks had important strategic strengths, or network economies. Individual sites could not afford the direct salespeople required to pitch agencies and clients, whereas networks could sell a portfolio. Also, running an effective ad-supported content operation would require significant investments in ad servers, measurement and profiling technologies, digital certificates, and personalization. Networks were able to leverage this investment across multiple sites, whereas single content sites could not.[126]

With the network economies, the new model enabled advertisers to minimize risk. In effect, the emerging ad networks shared certain affinities with investment activities and the stock market. The old top sites model of media buying was comparable to a naïve investor who put all the eggs into a single or at best a few baskets. On the other hand, a professional money manager diversified the risk by putting eggs in highly diversified baskets, according to the investment objectives; he or she also allocated investment funds dynamically and flexibly on the basis of the results and the performance.

Not only did networks have important strategic strengths compared with single content sites. They also offered advertisers significant advantages. First, even the most popular site could not deliver the traffic of a network. In 1996, PointCast populated more than one million desktops in six months, while DoubleClick attracted ten million unique visitors to its network. Unlike single content sites, networks could run the large databases required to track ads, content pages, and individuals—ensuring that an ad reached its audience as often as expected. Seeking trusted business relationships, clients and agencies liked to know who they were dealing with.[127]

As the number of marketing channels no longer accelerated in linear terms (the cable revolution), but would in time go through the roof (the Internet revolution), old practices of media planning would simply lose their rationales—they were decent procedures in *their* competitive environment. In the new environment, they would be as efficient as the Polish horsemen against German tanks in 1939.

Advertisers and agencies would be forced to changed with the new environment. They would have to find new ways of dealing with highly expansive and complex distribution webs. Presumably, networks could assist them in reaggregating the disaggregated sites and consolidating the fragmented audiences. Ad networks would create order into the chaos. It was DoubleClick that pioneered the concept of ad networks.

DoubleClick: "Building One-to-One Relationships Millions at a Time . . ."

The concept of ad networks emerged first at DoubleClick, Inc. The innovative interactive advertising agency pioneered the concept that, only a few years ago, was considered impossible—centralized media buying and selling vis-à-vis the highly distributed Internet. DoubleClick presented itself and was seen as the pioneering global Internet advertising solutions company. Combining state-of-the-art technology and media expertise, it had successfully centralized planning, execution, control, tracking, and reporting for high-impact, online media campaigns. It was the industry leader at leveraging technology to create solutions that helped advertisers and publishers unleash the power of the Web for branding, selling products, and building relationships with customers.[128]

The Genesis of DoubleClick. By the end of 1997, the New York–based DoubleClick had delivered approximately 6 billion ads on the Internet to over 25 million people in more than 80 different countries. After the mid-1990s, DoubleClick grew out of the interactive ad-sales division of Poppe Tyson, a pioneering interactive ad agency, and a unit of the privately held Bozell, Jacobs, Kenyon & Eckhardt (BJK&E), an international ad agency chain. When that division merged with Internet Advertising Network (IAN), an Atlanta software company started by Kevin O'Connor just a few months earlier, DoubleClick was formed in early 1996 and O'Connor became its chairman and CEO. The company was born from the marriage of Madison Avenue media savvy and cutting edge technology.[129]

In January 1997, DoubleClick signed an exclusive agreement allowing it to display ads on AltaVista, a subsidiary of Digital Equipment Corp. In effect, ads delivered on the websites of the top four Web publishers on the DoubleClick Network accounted for more than 61% of the company's revenues in 1997, while revenues derived from ads delivered on AltaVista represented some 45% of the total. DoubleClick was critically dependent on the partnership. In June of that year, DoubleClick also announced DoubleClick Direct, a results-based advertising network. Using sophisticated tracking and database capabilities (including "cookies," which gave a server such information as which websites a user had visited and what online purchases he or she had made), the company developed highly targeted ad delivery. It placed ads on more than 60 sites, including Travelocity and "USA TODAY." Most sites split ad revenues with the company. DoubleClick delivered ads online for such clients as Microsoft (about 10% of sales), AT&T, and IBM.

Trained as an electrical engineer, Kevin O'Connor, DoubleClick's chief executive, had always worked with software. To him, the Web's greatest potential was as a marketing vehicle. He anticipated the *interactivity* of the Internet to provide advertising opportunities not available in any other medium.[130]

Educating the Clients. With the company structure in place, the next step was marketing. DoubleClick was not a recognized name in the industry; it needed visibility. The industry did not understand its offering; it needed to educate the buyers. Based on the twin objectives of education and visibility, DoubleClick introduced its marketing plan. The company would educate the industry about the power of this new medium. With several key websites already aboard (such as The Dilbert Zone, Macromedia, and US News and World Report), its ubiquitous ad campaign explained how the Web allowed businesses to build one-to-one relationships between brands and consumers. The mini-seminars were accompanied by a more grassroots-level approach to marketing. DoubleClick employees spoke throughout the country at every venue from trade shows to ad agencies about the strengths of the Web as a marketing tool.[131]

Reportedly, DoubleClick spent more than $2 million through 1997 on the campaign, which included print advertisements, direct mail, and appeals on its own website. "We want to be a catalyst, if you will, for the industry to grow and realize its potential," said Lee Nadler, marketing director at Double Click. "We recognize the need to bring in the big advertisers and the big money," he added, "and that's going to take some time. Yes, we're selling now, but we're also educating for tomorrow's dollars." Nadler, who had also worked for Kirshenbaum Bond & Partners in New York and the online service Prodigy, said: "Door-to-door sales was the most effective marketing tool because you got to know the customer. You built a relationship, a dialogue. Now the Web has that same power and same efficiency, but some people feel they're coming in halfway through."[132]

After a few months of seminar circuits, DoubleClick was becoming synonymous with targeted Web advertising. As more and more companies recognized the benefits of this new media, a reputation for providing results spread throughout the growing industry, which came to know DoubleClick's cutting edge products—in particular, its ad network, DART (Dynamic Advertising Reporting and Targeting) technology, and direct-marketing services. DoubleClick DART was unbundled from the Network. This took place after repeated requests by sites with their own sales force for a full-service ad management system. By late 1997, DART clients included companies such as The Wall Street Journal

Interactive Edition, NBC, Excite Europe, and Reader's Digest. Double-Click had to educate the clients to see the potential of direct marketing by and on the Web. Often the company would use case samples to convey the critical lessons.

The Core Services: Technology, Network, and Direct. Since its inception, DoubleClick has been a leading provider of comprehensive Internet advertising solutions for advertisers and Web publishers. The company's technology and media expertise enabled it to dynamically deliver highly targeted, measurable and cost-effective Internet advertising for advertisers and to increase ad sales and improve ad space inventory management for Web publishers. Essentially, DoubleClick offered three distinct Internet advertising solutions:

- By 1998, the DoubleClick Network consisted of seven easily defined categories of interest, or affinity groups. These groups had been created to help advertisers create highly targeted campaigns. With over 70 premier sites in the Network (including Alta Vista, Dilbert, and US News & World Report), the company provided advertisers with a wide selection of ad vehicles. Double-Click perceived itself as a service provider in two critical markets for Internet advertising solutions, advertisers and Web publishers.

- DoubleClick's DART Service, an Internet advertising management solution for Web publishers with internal ad sales forces, which was currently being utilized by over 20 Web publishers, including NBC, The Wall Street Journal Interactive Edition, RealNetworks, and The Sporting News.

- DoubleClick Direct, the Company's recently introduced advertising solution designed specifically for direct marketers.

By 1998, in addition to these three solutions, DoubleClick had two additional components: DoubleClick International and DoubleClick Local.

In November 1997, the company estimated that more than 20 million users visited the websites of Web publishers that used the company's solutions, resulting in an aggregate of over 900 million requests received by DoubleClick for the delivery of ads (impressions). During the same period, DoubleClick managed approximately 7,000 Internet advertisements for over 600 advertisers, and over 100 Web publishers, representing an aggregate of approximately 350 websites that used the company's Internet advertising solutions. DoubleClick believed that advertisers would seek to take advantage of the attractive demographics of Internet users. It also thought that the Internet represented an attractive new medium for direct marketing, which had traditionally been conducted through direct mail and telemarketing, because now highly targeted product offers could be made to consumers *at the point-of-sale.* In 1997, some 61% of DoubleClick's revenues stemmed from ads delivered on the websites of the top four Web publishers on the DoubleClick Network.[133]

Moreover, the company anticipated that a substantial portion of its future revenues would be derived from ads delivered on the websites of a limited number of Web publishers.

According to Kevin O'Connor, technology was DoubleClick's key advantage, in particular DART.

Most people didn't see it, in particular traditional media companies. They wonder how to use a traditional media model on the Internet and ignore the latter's unique interactivity. Just as they neglect the fact that I can dynamically deliver an address and an ad just for you and then see how you react to it. That's not done in the media, so it was missed. They applied the norms of static advertising in the Internet where one can use dynamic advertising. They all missed it. At DoubleClick, we didn't know advertising, but we knew of what the *Internet* could do. So we developed the technology to manage dynamic advertising.[134]

If American media people struggled to understand the basics of the DoubleClick system, international buyers had hardly heard of it, not to speak of understanding its elements and functions. In order to sell cyberspace, then, one would have to invest into a physical sales force. To capitalize on the *global reach* of the Internet, DoubleClick established DoubleClick Networks in Europe, Asia, and other international markets. By the end of 1997, DoubleClick was operating networks in seven countries, enabling advertisers to place targeted global buys across numerous sites in multiple languages.

To enjoy the first-mover benefits, DoubleClick had to expand rapidly and flexibly, both of which translated to capital expenditures. By early 1998, the IPO was a necessity. On revenues of $20 million for the nine months ended 30 September, 1997, DoubleClick was still losing money. None of its rivals were too profitable either, including Softbank Interactive Marketing, Cliqnow, and Petry Interactive, which all offered advertisers the opportunity to buy a particular audience across many sites. Moreover, questions remained about the role that sellers of ad space across networks would play and whether they would be profitable. On February 20, 1998, DoubleClick leaped into the public market gaining 57% upon its debut. Having floated out three million shares in its IPO, DoubleClick raised a total of $51 million with the public offering. Still, the rivalry was rapidly intensifying.[135]

As ad networks struggled for clients and high margins, there were also nagging questions about the viability of their competitive strategies. As the "portal mania" of the early 1998 proved, the big sites like Yahoo! were looking to become their own content networks, and lots of money would go to them directly. Major aggregators (AOL) and software giants (Microsoft, MSN) posed a competitive threat to the prevailing players; since they were far more capital-intensive, they could consolidate the nascent industry and integrate the existing search engines with their operating systems, software applications, and so on. To make matters worse, many media buyers argued the price of Web ads was falling due to heavy discounting by big sites and competition from cut-rate space sold by companies such as FlyCast Communications Corp., which auctioned off the thousands of unsold ad spots that plagued websites.

O'Connor estimated the value of the worldwide ad market at $375 billion, including broadcast and print. DoubleClick's long-term goal was to prove the value of the Internet to advertisers. The company had to compete with print and TV in order to do so. The portal mania reflected an industry ripe for a shakeout, with weaker websites folding or merging with others. The survivors could potentially attract enough Web cruisers to make them a compelling ad venue for big marketers. While such forecasts were nightmare scenarios to many portals, they appealed to DoubleClick. The very same consolidation that threatened to demolish the minor portals offered a strategic objective to DoubleClick, even if it had to struggle more for margins than most of its Internet content site rivals.[136]

By late 1998, DoubleClick was known as one of the leading Internet companies. Naturally, its actions were keenly observed not only by industry visionaries but also by the incumbents. Yet, the company, by its very mission, blurred the existing industry boundaries. According to O'Connor,

A lot of people get confused by DoubleClick. They think we are an agency just because of our history. And, yes, we came out of an agency, but due to a mistake of history. We are not an agency. We are fundamentally on the sell side. True, our technology seems to operate on both sides because in some ways we are creating a kind of a NASDAQ system where the buyers and sellers may come together.[137]

After DoubleClick had developed and launched the concept of Internet-driven ad network, market research firms began to deduce the implications.

Types of Advertising Networks

By the end of 1997, the top ten most heavily trafficked websites accounted for more than 60% of all advertising revenue (Jupiter Communications). These sites tended to have an in-house sales staff, rather than turning to firms like DoubleClick to represent them. So the networks would be scrambling to lock up as much as possible of the remaining 35–40% of Internet advertising revenue. In practice that was expected to translate to $80 million if the networks' margins stayed high. Industry analysts estimated that firms like DoubleClick and Softbank took about 40% off the top of an ad buy, even if they expected that number to head down to 15–20%.[138]

In September 1996, Forrester Research released a study on Internet advertising and ad networks, based on the pioneering discoveries of DoubleClick, arguing that Internet dynamics favored the emergence of networks of sites, which would package the Web's dispersed content and traffic for advertisers.[139] Forrester noted that early reports indicated a healthy and growing market for Internet ads with online ad revenues at an estimated $80 million in 1996, growing to $4 billion by 2001. On the other hand, Forrester noted that advertisers were frustrated by pricing and reporting based on the old media models. Indeed, the firm predicted that advertising networks—not ad agencies—would become the dominant sellers of Web ads.[140] "Buyers crave far greater accountability from websites. Their needs will force a structural change in new media—away from individual sites and toward large networks of sites that sell advertising and run the huge database servers required to manage and analyze ads," said Mary Modahl, a respected Internet analysts who headed Forrester's new service.

Money and market power will flow toward networks. There will be several types, each with a unique pricing model and value proposition. You'll see content networks like CNET with commerce tied to content themes, and personal broadcast networks like PointCast selling on time and desktop penetration. Sites that aren't part of a network are going to get creamed.[141]

According to Forrester, the Internet was witnessing the emergence of five distinct types of advertising networks. Some of these networks were already known in the industry, some were not. While new types were emerging, older ones evolved to new directions. They could be described and exemplified in terms of certain crucial criteria: number/type of sites, value propositions, pricing models, industry rivals, and strategic groups of companies.[142] The classification was created on the basis of the pioneering work of several competing ad networks, in particular DoubleClick. Modified and updated from the original, Exhibit 5-10 presents their primary characteristics by the late 1990s.

1. *Ad-Reach Networks.* These networks came closest to the traditional mass media model. The players offered advertisers a selection from hundreds or even tens of thousands of vetted sites across a huge diversity of interest. The value proposition sought to provide the best of two worlds, mass marketing and one-to-one marketing; they used identification and personalization technologies to deliver targeted ads with a particular frequency, but they also offered mass reach deep into the Web.

When the ad-reach networks were used as traditional mass media, the

Exhibit 5-10
Five Types of Ad Networks

	Number/Type of Sites	Value Proposition	Pricing Models	Industry Rivals	Strategic Groups
1. Ad-Reach Networks	10s to 10,000s of highly varied content sites	Mass reach and individual targeting	CPM plus response rates	DoubleClick, BURST!, WebConnect, Commonwealth, Internet Link Exchange	Internet media brokers and Web direct marketers; small players
2. Local Networks	50 to 200 cities	Promotions tied to local retail classifieds	Response rates and percentage of sales	Digital Cities, Hometown Network, Sidewalk	Leading OSPs (America Online, MSN); major web sites (Microsoft); search engines (Yahoo!); newspaper sites
3. Personal Broadcast Networks	15 to 20 channels	Intrusion on the desktop	Mostly CPM-based	PointCast, IFUSION.com, Marimba	Small new media firms, software houses; strategic alliances with major Internet media players, OSPs, aggregators, and so on
4. Content Networks	10 to 15 sites per network; 2 to 3 networks per major content provider	Ads relate to content; support relationships between advertisers and consumers	Higher CPM based on context; response rates and percentage of sales for related direct marketing	CNET, ZDnet, Starwave, iVillage, Greenhouse, Pathfinder, CMP Techweb, Attitude Network	Online news providers; local aggregators; major OSPs; leading media and entertainment companies
5. Navigation Hubs	2 to 3 hubs	Mass traffic, short visits, key words	CPM only: response-based ads compromise their positions as independent guides	Yahoo!, Excite, Netscape, AltaVista, Magellan, WebCrawler, Infoseek, Lycos	Leading search engines; major aggregators; browser giants

Sources: Adapted, modified, and updated on the basis of DoubleClick Research; Mary A. Modahl and Ruth MacQuiddy, "Internet Advertising," *Media & Technology Strategies* 1(1), Forrester Research, September 1, 1996; and Mary Meeker, *Internet Advertising* (New York: HarperCollins 1997), pp. 6–11.

pricing models were CPM-based. But when the focus was on content sites with more targeted audiences, the models exploited direct-driven pricing models (click rates, response rates). Early contenders in this space included DoubleClick, BURST!, WebConnect, Commonwealth, and Internet Link Exchange. The strategic groups consisted of Internet media brokers, Web direct marketers, and smaller players.

2. *Local Networks.* If ad-reach networks were reminiscent of traditional broadcast media, geography-based networks tend to appeal to both national and local advertisers along traditional models seen in cable TV and print. Local affiliates sold store listings and classifieds, while national organizations brought in big brands that looked for reach; the ad model of the former was reminiscent of local city magazines, whereas that of the latter was more typical of national magazines. These rivals could offer advertisers 50 to 200 cities. Indeed, it was this characteristic that made them highly appealing to the new aggregators (search engines, online service providers), as well as software companies with powerful browser/home page presence (Microsoft, Netscape). The value proposition sought to tie promotions to local retail classifieds, which made the category critical in the nascent electronic commerce. To some observers, local networks represented a significant substitute threat to the old monopoly of classified advertising by local newspapers.

Depending on the nature of the ad objectives (media advertising/ brands, or direct response/promotions), the pricing models were based on click rates or response rates (conversion rates)/percentage of sales. Industry rivals in this space included Digital Cities, Hometown Network, and Microsoft's Sidewalk (formerly CityScape). Due to the perceived importance of the category, strategic groups involved all major portals: leading online service providers (America Online, MSN), major websites (Microsoft), and search engines (Yahoo!). Toward the late 1990s, leading newspaper players launched their home pages and websites, and experimented with local-network style solutions seeking to mark and defend their territory in classified advertising.

3. *Personal Broadcast Networks (PBNs).* The PBNs offered advertisers intrusion on the desktop. The business model resembled that of broadcast TV. Industry observers expected the PBN's to multiply to 15 to 20 channels each. These channels were expected to be increasingly programmed by major media companies that would sell ads and share revenues. Branded channels would cover the interests of the target audience, and the PBNs would take care of the rest; the pipelines were conceived of as a kind of "cable a la Internet." Consequently, the pricing models were mostly CPM-based. Industry rivals included companies like PointCast, IFUSIONcom, and Marimba. Strategic groups involved small new media firms and software houses, as well as strategic alliances with major Internet media players, online providers, aggregators, and so on.

After the mid-1990s, some industry observers expected PBNs to reaggregate the highly distributed Internet. But as we have seen, the notion of push as a single most powerful Internet advertising network originated from inflated hopes rather than realistic expectations. Certainly PBNs would remain a critical ad network—but just one among quite a few.

4. *Content Networks.* Unlike ad-reach networks that sought both mass and one-to-one marketing relationships, top content providers relied on focus strategies. Top content providers seemed to evolve in two distinct and separate directions. After the perceived failure of the Pathfinder site and its notion of the corporate home page as a brand umbrella (see Chapter 2), these content providers sought unified content themes and/or narrower target audiences. Also, some mutated into content networks with ten to fifteen thematically related site properties: ads related to content. As a result, the pricing model reflected high CPMs based on context, somewhat like with special magazines (more focused audiences translated to higher CPMs). On the other hand, certain major content providers sought to provide two to three networks that were oriented toward linking content themes (e.g., sports, entertainment, and so on) with advertising and commerce. The focus was not on content, but on supporting relationships between advertisers and consumers. In this category, the value proposition reflected the objectives of leading content providers to position themselves in electronic commerce. The narrower content network version emulated the direct model providing only two to three networks (sports, entertainment, etc.) per major content provider. Consequently, the pricing models reflected response rates and percentage of sales for related direct marketing.

Industry rivals included companies like CNET, ZD Net, Starwave, iVillage, Greenhouse (America Online), Pathfinder (Time Warner), CMP, TechWeb, and Attitude Network. Strategic groups consisted of online news providers, local aggregators, major OPSs, as well as leading media and entertainment companies. The heavy emphasis on computer-related rivals was not dictated by the network, but by the relatively low reach of the then-Internet—hence the focus strategies concentrating on "early adopters" and "early majority." In the long term, major OSPs and local aggregators, as well as America's leading media and entertainment companies were natural candidates for content networks.

5. *Navigation Hubs.* In 1996, Forrester expected search sites like Yahoo! and Excite to consolidate into two or three navigation hubs whose value would be in mass traffic. In retrospect, there was probably room for more hubs, perhaps enough for half a dozen or dozen mass players. By the spring and summer of 1998, the "portal mania"—the M&As of major Internet aggregators (search engines, ISPs, OSPs, etc.)—underlined the critical function of this category as the driver of mass traffic. The few and rare, big and huge navigation hubs were rapidly evolving into "des-

tination" sites that sought not only to attract traffic but also to retain the users within the hub itself.

The value proposition focused on mass traffic, short visits, and key word advertising. If the visits were brief, it would be futile to provoke appropriate conversion rates. Still, the negotiations between Procter & Gamble and Yahoo! on the use of click-through as the prevailing ad model for navigation hubs indicated that, along with CPMs, click rates could and would be applied with the major industry players. These networks consisted of dominant search engines, including Yahoo!, Excite, Altavista, Netscape, Magellan, WebCrawler, Infoseek, and Lycos.

NOTES

1. Michael Schrage, Don Peppers and Martha Rogers, David Dix, "Is Advertising Finally Dead?" *Wired*, February 1994.

2. Dan Steinbock, Interview with Lester Wunderman, chairman of Wunderman Cato Johnson, senior adviser to the board of directors of Young & Rubicam, and director of Dentsu Wunderman Direct in Japan, August 18, 1998.

3. Ibid.

4. Ibid.

5. Dan Steinbock, Interview with Fergus O'Daly, August 3, 1998.

6. Ibid.

7. Ibid.

8. Ibid.

9. Ibid.

10. Dan Steinbock, Interview with David Aaker, E. T. Grether Professor of Marketing Strategy, University of California at Berkeley, June 4, 1998. See also David A. Aaker, *Strategic Market Management*, 5th ed. (New York: John Wiley & Sons 1998).

11. Steinbock, Interview with David Aaker.

12. David A. Aaker, *Managing Brand Equity* (New York: The Free Press 1991).

13. Exploring the phenomenon of brand equity, Aaker provided a well-defined structure of the relationship between a brand and its symbol and slogan, as well as each of the five underlying assets, which clarified exactly how brand equity did contribute value. Importantly enough, Aaker opened each chapter with a *historical* analysis of either the success or failure of a particular company's attempt at building brand equity, including the Ivory soap story, the transformation of Datsun to Nissan, the decline of Schlitz beer, the making of the Ford Taurus, and others. Finally, citing examples from these and many other companies, Aaker showed how to avoid the temptation to place short-term performance before the health of the brand and, instead, to manage brands strategically by creating, developing, and exploiting each of the five assets in turn.

14. David A. Aaker, *Building Strong Brands* (New York: The Free Press 1996).

15. Steinbock, Interview with David Aaker. "In my third book on implementing brand strategy, I have done a lot of thinking on the Internet and building brands in the cyberspace," noted Aaker.

16. Steinbock, Interview with David Aaker.

17. Ibid.

18. Dan Steinbock, Interview with Regis McKenna, Chairman, The McKenna Group, September 18, 1998.

19. As a corollary, service brand equity criteria consist of references, reputation, experience, information, infrastructure, and evidence.

20. Regis McKenna, *Real Time: Preparing for the Age of the Never Satisfied Customer* (Boston: Harvard Business School Press 1997). Some of the basic themes of the book were first published in Regis McKenna, "Real-Time Marketing," *Harvard Business Review*, July–August 1995. See also "Board of a Different Breed," *Directors & Boards*, Fall 1995; "Stalking the Information Society," *Upside*, January 1995; "Know Thy Customer," *OEM*, October 1994.

21. On the Pampers Parenting Institute, see http://www.pampers.com/.

22. On these arguments, see Mary Meeker, *Internet Advertising Report* (New York: HarperCollins 1997), pp. 1–8 and 1–9.

23. In the marketers' popular parlance, one speaks of media advertising and sales promotions, just as one does about database marketing, relationship marketing, and direct marketing (direct mail and direct response are seen as applications of a broader notion). In the former case, the emphasis is on those aspects of the value chain that only focus on the immediate interface between the buyer and the product or service; usually it is conceived as an element of the marketing mix. In the latter case, however, that interface is considered a part of the marketing mix which is dictated by the marketing strategy; which is determined by the competitive strategy; which is subject to the overall (corporate) strategy. In the new marketing concept, relationship and direct marketing in particular are seen *as* an overall strategy, not technical instruments.

24. See *Banners and Beyond: Strategies for Branding, Driving Traffic and Sales*, Jupiter Communications, LLC, June 1997.

25. While the Jupiter model delineated most relevant tendencies in Internet marketing, it could be revised in four ways (theoretically, historically). (1) It was not based on the chronological evolution of the Internet. (2) It grouped into "alternative" platforms techniques (e.g., e-mail, chat groups), which were available for marketers even prior to the evolution of the Web. (3) It perhaps did not pay an adequate amount of attention to a consistent view of the virtual communities in the history of the Internet. (4) It may not have focused enough on the function of the ad networks in media buying and selling.

26. *1998 Online Advertising Report: Revenue Models, Market Strategies, Projections*, Jupiter Communications, August 1997.

27. Under the co-op program Intel ran with some 1,500 hardware makers that licensed its chips, Intel put aside 6% of the money and allowed the hardware makers to use the funds as part of their advertising budgets—so long as the ads produced with those funds incorporated the "Intel Inside" logo or theme. For example, Intel would reimburse Compaq for 50% of the cost of a television ad ending with the "Intel Inside" theme or 66% of a logo-bearing print ad. Lisa Bransten, "Intel's Program May Boost Internet Advertising by 40%," *The Wall Street Journal*, August 5, 1997.

28. Under the terms of the co-op agreement, $830 million would be available for "Intel Inside" advertising, and Intel would allow as much as $83 million to

be spent to fund half the cost of Web ads. But whether the money really got spent on Web ads was up to Intel's partners in the "Intel Inside" advertising cooperative. There was no guarantee the partners would want to switch.

29. On the early forms of Internet advertising the following is indebted to Mary Meeker, *Internet Advertising Report* chapter 6.

30. While the AT&T sound banner ads loaded almost instantly, the 20K applet took some 20 seconds to download via a 28.8-kbps connection and the ads themselves were somewhat intrusive.

31. See Janet Kornblum, "New Net Ads Make a Noise," CNET, September 3, 1997.

32. As a news organization, Time New Media was interested in NOW because it could turn banner ads into conduits for breaking story headlines. Darwin Digital also saw uses for the banner for non-news organizations, including the announcement of time-limited product promotions or the reporting of financial data or sports scores.

33. See Paul Festa, "Firm Promises Real-Time Banners," CNET, March 9, 1998.

34. Kim M. Bayne, "Narrative Impulse Service Targets Last-Minute Buys—Users Can Make Purchases in Banner Ads," *Advertising Age*, April 27, 1998.

35. See DoubleClick and I/PRO press releases, 1996.

36. See www.eyescream.com/yahootop200.html.

37. Yahoo!'s standard rate for context-based keyword advertisements ranged from $0.03 to $0.08 per impression, although discounts were provided from standard rates for high-volume, longer-term contracts. For comparison, the company's standard rates for banner advertisements ranged from $0.02 to $0.07 per impression, depending upon location of the advertisement within Yahoo!'s properties and the extent to which it was targeted for a particular audience.

38. Tim Clark, "Interstitials. '97 Web Ad Total Near $1 Billion," CNET, April 6, 1997.

39. Janet Kornblum, "Billboards on the Infobahn," CNET, November 8, 1996.

40. Ibid.

41. By June 1997, Hotwired, the online publication of *Wired* magazine, also started using interstitial ads. Rick Boyce, vice president and director of ad sales at Hotwired, said he hoped that the new ad form would stimulate more creativity on the part of advertising agencies, which had not embraced the Web enthusiastically. See Matt Richtel, "TV-Type Ads Emerge on the Web," *New York Times*, April 19, 1997.

42. *Banners and Beyond: Strategies for Branding, Driving Traffic and Sales*, Jupiter Communications, June 1997.

43. Ann Marie Kerwin, "NY Times' Web Site Lets Advertisers Get Personal: Profile Info from Users Allows Ads to Be Highly Targeted," *Advertising Age*, July 17, 1997.

44. For a similar classification, see US Web and Rick Bruner, *Net Results: Web Marketing That Works* (Indianapolis, IN: Hayden Books 1998), p. 300.

45. Like the finest high-quality travel and adventure magazines, Mungo Park's audience was passionate about travel, food and wine, luxury automobiles, and other disposable income products. Mungo Park was the first interactive adventure magazine to feature true exploration via the Internet. Headed by Richard

Bangs—award-winning author, multimedia producer, and founder of America's oldest adventure travel firm (Mountain Travel-Sobek)—Mungo Park featured live Internet-cast expeditions, original work by best-selling authors, and compelling editorial columns.

46. For more on portal sponsorships, see Meeker, *Internet Advertising*, chapter 6.

47. As with portals, CNET segmented hot corners into principal and section types. Another classic example of portal sponsorships was Happy Puppy (happypuppy.com), an online gaming and entertainment software site that used rapidly rotating rectangular banner ads on the screen (similar to CNET's portals). Ibid.

48. Dale Buss, "You Ought to Be in Pictures: Product Placement Isn't Only for the Big Guys," *Business Week*, June 22, 1998.

49. "Billboards on the Infobahn," CNET, November 8, 1996.

50. "AOL and 'Baywatch' Announce Marketing Agreement," America Online, Press Releases, Dulles, VA, August 26, 1998.

51. In 1996, the company generated 80% of its revenue from sponsorships/advertisements from pharmaceutical and healthcare organizations, such as Abbott Laboratories, Astra Merck, Pfizer, Bayer, Eli Lilly, Glaxo Wellcome, Hoechst Marion Roussel, Teva Marion, Aetna Health Plans, Cigna HealthCare, Oxford Health Plans, Humana, and Harvard Pilgrim Health Care.

52. On the interplay of pay-per-view and event promotions, see Dan Steinbock, *Triumph and Erosion in the American Media and Entertainment Industries* (Westport, CT: Quorum Books 1995), chapter 3.

53. On October 12, 1998, Yahoo! announced it would acquire Internet-based interactive direct marketer Yoyodyne Entertainment for about $29.6 million in an all-stock deal.

54. Jeff Pelline, "MTV, Yahoo Unfurl Music Site," CNET, July 16, 1997.

55. Jeff Pelline, "TV Guide and WebTV Click," CNET, January 13, 1997

56. Stephanie Miles, "ER" Premiere Hyped Online," CNET, September 26, 1997.

57. NBC; Nielsen Media Research, September 1997 (websites). In 1998, there were an estimated 98 million television households in the United States. A single ratings point represents 1%, or 980,000 households. Share is the percentage of television sets tuned to a specific program.

58. The experience suggested the agency, Fattal & Collins, could develop a larger business for delivering stories on the Web. It formed American Cybercast and began producing a science fiction drama called Eon-4.

59. "Firm Looks to Build Niche for Programs in Cyberspace," Associated Press, September 29, 1996.

60. Courtney Macavinta, "As the Web Turns," CNET, January 10, 1997.

61. Beth Lipton, "Dancing Baby in TV Encore," CNET, January 19, 1998.

62. The world's leading supplier of professional modeling and animation software with more than 200,000 animation customers and 62,000 3D Studio users, Kinetix was focused on the fastest-growing areas of the computer industry. According to the 1998 Roncarelli Report on Computer Animation, the global animation industry was expected to more than double in size by 2001.

63. By September of 1998, Dancing Baby was expected find a home on some

70 different items in stores throughout the world. The Dancing Baby music CD, for instance, sold close to 300,000 units in four weeks, while the CD single was No. 74 on the Billboard Top 100 chart after only two weeks of exposure. See Kinetics Press Releases.

64. Kevin Kelly and Gary Wolf, "PUSH! Kiss Your Browser Goodbye: The Radical Future of Media Beyond the Web," *Wired* magazine, March 1997.

65. *Banners and Beyond: Strategies for Branding, Driving Traffic and Sales,* Jupiter Communications, June 1997.

66. By 1998 Perlman held 11 patents and had 10 pending in conjunction with WebTV.

67. "WebTV Networks to Offer Internet Link Over TV Set," *Wall Street Journal,* September 5, 1996.

68. Steve Ditlea, "WebTV's Little Black Box: Net Ready for Prime Time," *New York Times,* November 29, 1996.

69. The company's backers included Microsoft and Vulcan Ventures, the venture capital firm of Microsoft's co-founder, Paul Allen. With the winter holidays of 1996, Sony Corp. and Philips Electronics NV, which made the devices, and WebTV Networks Inc., which developed the technology and sells monthly service, hoped the new hybrid would invade American TV homes.

70. "Dataquest Survey Shows U.S. Households Are Turned Off by Internet Television—New Program Examines the Convergence of the PC and Consumer Electronics Markets," Dataquest, December 16, 1996. See also Thomas E. Weber, "Slow Takeoff Suggests WebTV Isn't Ready for Prime Time," *Wall Street Journal,* January 2, 1997.

71. "WebTV-Type Devices Will Struggle for Three More Years," Forrester Research, April 17, 1997.

72. "IDC Finds Information Appliance Market Poised for Mass Market Acceptance," International Data Corporation, October 20, 1998.

73. While such estimates were not expected to be entirely accurate, most observers thought they had directional significance. In the mid-1990s, there were about 150 million PC users in the world, and over the next one to four years many PCs would be replaced by more powerful, communications-enabled PCs. See Mary Meeker and Chris DePuy, *Internet Report,* February 1996.

74. HarperCollins, the publisher, presented the book as "the bestseller that has fanned the flames of cyberspace controversy and remains the only guide to using the Internet to make money." See HarperCollins, Press Releases, and promotional materials on Amazon.com.

75. In many Internet dictionaries, the concept of *spam* derives from the words "spiced pork and ham." Actually, the nickname came from a Monty Python sketch in which people sitting at a table chant "Spam, Spam, Spam" endlessly until it drives everybody crazy.

76. Janet Kornblum, "Spam King Retreats," CNET, March 12, 1998.

77. Years before Mark Andreessen, the University of Illinois undergraduate, conceived Mosaic, Steve Dorner was working on Eudora on the computing staff of the University of Illinois at Urbana-Champaign, which gave the Eudora away. Unlike Andreessen who became a multimillionaire at age 24, Dorner was paid a salary until he left the university staff in 1992 to work on Eudora. See Jo Thomas,

"For Inventor of Eudora, Great Fame, No Fortune," *New York Times*, January 21, 1997.

78. Shaw & Co. had 400 employees in offices scattered around the globe and $800 million in capital, with annual returns averaging more than 20 percent. The firm wielded a $100 million technological toolbox of secret algorithms, and on a busy day it accounted for 5% of the total shares traded on the New York Stock Exchange. Compare Thomas A. Bass, "The Phynancier," *Wired*, January 1997.

79. The first goal was to deliver AOL e-mail and the AOL interface only to the AOL members. Even when the HTML version would become available, the company expected most users to opt for the non-HTML features.

80. Forrester Research, Inc., September 1997.

81. "Hotmail Provides Web-Based Free E-mail to the World on Independence Day," HotMail Corp., Sunnyvale, CA, July 1, 1996.

82. Another winner in the free e-mail craze was the venture capital firm of Draper Fisher Jurvetson—the financial backer of both Hotmail and Four11. See Andy Reinhardt in San Mateo, CA, with Heather Green in New York and bureau reports, "Microsoft and Hotmail: It's about Capturing Eyeballs," *Business Week*, January 19, 1998.

83. See Matt Richtel, "Microsoft Continues Buying Spree with Hotmail," *New York Times*, January 1, 1998.

84. Microsoft expected that Hotmail would generate more traffic at those popular sites and that, in turn, more advertising revenues would be generated as well. Concurrently, the Microsoft Network added pull-down menus to several of its sites that linked to all its Web properties in an effort to create "synergy."

85. Among its acquisitions, Microsoft spent $425 million to acquire WebTV Networks; it invested $150 million for a 7% stake in Apple and $1 billion for 11% in the cable concern Comcast. It also was buying portions of smaller and innovative startups. It acquired a 10% stake in Progressive Networks (Real Audio, Real Video); it spent $75 million to acquire Vxtreme (Web video). Overall, Microsoft invested heavily in Internet-related companies. The cash-rich company had more than $9 billion on hand to invest and a $160 billion market capitalization.

86. On the IRC and Jaakko Oikarinen, see the Web pages of FUNET (The Finnish University and Research Network): http://www.funet.fi/~irc/.

87. "The question is how to implement that message so it doesn't become annoying." After the mid-1990s, I/Pro and ichat began providing advertisers and member sites with I/Pro's verification of ad performance reporting, while the NetGravity AdServer sought to let sites manage ad inventory, dynamically target ads to audiences, measure results on demand, and automate sales efforts. See Kathleen Murphy, "Now Sites Can Tailor Ads to Chat, and Measure Results," *Web Week*, 2(18), November 18, 1996.

88. From April to July, cultural anthropologists observed the goings-on at 37 cyber-communities on various online services, which included Over 50 and Having Fun, Widowed World, Herpes Self-Help, Surflink, Romance Connection, and American Woodworker. The study also included news groups and other chat rooms devoted to television programs like "Friends" and "General Hospital." In addition, 24 to 30 chat fans were interviewed by psychologists, who focused on learning more about "the emotional needs" that motivated participation. See

Stuart Elliott, "Advertising: Using Internet As the Modern Marketplace," *New York Times*, November 25, 1996.

89. See Elliott, "Advertising: Using Internet as the Modern Marketplace."

90. For instance, computer-products retailer Egghead Inc. was holding chat sessions Monday through Friday in its online store, offering customers instant advice about software and helping them with their purchases. Similarly, ad agency Saatchi & Saatchi International used it to gather staff from around the world for brainstorming sessions. And Symantec Corp. was testing chat as a customer-service tool. See Lisa Bransten, "New Uses for Chat Software Could Improve Its Reputation," *Wall Street Journal*, December 15, 1997.

91. See Michel Marriott, "The Blossoming of Internet Chat—Moving from Gossip, Flirting and Worse to Education, Consumer Service and Even More Gossip," *New York Times*, July 2, 1998.

92. For the Mirabilis founders' original business concepts, see "About the Company," August 11, 1998. See www.mirabilis.com.

93. "A Letter to Our Users from the ICQ Team," Mirabilis Ltd., June 8, 1998.

94. If, after the acquisition, one were to go to Mirabilis's Web page, "About The Company," one could see a brief addition in the parentheses: "ICQ Inc., the successor of Mirabilis Ltd." The product name took over the company name. AOL needed an independent brand, but it was a company that skillfully exploited synergies; it did not need independent and autonomous companies—but a subsidiary with potent technology, expanding customer base, and attractive product platform.

95. "We do think this acquisition is a great launch pad for our broader Web portal strategy," said AOL spokeswoman Tricia Primrose. Yet, AOL remained quiet about how it would use the service as a portal offering. See Jim Hu, "What Will AOL Do with ICQ?" CNET, June 8, 1998.

96. "The Portal-Site Game," Wall Street Journal Interactive Edition, June [no date] 1998.

97. For a lucid introduction to issues and business models of online communities, see John Hagel III and Arthur G. Armstrong, *Net Gain: Expanding Markets through Virtual Communities* (Boston: Harvard Business School Press 1997).

98. For an interesting account on the first directories, agents, robots, and "spiders," see Andrew Leonard, *Bots: The Origins of New Species* (San Francisco: HotWired 1997).

99. For a brief account on the portal evolution, see "The Portal-Site Game," Issue Briefing.

100. Disney's objective was to build a site for such disparate Web operations as ABCNEWS.com, Disney Blast, ESPN.com, and the official league sites of the NFL, NBA and NASCAR.

101. Unlike such competitors as Infoseek and Excite, Yahoo! uses people rather than automated software to compile its directory, and the company's free navigational guide is available on several online browsers and networks, including Netscape Navigator and the Microsoft Network.

102. See Laurie J. Flynn, "A Search Engine That Charges for Top Billing," *New York Times*, March 16, 1998.

103. Account exec at BBDO, 1986–89; brand manager at Clorox Co., 1990–91;

director of marketing for video/business operations at Fox Broadcasting Co. in France, Italy, and Spain, 1992–96; current post, January 1996–. See Kim Cleland, "Karen Edwards: Yahoo!" *Advertising Age*, July 14, 1997. When first joining Yahoo!, part of Edwards' responsibilities included reading hundreds of user e-mails daily. The customer interaction proved invaluable to her success. With a background steeped in consumer branding, she saw a real opportunity to create a "really cool consumer franchise" in Yahoo! "Key to that end is not taking ourselves too seriously," said Edwards. "We're about keeping a very human face to the brand, which is why people smile when they hear the Yahoo! name."

104. Randall E. Stross, "How Yahoo! Won the Search Wars," *Fortune*, March 2, 1998.

105. Laurie Flynn, "Are Internet Search Engine Companies Still Hit or Miss?" *New York Times*, February 11, 1997.

106. According to a 1997 survey by Mediamark Research, in a typical month more than 25 million people used Yahoo! Some months, 40 million people visited. More people went to Yahoo! than to Netscape or AOL. More people searched at Yahoo! than watched MTV, Nickelodeon, or Showtime in any given week. Indeed, more people checked out Yahoo! than read the typical issue of *Time, Newsweek*, or *Life*. On the survey, see Mediamark Research and Stross, "How Yahoo! Won the Search Wars."

107. J. C. R. Licklider and Robert Taylor, and E. Herbert, "The Computer as a Communication Device," *International Science and Technology*, April 1968.

108. Howard Rheingold, *The Virtual Community: Homesteading on the Electronic Frontier* (New York: HarperCollins 1993).

109. Form 10-K for America Online Inc., filed on September 29, 1997, Securities and Exchange Commission, Washington, DC.

110. In the process of acquiring CompuServe's content operations, AOL sold to WorldCom its transmission network and operations business which had resulted in the notorious nickname, "America Offline," when the company had added more subscribers than it could handle.

111. See Marc Gunther, "The Internet Is Mr. Case's Neighborhood," *Fortune*, March 30, 1998.

112. Stung by the critics, AOL abandoned the practice and took a whopping $385 million write-off in October 1996. That wiped out its profits.

113. On Blockbuster, its meteoric growth strategy and controversial "creative accounting," see Steinbock, *Triumph and Erosion in the American Media and Entertainment Industries*, pp. 115–116.

114. Rebecca Quick, "AOL Will Open Chat Rooms to On-Line Advertisements," *Wall Street Journal*, March 5, 1997.

115. In the early 1980s, MTV Networks had charged highly targeted teen demographics. After the mid-1990s, AOL could pitch chat rooms as an "unparalleled opportunity for efficient and effective advertising to a significant percentage" of AOL users, who were upscale and well-educated—a more tightly defined demographic than television can offer advertisers. See AOL press release, February 1997.

116. Patricia Riedman, "AOL Taps Offline Databases in Ad Targeting Quest— Criticized by Privacy Groups, the Program Is Inspiring Similar Web Models," *Advertising Age*, October 20, 1997.

117. Ibid.

118. Websites could charge premiums up to 40% over base rates for targeted ads, Jupiter Communications analyst Marc Johnson said. "CPMs could just go through the roof," he added, "but where's the point of diminishing returns for marketers?" For instance, if a marketer picked all 300 criteria "selects" on which to target individuals, it would result in staggering cost-per-thousand rates. If publishers fully disclosed how they would using consumers' information, Johnson saw no reason why this would not become a staple of Web advertising. "This is a huge step forward in targeting," he said. Even better would be a mix of offline data and behavioral data, collected from users as they visit sites. "That's the ultimate home run." Ibid.

119. AOL also provided a variety of support mechanisms such as online support and telephone customer support services. The company believed that the adoption of flat-rate pricing would lead to increased subscriber acquisition and retention rates as compared to rates achieved prior to flat-rate pricing.

120. On the acquisition costs of new subscribers, see Gunther, "The Internet Is Mr. Case's Neighborhood."

121. Ultimately Borislow paid $100 million for exclusive access to AOL and its subscribers for three years. AOL also got warrants in Tel-Save and a share in the future profits from the long-distance business.

122. IBM had sought to profit by earning a percentage of World Avenue sales. Retailers said the mall flopped because IBM failed to promote it.

123. Thomas E. Weber, "AOL Plans to Collect 'Rent,' Not Commission, from Stores," *Wall Street Journal*, July 28, 1997.

124. Rebecca Buckman, "AOL Plans to Increase Rates Charged to On-Line Brokers," *Wall Street Journal*, June 12, 1998.

125. See Mary A. Modahl and Ruth MacQuiddy, "Internet Advertising," *Media & Technology Strategies*, 1(1), Forrester Research, September 1, 1996.

126. Also, networks could remain open to new site concepts, which could easily be added to existing systems for ad sales and service, whereas single content sites would not, without significant investments. As the industry migrated toward results-based pricing, content providers were expected to experience a win-some, lose-some pattern on advertising deals, whereas networks would be far more able to withstand the vagaries of the new pricing model. See Mary A. Modahl and Ruth MacQuiddy, "Internet Advertising." See also DoubleClick's research reports, from 1995 to the present.

127. No one wanted their ad running on a dead site or on one with inappropriate content. Networks would have to solve this problem by vetting sites. Ibid.

128. In addition to DoubleClick's Web pages and press information, this segment is based on Form S-1 for DoubleClick Inc. filed on December 16, 1997. (The S-1 filing is a pre-effective registration statement submitted when a company decides to go public, commonly referred to as an "IPO," i.e., initial public offering, filing.)

129. Spun out of Poppe Tyson, DoubleClick was a closely held, independent company with 45 employees. To get started, the company raised $2 million from Poppe Tyson's parent, BJK&E (which would soon be acquired by True North), and within its first two months of operations it had signed up 20 advertising clients and 20 sites. DoubleClick's major shareholders include chairman and CEO

Kevin O'Connor (15%); Bain Capital (14%); ABS Capital Partners II L.P. (8%); chief technical officer Dwight Merriman (8%); and ad firm True North Communications (5%).

130. Dan Steinbock, Interview with Kevin O'Connor, April 1998.

131. "Are you ready for classes in interactive advertising from A for Apple to Z for Ziff-Davis?" reported the *New York Times*. The lessons for marketers and agencies were in the form of a campaign for Double Click. The effort to promote the perceived potential of cyberpitches was being created by Digital Pulp, a small agency in New York, and carried the theme "Building one-to-one relationships millions at a time." Stuart Eliot, "An Interactive Advertising Network Offers Tutorials," *New York Times*, January 20, 1997.

132. The first ad in the Double Click series makes that same comparison to how Fuller brushes and vacuum cleaners were peddled: "An introduction is made, interaction begins, questions are asked and answered, products are sold." The ad goes on to present tips on how to get the proverbial foot in the door, suggesting for instance that the creative content of interactive advertising "be tested before you spend big money on placements." See Eliot, "An Interactive Advertising Network Offers Tutorials."

133. For the year ended December 31, 1997, according to a filing with the Securities and Exchange Commission.

134. Steinbock, Interview with Kevin O'Connor.

135. None of DoubleClick's direct competitors offered a comparable service, but the ad service started a rivalry with companies that sold ad serving software, like NetGravity and ClickOver, which were already mounting an offensive. Moreover, agencies and sites were concerned that the tools they used not have bias in them.

136. Unlike Yahoo!, Excite, and other Internet content sites, however, the company doesn't own the sites that were included in its ranking. Instead it takes a small cut of the revenue from serving up ads on those sites and so has much lower margins than those sites.

137. Steinbock, Interview with Kevin O'Connor.

138. Scott Kirsner, "DoubleClick: The Big Fish in a Murky Pond," CNET, December 17, 1997.

139. The following discussion is based on and extends the lessons of Mary A. Modahl and Ruth MacQuiddy, "Internet Advertising."

140. "Forrester's New Media & Technology Service Predicts Dominance of Networks for Web Advertising," Forrester Research, November 7, 1996.

141. Ibid.

142. Forrester's classification was created on the basis of the pioneering work of several ad network rivals, in particular DoubleClick. In the following, some categories have been slightly modified and updated with more recent trends and information.

6

World Wide Web—Global Marketing and Global Marketers

After World War II, American multinational companies (MNCs) found great opportunities in Europe, Asia, and Latin America. While marketing was technically far less advanced than in the late 1990s, products were adapted to local markets since production was often localized. Gradually, *multinational marketing* came to mean marketing to different countries with local adaptation of products and promotions. That certainly contributed to the rise of new approaches in marketing disciplines. In the end of the 1950s, market segmentation gave marketers a tool to divide given markets into more homogeneous subgroups. The early 1960s witnessed the conceptualization of the marketing mix with its "4Ps" of marketing (product, price, promotion, and place). Starting in the late 1960s, product positioning enabled marketers to place a product or brand in a specific location in the consumer's perceptual map of a product category. Concurrently, marketing research techniques grew increasingly sophisticated.[1]

The early 1970s saw the beginning of the global phase which involved far more standardization of products and integration of activities across countries than had been the case in the multinational phase. Due to the energy crisis, inflation, and currency devaluation, international ventures became less attractive to U.S. companies in the mid-1970s, while foreign multinational corporations began to operate in the American market. As Americans began driving Hondas, loading Konica cameras from Japan with Fujitsu film, watching Sony televisions, and drinking beer from Germany, U.S. industry lost one foothold after another in the technology and consumer electronics sector. As U.S. big business retreated, American advertising was bound to follow.

TOWARD GLOBAL MARKETS

Drivers Toward Globalization

At the close of the 20th century, many marketers recognized four classes of determinants that propel companies toward globalization: market, competition, cost, and government policies.[2] What is not yet acknowledged is the force of the Internet, which seems to serve as a globalizing force through all of these basic determinants. It affects all four classes.

Competitive Drivers. In general, competitive drivers refer to the emergence of global competitors, which has forced a number of firms to develop the necessary facilities and infrastructure for domestic companies to go global. Companies no longer just sell abroad, but also transfer skills and technology across countries, making it easier for domestic companies to expand globally. Many pure Internet plays exemplify this category, from software houses like Netscape to Web retailers such as Amazon. Even for those firms that are active in most foreign markets already, the competitive synergy achieved from synhronizing marketing across countries can be significant. This, indeed, is one of the great assets of the Internet, as demonstrated by Netscape's Navigator, which became a world class product without an advertising budget, or the ICQ of Mirabilis, a tiny Israeli software startup that captured an installed customer base of millions in just a few months. As Internet skills gradually proliferate in other industries and companies, similar coups are inevitable. Like globalization, the Web serves to push further the boundaries of operational effectiveness in competitive markets.

Cost Drivers. In his classic essay, Levitt paid special attention to cost drivers in globalization, associating them with the rise of new technology ("the vector of technology and the vector of globalization"). With the convergence of preferences, globalization shapes markets into magnitudes that allow great economies of scale and therefore reduction of costs and prices. The Internet was likely to accelerate these processes—from the attainment of scale and scope economies to global sourcing advantages.

Government Drivers. The government globalization drivers include favorable trade policies, acceptance of foreign investment, compatible technical standards, and common marketing regulations. In the past, governmental barriers to foreign market entry kept local markets protected, which made global marketing an impossibility. With the demise of old-style protectionism, governments have exploited nontariff barriers to attain similar objectives. Due to the complexity and high initial capital outlays of the Internet infrastructure, government drivers have played a critical role in Silicon Valley and internationally. Between 1996 and 1998, for instance, the struggle for compatible industry standards in electronic commerce provided an excellent example of national efforts to gain advantage through standards policies.[3]

Market Drivers. The strongest driver of global marketing consists of market factors: common customer needs, global business customers, global channels, transferable marketing, and leading markets. As U.S.-based Internet surveys were compared with those in the overseas markets, the early-adopter categories proved quite similar: predominantly male, white, mobile, upper middle class, highly educated, and so on. In the long run, the Web was bound to intensify *common customer needs*. Moreover, as *global business customers* preferred to do business with suppliers or vendors providing global service, these companies tended to have needs across several countries. Unsurprisingly, perhaps, global hotel chains like Hilton and transportation companies like Federal Express emerged among the early entrants in the Internet business-to-business markets. Similarly supplier firms in the automobile industry (General Motors, Ford, and so on) that went abroad decades ago were among the first in developing intranet and extranet systems.

Just as *global channels* have had a reinforcing effect on the emergence of global marketing strategies, they have also tended to accelerate business activities on the Web to the extent that the Web is likely to have a positive effect on global marketing strategies. When the Internet was enhanced with graphic user interfaces in the early 1990s, the creators did not call their accomplishment a *World Wide* Web without a reason. Naturally, the first companies to experience the full impact of the Web potential in the globalization of operations have been those firms that have a crucial role in the nations' infrastructure—telecommunications (the substitute threat of Internet telephony) and logistics (the Web's impact on transportation and retail). In *transferable marketing*, similar marketing ideas have been used in different countries, irrespective of the component of the marketing mix (brand, price, promotion, delivery).

The Internet is a powerful enabling force that enables the use of similar and identical ideas in different corners of the world. It also moves transferable marketing into real time and forces marketers into an interactive mode. Indeed, one might make the case that, since the early 1990s, the Clinton administration's technology policy, the emergence of the Internet, and the rapid globalization of macroeconomic environments have served to "tighten" the dynamics of America's competitive advantage in global competition. Individually and as a system, these determinants have accounted for the *pressures* on firms to invest and innovate. As a system, this "diamond" has become expansive, thick, and self-reinforcing.[4]

In effect, each determinant of the "diamond" framework supports and reinforces the other. America's *factor conditions*, (i.e., skilled labor and infrastructure) dominate both Internet traffic and transactions worldwide. The U.S. *demand conditions* (i.e., the nature of domestic demand for the Internet products and services) are most extensive and sophisticated worldwide. Due to the expanding marketplace, the nation also leads in *related and supporting industries* that dominate infrastructure, hardware, and software, as well as content/agglomeration worldwide. Patterned according to the Silicon Valley model, America's domestic rivalry—*firm strategy, structure, and rivalry*—in the technology sector was more intense than anywhere else in the world.[5] By the late 1990s, even a superficial glance at the top 20 major Internet and Internet-related industries demonstrated quickly the overwhelming dominance of the U.S.-based rivals and the relative absence of Asian and European players.

In addition to these systemic variables, two additional determinants have operated significantly in the Internet-related areas. By definition, *chance events* are developments outside the control of firms and usually the nation's government. The end of the Cold War has been a critical variable in the deregulation of markets, globalization of business, and resurgence of new technology, which all have provided a crucial boost to the Internet, separately and as a system. In addition to general macroeconomic policies, the *government*, in particular the Clinton administration's reconversion and technology policy, coupled with the national information infrastructure and electronic commerce initiatives, were well-timed to embrace the change rather than fight it.

In *leading markets* customers tend to be particularly sophisticated and demanding. These markets and the need for the firms to be in such markets serve as powerful drivers of global strategies in order to exploit the first-mover benefits in leading markets. Typically, firms with the capabilities of implementing a global marketing strategy can draw on lessons from competitors and customers in leading markets to design their strategy. In this regard, the U.S. online marketplace—or more widely, the U.S. technology sector and the highly effective and liquid financial exchanges (stock markets, venture capital) as its great enablers—has a unique and historical position. Toward the end of the 1990s, this characteristic was particularly poignant in the emergence of the U.S. Internet economy as a global first mover.

U.S. Internet Economy as a Global First-Mover. By the end of the 1990s, a worldwide population explosion on the Web was under way, with the number of Web users growing from 50.2 million in 1997 to a projected 174.5 million in 2001. In 1997, the United States dominated (58%), but its percentage of the Web population was dropping (an estimated 54% in 2001). IDC forecasted Asia/Pacific would "leapfrog" Western Europe in Web population by 2001, replacing Europe as number two behind the United States. The greatest, albeit not the only, payoff for corporations that invest in the Internet was expected to come from conducting business on the Internet. In 1997, IDC estimated that there would be more than $10 billion in Internet transactions, less than 0.05% of the global economy. By 2001, Internet commerce volume was expected to surge to over $220 billion, or just under 1% of the global economy. While the United States was expected to dominate Internet commerce through 2001, its market power would likely slip from about 80% of volume in 1997 to less than 70% in 2001.[6]

In the long run, electronic commerce should succeed in moving economic activity closer to some of the ideals of perfect competition: low transaction costs, low barriers to entry, and improved access to information for the consumer. In the short run, however, electronic commerce has been a relatively minor part of most economies—about the size of mail order catalog sales in the United States. Moreover, it has penetrated sectors unevenly. In the business-to-business markets, transactions of just a few firms have exceeded all estimates of the business-to-consumer market, where sales were dominated by services and intangibles: travel and ticketing services, software, entertainment and financial services. For intangible products such as audio, video, information services, real estate services, and some business services, the economic impact of electronic commerce was expected to be significant and relatively swift. Further out, any easily digitized economic activity—including health, finance, education, and many government services—would be affected.

Intense interest in the economic impact of electronic commerce was linked to the fundamental fact that it shrank the economic distance between producers and consumers. *In theory*, consumers could go directly to producers without the need for traditional retailers, wholesalers and, in the case of intangibles, distributors. *In practice*, the available evidence indicated that, by the close of the 1990s, electronic commerce was thriving mostly in the United States, although the relative growth figures continued to climb in Asia and Europe.

The Globalization of Markets

By the 1980s, mass advertisers were faced with the challenge of developing and coordinating extensive ad campaigns, not just on a national scale but in a number of foreign markets. As global marketers pushed international advertising expenditures on unprecedented levels, advertising in overseas markets grew very rapidly. "Globalization of marketing became so important that a number of foreign firms made significant investments in U.S. companies," notes one observer. "Foreign-based multinational corporations even began manufacturing their products entirely in the United States, such as the Honda Accord in Marysville, Ohio. Other global corporations acquired shares in such major retailers as Fedmart, A&P, F.A.O. Schwarz, and Gimbels."[7]

The evolution of aggregate expenditures confirmed some popular perceptions. Between 1983 and 1988, U.S. ad expenditures climbed from $76 billion to more than $118 billion, while annual change actually slowed from 14% to 16% to less than 8%. Simultaneously, annual change in overseas markets leaped from less than 0% to 20% to 30%. In 1988, overseas ad expenditures *outpaced* the growth in the U.S. market. It was the first time, historically. In 1983, U.S. ad expenditures had accounted for almost 57% of total world ad expenditures, whereas by 1998—some fifteen years later—the U.S. portion was less than 48%. Concurrently, the portion of overseas ad expenditures of total world ad expenditures soared from 43% to 62%. After the recession of 1990 and 1991, the leadership of the Clinton administration resulted in the strong performance of the U.S. economy. That did slow the erosion of the U.S. ad expenditures as a portion of total world ad expenditures, but it did *not* reverse the directional significance (Exhibit 6-1). By the mid-1990s, only four of the top ten global advertisers were headquartered in the United States. By 1998, one-third of the top ten global ad organizations were headquartered outside the U.S. marketplace.

By the late 1980s, a national debate emerged on foreign ownership in different sectors of the U.S. economy. Another and more specific debate on the role of globalization in American marketing was all but inevitable. In effect, as the fate of Madison Avenue and Wall Street often anticipate the national issues of their crucial clients—American big business—one might expect that this debate preceded and anticipated the national one. That, indeed, was the case.

Global marketing is typically defined as marketing activities integrated across multiple country markets.[8] The first signs originated from the late 1960s, when Robert Buzzell published a prescient essay that anticipated (and, at least partly, framed) the future debate on globalization, "Can You Standardize Multinational Marketing?"[9] The title reflects his primary concerns, which were those of the multinational marketing era. The primary issue was to standardize *multinational* marketing, not yet to find proper standards for *global* marketing. Still, the new phase did not really get recognized until 1983, when Theodor Levitt published a significant essay on "The Globalization of Markets." It was controversial and provoking, and intended to be both:

A powerful force now drives the world toward a single converging commonality, and that force is technology. It has proletarianized communication, transport, and travel, making them easily and cheaply accessible to the world's most isolated places and impoverished multitudes. Suddenly no place and nobody is insulated from the alluring attractions of modernity. Almost everybody everywhere wants all the things they have heard about, seen, or experienced via the new technological facilitators that drive their wants and wishes. And it drives

Exhibit 6-1
Worldwide Advertising Expenditures: United States and Overseas Markets,
1983–1999 (estimated)

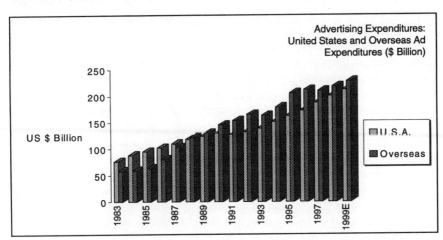

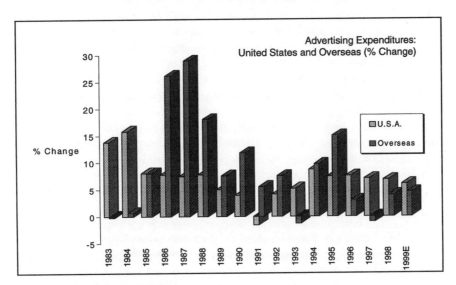

Source: McCann-Ericksson (1998).

these increasingly into global commonality, thus homogenizing markets every-where.

The result is a new commercial reality—the explosive emergence of global markets for globally standardized products, gigantic world-scale markets of pre-viously unimagined magnitudes.[10]

In developing a marketing strategy, the world's largest mass marketers had two basic options: a multinational or a global marketing strategy. In the former, each market was assumed to have a unique culture and competitive environment. Consequently, advertisers would opt for a more or less customized marketing program with optimal modifications for different localities. This had been the traditional multinational strategy. In the latter, each market was assumed to have more and more converging commonalities with other cultures and competitive environments. Consequently, the advertisers would adopt a more or less standardized marketing program with minimal modifications for different localities. This was the essence of the new global advertising ethos which was embraced by Saatchi & Saatchi, the legendary ad agency of the booming 1980s. It was implemented by companies like Benetton, with its line of Italian knitwear and cosmetics; Coca-Cola, which used near-identical TV ads with local languages dubbed in ("one sight, one sound, one sell"); and many others.

In the 1980s, Levitt was at the peak of his career. He was chairman of the department of Marketing at Harvard Business School, an author of marketing books that had pioneered the discipline, an editor of *Harvard Business Review*, and a longtime consultant to and director in a number of large U.S. and global corporations.[11] He was influential and his words carried weight. His academic contributions also prompted a controversial business relationship with Saatchi & Saatchi. His essay was bound to trigger an intense debate on the *extent* of the globalization of markets among U.S. marketers and managers. The emergence of the discourse reflected shifts in the U.S. and international aggregate ad expenditures, the ensuing agency consolidation, and the so-called "mega-merger activity." The debate, however, soon narrowed down to one on global brands. That issue, naturally, was close to the hearts of the worldwide ad agency networks, but it was only an element of the total picture—that is, the globalization of *markets* (Exhibit 6-2).

Technology and Globalization

With the launch of the Web and the browsers, the Internet entered an era of user-friendly interfaces. As much as Levitt's original essay caused commotion among marketers, advertisers, ad agencies, and market researchers, its logical extension—the idea of the *World Wide* Web as an ultimate technological facilitator, driver of global commonality and thus the homogenizer of markets everywhere—was hardly grasped by the late 1990s.

Levitt suggested that, due to the globalization of markets, all parts of the world want the most advanced things that the most advanced sectors already have; they also want them in the most advanced states of functionality, quality, reliability, service levels, and price competitiveness. *That*, he argued, means "the end of the multinational commercial world"

Exhibit 6-2
"The Globalization of Markets"—In Retrospect

In 1998—some fifteen years after the original publication of his famous essay, "The Globalization of Markets"—the booming years of the 1980s were well behind. Madison Avenue had been restructured after the stock crash of 1987, and then restructured again after the second crash in 1989. The ad agency networks had grown into worldwide chains of integrated marketing communications. The globalization of the business was a reality, yet it had proven far more complex to create and build worldwide corporate organizations than most observers had anticipated.* In the light of such context, "The Globalization of Markets" was bound to trigger debate and dispute. From Levitt's standpoint, however, the worst mistake had been to *narrow* the debate to the issue of "global brands."

> The first publication of "The Globalization of Markets" led to some big distortions. The major one was created in the professional advertising community, mostly the agency business. The original debate was about the *globalization of competition and markets*. The distortion converted the debate into one about the *globalization of brands*. The agencies talked about brands, the globalization of brands. They argued that there are some severe limits on the globalization of brands. In effect, that's what *I* was arguing, mostly based upon differences in local cultures and laws abiding practice. The essay made no argument about the globalization of brands. I did suggest that with the help of the economies of scale you could finance a more effective branding strategy that is global.**

> In "The Globalization of Markets," Levitt did emphasize that he did "not mean to advocate systematic disregard of local or national differences. . . . sensitivity to them does not require one to ignore the possibilities of doing things differently or better." The issue was not about execution only; it was about the fundamental strategy; not to do things right, but to do the right things.***

*In the 1980s, Professor Levitt himself had accepted an offer to sit on the board of Saatchi & Saatchi, certainly the most interesting and controversial agency of the boom decade—but by the mid-1990s Levitt would be ousting the brothers from their agency.
**Dan Steinbock, Interview with Theodor Levitt, Professor Emeritus, Department of Marketing, Harvard Business School, September 18, 1998.
***See Theodor Levitt, "The Globalization of Markets," *Harvard Business Review*, May–June 1983. See also his criticism on narrowing (and distorting) the debate to issues of global brands, in the preface to Theodor Levitt, *The Marketing Imagination* (New York: The Free Press 1986).

and "the globalization of markets." If, as Levitt argued, corporations geared to the globalization could generate enormous economies of scale in production, distribution, marketing, and management, one might expect the Web to cause similar gains in "speed economies." And as globalization would translate these economies into equivalently reduced

Exhibit 6-3
The Critique of the Globalization Thesis

After the mid-1980s, critics pointed to three assumptions and pitfalls of the globalization thesis:

1. **Pro:** Customer needs and interests are becoming increasingly homogeneous worldwide.

2. **Pro:** People around the world are willing to sacrifice preferences in product features (functions, design, and the like) for lower prices at high quality.

3. **Pro:** Substantial economies of scale in production and marketing can be achieved through supplying global markets.

1. **Con:** Lack of evidence of homogenization; growth of intracountry segmentation; price sensitivity.

2. **Con:** Lack of evidence of increases in universal preference for low price at acceptable quality; low price positioning was a highly vulnerable strategy; standardized low price could be overpriced in some countries and underpriced in others.

3. **Con:** Developments in flexible factory automation lessened the significance of economies of scale in production and marketing; production costs are often a minor component of total cost; the standardization philosophy is primarily product driven.

Source: On the globalization thesis, see Theodor Levitt, "The Globalization of Markets," *Harvard Business Review,* May–June 1983; on the critique of the thesis, see Susan P. Douglas and Yoram Wind, "The Myth of Globalization," *Columbia Journal of World Business,* Winter 1987; on Levitt's responses to the critics, see the preface to Theodor Levitt, *The Marketing Imagination* (New York: The Free Press 1986).

world prices, the Web could conceivably threaten to shatter many mature markets with intense price competition.

In the late 1980s, the intense debate on globalization downplayed the emphasis on *technology* that permeated and largely motivated Levitt's original essay (Exhibit 6-3). In effect, he cited the author of *The Americans,* Daniel J. Boorstin, who had characterized the contemporary age as driven by "The Republic of Technology," whose "supreme law . . . is convergence, the tendency for everything to become more like everything else."[12] *In business,* that had translated into global markets, with global corporations selling the same standardized products—autos, steel, chemicals, petroleum, cement, agricultural commodities and equipment, industrial and commercial construction, banking, insurance, computers, semiconductors, transport, electronic instruments, pharmaceuticals, and telecommunications, to mention only a few of the obvious examples—largely in the same single ways everywhere.[13]

What is so fascinating about these two examples and many other similar ones is the fact that they reflected *and* accelerated the interplay of technology and globalization. Or as Levitt put it,

two vectors operate simultaneously to drive the world: the vector of technology and the vector of globalization. The first helps powerfully to shape human preferences. The second shapes economic realities. With preferences converging, regardless of how much they constantly evolve and also diverge, markets are shaped into magnitudes that allow great economies of scale and therefore reduction of costs and prices.[14]

While preferences are constantly being shaped and reshaped, the significance of modernity resides in how *technology* is shaping the world's preferences into homogenized commonality (i.e., global standardization). That does not imply the demise of heterogeneity. On the contrary, *within* that commonality enormous variety would continue to assert itself and thrive, as evidenced by America's economy, the world's single largest and highly diverse and specialized domestic market. But not everything would thrive. The vehicles of the classic marketing mix would have to change in the process, even if their underlying and dynamic interplay would remain. Not every product, price, place, or promotion would survive in the new marketplace. People would prefer lower-priced and more-or-less standardized quality products over higher-priced, customized products. Distribution channels would have to ride the momentum of technology, just as promotion would have to adjust to new channel structures. The vectors of technology and globalization implied the expansion of modern markets into cost-reducing global proportions. A "new economics of the digital revolution" might be conceivable in certain, perhaps even many, industry segments. But if, in due time, these new technologies would be available to all companies, they would not make or break strategy—precisely *because* they would be available to all players.[15] Instead, they would be part of the rules of the game, the "cost of doing business," not an adequate means to win business. They would boost operational effectiveness, not strategic positioning.

Nowhere has this phenomenon been as poignant as on the Web. And yet, in most literature of the late 1990s, it was treated only incidentally or anecdotally, if at all, without deeper understanding or consideration of the implications. When, for instance, Hotmail emerged out of nowhere on the Independence Day of 1996, it had, literally, no clients. A year later, its subscriber base surpassed five million. This made it the second largest e-mail provider in the world; it was right behind America Online. "We started as just two people with an idea, and today 30,000 new users sign up for Hotmail daily," said Sabeer Bhatia, CEO and president of Hotmail.[16] By the end of 1997, the customer base amounted to ten million subscribers and it was acquired by Microsoft for $385 million. The case of Mirabilis may have been even more interesting. As Hotmail began its operations, three twentysomethings from Tel Aviv, Israel, visited Silicon Valley and decided thereafter to launch ICQ, an Internet-based pager that lets users know when their friends are on-line. They saw an opportunity: millions of people had been connected to the Internet, *but not interconnected*. They would supply the single missing component to enable the surfers to interact *with each other*. Mirabilis was not doing things better; it was doing things right.

Globalization of "Miniature Markets" and Strategic Use of Speed

Levitt saw the technology homogenizing world tastes, wants, and possibilities into global-market proportions, which allowed for world-standardized products, giving global producer powerful scale advantages. Some readers interpreted the statement simplistically as a prophecy on the eclipse of segments. That was not the point at all. On the contrary, as Levitt noted, "globalization does not mean the end of segments. It means, instead, their expansion to worldwide proportions." In this massive process, the transition itself provided ample opportunities of bold enterpreneurship: "What is seldom even imagined are the possibilities of vigorous and yet patient intervention to modify, transform, or bypass established channels and practices."[17]

"Ironically, over the years, we have seen the simultaneous growth of global preference structures and particularly on certain kinds of high-touch consumer goods. These have become global in their presence and in their predominance," commented Levitt fifteen years after the original essay.

Since the debate about "the globalization of markets," I have made the argument that this is not so surprising, given that we've had global preference in other high-touch products for a long, long time. In classical music, for example, Mozart and Vivaldi are global. So is architecture. All these high-touch products have always been global.

As to popular music and television, pop culture, Hollywood, food cultures, soft drinks—these, for the first time, represent the globalization of preference structures of people who are *not* well educated and highly educated. They don't have a history of elite preference structures that they inherited from their families, just the opposite. In addition to common global preferences with respect to the high-touch products that pick up mass markets around the world, what is really interesting and a big surprise is the following: We have seen the globalization of *miniature markets* in these categories. Take, for example, foods all over the world. Now you can get sushi, pizza, Chinese food, and pita bread all over the world. It is all over the world; it is not just for the wealthy few any longer.

So you've got this simultaneous development of global mass markets and developments of multiple miniature markets; they thrive simultaneously. I don't know how to explain why they have developed how they have. It may have a lot to do with communication; like economics, it has driven those preference structures. Technologies for producing are also very low cost and available all over the world.

The mass markets in the popular arts or popular products categories have globalized because the consumer speaks the same global language, the global language of commonality. That is translated by these new technologies, telecommunications specifically. We are seeing the digitization of everything. In the article back in 1983, I mentioned that mathematicians and chemists think the same common language all over the world. Since the times of modern chemistry, the chemical industries have been global industries. Similarly, the electric industries have always been global industries—take for example Siemens or General Electric. They are based on the common language of science and engineering. Now we see with the popular arts that there is a common language, too; this common language is transmitted through communication.[18]

The Internet, notes Levitt, should *not* be seen as "just another new technology," but something that is more akin to the massive infrastructural changes in the economy and society, such as the revolutionary changes in transportation and communications in the 19th century. If, however, one were to assess the significance of the Internet from the standpoint of marketing only, Levitt would approach it mainly as

an *information source* on various products and prices available. It is itself an instrument "competing" in the sense of serving the buyer, knowing the buyers and the sellers, and providing a medium of exchange that enables funds to be transported from the buyer to the seller through credit cards and other transactional information. Information is a critical thing.[19]

In "The Globalization of Markets," Levitt argued that technology would accelerate commerce very rapidly. The Internet confirms the thesis. "The change will continue to energize these technologies that will facilitate and lead to more and more globalization in one form or another."[20]

By the late 1990s, Levitt considered it heroic but too early to make suggestions on viable business models on the Web. "It may be one thing today and something else this evening. Who knows?" He expected the change to take a long while and be continuous by nature.[21]

After the mid-1990s, Internet marketing attracted wide attention in the nation's research universities, even though the subject was only arriving in the established curricula (see Exhibit 6-4). Still, early research evidence supports many of Levitt's conclusions. In the spring of 1996, John A. Quelch and Lisa R. Klein published their "The Internet and International Marketing" in the *Sloan Management Review*.[22] Among other things, the

Exhibit 6-4
Internet Marketing and American Academia: A Transitional Period

By the late 1990s, as chairman of the Department of Marketing at New York University, Professor C. Samuel Craig taught in one of the nation's leading universities. Located next to Silicon Alley, NYU also—like Columbia University, New School for Social Research, Baruch College, and many others—participated in the training of the new media talent. Specializing in international marketing, Craig had a privileged position to evaluate the arrival of Internet and interactive marketing to American academia.

Professor Craig's own research ranged from international and global marketing to consumer behavior, marketing, and consumer research. "One of the things that makes us unique is location," says Craig. "We are in New York City and in close proximity to the media, marketing, and communications industries. We have a fairly large group of scholars and faculty. Due to the location, many of our people also interact and consult with businesses and bring that back into the classroom.

"The interesting thing about the Internet is that, from the standpoint of the academia, it spans a number of disciplines," Craig says. "The department of information systems, for example, is concerned about the technology and its use. The department of marketing, on the other hand, is more interested in the consumer perspective and their use of the technology. For real progress to be made, there will have to be more truly joint undertakings to develop technologies such as user-friendly interfaces.

"Across the United States, marketing departments are embracing the Internet. Many are offering courses in Internet marketing. In due time, there will not be a need for an Internet marketing course because it will just be folded into the courses on advertising, consumer behavior, and marketing research; they will be fused throughout the curriculum. The contemporary situation is a transitional period.

"In terms of the effective use of the Internet, the limiting factor is computer penetration and demographic access. In 1998, you can reach roughly 25% of the U.S. households and that means that you will miss 75%. If you do a telephone survey, you would reach 98%. Numbers alone, of course, do not tell the story. For a lot of technology-based products and some upscale consumer households, that 25% may be quite relevant. If, however, you would like to conduct similar Web-based consumer research globally, you will find that the household PC penetration and Internet connections remain miniscule in some countries."

Source: Dan Steinbock, interview with C. Samuel Craig, Chairman, Marketing Department, New York University, August 7, 1998.

authors emphasized that the rise and increasing penetration of the Web underlined the new potential of enterpreneurial firms. In particular, they made note of several challenges for international marketers eager to launch Web activities. The management of global branding and corporate name or logo identification posed a major challenge for MNCs. The reduction of the competitive advantage of scale economies in many industries was about to make it easier for small marketers to compete worldwide. For companies marketing on the Internet, *technology* would be a more important source of competitive advantage than *size*. Because the Web's speed and worldwide presence made its users intolerant of inconsistencies and slow response, it presented serious organizational challenges for MNCs attempting to convert their global businesses to the new medium. It would be even harder to contain news of product quality problems and cross-border differences in quality, price, and availability. The creation of a website was not a one-time effort and would require global marketers to continually assess the perceived value of their Internet sites among target groups across countries. And even if the Web promised to reinforce the trend toward English as the lingua franca of commerce, cultural barriers would remain.[23]

The Strategic Use of Speed. In addition to the early research evidence, recent developments in marketing theory supports indirectly many of Levitt's theses. In his *Marketing Strategy*, Steven P. Schnaars makes note of speed as "a strategic thrust of the 1990s," when hurrying new products to market and speeding up the flow of goods through channels of distribution became goals for large and once-stodgy operators. "Speed," as he puts it provocatively, "replaced size as a perceived competitive advantage."[24] Speed as strategy, he notes, started as an outgrowth of the "just-in-time" inventory methods of the early 1980s. It began in the auto industry, where U.S. sellers sought to catch up with the cost and quality advantages held by Japanese brands. By the mid-1980s, it had expanded to include "quick-response systems" in retailing and apparel. In particular, speed played a strategic role in innovation and distribution. In the former, the focus was on *new* products and ideas (think of Mirabilis and Hotmail). In the latter, it was on *existing* goods and information through channels of distribution (think of Amazon.com and FedEx).

Schnaars saw several reasons for the rise of speed as a source of competitive advantage. A truly sustainable competitive advantage had proved an elusive goal for companies. Speed sidestepped the need to predict the future by moving quickly with markets. It allowed the market test to decide which products were to be successful and which would fail. It boosted the fates of new products which were the life-blood of future earnings. Shorter product life cycles made speed necessary. It was critical in growth markets, which were crowded with competitors and were intensely competitive. By acting rather than analyzing, speed suppressed copycats. It also made it possible to gain limited retail shelf space early. And it promoted an enterpreneurial culture of doing and trying rather than a bureaucratic culture of analysis and testing.[25]

The Web would boost all of these characteristics, very rapidly as some evidence already indicated.[26] Yet, it would also frustrate inflated hopes and optimistic scenarios. Certainly, "speed as strategy" became a common phenomenon prior to and with the surge of the Web. But, really, was it a "strategy"? In the 1990s, the fortunes and failures of Internet marketing indicate that while speed was used as strategy, it did not function in that capacity. The pioneers of the Internet did seize speed as a way to gain early entry in the marketspace. They also hoped that this entry would enable them to better position themselves against the incumbents of the marketplace that would follow their trail. An offensive entry strategy was coupled with a defensive positioning strategy. In this struggle for market power, speed was *used strategically*, and it served as an instrument of *strategic opportunism*. But it might be exaggeration to conceive of speed itself as strategy. Essentially, it meant doing things right fast; it did not necessarily or always mean doing the right things. In the former capacity, speed served as an element of operational effectiveness; in the latter, it functioned as strategy, or as an element of strategic positioning.[27]

These Web-driven changes did not take place as fast as the Internet visionaries had predicted. Nor did they occur as slowly as the incumbent media had assumed (or hoped). The early history of television is a case in point. Yet, any efforts to use that past to extrapolate future trends would be doomed—hence the evasions of the Internet pundits and the initial puzzlement of the incumbent media. Indeed, the case is instructive and serves as a guide for other future developments because it throws light on the *nature* of the inflated expectations and often grim business realities.

EPILOGUE: "THE WAR FOR EYEBALLS"

There are curious parallels between the early years of television and the first years of the Internet bursting onto the American scene. In both cases, a new technology took the nation, as contemporary observers would often put it, "like a delayed time bomb." Yet, there were significant differences, too.

Television and the Internet: Historical Similarities

Late in 1948 the FCC, having issued some 100 TV licenses, called a sudden halt to study interference problems. The television "freeze" constrained the evolution of the new media at the turn of the 1950s.[28] Initially, the Web faced similar regulatory barriers. As long as the evolution of the Internet remained constrained by the mission of the NSFNet, commercialization could not proceed properly. With the phased privatization of the infrastructure, the transition accelerated significantly. Meanwhile, the development of the user-friendly technologies set the stage for the nation's Web-driven business-to-business and consumer markets.

Broadcast television originated from the pre–World War II era. Just as World War I had set the stage for radio, wartime advances in electronics set the stage for a TV explosion. The television freeze gave sponsors and ad agencies time to experiment with programs and commercials. The sponsor-supported system of the radio era offered a pattern for the age of television. Still, the decade of 1945 to 1955 became one of constant upheaval and conflict, with numerous overlapping transitions.[29]

The Internet, on the other hand, originated from military projects launched at the onset of the Cold War in the late 1950s. The transition came only with the late 1960s and early 1970s, which saw the first international conferences on the Internet, the evolution of the primary standards, and the shift of the research from Pentagon to the nation's defense contractors and research universities. By the late 1980s, the nonprofit infrastructure was rapidly turning commercial. With the launch of the Web and the first browsers, the change accelerated exponentially. Starting in 1993 and 1994, the nation entered a period of constant upheaval and conflict, with numerous overlapping transitions.

At the turn of the 1950s, the main transition was from radio to television, as television erupted in "a gold rush atmosphere." Several factors contributed to these massive shifts, including a pent-up demand (a transition from war production to the production of consumer goods), massive demographic changes (the postwar baby boom, the flight to suburbia), increasing competition (eclipse of most institutional advertising in favor of merchandising competition in domestic and overseas markets), and the rise of multinational U.S. corporations.

At the turn of the 1990s, the transition was from the "old" media to the "new" media. Now the so-called "Internet mania" erupted in a gold rush atmosphere from California's Silicon Valley to New York City's Silicon Alley, as well as the nation's thriving technology sector and IPO markets. Several determinants drove the process. The Cold War had eclipsed. With the arrival of the Clinton administration, the government purposefully accelerated the expansion of the national information infrastructure as well as the emergent electronic commerce. Baby boomers had given birth to a new baby boom. International markets were soaring.

As the freeze ended in 1951 and 1952, almost all TV cities reported a 20% to 40% drop in movie attendance. "The tendency for national sponsors was therefore to hang onto a coast-to-coast radio network program, while getting a foothold in television," writes Eric Barnouw in his classic history of American broadcasting. "It was a time for straddling. Soon— after the freeze—they would make the big jump. Thus network radio, with a sense of doom, had a final fling. Many programs sounded the same. As audiences shrank, battles for the remnants grew fierce."[30] In 1949—even amidst the freeze—*Printer's Ink* had started to keep statistics on advertising revenue from television. "An advertising agency cannot ignore television," said one adman in 1950. "But television affords little profit for advertising agencies since most TV appropriations are small compared with those for other media." "We don't know yet that it pays," agreed Clarence Goshorn of Benton & Bowles. "We have a lot of fragmentary success stories, but no continuity of measurement by even imperfect sales."[31]

How similar were the concerns on Madison Avenue in the mid-1990s when the national mass marketers sought to hang onto the network television while trying to get a foothold on the Internet![32] By 1994 and 1995, trade journals, ad agencies, and market research firms began to keep statistics on ad revenue from the Internet. According to conventional wisdom, agencies could not ignore the new media. But since the Web provided so little profit for agencies, many doubted it paid. Anecdotal success stories were abundant, but the absence of proper long-term counting and auditing statistics, technologies, and standards made all data suspect. By the spring of 1994, *Advertising Age* began to publish its "Interactive Media & Marketing" section, while *Broadcasting & Cable* followed suit with its "Telemedia Week" supplement focusing on "the interactive world of voice, data and video." Meanwhile, even NBC lined up major online services to carry a new programming and marketing service, NBC Online, while CBS Marketing Interactive intended to make use of a variety of interactive media technologies to deliver CBS programming, promos, and advertisers' messages.[33]

Back in the 1940s, those who saw the television explosion coming were able to enjoy the first-mover benefits. By 1949, BBDO's Ben Duffy spent 80% of his media time on TV, only 20% on radio; a year later, the BBDO TV department had grown from 12 employees to 150, and the agency was billing $4 million in the new medium. The lines were blurred between ad agencies and TV networks as many top executives shuttled back and forth between the two. Even under the FCC freeze the industry's total TV business went from $12.3 million in 1949 to $128 million in 1951, a level that radio had taken sixteen years to reach.[34]

With the Internet, old-style ad agencies became bystanders. However, flexible and ambitious new media enterprises and interactive ad agencies saw the explosion coming and were able to enjoy the first-mover benefits. In 1991, CKS Group generated $5.2 million in revenues but hardly any net income; five years later, the agency pocketed $136 million in revenues and almost $8 million in net income. (However, as an integrated communications agency, it garnered a major portion of the revenues from non-Internet related segments.) By 1998, USWeb acquired CKS in a stock swap valued at about $340 million. Meanwhile, the lines were blurred between the old and the new media; many top executives shuttled back and forth between the two, as well as trade associations and software and telecommunications companies. Even without adequate counting or auditing solutions, the Internet advertising revenue soared from a zero point in 1994 to an estimated $2.1 billion in 1998 and was expected to boom to $9 billion by 2002.[35]

For Madison Avenue, television had meant a new kind of advertising. After technical problems, dozens of big clients had switched agencies to find creative departments adept at the new techniques. Like print, TV was visual; like radio, it was intrusive and had audio; like neither, it was kinetic and immediate. On TV, "you can jump right into the selling copy without having to snag attention first," George Gallup pointed out. Now products could be demonstrated in use, with a voice-over describing the action. Young & Rubicam bragged about the "dramatic demonstration" in its early TV ads: a Goodyear tire being crushed and returning unblemished. The 1950s were "the age of the eye."[36]

For Silicon Valley and Silicon Alley, the Internet represented a new kind of advertising with *its* own technical problems. By the late 1990s, major clients favored interactive ad agencies that were more adept at the new techniques. Like print, the Web was visual; unlike print, it also offered an endless potential of links for data and information. Like radio, the Internet would become intrusive and had audio; unlike radio, it had video and seemingly endless cost-efficient applications, from local radio to global radio. Like television, the Web had audio, video, and immediacy; unlike TV, it was far more cost-efficient and direct. And unlike all of its predecessors, the Web was not only real time, but also interactive, offering full-scale points-of-sale capabilities. It could provide interactive demonstration and immediate delivery for digital intangibles. It not only offered a copy for sale, it could make a sale. The 1990s would be the decade of the Web.

So there were many parallels between the early years of television and the first years of the Internet. But the similarities are *not* the moral of the story—instead, the *dis*similarities are.

Television and the Internet: Historical Dissimilarities

After the TV freeze was lifted in the spring of 1952, new TV retail stores opened at the rate of a thousand a month. CBS Television made its first net profit in 1953, and a year later it became the largest ad medium in the world, with a monopoly of the top-rated shows. In three years, TV's share of billings at the Leo Burnett agency went from 18% to over half. Overcoming its earlier skepticism, even Benton & Bowles was deriving 60% of its revenue from TV.[37]

On the Internet, the portals were the primary ad allocators in the late 1990s. America Online had made profits since the late 1980s, but its profitability accelerated drastically from $40 million to almost $1.7 billion between 1993 and 1997, when its market value was estimated at $5.6 billion. In 1994, Yahoo! made $1.4 million in revenues; in 1997, it generated $67.4 million, but net losses accelerated from $0.6 million to $22.9 million. Yet, its market value exceeded $3.2 billion. Among the Web retailers, Amazon.com generated $148 million in revenues and $28 million in net losses by 1997, when its market value exceeded $1.4 billion. True, its annual growth rate exceeded 840%, but even that was no assurance of its survival. Among the old-style ad agency networks, the Web revenues continued to play an insignificant role in the late 1990s.

Why was it so hard to gain profitability? If the market growth was "explosive," why were the firms not thriving? The primary reason involves the characteristics of the competitive environment.

In the 1950s network era, the structure of marketing channels was simple. Briefly put, the alternatives were few and scarce. The peak years of "classic Hollywood" had ended with the Paramount decrees that forced the vertically integrated studios to divest their theatrical segments. Concurrently, the rise of broadcast television, as well as shifts in demographics and lifestyle, led to Hollywood's demise and the growth of the independents. As classic Hollywood lost its exhibition pipeline, more extensive distribution emerged through the explosive growth of broadcast television. With their vast film libraries, the studios survived as production houses for broadcast TV, just as they would later thrive in syndication and foreign markets. As the "Big Three" broadcast networks gained the role of the "Big Five" studios in American lives, Hollywood studios were taken over by diversified conglomerates. In the network era, the TV channel capacity encompassed only ten channels. This barrier enhanced the oligopoly of the "Big Three." Until cable deregulation, NBC, CBS, and ABC remained as invulnerable as once Detroit's three mighty automakers were. In the process, they also became as complacent.[38]

By the late 1990s, the structure of marketing channels had rapidly not only become complex, it was being digitized and moving toward the Web applications. Most importantly, channel alternatives were many (Exhibit 6-5). Now half a dozen major media and entertainment conglomerates (Time Warner, Sony, Viacom, News Corp., Walt Disney, Seagram, and DreamWorks) owned large film libraries and controlled TV programming. Most of these companies had significant interests in TV shows and dominated the distribution of new products.

The "Big Three" were not so big any longer; Fox, independent stations, and syndicators had joined them, as well as dozens of basic cable, pay cable, home shopping, and pay-per-view channels. Most studios had, directly or indirectly, interests in direct broadcasting satellites (DBS). Local telcos had sought access to the marketplace since the late 1980s, and while they were not involved in the content production, they did, as a strategic group, invest in DSL to garner cable audiences and high-speed Internet users. International carriers entered the fray in the summer of

1998, when AT&T acquired TCI, seeking access to households (and breaking the telcos' bottleneck front) *and* joining the strategic group of cable-modem providers (@Home, RoadRunner). In return, major studios like Time Warner were seeking entry into local telecommunications. With the rise of the Internet, even infrastructure firms such as Intel were investing $300–$400 million a year into software and new media firms that provided content and solutions to major players. Software giants like Microsoft had ensured entry though online service (MSN), navigation (Internet Explorer), and access (WebTV). Content and agglomerator providers, such as Yahoo! and America Online, had positioned themselves as portals that controlled access to masses of online users.

The media marketplace in the 1950s and the 1990s represent two entirely different competitive environments. In the first, the technologies were continuous and the channel structure was simple, "thin," maturing, domestic, and ruled by two to three critical strategic groups of companies (TV networks, Hollywood studios, publishers). In the second, the technologies are discontinuous, and the channel structure is complex, "thick," growth-oriented, multidomestic or international, and ruled by a handful of critical strategic groups (Hollywood studios, publishers, software firms, telcos and carriers, pure Internet players, consumer electronics). Moreover, each group is no longer a "cozy" oligopoly but an unregulated (e.g., computers) or deregulated (telecommunications) cluster of warring sub-groups. Also, each has its differentiation and cost-leadership leaders, and smaller focus players. Many are critically dependent on exports or foreign direct investment. By 1994, even John Malone, the legendary chief executive of TCI, noted that the big players had become "octopuses all with their hands in each other's pockets. Where one [industry] starts and the others stops will be hard to decide."[39]

Whatever the alleged blessings of the Internet (and they *are* many), it would be impossible to initiate a frontal launch in such a marketplace (like television did in the 1950s). Nor could a single strategic group initiate Web-driven strategies without other players having to follow them. (These comparisons of the network era and the pre-Web era exclude the rise and functions of nonmeasured media advertising and direct marketing in the marketplace; the role of each was minimal in the early 1950s. Similarly, these considerations bracket the rise of trade and consumer promotions since the 1980s.) In a dynamic system, one strategic move is bound to trigger others. The system had become so complex that even scenario forecasts would find it difficult to reliably predict the course of developments.

Change was inevitable, and mass marketers were preparing themselves for it. However, they would do little before more precise (measured) information on the Internet marketplace became available. Until

Exhibit 6-5
Marketing Media and Channel Structure: From Network Pipelines to the Internet Era

1. Network Pipeline: From 1950s to Late 1970s

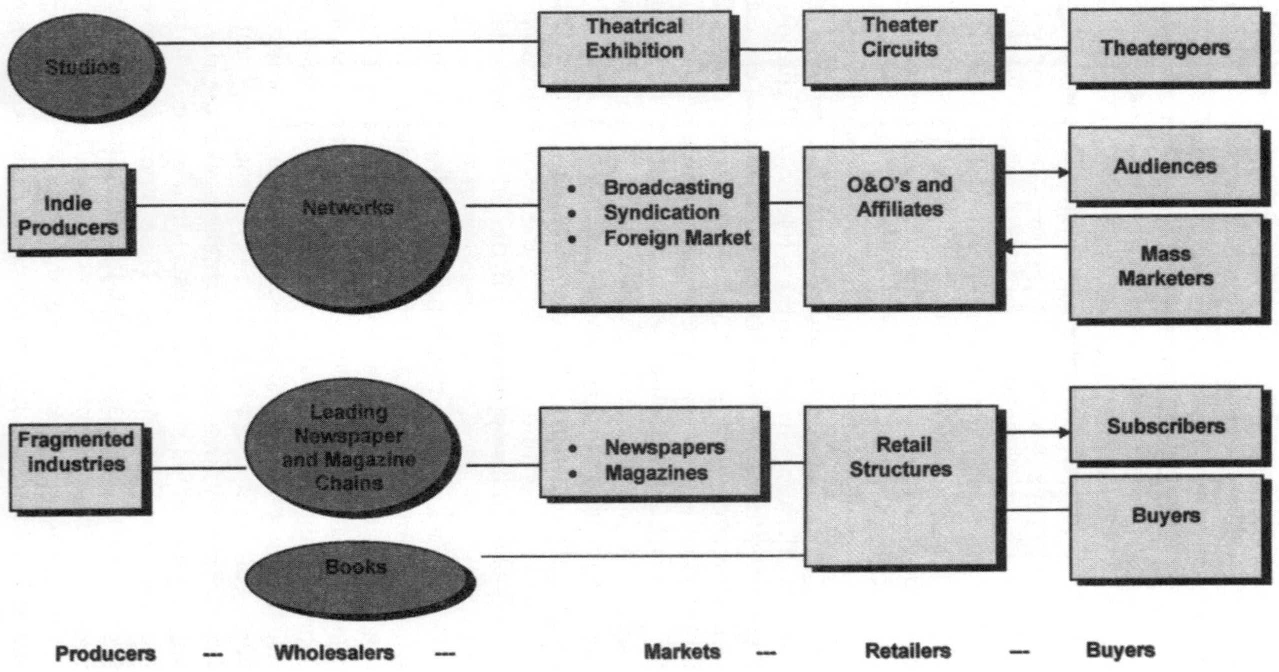

| Producers | — | Wholesalers | — | Markets | — | Retailers | — | Buyers |

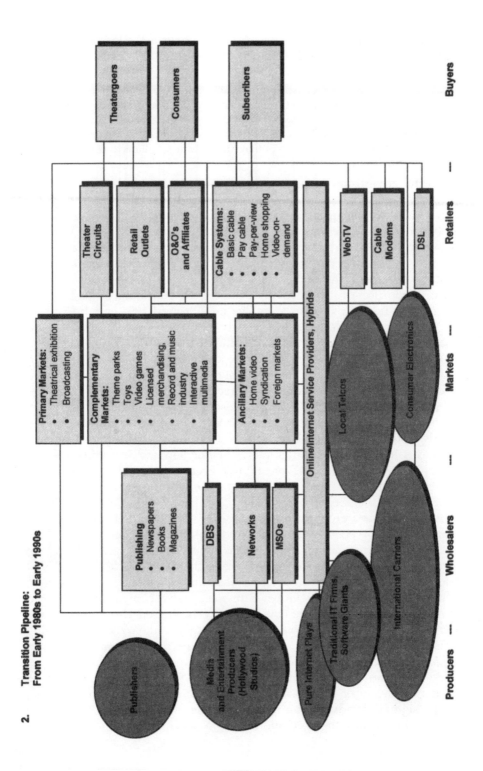

2. Transition Pipeline:
From Early 1980s to Early 1990s

291

the mid-1990s, the Internet surveys were not exactly known for their reliability or validity. As *Time* put it,

while there's nothing especially vaporous about the 26-year-old global computer network known as the Internet, the estimates of its size that have been tossed around during its meteoric rise to celebrity over the past two years have been pretty mushy. As seemingly straightforward a question as how many people use the network has produced answers that range from 3 million to 60 million.[40]

As the advertisers rushed to the Web in 1994 and the investors followed a year later, educated guesses no longer served as substitutes for statistically significant audience research demanded by marketers, Web publishers, and investors who considered the Internet history's fastest growing market and a new communications medium. The hard data arrived in November 1995, when Nielsen Media Research unveiled the results of perhaps the first solid, scientific survey of the Internet (or at least the portion of it that covered the United States and Canada).[41] Indeed, even the terms began to evolve only around 1994 and 1995.

According to Nielsen, approximately 37 million people in the United States and Canada had access to the Internet, either directly or indirectly (e.g., through a friend, a colleague, or a commercial OSP, such as CompuServe, Prodigy or America Online). Some 24 million people had used the Internet during the past three months (i.e., 11% of the population 16 and older). On average, those users logged nearly 5.5 hours online each week.[42] Counting heads is an inexact science; and counting heads on the Internet in the mid-1990s was more of an art than a science. Unsurprisingly, three months later, another new survey estimated that 17 million American adults, or one in eleven, had used the Web—twice the most widely accepted previous estimate of Internet use, but still unacceptable to the skeptics.[43]

As the demand grew for reliable research data, market research firms rushed to the Web.[44] A flood of surveys followed while the numbers were debated for reasons of science as much as for business rivalry. In April 1996, Nielsen released a new research study which reported that there were 22 million adult Internet users in the United States. As these numbers inflated the previous estimates, many companies embraced them to instigate electronic commerce. Even Nielsen was swept by the debate.[45] Still, marketers could no longer ignore the Web. The writing was on the wall—some of that time was taken out of hours these users *could* have spent watching TV.

By 1997 and 1998, marketers, media, and new media companies, as well as ad agencies had come to believe that the Internet was evolving into a significant advertising medium as the owners of PCs spent more time online surfing the Web and less time watching television. "The average hours per week on the Internet has doubled in the past year in the United States, rising to about 13 to 14 hours a week (per Internet user)," said Ira Carlin, executive vice president and media director of McCann-Erickson Worldwide during the annual congress of the World Federation of Advertisers in October 1997. "Think about the impact that has when you're trying to reach your customers in the United States." Revenues from advertising on the Web hit an annualized rate of $850 million in the third quarter in the United States. Although Web advertising remained just a fraction of television ad revenues, it was about to exceed radio ad revenues, Carlin said. And while much contemporary Web advertising was of poor quality, that did not mean it would not improve. "Hey, we were lousy at the beginning of television," Carlin said. "So don't complain to me about the quality of the World Wide Web. It's only three years old."[46]

By August 1998, America Online and Nielsen Media Research revealed that households wired up to the Internet watched 15% less television than households without Internet access. In the past, industry observers had made educate guesses of 10% to 30% audience shifts, but the AOL/Nielsen numbers were the first more reliable ones.[47] Unlike most Internet companies whose usage went up during daytime, AOL's peaked on prime time. "The Web is a daytime phenomenon," acknowledged Ted Leonsis, then-president of the AOL Studios. "AOL is a primetime medium. What strikes me most is our usage pattern. Thursday night is the highest TV viewership, and it's our worst night. We're competing with Jerry Seinfeld, so I'm much more concerned about Seinfeld than I am about Bill Gates."[48]

That made America Online more threatening to the incumbent old media.

The Future of Internet Marketing?

In the mid-1990s, Procter & Gamble was the leading American mass marketer whose international ad spending amounted to some $5.4 billion. As the industry leader, P&G's strategic decisions had a significant impact on the industry evolution and on the strategies of other mass marketers. In 1994, Edwin Artzt, then-chairman and CEO of P&G, had awakened Madison Avenue to the challenge of interactive advertising. Starting in the fall of 1995, John Pepper, P&G's new chairman and CEO, would have to steer the mass marketer to the 21st century in an environment that seemed to threaten the very existence of all mass marketers. Insofar as Pepper was concerned, P&G's Internet strategy was subject to two strategic objectives that dictated the overall corporate strategy: price-conscious marketing goals and a revenue-driven corporate strategy. By 1996, the marketer's vision included moving toward pay-for-performance for ad agencies and squeezing more value per dollar from media spending. The changes were triggered by the decline of growth. The objective was to double the sales to $70 billion by 2005—at least before Asia was swept by financial turmoil in 1998.[49]

As important as the Web would be in the *future*, the Internet or its potential was only *one* of Pepper's *present* concerns—and ultimately subject to the overall corporate strategy. *That* would be the "natural" pattern with other mass marketers, too, as they began to position themselves strategically on the Web.

On August 20, 1998, some of the world's biggest advertisers, invited by Procter & Gamble, gathered in Cincinnati's "Future of Advertising Stakeholders Summit" (FAST). The abbreviation was not incidental. The stated motive was to quickly reverse what many saw as the failure of Internet advertising to date. The participants included America's top mass marketers, including executives from Coca-Cola, Levi Strauss, Unilever, and AT&T. But as the business press was quick to point out, what was even more interesting was that P&G did *not* invite the most senior executives of its main ad agencies to the session.[50] Reportedly, Denis F. Beausejour, P&G's VP in charge of worldwide advertising, who had orchestrated the summit, did not think that Madison Avenue was very tuned in to what was going on in new media. Only a week before Cincinnati, Richard A. Goldstein, president and CEO of Unilever's U.S. operations, set the tone by calling banner ads "more of a nuisance and clutter than an attraction."[51]

Leading packaged-goods advertisers were frustrated. Where was the wonderful future of the Web? Online advertising certainly did not deliver what *they* wanted. Fueling the advertisers' concerns were the steadily shrinking audience numbers at the big broadcast networks, long the cheapest and easiest way for companies such as P&G and Unilever to reach consumers. In the mid-1950s, the Big Three still commanded 25%–30% of the prime time audience *each*. By 1998, each had to struggle to garner a 10% cut. Ironically enough, demand for network advertising had *grown* briskly since 1991 as new buyers—technology companies like Intel, financial services giants like Fidelity, telecom firms like Sprint—were clamoring to reach mass audiences. By auctioning up to 80% of their prime-time inventory during a frenzied week of "upfront" buying in May 1998, the networks had been able to drive up the cost of what remains a scarce commodity. "We call it the less-is-more syndrome," says NBC's Robert C. Wright. "It isn't necessarily value pricing." It was not. NBC was able to raise prices by 14% the previous spring after *losing* 5% of its prime-time target audience, and the other networks followed suit.[52]

But the value was concentrated in the highest-rated broadcast shows, not at the low end of the Nielsen ladder. Mass audiences garnered less and less and cost more and more. Yet, the demand was soaring and prices were climbing on the top product. Perhaps mass broadcasting had become grossly inefficient, but it was still, well, *mass*. Value, of course, had fled to segments like cable or to fragments like online. Mass marketers wanted to build and nurture brand loyalty, as well as broad reach. Until the mid-1980s, they had had both. Now, just a few years later, they had neither. TV networks delivered mass but with overpricing. Cable gave value but segments only. The Web promised to change "everything," and yet it threatened to destroy even the rest.

Little had changed in the four years since former P&G chief Ed Artzt had energized ad agency executives to wake up and embrace new media. Numbers told the story. By 1998, P&G spent $3 billion a year on advertising; it had been recently spending only $3 million a quarter on interactive ads. But things were changing, and they were changing fast. If Gates had been willing and able to conduct a strategic U-turn, why not P&G?

At Cincinnati's summit, P&G did its outmost to persuade and force tradition-bound advertisers to confront the problems hobbling the Internet-advertising market. "The results amazed the assembled flock of old-line consumers-products experts, new-media types and on-line agencies," reported the *Wall Street Journal*. Rivals such as Unilever, Clorox, Nestle, and Johnson & Johnson also attended the summit and stopped duking it out long enough to agree on a new fifteen-member steering committee and a game plan."[53] The list urged mass marketers to draft standards for measuring online audiences by November 1998 and then establish a set of ad types that websites would accept. By April 1999, America's mass marketers intended to develop a way to reconcile contradictory data supplied by various online services.

If Cincinnati's fragile consensus were to hold, billions of dollars in advertising revenue could move toward cyberspace and away from network television. Some estimates put the combined ad-buying power assembled under P&G's roof at more than $50 billion a year. "Let's face it; there's a massive revolution in consumer habits," said Denis Beausejour, P&G vice president in charge of worldwide advertising. "No one organization, or even a handful or organizations, can be the driver. No one is in control, and that's really disrupting the marketing landscape—in a really positive way." P&G itself envisioned that in five years as much as 80% of its $3 billion ad budget could be spent on what it broadly defined as "interactive digital media," including the Internet, cable, interactive television and high-definition TV.[54]

As important as these developments were and as much as they bespoke of the coming maturity of the Web, they represented only the very beginning of realizing the Internet's *potential*. After all, one could hardly apply the tools, methods, and standards of the past broadcast era (centralized, top-down, one-way, packaged communications) to measure progress of a quite different era of dialogue and interactivity (distributed, bottom-up, two-way, real time communications). Even a decade before the rise of the Internet, American media advertising had come to an end of an era. After deregulation, market segmentation, new technology, and alternative media outlets and ad options, mass marketing was simply a thing of the past, as evidenced by the rapid erosion of brand loyalty and the equally rapid proliferation of promotions. The Web would aggravate the fragmentation—and, perhaps, provide the last nail for the coffin.

Moreover, the emergence of database and relationship marketing— first in business-to-business markets, later in consumer markets—had been transforming the traditional "rules of game" since the 1970s and 1980s. The impact of direct marketing originated from the 1950s and 1960s. All of these approaches had questioned the very ground of traditional media advertising, from inaccuracy to accountability. If, as most Internet marketers argued, the Web represented a powerful drive of technology integration, they did *not* mean that this integration would take place on the terms of Internet advertising (at best, a small segment of all actual *and potential* Internet applications). Instead, if anything, such integration would have to proceed on the terms of a *new marketing concept*—one that the pioneer marketers, such as Regis McKenna and others, had been developing for years (Exhibit 6-6).

By the close of the 1990s, this interactive future was approaching rapidly. After all, Silicon Valley was doing its utmost to boost the expansion of the interactive marketplace. Its dream of total connectivity had won. Mass marketers would have to deal with the ensuing nightmare of potentially infinite marketing channels.

Two months prior to the Super Bowl of 1997, Intel's then-CEO Andy Grove delivered a keynote speech at the Comdex computer show predicting a war "for eyeballs." He argued that the industry's next struggle was to capture a sizable chunk of the time consumers spent watching television. In fifteen years, microprocessors would be 250 times more powerful than they were in 1997, which would provide enough muscle to put the PC into head-to-head combat with TV and any other type of electronic entertainment device. In the "war for eyeballs," high-powered computers would assume communications functions such as high-quality video phones, television programming, and interactive games, Grove said. "In this war, he who captures the most eyeballs wins."[55]

As the leading maker of semiconductors, Intel naturally intended most of these computers to be powered by its chips. In 1997, there were only about a third as many PCs in homes as TV sets. But Grove expected that balance to change as new technologies would enable the PC to capture the attention of TV audiences. Already, Grove noted, the 15 million to 20 million users of the Web represented an audience to rival a traditional

Exhibit 6-6
Some Characteristics of the New Marketing Concept: A Sketch

Marketing Concept	Sales-driven	Customer-driven	Market-driven
Role of Marketing	Marketing as departmental function	Marketing as buyer orientation	Marketing as real-time feedback loop
New Product Development	Technically driven product development	Marketing-driven product development	Knowledge- and experience-based marketing
Forms	Change customers to fit product ("one color")	Change products to fit customer ("tell me which color")	Adapting products to layer strategies ("let's figure it out together")
Strategic Objective	Making things	Selling things	Owning market
Demands on Company	Control costs Competitive production	Competing on products Competitive differentiation	Serving customers Competitive customer relationships
Center of Gravity	Engineering	Finance	Marketing
Competition Model	Mass marketing	Flexible marketing	"Anything, any way, anytime" (customization)

Source: This sketch has been drawn on the basis of the characteristics presented in Regis McKenna, "Marketing Is Everything," *Harvard Business Review,* January–February 1991. It does not appear in the essay itself.

broadcast network. "We need to look at our business as more than simply the building and selling of personal computers," said Grove. "Our business is the delivery of information and lifelike interactive experiences."[56]

In the long term, Silicon Valley's dream of interactive media would be *the* winning reality. By the fall of 1998, willing to exploit that future, America's greatest mass marketers began to reposition themselves strategically on the long and tortuous road. Edwin Artzt's crisis speech had framed the agenda in 1994. Now others would have to implement it. In the early 20th century, Procter & Gamble had pioneered mass marketing in America. Now marketing—whatever it would be like in the next millennium—would have to adapt to Silicon Valley's pace of change.

A little silicon chip prepared to tackle and sweep through Madison Avenue. It looked innocent and innocuous. One could hardly see it anymore. But after it finished its job, marketing and advertising would no longer be the same—in America or worldwide.

NOTES

1. For this periodization—from the multinational to the global phase—see Johny K. Johansson, *Global Marketing: Foreign Entry, Local Marketing, and Global Management* (New York: McGraw-Hill 1997). On the issues of global marketing, see also Susan P. Douglas and C. Samuel Craig, *Global Marketing Strategy* (New York: McGraw-Hill 1995).

2. For this classification and account of globalization drivers, see Johansson, *Global Marketing*, especially pp. 8–16.

3. By Elizabeth de Bony, "United States, EU Differ on Global Standards for the Net," *InfoWorld*, October 2, 1997. On the differences between U.S. and EU views on global electronic commerce, see my OECD report, Dan Steinbock, *Dismantling the Barriers to Global Electronic Commerce*, An International Conference and Business-Government Forum Organized by the OECD and the Government of Finland in Co-operation with the European Commission, the Government of Japan, and the Business and Industry Advisory Committee (BIAC), Turku, Finland, 19–21 November 1997 (published in February 1998).

4. On the basics of the determinants of national advantage, see Michael Porter, *The Competitive Advantage of Nations* (New York: The Free Press 1990), pp. 71–73.

5. Ibid.

6. See IDC, Press releases, July, 1997. On the U.S. first-mover benefit in the emerging global electronic commerce, see my OECD report, Dan Steinbock, *Dismantling the Barriers to Global Electronic Commerce*. On the National Information Infrastructure (NII) initiative, see U.S. Government, *The National Information Infrastructure: U.S. Government, Agenda for Action*, Information Infrastructure Task Force. September 15, 1993. On the emergence, formulation, and implementation of the NII initiative, see, e.g., Brian Kahin, "The U.S. National Information Infrastructure Initiative, the Net, and the Virtual Project," in Brian Kahin and Ernest

Wilson (eds.), *National Information Infrastructure Initiatives: Vision and Policy Design* (Cambridge, MA: MIT Press 1997).

7. Juliann Sivulka, *Soap, Sex, and Cigarettes: A Cultural History of American Advertising* (Belmont, CA: Wadsworth 1998), p. 360.

8. See Johansson, *Global Marketing.*

9. Robert Buzzell, "Can You Standardize Multinational Marketing?" *Harvard Business Review*, November–December 1968.

10. Theodor Levitt, "The Globalization of Markets," *Harvard Business Review*, May–June 1983. A slightly different version is included in Theodor Levitt, *The Marketing Imagination* (New York: The Free Press 1986), chapter 2.

11. For Levitt's contributions in marketing, see, e.g., his *Innovation in Marketing* (New York: McGraw-Hill, 1962); *Industrial Purchasing Behavior* (Boston: Harvard Business School 1965); *The Marketing Mode: Pathways to Corporate Growth* (New York: McGraw-Hill 1969); *Marketing for Business Growth* (New York: McGraw-Hill, 1976); *The Marketing Imagination* (New York: The Free Press 1983, expanded edition in 1986); *Thinking About Management* (New York: The Free Press, 1990).

12. Daniel Boorstin, *The Americans, The Colonial Experience* (New York: Random House 1964).

13. See Levitt, "The Globalization of Markets."

14. Ibid.

15. "The new digitized equipment and process technologies are available to all. This will enable those with minimal customization and narrow product-line breadth to drive their costs, as in old-fashioned mass production, far below those with more customization and wider lines." See Levitt, "The Globalization of Markets."

16. "Hotmail Celebrates One Year Anniversary and Five Million Users," Hotmail Corp., July 7, 1997.

17. See Levitt "The Globalization of Markets."

18. Dan Steinbock, Interview with Theodor Levitt, Professor Emeritus, Department of Marketing, Harvard Business School, September 18, 1998.

19. Ibid.

20. Ibid.

21. Ibid.

22. John A. Quelch and Lisa R. Klein, "The Internet and International Marketing," *Sloan Management Review*, Spring 1996, pp. 60–75.

23. Ibid.

24. Steven P. Schnaars, *Marketing Strategy: Customers & Competition* (New York: The Free Press 1998), pp. 26–27.

25. Ibid.; see chapter 12, "Speed As Strategy."

26. See in particular Marco Iansiti, *Technology Integration* (Boston: Harvard Business School 1998).

27. On this crucial distinction, see Michael E. Porter, "What Is Strategy?" *Harvard Business Review*, November–December 1996. Ultimately, it is vital to reassess the significance of the economies of scale and scope, two crucial notions in industrial organization, and explore them against the context of speed, or speed economies. This is one of the tasks I hope to conduct in a future study.

28. On the television "freeze," see in particular Christopher H. Sterling and

James M. Kittross, *Stay Tuned: A Concise History of American Broadcasting*, 2nd ed. (Belmont, CA: Wadsworth 1990), pp. 295–302.

29. On this transition, see Erik Barnouw, *The Sponsor: Notes on a Modern Potentate* (New York: Oxford University Press 1978), pp. 41–48.

30. In *non*-TV cities, movie attendance continued to hold firm or rise. Areas well saturated with TV were reporting movie theater closings in waves. While the rise of outdoor drive-in theaters played a role in the shift, television was considered the primary cause. A drastic decline at sports events was seen in most TV cities. Restaurants and night clubs felt the impact. Radio listening declined sharply in all TV cities, even though a sponsor wanting national coverage could not yet get it in television. See Eric Barnouw, *The Golden Web: A History of Broadcasting in the United States, Vol. II—1933 to 1953* (New York: Oxford University Press 1968), pp. 286–287.

31. Stephen Fox [1984], *The Mirror Makers: A History of American Advertising & Its Creators* (Urbana: University of Illinois Press 1997), pp. 210–211.

32. In the early 1950s, the growth of "bolder" network radio programming had gone hand in hand with the flight of national advertisers to broadcast television. As money got tight, content standards began to shift; as audiences shrank, battles for crumbs got fiercer. More was allowed. It would be the same in the early and mid-1990s when "reality programming" swept through program schedules and talks shows became a national craze and controversy.

33. Dan Steinbock, *Triumph and Erosion in the American Media and Entertainment Industries* (Westport, CT: Quorum Books 1995), p. 268.

34. Fox, *The Mirror Makers*, pp. 210–211.

35. *1998 Online Advertising Report: Revenue Models, Market Strategies, Projections*, Jupiter Communications, August 1997.

36. Fox, *Mirror Makers*, pp. 210–211.

37. Ibid.

38. On the demise of the simple channel structure and the rise of the complex one, see Steinbock, *Triumph and Erosion*, especially chapters 6–7.

39. Ibid, p. 259.

40. Julian Dibbell, "Nielsen Rates the Net," *Time*, November 13, 1995.

41. In the past, surveys had relied on figures obtained through questionnaires or by counting the number of Internet host computers and multiplying that by an estimated number of users per host. Since an Internet host computer could be anything from a single workstation to a gateway computer serving an entire university, such numbers were hardly reliable. By contrast, the Nielsen survey used the random phone-calling techniques employed by political pollsters and marketing firms. Commissioned by CommerceNet, an industry consortium looking to boost business online, the study was based on interviews with more than 4,200 North American households. The sample was large enough to be taken seriously.

42. Nielsen Media Research, Press Releases.

43. These figures came from a collaboration of researchers at the Baruch College School of Public Affairs and the polling company Louis Harris and Associates. See Howard Goldberg, "Survey Doubles Estimate of Web Use to 17 Million American Adults," *New York Times*, February 17, 1996.

44. I intend to explore the evolution of the new market and audience research in a forthcoming work on marketing strategy and new media planning.

45. The ambitious telephone survey was designed by Nielsen Media Research and Professors Donna L. Hoffman and Thomas P. Novak of Vanderbilt University in Nashville. In December 1995, Hoffman publicly disavowed the Nielsen report, saying that its conclusions were invalid. A number of similar surveys conducted by Internet companies and market research companies at about the same time indicated that there were fewer than ten million Internet users in the United States and Canada *combined*. See Peter H. Lewis, "New Estimates in Old Debate on Internet Use," Reuters, April 17, 1996.

46. "Net Diverts TV Viewing, Execs Say," Reuters, October 21, 1997.

47. According to Nielsen, most households connected to the Internet were generally categorized as "upper-demographic"—that is, their age and income levels were higher than those of average Americans. In this regard, the demographic shift was reminiscent of the early years of the cable. While Nielsen could not show that households were watching less television *as a result* of Internet usage, AOL found the study a useful tool to wave flags at advertisers still skeptical about the Internet's effectiveness as a marketing tool. See Jim Hu, "Study: Net Users Watch Less TV," CNET, August 12, 1998.

48. See John Brockman, *Digerati: Encounters with the Cyber Elite* (San Francisco: Hardwired 1996), p. 183; Amy Barrett, "We Have to Be Prime Time," *Business Week*, April 15, 1996.

49. See Jack Neff and Pat Sloan, "P&G, No. 1 Again, Aims to Reinvent Marketing," *Advertising Age*, September 30, 1996. On Pepper's strategic objectives and decisions, see, e.g., Peter Galuszka, "John Pepper: His Gamble for Procter," *Business Week*, September 14, 1998.

50. Indirectly, however, established agencies did have a role; P&G did invite a number of executives from interactive shops, some of them owned by old-line ad agency networks.

51. Sally Beatty, "P&G and Unilever Brainstorm: How Can Internet Ads Be Better?" *Wall Street Journal*, August 13, 1998.

52. Marc Gunther, "What's Wrong with This Picture?" *Fortune*, January 12, 1998.

53. Sally Beatty, "P&G, Rivals and Agencies Attempt to Establish On-Line Ad Standards," *Wall Street Journal*, August 24, 1998.

54. Ibid.

55. "Intel CEO Andy Grove Tells Comdex Attendees the Microprocessor Revolution Is Still in Progress," Intel press release, November 18, 1996.

56. Ibid.

Index

About the Author

DAN STEINBOCK is Affiliate Researcher at the Columbia Institute for Tele-Information (CITI), Columbia Business School. He also serves as a visiting professor at the Helsinki School of Economics in Finland. He consults for leading Finnish and European high-tech companies and has been engaged in a joint videoconferencing project with Intel Corporation. Dr. Steinbock publishes widely in English and his native Finnish, and is the author of *Triumph and Erosion in the American Media and Entertainment Industries* (Quorum, 1995).